EDUCATION for MARRIAGE

Education
for
Marriage

---

by

JAMES A. PETERSON

*Associate Professor of Sociology
and Marriage Counselor of the
University of Southern California*

Charles Scribner's Sons

NEW YORK

To My Family

AUDREY, JON, MARY, AND NANCY

for their many contributions to
the experience and insight
which have gone
into this book

Foreword

HENRY J. WEGROCKI, M.D.*

IT IS A PARADOX THAT, IN AN AGE WHEN ENTRY INTO EVEN SIMPLE OCCUPATIONS NECESSITATES SOME TRAINING AND PREParation, the initiation of the complex interrelationships which constitute marriage is often accomplished blithely and without much real forethought. The practicing psychiatrist, who sees a parade of pathetically incompatible couples, too often realizes that he could have been helpful if he had been consulted *before* marriage.

The prevention of potentially unsuccessful marital unions, and of the misery they bring to all concerned, is one of the aims of Dr. Peterson's *Education for Marriage*. The broad range of factors that make for future compatibility, or incompatibility, is set forth comprehensively, yet pithily. It is difficult for any author, unconsciously anchored, intellectually and emotionally, in the conceptual system of his particular discipline or field of endeavor, to visualize marital problems except in terms of his own familiar frame of reference. Dr. Peterson's background in religion, psychological counseling, and sociology, as well as the breadth of his own personal understanding, enable him to surmount this tendency to unilateral emphasis. The comprehensiveness which results is not, however, achieved at the cost of unity or organization, and the book is unique, not only in its scope, but also in its organic wholeness and its steady, and steadying, sense of direction.

* Associate Clinical Professor of Psychiatry, School of Medicine, University of Southern California and Chief, Psychiatric Service, California Hospital, Los Angeles, California.

vii

Unique also, as a specific contribution, is the series of exercises in self-analysis appended to the various chapters. These are non-threatening in nature, but are provocative of further and deeper reflection on the issues of potential compatibility. If they only *raised* questions and doubts without pointing to a solution, they would still serve their purpose of increasing awareness of the various aspects of interpersonal adjustment that need to be evaluated before marriage is decided upon.

This preventive orientation is, however, secondary to a more basic, positive attitude toward the potentials of marriage. Dr. Peterson's effort represents a mental-hygiene approach in the fuller sense by its emphasis on the values and the development of togetherness in marriage. *Education for Marriage* succeeds excellently in prescribing the circumstances that make marital union an opportunity for a growing, greater, "other-centered" self-realization. Education, in any real sense, is a constantly evolving process. To deepen one's understanding is as important as to gain it. From this standpoint, this book has as much value for the already married as for the unmarried.

H. J. W.

Foreword

HARVEY J. LOCKE*

NATURAL SCIENTISTS AND THE LAY PUBLIC OFTEN COMPLAIN THAT SOCIAL SCIENTISTS, WHO PRESUMABLY HAVE ACQUIRED various kinds of knowledge from carefully designed investigations, do not make this knowledge available to the public. The hesitation to publicize such knowledge is due to two things: (1) Social scientists emphasize the tentative nature of all knowledge and particularly that of social science; (2) Since the folkways of social science are against popularizing research knowledge, one might lose status among one's colleagues by so doing. This reluctance on the part of social scientists has resulted in a lag or gap between the knowledge relevant to human problems which scientists possess and the information which is being used to deal with these problems. Dr. Peterson's book bridges the gap by collating the research findings on marriage and the family and then applying it to education for family living. Those who use this book will find an excellent, frank, and dignified treatment of such various phases of family living as childhood experiences, dating in preparation for going steady, behavior during engagement, sex relations and the process of reproduction, and problems of living together.

H. J. L.

* Professor of Sociology, University of Southern California.

Preface

PSYCHOLOGISTS AND SOCIOLOGISTS HAVE KNOWN FOR SOME
TIME THAT THERE ARE BASIC CULTURAL AND PERSONALITY
factors—many of them largely unconscious—which operate to draw
young people together, impel them into marriage, and determine their
adjustment in marriage. Much as any young person may desire to make
a rational choice and find happiness in marriage, the degree of success
will depend primarily upon the individual's background and personality
configuration and not upon his or her ability to evaluate those traits
in another which, theoretically, should contribute to a happy marriage.
Consequently, in preparation designed to bring about a wise choice and
a satisfactory marital adjustment, primary emphasis must be placed
upon growth in the maturity and insight of the individual.

Education for marriage involves, then, not only a mastery of the facts
provided by research, but, equally important, the modification of attitudes and the recognition of membership in socio-cultural classes and
groups with their various marital expectations. This book attempts to
present both sociological and psychological data which might contribute
to the process of growth. The sequence of chapters, the text material,
and the exercises in self-analysis which follow the chapters have been
planned with this development in mind. In this respect the book differs
somewhat from previous books in the field; and its basic goals may be
defined as follows:

1. To help the student develop a point of view toward pre-marital dating
and sexual behavior that will contribute to and not diminish his or her
chances for marital adjustment.
2. To help the student identify attitudes and expectations which he has
taken over, largely unawares, from socio-cultural sources such as the ro-

mantic complex or ideal images, and to deal more objectively with these attitudes and their relation to wise marriage choice.

3. To contribute to the elimination of social and sexual inhibitions and to substitute wholesome acceptance of the physical opportunities of marriage and parenthood.

4. To help the student develop the ability to share emotions and ideas with his or her future mate.

5. To contribute to the growing ability of the student to make his own choices thoughtfully and to depend upon his own resources.

6. To share with the student an appreciation of the utility of the results of experience, case studies, and research regarding mating, and the problems—economic, recreational, in-law, religious, sexual, and reproductive—which have a bearing on adjustment in marriage.

7. To share with the student an appreciation of the utility of the various counseling facilities which are available to him.

[Additional research material of value to the teacher will be found in Appendix III.]

It is obviously impossible to express here the author's indebtedness to those whose earlier studies constitute the body of insights on this subject, or to express appreciation to all who have given assistance in the writing of this book. Of the many who have helped, Dr. Harvey Locke has consistently given encouragement and criticism. He read all of the manuscript once and some of it twice, and his vast background in the subject, including his extensive research, was generously shared with the author. Dr. Emily Mudd read the entire manuscript with great care, and contributed many helpful suggestions. Dr. Henry Wegrocki read the entire manuscript from a psychiatric point of view, and his comments sharpened many passages. He also contributed much to the chapter on the psychological factors involved in wise marriage choice. Dr. Nadina Kavinoky helped with the chapter on reproduction. Dr. Martin Neumeyer read the chapter on recreation, and Dr. Francis Christensen reviewed the entire manuscript with critical care. Helen E. F. Jenkins and Pat Glanz read and typed the entire manuscript. Thomas J. B. Walsh of Charles Scribner's Sons and Dr. Tracy Strevey have contributed much in encouragement and human understanding. Audrey Peterson provided some of the charts and diagrams. Finally, the author is grateful to a generation of students who have helped him to recognize needs and to experiment in ways of meeting those needs.

JAMES A. PETERSON

Contents

Figures

Tables

For the Student

COLLEGE STUDENTS AT THE MIDPOINT OF THE TWENTIETH CENTURY ARE AWARE THAT THE MARRIAGES OF THEIR OLDER brothers and sisters were the most fragile in history. Those marriages were broken at the rate of about one divorce for every three marriages. Statisticians indicate that the trend is toward more and not less frequent divorce. Yet, other factors—the trend toward equality and companionship in marriage, more adequate knowledge of reproduction and sexual adjustment, the spectacular decline in maternal and infant mortality, better management of sterility problems, the growing accumulation of insights into child psychology, consumer education, and other related phases of family life—promise for those who are adequately prepared a longer and more satisfying marital experience than that enjoyed by any past generation. It depends entirely upon the individual whether his marital venture will end in bitter frustration or a vital and enduring relationship. This book was prepared to help students achieve the personal adjustment and the broad insight necessary for a permanent and happy marriage today.

Parts I and II of this book are devoted primarily to an understanding of the way our early experiences condition our expectations of the roles we are to play and our psychological readiness for marriage. This part of the book will have a double meaning for each student. It will help him to become a better parent when it is his turn to guide his children toward maturity. Also, by enabling him to analyze his own background, it may assist him to eliminate inhibitions, clarify his sense of his role, and grow in his ability to adjust to others—and to that extent help him to determine his own marital destiny rather than act the part of a puppet manipulated by strings attached to his past and to his culture. Parts III and IV of the book deal with adjustment in marriage and consider ways in which the individual may consciously adapt himself to his changing culture.

This book relies in part upon sociological studies of the family, in part on psychological theory, and in part upon the opinions of family counselors and others who are considered experts in the field. Material drawn from sociological or psychological studies is often misused. From their experience in dealing with social phenomenon, social scientists know that every condition or fact is the product of a multiplicity of causes. Hence in their research reports they are careful to say that a single factor is "associated" with another factor or is symptomatic of it; they rarely use the term "causes" to indicate that a single factor is responsible for another. But others who quote these studies often change the language of the scientist and imply that one social fact "causes" another. An illustration of this misuse of scientific data can be found in the association of attendance at Sunday School with marital adjustment. Several studies have shown that individuals who attend Sunday School until they are eighteen or older are found in greater numbers in the well adjusted group than in the poorly adjusted group. But there are many other facts which are also true of the well adjusted group as compared with the poorly adjusted group. Therefore it is not possible to generalize and to say that it was attendance at Sunday School that *caused* the marital adjustment. Attendance at Sunday School may be only one outward sign of a general type of personality which successfully adjusts to marriage.

It is important for the student to understand the value—and the limitations—of the research studies which will be quoted. Dr. Locke, in the first three chapters of his book, *Predicting Adjustment in Marriage*, clearly presents the methodology used in marriage studies as well as an analysis of the usefulness of such studies.

The final value of the present book does not lie in its ideas, its speculations, its statistics, or its quotations. It will mean much or little to the student in direct proportion to the extent that it stimulates him to become aware of his own needs and inhibitions, to clarify his expectations of role, to expand his capacity to relate to others, and to eliminate negative attitudes. If it is true that modern man is nervous and neurotic, anxious and fearful, it is also true that he is the most malleable creature on earth. He has the capacity to grow, to learn, and to adjust. This book proposes to help the student become the kind of person who can adjust well to marriage in an age when rapid social change puts a premium upon adaptability and creativity.

Each chapter is followed by an exercise called "Self-Analysis." The purpose of this exercise is to enable the student to develop the ability to meet the demands of modern marriage that have been outlined in the chapter; to discover the degree to which he has acquired a mature definition of affection; to uncover his own expectations of role which may previously have been hidden and unexpressed; to overcome inhibitions due to ambivalences in his background at home and in society; to learn about modern family life so that he will adopt attitudes which will be productive of adjustment; and to analyze his own past in terms of becoming the kind of adaptable and creative person who can find success in the companionate and democratic family.

EDUCATION for MARRIAGE

CHAPTER 1

Marriage in Transition

INTRODUCTION: THIS IS A BOOK ABOUT THE ONLY REALLY IMPORTANT THING IN THIS WORLD—HUMAN BEINGS. NOTHING ON earth is as intricate or as sensitive as the human mind; nothing is as complex or as creative as personality. Man in his early years of existence can incorporate the learning of past centuries into his life and anticipate the future in his values. In this sense he is bound by neither time nor space. Generation after generation adds new dimensions to man's understanding and new conquests of his environment. Today his creativity has resulted in the awful Frankenstein of the hydrogen bomb. Many young people living in the shadow of the bomb fail to realize that the scientific method of thinking that produced it has also developed more adequate ways for individuals to achieve the fulfillment of personality. The tools of science, the insights shared in education, and the freedom of democracy provide means for greater development than ever before in history. These chapters focus on growth sequences which may help young men and women to live full lives; to build a constructive future, unfettered by fears from their past; and to develop personalities so strong that they cannot be submerged by another in marriage and so mature that they can contribute to the growth of their mates and their children.

This is a book about the most important decision human beings ever make—the choice of a life partner. That single decision has many and extended results. In choosing a mate one chooses the ancestors of his children; he chooses the mood and atmosphere of his future home; he

1

chooses the level of his future intellectual, aesthetic, and recreational life; he chooses friends and family. In selecting his lifetime companion he is limiting or expanding his own possibilities for personality enrichment in so far as one possible mate would stifle while another might inspire him. He will live the greater part of his life in intimate relation to the one who walks with him up the marriage aisle. Whether that choice is for "better or worse" depends upon wise and mature attitudes.

This is a book about the way human beings can adjust to the most important relationship in life—marriage. Society never automatically guarantees either success in marriage or good parenthood. Marriage today has much potentiality for shared happiness among husband, wife, and children; in a complex and changing social environment, that happiness must be achieved by effort. To understand the conditions and attitudes which promote happiness in marriage is a prerequisite to good adjustment. No other area of life is as crucial as marriage for individual serenity and satisfaction. No economic success, no material achievement, neither fame nor glory, can purchase love, trust, and tenderness. These are the rewards of unselfish devotion. Without them life is cold and empty. Marriage is never a means for economic security; it is a shared effort to win shared goals. Marriage is never a means for sexual convenience or satisfaction; the physical part of marriage only expresses the tenderness that exists. Marriage is the fulfillment of our deepest needs to be an intimate part of another's life, to be trusted by someone who knows us year after year; to be loved and to be regarded tenderly by someone who cares—this is the meaning of marriage.

Marriage of one type or another has been a part of every known culture, primitive or advanced. The most epochal as well as the most intimate experiences of life occur within the framework of marriage. There are many expectations that are not verbalized when two people stand before the minister and pledge their loyalty "until death do us part." The miracle of motherhood and fatherhood will be shared by most couples. Later will be added the anxiety over illness, the concern for development, and eventually the poignant sense of loss when children marry. Throughout life, husband and wife experience together success and sorrow, joy and disillusionment. Moreover, they will share themselves, spiritually, mentally, physically, in a more complete way than in any other relationship they will have. Monogamous marriage in one form or another seems to be the universal way in which our most basic affectional and social needs are met. Marriage is the most profoundly important venture of life. How adequately we are prepared for that venture will determine not only the success of our marriage, but also the quality of most of life's experiences.

The functions of marriage vary according to cultures, so that it is difficult to define either marriage or the family in terms other than those of distinctive types of association. For this reason the definitions offered by Burgess and Locke seem most appropriate. They define marriage as "the union, sanctioned by society, of men and women as husbands and wives."[1] The family is " . . . a group of persons, united by ties of marriage, blood, or adoption, constituting a single household; interacting and communicating with each other in their respective social roles of husband and wife, mother and father, son and daughter, brother and sister; and creating and maintaining a common culture."[2]

THE FAMILY IN TRANSITION

Sociologists recently have emphasized the evolution of the family from an institution to a companionship. Such evolution means that the family is in a state of transition of form and function. The shifting nature of the contemporary family is expressed in this summary sentence from Burgess and Locke:

> The basic thesis of this book is that the family has been in historical times in transition from an institution with family behavior controlled by the mores, public opinion and law to a companionship arising from the mutual affection and consensus of its members.[3]

Whenever basic institutions are in process of change, individuals who are conditioned by and participate in those institutions change too. They develop different functions, new attitudes, changing roles and expectations. They must also adjust to the new roles and expectations of others. In this book the term "role" is frequently used. By role we mean the way an individual thinks of his part as he interacts with others. This concept of his part comes from the way he has reacted to what others have expected of him. Obviously a person will take a different part in life, or play a different role, depending upon the group he is in at the moment. Thus, a student plays differing roles in the classroom, in a

[1] Ernest W. Burgess and Harvey J. Locke, *The Family, From Institution to Companionship*, New York, by permission of The American Book Company, 1953, p. 6.
[2] *Ibid.*, pp. 7–8.   [3] *Ibid.*, p. 22.

fraternity, or on a date. Some individuals are conscious of some of their role expectations, others are totally unconscious of them. Certain segments of the population accept new roles easily because, for many reasons, individuals in those groups are more adaptable. Other segments resist change and cling to old attitudes. Some adjustment difficulties in contemporary marriage stem from this differential in the rate of accepting new attitudes and new roles; some come about because the new roles are not yet articulated clearly; problems arise when individuals with old attitudes mate with individuals with new attitudes.

Family conflict over the matter of careers for wives reflects one of the problems related to this shift in family function. The woman's role, according to the mores of the institutional family, was to keep the house, bear the children, bake the bread, and serve the husband. The woman's role, in the emerging pattern of the companionship family, is one of equality with her husband in decision-making, in pursuing a profession, in functioning as a citizen, and as a creative individual. It is obvious that if a man who expects his wife to function according to the institutional mores marries a woman who conceives of her role in terms of the companionate family they will have very basic conflicts. If both of them hold to these expectations with tenacity after they are married, adjustment may be impossible.

It is important to visualize and to ponder on the profound contrast between the institutional and the companionship family. Wise marriage choice and later marital adjustment depend partially upon an understanding of the transitional nature of today's family. The following chart shows some of the more important shifts in function, in role-playing, and in attitudes of these two types of families. The two headings, "Traditional and Companionship," describe the old and the new aspects of family functioning. Each item in the chart represents an important shift in family life. The horizontal arrow represents the movement or the direction of that shift. The vertical lines lead in each case to resultant attitudes or role expectations which are correlated with the type of family organization above them. The quotation in the center of each chart is a statement by some authority in the field of family life indicating the importance he attaches to this particular change. The purpose of the chart is to clarify and to stress the essential concept of the transitional nature of family life today.

This chart of the trend toward the companionship family by no means exhausts the significant shifts that are occurring in the structure and

4

functions of the contemporary family. It merely emphasizes the complexity and the scope of the transition as well as the sharp contrasts in attitudes associated with the traditional and companionship patterns. The changes it records have not only limited the functions of the family but have altered the types of satisfaction associated with family living.

FIGURE 1. The Traditional and the Companionship Family

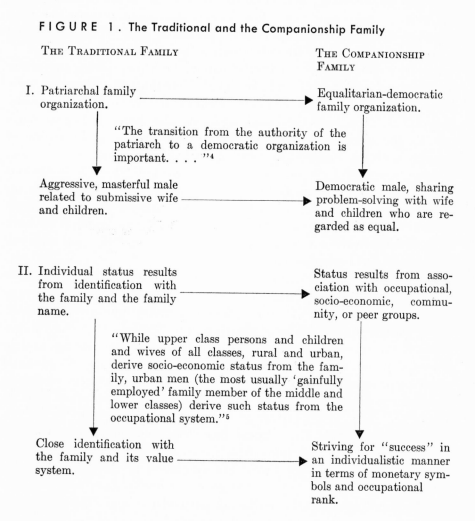

THE TRADITIONAL FAMILY

THE COMPANIONSHIP FAMILY

I. Patriarchal family organization.

Equalitarian-democratic family organization.

"The transition from the authority of the patriarch to a democratic organization is important. . . ."[4]

Aggressive, masterful male related to submissive wife and children.

Democratic male, sharing problem-solving with wife and children who are regarded as equal.

II. Individual status results from identification with the family and the family name.

Status results from association with occupational, socio-economic, community, or peer groups.

"While upper class persons and children and wives of all classes, rural and urban, derive socio-economic status from the family, urban men (the most usually 'gainfully employed' family member of the middle and lower classes) derive such status from the occupational system."[5]

Close identification with the family and its value system.

Striving for "success" in an individualistic manner in terms of monetary symbols and occupational rank.

[4] *Ibid.*, p. 26.
[5] From *The Modern Family* by Robert F. Winch, p. 175. By permission of Henry Holt and Company, Copyright, 1952.

5

FIGURE 1. The Traditional and the Companionship Family (Cont.)

III. Family as an interdependent, productive economic unit. ⟶ Family supported by a "gainfully employed" person whose economic life is spatially and functionally divorced from the rest of the family.

"This has resulted in a shift from a family in which the members were economically interdependent, to one in which one or more are economically independent while the others are classified as dependents. Thus the economic bond which has been regarded as central to marriage and the family has been greatly weakened."[6]

Number of children large because they are economic assets. Cohesion through sharing in common work. ⟶ Small family in which all members except the "gainfully employed" are "dependent," and economic liabilities.

IV. Unrestricted child bearing; family emphasis on procreation. ⟶ Planned parenthood.

"Quantitatively speaking, the significance of the reproductive function as a bond holding the family together has decreased."[7]

Socialization due to multiplicity of interactions in the large family. ⟶ Families are becoming smaller and smaller; with a minimum of interaction. Sociability or socialization more and more the province of non-family agencies.

[6] *Ibid.*, pp. 81–82. [7] *Ibid.*, p. 134.

FIGURE 1. The Traditional and the Companionship Family
(Cont.)

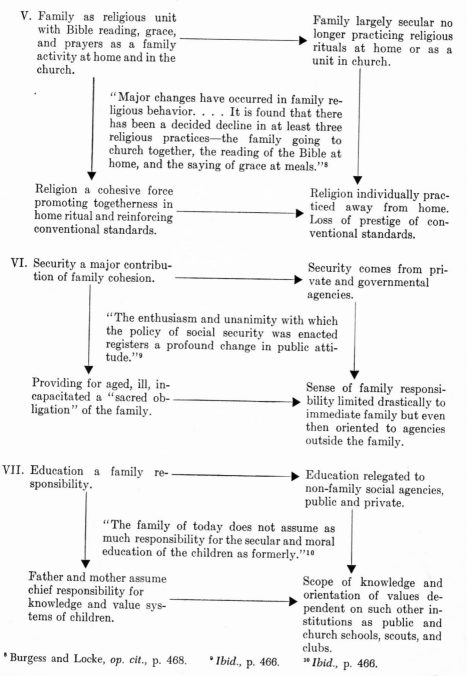

V. Family as religious unit with Bible reading, grace, and prayers as a family activity at home and in the church. ⟶ Family largely secular no longer practicing religious rituals at home or as a unit in church.

"Major changes have occurred in family religious behavior. . . . It is found that there has been a decided decline in at least three religious practices—the family going to church together, the reading of the Bible at home, and the saying of grace at meals."[8]

Religion a cohesive force promoting togetherness in home ritual and reinforcing conventional standards. ⟶ Religion individually practiced away from home. Loss of prestige of conventional standards.

VI. Security a major contribution of family cohesion. ⟶ Security comes from private and governmental agencies.

"The enthusiasm and unanimity with which the policy of social security was enacted registers a profound change in public attitude."[9]

Providing for aged, ill, incapacitated a "sacred obligation" of the family. ⟶ Sense of family responsibility limited drastically to immediate family but even then oriented to agencies outside the family.

VII. Education a family responsibility. ⟶ Education relegated to non-family social agencies, public and private.

"The family of today does not assume as much responsibility for the secular and moral education of the children as formerly."[10]

Father and mother assume chief responsibility for knowledge and value systems of children. ⟶ Scope of knowledge and orientation of values dependent on such other institutions as public and church schools, scouts, and clubs.

[8] Burgess and Locke, *op. cit.*, p. 468.   [9] *Ibid.*, p. 466.   [10] *Ibid.*, p. 466.

FIGURE 1. The Traditional and the Companionship Family (Cont.)

VIII. Leisure time limited but ⟶ Leisure time expanded in centered in the home. scope and spent in commercialized activities.

"Formerly recreation was largely centered in the home whereas today it is increasingly outside."[11]

The family reinforced by sharing group recreation at ⟶ home.

The family divided by recreation outside the home in pursuits differentiated into age and sex groups.

IX. Mate selection a family concern with parents exerting profound influence. ⟶

Mate selection a highly individualistic matter with parents expected to play little part in choice of life partner.

"In the United States. . . . young people have secured almost complete freedom of mate selection. . . ."[12]

Emphasis upon common backgrounds, compatible personality configurations, ⟶ family status, and future economic security. Dependency on parents essential for this type of choice.

Emphasis on courtship and romantic love. Independence an essential psychological attribute to this type of choice.

X. Pre-marital companionship limited to group activity or closely chaperoned pairs. ⟶

Rise of unchaperoned dating.

"Dating is a relatively new phenomenon in American culture. . . . In American society before World War I, except in the upper classes, even the initial request for the company of a young woman to or from a social event, was interpreted by the girl, her family, and the community as evidence of the man's serious intentions."[13]

Rigid social control of ⟶ heterosexual behavior.

Self-control of heterosexual behavior.

[11] *Ibid.*, p. 468.   [12] *Ibid.*, p. 345.   [13] *Ibid.*, p. 331.

FIGURE 1. The Traditional and the Companionship Family (Cont.)

XI. Relatively close family and friendship groups on homogeneous socio-cultural levels. → Relatively free family and friendship group interaction on heterogeneous socio-cultural levels.

"Differences in religion thus constitute one of the most important phases of cultural conflict. . . . [In Chapter IX] we considered some of the trends in such mixed marriage and found that the principle of homogamy seems to be ignored to an increasing degree in the matter of religion."[14] "Marital conflict based upon ethnic differences is so common in our heterogeneous society that only brief mention is necessary in this context."[15]

In-group marriages in terms of economic, social and economic class, nationality and religious marriage with consequent similarity of background factors in family life. → Out-group marriages involving serious divergencies in values, role-playing, and habit systems resulting in conflict situations.

XII. Child training defined as acculturation to fixed values. → Child training defined as development of creativity and achieving the greatest development of unique potentialities of each child.

"This is perhaps the essential difference in the way our ancestors and ourselves regard the child. Our ancestor saw these earliest years as a negative period of life, a sort of necessary evil full of idle deviltry and cantankerous mischief; the child survived it and his parents endured it as best they could, until late adolescence when life hesitatingly began. We, of a later vintage, regard childhood as a foundation period of great importance, a period of twig bending during which the shape of the future tree is determined."[16]

Stable and rather rigid social and moral values. → Unstable and diversified moral and social value systems.

[14] Andrew G. Truxal and Francis E. Merrill, *Marriage and the Family*, Copyright, 1953, by Prentice-Hall, Inc., p. 478. Reprinted by permission.   [15] *Ibid.*, p. 481.
[16] James H. S. Bossard and Eleanor S. Boll, *The Sociology of Child Development*, by permission of Harper and Brothers, 1948, pp. 654–655.

FIGURE 1. The Traditional and the Companionship Family (Cont.)

XIII. Role of the wife as the homemaker, and mother. | wife as the housekeeper ⟶ | Role of the wife extends to employment and community leadership outside the home as well as to companionship with husband and children inside the home.

"In a simple, agrarian society, the role of the wife is well-defined. The same cannot be said of an industrial, urban society. During the early years of marriage and later in times of economic stress, the modern wife may contribute to the family income through gainful employment. Depending upon the social level and the nature of her husband's work, she may also have the important role of hostess at social functions. She is also expected to be a companion to her husband at all times, in which capacity she may run the gamut from sexual partner to practical nurse. In addition to these role patterns, the middle class urban wife not only bears the children but assumes the major responsibility for their care. Finally she is the household manager and general purchasing agent, which functions require their own skills. This pattern of role expectations of the wife is the most complex that any family system has ever seen. The possibilities of failure are greatly enhanced by this complexity."[17]

Wife was subordinated to husband but had well-defined rewards as the result of fulfilling well-defined roles. ⟶ Wife tends to be independent, to have many interests besides husband and children, and to be confused in terms of expectations. She often does not have a sense of security from fulfilling her role expectations because they are vague and transitory.

[17] Truxal and Merrill, *op. cit.*, p. 197.

AFFECTION AND COMPANIONSHIP AS CORE FUNCTIONS
OF THE CONTEMPORARY FAMILY

As the new family has emerged, many previous functions of family life have been assumed by other, non-family institutions. The family is no longer the religious, social, recreational, and economic center it once was. Nor does it perform the educational, security, or protective functions it once did. The two remaining functions, giving affection and sharing companionship, have become even more important today because of other trends in society. The industrialization of the Western world, the growth of urban centers of living, the emergence of scientific thinking, and the rise of secularization—all these have combined to produce other patterns of societal change. Modern urban man is an isolated and lonely creature. Previously men worked and worshiped, played and grieved, in a primary, or face-to-face, relationship with many individuals they knew and trusted well. These contacts provided support and close personal relationships which are not present in the great city or even the modern suburb. Burgess and Locke summarize the importance of these core family functions as follows:

> In spite of the loss of the historical functions of the family—economic, protective, educational, recreational and religious—it is necessary to realize that the family still retains two intrinsic functions. While various forces are shearing from the family its institutional significance, it still maintains its affectional and cultural activities. More and more the American family is becoming a union of husband and wife, parents and children, based upon the sentiment of love, common interests, and companionship. Child development is affected by varied and important home activities. Perhaps most significant are the attitudes, behavior, and relationships of the family that may be summed up in the descriptive phrase, "home atmosphere." Family affection is, of course, the chief ingredient here, but others of vital import are family events and celebrations, family traditions and memories, common interests and activities, and informal methods of family control.[18]

It is precisely the pivotal importance of affection and companionship in happy marital adjustment that makes a pseudo-affectional philosophy so insidious a threat to wise marriage choice. We are referring to what is generally known as "romantic love." Romantic love is a form of camouflaged physical attraction which seems to preclude consideration

[18] Burgess and Locke, *op. cit.*, p. 470.

of other more permanent phases of companionship and adjustment. Waller ascribes the rise of romantic love to the frustration of the sexual drive with a consequent idealization of the future mate.[19] Burgess and Wallin think that it is the result of the basic attempt of each individual to find security and self-esteem.[20] Winch regards romantic love primarily as a cultural product:

> . . . there are so many facets of our culture which impinge upon our daily life and which spell out so continuously and so repetitiously the story of romantic love that there is no shortage of informal indoctrination of this point.[21]

The theme of romantic love is central to almost every movie, radio serial, or popular song. The floral, perfume, garment, music and recreation industries have a vested interest in promoting this view of love. The strength of the response to the theme of romantic love comes both from the unfulfilled sexual needs of the unmarried and from the insecurities and anxieties that derive from urban life. The loneliness of city living accentuates the search for any type of response. Romantic love not only superficially meets this need but adds the thrill of dreams besides. While romantic love seems to be related to the emerging function of the family as an affectional group, it actually distorts reality so far that a later and more permanent type of affection is difficult to achieve. Burgess and Locke summarize this problem as follows:

> Naturally, even where passion was deep and sincere, there was disillusionment when romantic impulses led to unions of persons of widely different temperaments, different cultural backgrounds, and different philosophies of life. It became evident that in many marriages, even if respect remained, romance had faded. The affinity theory was modified to demand either the continuance of romantic love in marriage or the dissolution of the marriage . . . Increasingly in America and to some extent in other countries, the philosophy of romantic love is itself a major factor in the disillusion of one relationship and the consummation of a new union.[22]

The first characteristic of romantic love is its emphasis upon the automatic nature of wise marriage choice. The "right one" exists and at the proper time will appear. He will appear, it might be added, under

---

[19] Willard Waller (Revised by Reuben Hill), *The Family: A Dynamic Interpretation*, Copyright, 1951, by The Dryden Press, Inc.
[20] Ernest W. Burgess and Paul Wallin, *Engagement and Marriage*, J. B. Lippincott Company, Philadelphia, 1953.
[21] Winch, *op. cit.*, p. 361.   [22] Burgess and Locke, *op. cit.*, pp. 321–328.

the most favorable romantic conditions. The second characteristic of such a love is that it is spontaneous. As soon as the two perfectly matched individuals come together they know that they are destined for an exquisite and eternal love experience. Thus, a mother told her doubting daughter that if the daughter had any reservations about her lover being the right one, then she should not marry him because one always knew, without question, when the right one appeared. A third aspect of this type of love involves a deep faith concerning the future. If one wishes for and then marries the predestined mate, one's marriage must inevitably be superbly successful. Many stereotypes are associated with romantic love. The man is always handsome, strong, and reliant; the girl—mysterious, alluring, and beautiful; the house—luxurious, chic, and commodious (a change from 25 years ago when the house was small and cosy, with porches and roses). No mundane problems of finance, illness, or conflict can ever upset this family unit, for somehow love immunizes the couple from all the negative aspects of common experience.

In varying degree, this is the formula of the modern song, movie, soap opera or serial, radio play, television play—and consequently of adolescent talk and expectation. It is far removed from such concepts as mutual problem-solving, from such concerns as the budgeting of time and money or the care of children. On the contrary, since happiness is inherent in the magic match, any study of marriage, babies, or sex problems is irrelevant. It is obvious that this approach itself has become a factor in the deterioration of marriage, since it provides no rational, responsible view with which a couple may meet the impact of reality.

A couple recently counseled by the author illustrates this point. The girl had taken a pre-marital counseling class. She was a very good student, driven to study by the knowledge that her parents expected her to get straight A's. She spent too much time on her studies and too little in developing her social facility and acquiring her share of friends. Consequently, after graduation, when all of her classmates were getting married, she was without a fiancé. She had had two or three affairs; she had counseled about them and in the calm atmosphere of the counseling office had soon found that she had exaggerated their significance. Then, one day she came singing into the counselor's office. She had come, she said, not for counsel but to announce that she had found the one and only. She quickly recovered herself; she knew, she said, that ordinarily this meant that a couple was under the spell of the romantic notion of love and had temporarily lost any sense of perspective. But, she went on, their case was different. She had been standing on a pier when a small motor boat came rushing by. As it came close to her, it coughed and wallowed. The handsome youth standing in the boat looked up and caught her smiling at his dilemma. In that first glance, she said, there was so much mutual understanding that she knew they were destined for each other. Evidently he felt it, too, for he quickly leaped from the boat and stood beside her. This had been only ten days ago and they were to be married in three weeks. She wanted to invite the counselor to the wedding because, she said, he had taught her so much about love and marriage. Growing more confidential, she asserted that this was truly the work of God who had revealed that she and her fiancé were meant for each other. They were duly married. Three weeks later they were in the counselor's office with serious problems. The marital-adjustment-risk group into which this couple falls is low.

The belief in romantic love is most pervasive. While it is especially characteristic of the adolescent, it colors the attitudes of all groups. In order to deal intelligently with marriage choice it is important that an individual become aware of his own motivations and his own definitions of love. One of the tasks in preparing for marriage is to clarify one's knowledge of the kind of affection which is related to good marital adjustment.

In contrast to romantic love there is a type of affectional relationship which has far greater promise for marriage. In this book we shall designate it as companionship love. It is the product of basic interaction in which each love partner complements the other, meets his needs, and adds to his essential satisfactions. Burgess and Locke stress three contributions of companionship to the sentiment of love: (1) participation in common interests, (2) exaltation of the sympathies, and (3) mental interstimulation and response.[23] Truxal and Merrill contrast the essential elements of romantic and companionship love:

> One reason for the current instability of marriage is the confusion between affection and romance. Couples who come to the parting of the ways for reasons of incompatibility are often disillusioned romantics whose marital experience has failed to measure up to their expectations. Erotic ties, viewed in the narrow sense, are a tenuous foundation upon which to build the superstructure of the family. These ties are inevitably less stable than those forged about making a living, building a home, educating the young, or worshipping God.[24]

[23] Burgess and Locke, *op. cit.*, p. 324.   [24] Truxal and Merrill, *op. cit.*, p. 349.

After relating the difference between romantic and companionship love to an independence-dependence scale, Winch contrasts these types of affectional relationships as follows:

> Having gone this far in our explanation of companionship love, can we now tie the threads together and say what it is? As indicated, it is presented as the opposite of romantic love. This contrast is viewed as lying in the independence-dependence dimension of personality. The romantic lover is viewed as dependent, diffident, insecure—emotionally as an adolescent. The companionship lover is viewed as independent, confident, secure—emotionally an adult. The romantic lover tries to gratify all of his needs in one all-consuming passion but perhaps sensing that such totalitarian need gratification in a single love-object is impossible, he staves off disillusionment by keeping the love-object inaccessible. The companionship lover seeks to make relatively more modest claims on his love-object. Since his claims are modest, the likelihood of gratification is greater, and he can admit that the love-object, like himself, is mortal. Redundant and obvious as it may sound, companionship love is distinguished by the capacity to be a companion, a friend, an intimate. In companionship love one is able to say: "Not only do I love her; I like her."[25]

Let us hasten to say that these quotations do not imply that romance or sexual attraction should play no part in normal courtship. But because of the difficulty of adjustment owing to the transitional nature of the modern family, romance must be tempered by realism and sexual attraction by good sense.

CONFLICTS BETWEEN HUSBAND AND WIFE DUE TO DIFFERENCES IN MARRIAGE EXPECTATIONS

One of the important considerations often overlooked by individuals who are romantic is that in a heterogeneous society there are a great many divergent views as to what constitutes good and proper behavior in marriage. Modern marriage takes place in a social environment where the changes in family structure and function previously described leave different imprints upon the roles individuals expect to play in marriage. If two individuals with rather divergent role expectations fall in love and marry, the result is poor adjustment. Insight into the shifting functions of contemporary marriage may assist one to act more successfully in making a wise marriage choice and in achieving greater marriage stability. Each of the shifts presented in the charts may be regarded

[25] Winch, *op. cit.*, pp. 399–400.

as polarities and may be arbitrarily scaled for the purpose of graphic presentation. We may represent the "institutional-companionship family transition" in the following way:

INSTITUTIONAL   COMPANIONSHIP

| 0 | 10 | 20 | 30 | 40 | 50 | 60 | 70 | 80 | 90 | 100 |

All of the other processes of transition may be similarly scaled. In analyzing a case study it is possible to assign a hypothetical score of such scales to a man and a woman. Suppose that Mary Smith and Harry O'Brien, an engaged couple, be used as an illustration on the following scales.

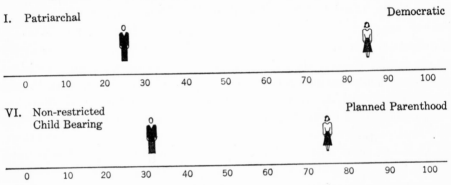

I. Patriarchal   Democratic

| 0 | 10 | 20 | 30 | 40 | 50 | 60 | 70 | 80 | 90 | 100 |

VI. Non-restricted   Planned Parenthood
     Child Bearing

| 0 | 10 | 20 | 30 | 40 | 50 | 60 | 70 | 80 | 90 | 100 |

It is obvious that these two individuals will have to face and resolve important differences before much cohesion is achieved in their marriage. Similar scales could be drawn from this case study to represent closeness or distance between the two principals in their role expectations and in their marriage philosophies, in their views of child guidance and discipline, in their social and religious attitudes, even in their ideas about recreation.

Our population is so heterogeneous that individuals who would be ranked at the opposite poles of these basic scales may be physically attracted and "fall in love." The idealization which goes with romantic love tends to obscure the significance of basic differences until after marriage. The differences will then appear, in the early months of marriage, as very unwelcome surprises.

Part of the task in preparing for a wise marriage choice and later marital adjustment is to learn the significance of the roles we must play, to become aware of our own unconscious expectations and then become reflective about them. One of the purposes of this book is to help students discover where they rate on these scales and what meaning this rating has for their future adjustment in marriage. This type of self-analysis will do much to help individuals avoid unions with people who have values and attitudes so contradictory that conflict is inevitable.

ROLE-CONFLICT AND CHILDREN

Suppose that Harry and Mary never come to understand the basic differences that separate them but, instead, drawn to each other by a "great love," get married. In due course, they have a child, Helen. Even before Helen is born, they have discovered that their thinking is very different on how decisions should be made, how children should be reared, what church they should attend, and so forth. While Helen is growing up, she finds no unified parental accord on her own behavior or on family matters. Her parents cannot even agree on how such accord should be reached because her father thinks that the man should be dominant and "lay down the law," while her mother thinks that the family should sit down together and discuss each problem as it arises, and that even the children should have some voice in the final decision. So Helen never learns what place either father or mother should have in the home. Beyond this, Helen goes to a school where there is little difference in the instruction given to boys and to girls. Some of the boys take homemaking and some of the girls take shop. And when Helen visits the home of her friends she finds the same kind of vagueness as to what men are expected to do and what women are expected to do. We may now indicate on the first scale what this conflict will mean to Helen.

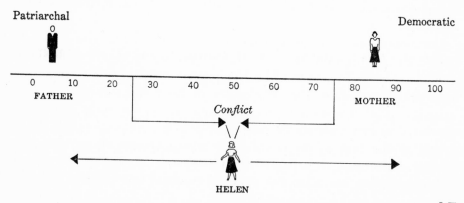

Patriarchal
0

Democratic

| 0 | 10 | 20 | 30 | 40 | 50 | 60 | 70 | 80 | 90 | 100 |

FATHER

MOTHER

Conflict

HELEN

Helen is pulled in many directions. The ambivalence in her family becomes part of Helen. She may desire to play the right role but she has no way of knowing what it is. When she begins to associate with males, she may not be sure how they should act. She knows how her father acted and she knows that this resulted in conflict. She does not know how she should act. She knows what role her mother tried to play, and, consciously or unconsciously, she is apt to reject this role because it, too, led to conflict and unhappiness. Thus the original conflict of roles in her own family has weakened the presentation of family models for her guidance and caused her to reject what she did see.

A great many young people today find themselves in Helen's predicament. Of course, other factors also play a part in this problem. Consider Helen's ability, or lack of it, to adjust sexually. She has been brought up in a society which has shrouded sex with the shadows of shame and silence. She knows little about it, and even what she knows may not be operative because of inhibitions derived from her parents and her peers. She is a victim of cultural lag. Society has set before her the goal of achieving more in her sex life than her mother or grandmother ever envisioned, but society has also presented her with attitudes which make it difficult for her to reach that goal. Likewise, in many other areas, conflicts between her parents and conflicting attitudes in society have now become conflicts within Helen herself. In some cases, these conflicts, in the family or in our culture, mean that no information is shared with young people. In this case, the need is to provide accurate and pertinent facts. This means that part of the purpose of education for marriage is to help young people orient themselves in a world of change. By being sharply aware of the ambivalences in their homes and in society, they are in a better position to deal intelligently with the problem of defining their own roles and values.

ANXIETY AND INSECURITY DUE TO CONFLICTING ROLES OF PARENTS

Suppose now that something different had happened in the social environment of Helen. Let us assume that the conflict in her home was so severe that her parents decided to separate. The environment during her first seven years was one of bitter quarreling, raging conflicts, and profound unhappiness. Then, at seven, she went through the trying experience, first of the separation and, later, of the divorce of her parents. She had already, at seven years of age, become a fearful and anxious child because of these conflicts. Thereafter she lived only with her mother who was bitter over the divorce and who resented Helen. Helen knew neither the serenity nor the affectional responses which would have made it possible for her to develop a normal personality configuration. This chain of circumstances affected her in two ways. It gave her a morbid fear of marriage and a suspiciousness of men, instead of a happy image of what marriage might be. She developed a neurotic personality as a result of the stresses in her early life. In varying degrees, Helen's story parallels that of many young people who must themselves adjust in marriage. How valid this generalization is may be seen from the following chart which depicts the increase of divorce in the United States. These statistics are taken from the *Statistical Abstract of the United States.*

F I G U R E 2. Divorces in the United States per 1,000 marriages, 1885–1950*

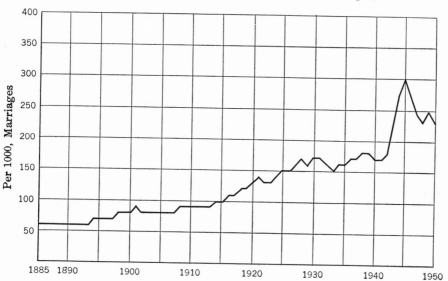

* Data from the *Statistical Abstract of the United States,* 1952, p. 59.

Of course, not all divorces are due to conflicts of role or to the anxieties associated with the neurotic personality, but they are important among the factors associated with divorce. They are also associated with many of those marriages which remain legally intact but which have little cohesion and which offer little in the way of opportunities for the development of the personalities of parents and children. While the extent of emotional problems in contemporary society is difficult to measure, studies indicate that one family out of five will face an emotional problem of such severity that one of its members will have to be placed in an institution or require long psychiatric care. There is a direct relationship between immaturity and maladjustment in marriage.

In a very true sense one must "become" a capable marriage partner. One must be aware of his shortcomings and try to correct them in order to attract and retain the kind of person one desires. One must remember that one is a part of his social scene and already has a history by the time he is ready to be married. The reflective person will not allow romantic love to cloud realistic considerations. He will be aware of the lasting values in other persons. He will have given attention to his or her projected role. He will have faced personality problems originating in his childhood and adolescence so that they no longer have the power to destroy his future happiness.

CONCLUSION

The basic goal of this chapter has been to give the student something of a perspective on the basic changes involved in contemporary family life and to indicate some of the ways these changes influence individuals as they prepare for and experience marriage.

In the next chapters, we will look at general and specific ways in which childhood, youth, dating, and such conditioning factors as recreational, religious, and socio-economic attitudes have prepared us for happiness or disillusionment in marriage. If the reader will be faithful in relating these conditioning factors to himself, he may develop an awareness of those aspects of his personality which will be hindrances or assets in adjusting to marriage. The experience of relating his own background to the objective data presented may help to eliminate potential inhibitions or aid in achieving more wholesome attitudes. The experience of locating his own specific conditioning in terms of his religious and socio-economic background and his basic role expectations should be helpful not only in forming a broader base for future growth but in realizing some of the non-verbalized expectations that necessarily play a part in marriage adjustment.

READINGS

James H. S. Bossard and Eleanor S. Boll, *The Sociology of Child Development*, New York, Harper and Brothers, 1948, Part 7.

ERNEST W. BURGESS and HARVEY J. LOCKE, *The Family, From Institution to Companionship*, New York, The American Book Company, 1953, Chapter I.

HARVEY J. LOCKE, *Predicting Adjustment in Marriage: A Comparison of a Divorced and a Happily Married Group*, New York, Henry Holt and Company, 1952, Chapters 1–3.

ANDREW G. TRUXAL and FRANCIS E. MERRILL, *Marriage and the Family*, New York, Prentice-Hall, Inc., 1953, Chapter 16.

ROBERT F. WINCH, *The Modern Family*, New York, Henry Holt and Company, 1952, Chapter 14.

PART ONE

PREPARING

FOR MARRIAGE

CHAPTER 2

Factors in Infancy

INTRODUCTION: HARRY EMERSON FOSDICK, ON A CHRISTMAS CARD HE SENT OUT DURING WORLD WAR II, EPITOMIZED OUR feeling for the potentialities of all children: "Christmas reminds us that a baby may be mightier than a battle." The tumult and the shouting of first-century conquests have faded away, but the influence of Jesus' life becomes each year more widespread and decisive.

A baby is a multiplicity of potentialities. The whole human past—centuries of constant growth of sensitivity and adaptation—is funneled to each infant. Twelve billion nervous cells have already "in utero" begun to develop patterns of responsiveness. The vast microscopic network of neurons provides both for automatic reaction and for poetic imagination. But a sterile or negative environment may blanket rather than fan the fires of creative growth.

Levy and Monroe say: "The child prepares for marriage during every moment of his waking hours, and perhaps also in his dreams."[1] How expectant parents feel about their coming child will determine how much love they will share with him. How much love they give the child is important in determining the child's growing capacity to show affection himself. The rejected child does not develop the response patterns that are essential for the intimate sharing of marriage. Initial child-training practices have an important bearing on later emotional development. In this chapter, important aspects of child-rearing that have meaning for later adjustment are studied. Its conclusions are widely held by psy-

[1] John Levy and Ruth Monroe, *The Happy Family*, Alfred A. Knopf, Inc., Copyright, 1946, p. 18.

chologists who deal with the developmental problems of children; they are confirmed by the main body of experimental studies,[2] though further research is needed on each of the points to be considered.

DESIRE FOR CHILDREN AND MARITAL ADJUSTMENT

Not all children are planned for or wanted. Two studies of marriage adjustment have asked questions about the wish for children and marital happiness. Burgess and Cottrell reported that couples having no children but desiring them had the highest adjustment scores, couples having one or more children and wanting them had the next highest adjustment score, and couples having unwanted children had the lowest adjustment score.[3] In a subsequent study, Locke decided to test the validity of this conclusion by asking the following series of questions:

> Did the husband want the child or children or the marriage in question: yes_____; no_____. Did the wife want the child or children; yes_____; no_____. If no children, did the husband want children: yes_____; no_____. Did the wife: yes_____; no_____.[4]

Locke's findings confirmed those of Burgess and Cottrell, for he found that the desire for children is correlated with happiness in marriage.[5] Where children are wanted, they are born into better-adjusted families than are children who come into homes where they are unwanted. This means that wanted children enter a better conditioning environment than those who are unwanted. The unwanted child often, though not always, becomes the rejected child, and his emotional deprivation marks him for life. On the basis of these studies we must conclude that parental readiness for the advent of a child is an important factor in that child's psychic growth.

PRE-NATAL INFLUENCES ON PERSONALITY

Recent studies have speculated about the influence of a mother's attitudes during pregnancy upon the child's personality. We are not

[2] An interesting critical review on the studies in this area has been made by Harold Orlansky in the *Psychological Bulletin*, 46 (1949) in which Orlansky concludes that present experimental research contradicts the thesis that infant care is largely determinative of later personality, concluding that what happens during other periods is likewise important.

[3] Ernest W. Burgess and Leonard Cottrell, *Predicting Success or Failure in Marriage*, Copyright, 1939, by Prentice-Hall, Inc., New York, pp. 260–261.

[4] Harvey J. Locke, *Predicting Adjustment in Marriage: A Comparison of a Divorced and a Happily Married Group*, p. 167. By permission of Henry Holt and Company, Copyright, 1951.   [5] *Ibid.*, p. 169.

thinking of the old wives' tale that the way a mother acts or thinks may mark the baby physically. Bowman deals with this belief, by the way, and reports the following cases:

> As is common during pregnancy a woman developed a persistent craving for a particular food, in this case, cherries. At the market she found that cherries were expensive, because out of season, and she could not buy any. When the baby was born it had a growth like a cherry on its upper lip. A woman was chopping wood, holding a small ax in her right hand. The ax slipped and cut her left hand. She grasped her left hand with her right one to stop the bleeding. When her baby was born it had no fingers on its left hand.[6]

Bowman, of course, rejects the implication of any relationship between these phenomena and accounts for them as pure coincidence, saying that there is no way known in which such experiences can affect the fetus.

Sontag studied pre-natal influences from the standpoint of both nutrition and emotions, and concluded that there are ways in which the attitudes of the mother may make a permanent imprint upon the psychic growth of the child. He also discusses the role of adequate nutrition in pregnancy and the relationship of this factor to ease of labor and the growth and health of the child.

> More recently investigators in Toronto compared the records of two different groups of infants. The mothers of both groups of infants lived during pregnancy on diets which were poor from the standpoint of vitamins, proteins and minerals. One group of mothers, however, had their pregnancy diets supplemented by large amounts of vitamins. The infants of this group showed better growth during the first year of life and much less illness and in general were healthier children than those of the mothers whose diets had not been supplemented by vitamins. An additional fact of interest was that the labors of the mothers on the supplemented diets were easier and shorter than those of the women whose diets were non-supplemented.[7]

Modern nutritional science has enhanced the health of both the infant and the mother. It is no longer necessary for a mother to lose her vitality with each pregnancy. She is also healthier and happier because her obstetrician sees to it that she protects her own health as well as that of her child.

---

[6] By permission from *Marriage for Moderns*, by Henry A. Bowman, p. 404. Copyright, 1948, McGraw-Hill Book Company, Inc.

[7] Lester Sontag, "War and the Fetal-Maternal Relationship," *Marriage and Family Living*, 6, 1944, p. 3. Reprinted by permission.

Sontag goes on in his article to consider what he terms "endogenous factors." He speculates about the possibility that the emotional reactions of the mother will produce physiological reactions which will in turn affect the fetus. Anxiety is not only a condition of the mind, it is also a state of the body. He thinks that he and his co-workers have discovered significant relationships between the body movements of the fetus and emotional stress in the mother:

> Another change which is apparent at birth in infants of mothers undergoing severe emotional stresses is in behavior, in total activity level. Such an infant is from the beginning a hyperactive, irritable, squirming, crying child who cries for his feeding every two or three hours instead of sleeping through his four-hour feeding. Because his irritability involves the control of his gastro-intestinal tract, he empties his bowels at unusually frequent intervals, spits up half of his feedings and generally makes a nuisance of himself. He is to all intents and purposes a neurotic infant when he is born . . . the result of an unsatisfactory fetal environment. In this instance, he has not had to wait until childhood for a bad home situation or other cause to make him neurotic. It has been done for him before he has ever seen the light of day.[8]

Mothers who resented their pregnancies and then felt guilty about that resentment would certainly be in such conflict that much anxiety would result. This anxiety in turn might affect the fetus as Sontag has indicated above. However, comparative studies need to be made in this area of pre-natal influence before this conclusion can be recorded as truly scientific.

THE BIRTH TRAUMA AND PERSONALITY DEVELOPMENT

At birth, one leaves the comfortable security of the uterus and is suddenly in a world where one must labor to breathe and exert oneself to be nourished, where one experiences heat and cold, pain and discomfort. Birth is a formative crisis of life. The conditions which offset that shock are the warmth, the play, the tenderness, and the cuddling of the mother or substitute mother. Where those conditions are not present, the baby does poorly and, under severe circumstances, may die. At the turn of the century, a great many babies in the most privileged homes and in the best hospitals were dying in alarming numbers. No specific germ or genetic factor could be isolated to account for this mortality.

[8] *Ibid.*, p. 4.

28

The disease was known as Marasmus, which is a Greek term meaning "wasting away." The only etiological factor that distinguished the care of these children from that of others observed to be husky was the fact that the carefully sterilized and scheduled babies were not rocked, cuddled, or loved. The disease came under control when a famous pediatrician wrote, so it is said, on the charts of such babies: "This baby is to be loved one hour a day." Today this discovery has resulted in the well-known formula, TLC, or "Tender, Loving Care." Margaret Ribble is the most outspoken advocate of "mothering." In both an intensive study of 600 babies in New York and in a follow-up study in Berlin, Dr. Ribble found that babies which were not loved developed negativism in feeding habits and a depressive tone which she identified as infantile atrophy. Ribble's thesis has been widely accepted by child psychologists and pediatricians. The case study presented below illustrates her viewpoint:

> Little Bob was born in the maternity hospital where the writer was making studies of infants at the time. He was a full term child and weighed six pounds three ounces at birth. During the two weeks' stay in the hospital the baby was breast fed and there was no apparent difficulty with his body functions. The mother, a professional woman, had been reluctant about breast feeding because she wished to take up her work as soon as possible after the baby was born, but she yielded to the kindly encouragement of the hospital nurses and the feeding was successful. Both mother and child were thriving when they left the hospital.
>
> On returning home the mother found that her husband had suddenly deserted her—the climax of an unhappy and maladjusted marriage relationship. She discovered soon after that her milk did not agree with the baby. As is frequently the case, the deep emotional reaction had affected her milk secretion. The infant refused the breast and began to vomit. Later he was taken to the hospital and the mother did not call to see him. At the end of a month she wrote that she had been seriously ill and asked the hospital to keep the child until further notice.
>
> In spite of careful medical attention and skillful feeding, this baby remained for two months at practically the same weight. He was in a crowded ward and received very little personal attention. The busy nurses had no time to take him up and work with him as a mother would, by changing his position and making him comfortable at frequent intervals. The habit of finger sucking developed, and gradually the child became what is known as a ruminator, his food coming up and going down with equal ease. At the age of two months he weighed five pounds. The baby

at this time was transferred to a small children's hospital, with the idea that this institution might be able to give him more individual care. It became apparent that the mother had abandoned the child altogether.

When seen by the writer, this baby actually looked like a seven months' foetus, yet he had also a strange appearance of oldness. His arms and legs were wrinkled and wasted, his head large in proportion to the rest of the body, his chest round and flaring widely at the base over an enormous liver. His breathing was shallow, he was generally inactive and his skin was cold and flabby. He took large quantities of milk but did not gain weight since most of it went through him with very little assimilation and with copious discharges of mucus from his intestines. The baby showed at this time the pallor which in our study we have found typical of infants who are not mothered, although careful examination of his blood did not indicate a serious degree of anemia. He was subject to severe sweating, particularly during sleep. A thorough study showed no indication of tuberculosis. The child's abdomen was large and protruding, but this proved to be due to lax intestinal muscles and consequent distention with gas and to a greatly enlarged and distended liver, which was actually in proportion to that of the foetus. There was no evidence of organic disease, but growth and development were definitely at a standstill, and it appeared that the child was gradually slipping backward to lower and lower levels of body economy and function.

The routine treatment of this hospital for babies who are not gaining weight is to give them concentrated nursing care. They are held in the nurses' laps for feeding and allowed at least half an hour to take the bottle. From time to time their position in the crib is changed and when possible the nurse carries them about the ward for a few minutes before and after each feeding. This is the closest approach to mothering in a busy infants' ward. Medical treatment consists of frequent injections of salt solution under the skin to support the weakened circulation in the surface of the body.

With this treatment the child began to improve slowly. As his physical condition became better, it was possible for our research group to introduce the services of a volunteer "mother" who came to the hospital twice daily in order to give him some of the attention he so greatly needed. What she actually did was to hold him in her lap for a short period before his 10 A.M. and 6 P.M. feedings. She was told that he needed love more than he needed medicine, and she was instructed to stroke the child's head gently and speak and sing softly to him and walk him about. Her daily visits were gradually prolonged until she was spending an hour twice a day, giving the baby this artificial mothering. The result was good. The child remained in the hospital until he was five months of age, at which time he weighed nine pounds. All rumination and diarrhea had stopped, and he had become an alert baby with vigorous muscular activity. His motor coordinations were of course retarded. Although he held up his head well and looked about, focusing his eyes and smiling in response to his familiar nurses, he could not yet grasp his own bottle or turn himself over, as is customary at this age. The finger sucking continued, as is usually the case with babies who have suffered early privation.

In accordance with the new hospital procedure, as soon as the child's life was no longer in danger, he was transferred to a good, supervised foster home in order that he might have still more individual attention. Under this regime, his development proceeded well and gradually he mastered such functions as sitting, creeping and standing. His speech was slow in developing, however, and he did not walk until after the second year. The general health of this child is now excellent at the end of his third year; also his "I.Q." is high on standard tests, but his emotional life is deeply damaged. With any change in his routine or with prolonged absence of the foster mother, he goes into a state which is quite similar to a depression. He becomes inactive, eats very little, becomes constipated and extremely pale. When his foster mother goes away, he usually reacts with loss of body tone and alertness rather than with a definite protest. His emotional relationship to the foster mother is receptive, like that of a young infant, but he makes little response to her mothering activities except to function better when she is there. He has little capacity to express affection, displays no initiative in seeking it, yet fails to thrive without it . . . [9]

This case illustrates the emotional factors which Ribble feels influence all children in their physical and psychological health. Rena Spitz reports a study which not only confirms Ribble's interpretation but gives statistical evidence about the physical results of mothering and the lack of it. She compared the rate of development and the mortality of babies in two institutions. The institutions were evenly matched so far as adequate nutrition, adequate medical care, hygiene and asepsis, and housing were concerned; but one kept the babies with their mothers and the others cared for them without the help of mothers. The mother-child relationship was then the independent variable. The children cared for with mothers were in an institution called "Nursery," those without mothers in an institution called "Foundlinghome." At the end of the first

[9] Margaret Ribble, *The Rights of Infants*, quoted by permission of Columbia University Press, Copyright, 1943, pp. 4–7.

year, the "developmental quotient" for "Nursery" children was about 98 and for the children in "Foundlinghome" about 70. But by the end of the second year, the quotient of the children in "Foundlinghome" had decreased to 45; and the difference in mortality was so striking that we quote Spitz directly:

> The most impressive evidence probably is a comparison of the mortality rates of the two institutions. "Nursery" in this respect has an outstanding record, far better than the average of the country. In a five years' observation period during which we observed a total of 239 children, each for one year or more, "Nursery" did not lose a single child through death. In "Foundlinghome" on the other hand, 37 per cent of the children died during a two years' observation period.[10]

These studies indicate the importance of love at the beginning of life. There is reason to believe that love continues to be an essential, if not the most essential, ingredient in healthy living. The early relationship of a mother and child is of paramount importance in influencing the health and response patterns of her child. This relationship conditions the child's later ability to give and receive affection. We may agree with Orlansky that other periods of training are important for the adult personality and still find with Ribble and Spitz that treatment in infancy is important. And for our purposes, in preparing our children for marriage or in reviewing our own backgrounds to determine our own preparation for marriage, it is not essential to say that one period or another is the most crucial.

CULTURAL DETERMINATION OF THE STYLE
OF AFFECTIONAL RELATIONSHIPS

Maleness, femaleness, sex, and their interrelationship mean different things in different cultures. Our expectations in regard to specific patterns of sexuality depend in conspicuous degree upon the culture in which we live. Because cultures tend to bring their customs, their forms, and their expectations into alignment, we may find adult sexual roles symbolized and also created during infancy. We will now consider the specific way infant-training conditions our style of affectional relationships as men and as women. A given culture expects a particular type of affectional response and, so to speak, selects the type of training

[10] Rena A. Spitz, "The Role of Ecological Factors in Emotional Development in Infancy," *Child Development,* 20, 1949, p. 149. Reprinted by permission.

that will produce that response. Only in our century, when there is such confusion of expectations and when so much thought is given to childhood training, do we have an opportunity to influence consciously the way our children will regard sex. By analyzing other cultures, Mead clarifies the way sexual responses are formed.[11] In developing her analysis of different types of sexual attitudes, Mead first studied infancy in the cultures of the South Seas.

The Arapesh carry their infants in soft net bags slung from their mothers' foreheads or on their fathers' shoulders. The baby to them is a fragile object. In the early months both mother and father concentrate on protecting and nourishing this vulnerable addition. The baby is fed at the breast often and tenderly, whether it demands food or not. Because it is satiated with food and because it is always tenderly carried, the focus of attention is upon its receptive mouth, a pattern which Margaret Mead thinks is easily transformed in the case of girls to sexual receptivity. On the other hand, boys who have learned only to receive, never to grasp or demand, become frightened lovers, hunters, or entrepreneurs. The early training that so well conditions women for their role sexually and socially by stressing the complementary nature of human interaction prohibits men from those male forms of aggressiveness that in other cultures bring inventiveness and wealth.[12]

In contrast, the Iatmal baby is taught to demand. After the first weeks, it is placed some distance from the mother and must cry lustily to get any attention or food. Once it has attracted the mother's attention, it is fed with interest and adoration, but even though it is fed amply after its screeching insistence, its relationship with the breast is more energetic. Two other factors operate to make the mouth not only a receptive organ but also a demanding one. The infant is early given hard pieces of bird-meat and, later, cuts its teeth on shell ornaments. The child learns that anger and self-assertion are the attitudes that gain rewards. The child is regarded as an individual from birth. There is added to the receptive mood a demanding one, so that both the male and female learn to play more aggressive and positive social and sexual roles in life.[13]

Among the Mundugumor, women have a rejecting attitude toward both child-bearing and nursing, and the way the child is handled depicts symbolically this rejection. The child is carried in a rough basket that is harsh to the skin, and nursing is brief and without tenderness. Out of this

[11] Margaret Mead, *Male and Female*, New York, William Morrow and Company, Copyright, 1949.   [12] *Ibid.*, pp. 65–67.   [13] *Ibid.*, pp. 68–69.

contest between mother and child come angry, conflict-minded adults, so that in later life "biting and scratching" are part of the foreplay of sexual activity. The acquisition of another wife by trading a daughter brings the father, who wants a young mate, and the son into early enmity. The father, remembering his own bitter initiation into life, will treat his son harshly. The son, too, learns to be adequate in a desperate world where one may laugh while succeeding through conflict and anger.[14]

Thus every culture has a definite pattern of relationship between the sexes, and in every culture this pattern is both symbolized and perpetuated by the way babies are guided in their growth sequences. But what of our own culture—so much in flux? Does it exhibit a characteristic manner of molding response patterns?

In America, children are generally born to a mother who is either completely or partially under an anesthetic. She can consciously share very little of the birth experience. As soon as the baby is born, it is taken some distance from her and is placed in a nursery where it does not have that immediate closeness to its mother that Ribble has indicated is so important. Later this separation will be more obvious when the "mechanical perfection of a bottle" is substituted for the mother's body as the source of food and comfort.[15] Thus, instead of a complementary relationship between the mother's body and the child, there develops a dependence on an external device (the bottle) for meeting basic needs.[16] The baby early learns that mouths are not a way of "being with someone" but a way of existing in an impersonal environment.[17] So almost from birth the "deep structural difference between masculine and feminine roles is lost."[18]

These childhood conditioning experiences are only a small part of larger behavior patterns. Certainly, in America, we must take into account the Puritan heritage to explain the rejection of the body that is expressed by every attempt to substitute mechanical processes for bodily ones. What concerns us is the fact that in our culture the sense of maleness and femaleness is obscured in a general cultural emphasis on early denial of sexuality and sensuality. A student reported recently that, until she was sixteen, whenever her mother took her to visit a house where there was a baby, they quickly departed if the baby was having a bath or was nude. Happily, the modern trend is away from these

[14] *Ibid.*, pp. 69–70.   [15] *Ibid.*, p. 260.   [16] *Ibid.*, p. 270.
[17] *Ibid.*, p. 272.   [18] *Ibid.*, p. 273.

3 4

traumatizing methods and toward closer physical and psychological relationships between parents and infant. Following the notable work of Grantley Read, many obstetricians are helping young mothers to face childbirth without fear. By becoming aware of the basic adequacy and preparation of their bodies for bearing children, these young women come to view childbirth as a natural, healthy process and not as a threatening consequence of a long illness. Again, the institution of rooming-in procedures, by which the baby is placed in a crib beside the mother's bed shortly after birth and the nurse acts as teacher for both husband and wife, insures healthier emotional relationships. Again, the trend is away from mechanical methods of nourishing the child and is moving toward breast-feeding, for it has been found that breast-feeding not only immunizes the child against infant diseases but also against anxiety and fear.

SPECIFIC AREAS OF INFANT BEHAVIOR AND THEIR RELATIONSHIP TO LATER MARITAL ADJUSTMENT

The reader will remember that Margaret Mead felt the differences in satisfying the sucking need made for differences in later love relationships. Sucking seems to be a normal instinctive behavior pattern. It is the mechanism whereby the child receives nourishment. Since this is his primary concern in his first weeks, it is of primary importance from a nutritional point of view. Beyond this, sucking is also the first of the infantile bodily pleasures. Travis and Baruch say:

> Besides having his physical hunger satisfied, the baby also needs to suck for the pleasure of sucking. Sucking brings him closeness. It brings him comfort, it brings him his first sensory gratifications. Not only is sucking a means of livelihood, it is also a source of satisfaction in itself. He sucks not only to fill his stomach with food but also to fill his soul with peace.[19]

Ribble adds another thought about the emotional value of sucking:

> The mouth of the baby must have special consideration as an organ, the use and stimulation of which arouses the first sense of well-being and pleasure and definitely furthers mental development.[20]

Literally, the mouth furnishes the first "taste" of the outside world. Ribble concludes that the baby's initial security, or pleasure, satis-

[19] Lee Travis and Dorothy Baruch, *Personal Problems of Everyday Life*, New York, Appleton-Century-Crofts, Inc., Copyright, 1941, p. 46. Reprinted by permission.
[20] Ribble, *op. cit.*, p. 32.

faction and success, is closely linked with his mouth activity.[21] Travis, Baruch and Ribble all are saying that sucking conditions the baby to regard the body as a source of pleasure and to accept life as good. It may thus have not only general but specific correlations with later acceptance of the mouth—as an erotic zone of kissing—as pleasurable and good.

BREAST-FEEDING

If sucking is of vital importance in giving a child a sense of security and pleasure, it is reasonable to believe that this is related to the fact that such activity brings the child in reassuring and warm contact with the mother. This raises the question whether or not breast-feeding is superior to bottle-feeding. Ribble thinks that there is no room for doubt about this:

> Since sucking is a function which will soon be replaced, the best arrangement, where possible, is to follow Nature's clue. In normal breast feeding, which is without question the ideal form, at least until the teething period, the various instinctual hungers are self-regulated. The amount of flow of the mother's milk and the time and effort needed by the baby to extract it usually correspond nicely with his needs. The contact and fondling give the necessary passive stimulation. Artificial feeding immediately introduces the necessity for a careful regulation of sucking time coordinated with the flow of milk from the bottle. Holding, before and during the bottle feeding, is obviously necessary.[22]

Others are not quite so dogmatic about the importance of breast-feeding as compared to bottle-feeding when the bottle is held by the parent and the child is handled in a tender, loving way. Ross and Johnson summarize this point of view when they say:

> What happens to the infant in his first activity, eating, may lay down the basic pattern of behavior. When the child has a basic confidence in people, he no longer needs to waste his energy in trying people out, but can turn his interests to creative, productive pursuits. While breast feeding has advantages in that the mother has opportunity to be closer to the baby and thus to express her friendliness, bottle feeding can accomplish the same if the mother really loves her child and gives freely of her time and interest.[23]

[21] *Ibid.*, p. 23. [22] *Ibid.*, p. 33.
[23] Helen Ross and Adelaide Johnson, "A Psychiatric Interpretation of the Growth Process in the Early Years," *Journal of Social Casework*, Volume 30, 1949, p. 88. Reprinted by permission.

Ross and Johnson might profitably have reviewed the differences in results of the varieties of breast-feeding in the tribes studied by Margaret Mead, for analysis of the experience of these tribes indicates that it is not breast-feeding itself but rather the attitude expressed by means of breast-feeding which determines the behavior patterns.

There are many unanswered questions about breast-feeding. We wonder if the modern emphasis does not make many women who cannot breast-feed their children feel guilty and actually mar their relationship to their children. We wonder what validity there is to the psychiatric interpretation of bottle-feeding—that it may represent, for women, a type of symbolic rejection of either their femaleness or of their children. We wonder what substance there is to claims the breast-fed children develop substantially fewer thumb-suckers than bottle-fed children. We wonder to what extent mothers' milk does immunize the baby to many diseases of childhood. The physiologists give some answers to this last question. Some of their research is indicated in the following quotation:

> Human milk is specially adapted to the requirements of the human infant and so differs in some respects from that of all other animals. Cow's milk is most frequently substituted for human milk. The relative composition of the two can be seen in the following table.

T A B L E 1. Composition of Human and Cow's Milk

	Human (Average) %	Cow's (Average) %
Water	88.4	87.1
Proteins	1.5	3.2
Fat	3.3	3.9
Lactose	6.5	4.9
Salts	0.3	0.9

In substituting cow's milk for human milk, the differences that must be taken into consideration are not only the different relative proportions but also the following: The difference in the proteins; the protein of human milk is one-third caseinogen and two-thirds lactalbumin, and that of cow's milk is five-sixths caseinogen and one-sixth lactalbumin. The difference in the curds formed in the stomach; human milk curdles in small flocculi, and cow's milk curdles in large, heavy curds. The reaction of human milk is practically neutral, pH 7.0 to 7.2; cow's milk is slightly acid, pH 6.6 to 6.8 when first drawn, but the acidity increases on standing. Human milk is sterile, and cow's milk, due to the handling it undergoes, contains a large number of microorganisms. Pasteurization destroys the microorganisms usually found in milk, but unless it is done very carefully, it also destroys the vitamins. Human milk contains antitoxins and antibacterial substances that have been formed in the mother's blood; and as it is ingested directly from the breast, its germicidal power is at its height. Cow's milk may have germicidal value, but this soon deteriorates and usually is lost by the time it is given to the child.[24]

We wonder what statistical proof there is for Ribble's assertion that breast-feeding is "the most important means of immunizing the baby against anxiety."[25] Since anxiety is the core problem of modern personality adjustment, such a sweeping statement is challenging, but no proof is offered to substantiate it. We wonder really how much validity there is to Mead's suggestion that "for the complementary relationship of the child at the breast is substituted a pattern that can easily be made an alternating one—'Give baby a cracker, baby give mother a cracker'—in which a satisfying object intervenes between the two, and deep structural differences between their masculine and feminine roles are lost."[26] There are a great many intriguing avenues for speculation in this area. Our conclusion is that in whatever way it may be performed—whether by fondling when feeding the baby from the bottle or by gentle handling when breast-feeding the baby, or by any of the subtle, unrecorded methods by which a mother influences her children—the ability to love must be developed.

THUMB-SUCKING

The only importance of thumb-sucking is the anxiety it produces in parents and the conflict that that anxiety creates between parent and child. Thumb-sucking may be thought of during its earlier manifestations as a natural response to the sucking need. Several studies indicate this. David Levy found that babies who were fed once every four hours sucked their thumbs at about twice the rate of babies who were on a three-hour schedule.[27] In her study of 500 infants, Ribble found that babies fed on a three-hour rather than a four-hour schedule "were better organized

[24] Diana Clifford Kimber and Carolyn E. Gray, A.M., R.N., *Textbook of Anatomy and Psychology,* Copyright, 1952, pp. 703, 704. Reprinted by permission.
[25] Ribble, *op. cit.,* p. 34.   [26] Mead, *op. cit.,* pp. 272–273.
[27] David M. Levy, "Finger Sucking and Accessory Movements in Early Infancy: An Etiological Study," *American Journal of Psychiatry,* May, 1928, 7, pp. 881–918.

and much less restless."[28] In still another study, children who had sucked over a longer period (seven or eight months) were compared to those who had sucked for a shorter period (three to four months).[29] Those who had sucked longer had fewer behavior problems later. In early childhood, if thumb-sucking persists, it is generally a comfort-giving behavior pattern. Thumb-sucking worries many parents because they think it is unhygienic, unsightly, and productive of dental malocclusion. But dental damage rarely occurs when thumb-sucking is confined to the first two or three years before permanent teeth arrive. Furthermore, there is evidence to indicate that if the child is not thwarted in his early sucking needs, he will not thumb-suck later. Travis and Baruch report on the study of a dentist, Samuel J. Lewis, as to the part thumb-sucking plays in producing unsightly teeth:

> One clever dentist investigated. His method was not to see only children with crooked teeth, but quite a different one. He took casts of children as they grew. Some of the teeth became crooked. Some stayed straight. It was a fact, he saw, that when children sucked their thumbs, their baby teeth were pushed out of alignment. But he saw, too, that when the second, permanent teeth came in, just as many of the non-thumb-suckers had crooked teeth as did the thumb-suckers. What had happened was this. If the thumb-sucking had stopped prior to second dentition, often the teeth would correct themselves. One important thing, then, is to see that thumb-sucking stops before the child's permanent teeth come in, not that he is prevented from sucking in his infancy or at two or three. In fact when infants and two- and three-year olds are allowed to suck all they wish, they stop gradually of their own accord without the same hurt that "breaking them" creates. They stop, that is, unless they need to cling to sucking as a means of comfort which their environment makes necessary. And, of course, the only safe cure lies not in taking sucking away from the child, but in taking away the pressures and the hardships that are driving him to seek solace.[30]

Primitive cultures recognized this need of sucking by furnishing the child with various types of pacifiers. Today the emphasis is generally to thwart any mouth activity—which is unfortunate in so far as it causes irritation to the child and a lack of oral satisfaction that may later interfere with normal affectional mouth activity.

[28] Ribble, op. cit., p. 31.
[29] Joel Hill, "Infant Feeding and Personality Disorders," Psychiatric Quarterly, 1937, 11, pp. 356–382.   [30] Travis and Baruch, op. cit., p. 182.

TOILET TRAINING AND ATTITUDES TOWARD SEX

The psychoanalytical school of thought holds that another important aspect of infantile experience which is directly related to sexual attitudes in the mature person is that of bowel- and bladder-training. Two specific problems arise during toilet training. The first has to do with the attitudes of the parent toward the training, and the second has to do with the accommodation of the parent to the child's interest in his bodily processes. Educators have an important term to describe the situation in which there is a complex of factors in a learning situation. They say that "concomitant factors" are being learned. Bowel-training involves other factors besides the control of the bowels in a manner approved by society. Because the evacuation organs are so closely associated with the genitals, any attitude associated with evacuation will tend to be transferred to sexual interests as a concomitant learning. Thus, when a mother teaches her child to conform in bowel-training by shaming him for his mistakes or when she uses such terms as "nasty," "dirty," "bad" to describe her soiled child, she is unconsciously teaching him attitudes toward anything sexual in nature.

If, because of social pressure, she feels compelled to establish training at an age when the musculature of the child is not ready for such effort, this experiment may result in permanent damage to the child's elimination apparatus. The watchwords for toilet training are casualness and patience, for toilet training that is premature or carried on with rigid and harsh attitudes may result in lifelong preoccupation with evacuation, compulsive ideas of cleanliness, stubbornness and stinginess, hesitation in sexual acceptance.[31]

Closely related to the matter of toilet training is the handling of the child during that period when his attention is focused directly upon elimination as a pleasure. During this time he may dawdle over his performance and take pleasure in his productions. Sometimes he will smear, and at other times show attitudes towards his stools which are completely antithetical to the adult expectations of his mother or father. If they condemn the child as "naughty" or "bad," he may carry over into adult life an unconscious conclusion that all other activities of the same organs are "naughty" and "bad." Again, if the pleasure associated with defecation is described as bad, the child tends to generalize that all

[31] *Ibid.,* p. 148.

pleasure is bad.[32] The wise parent is aware that the process of acculturation is a lifelong process and that attitudes of society will be accumulated later when the child is ready for social control.

CONCLUSION

American child care, in some of its phases, tends to use substitutes for the close body contact that Mead considers so essential to the development of our sexual selves. Insistence on cleanliness and bodily care has resulted in the daily bath, followed by an oil rub and the application of powder. During all this time, the baby is undergoing skin stimulation which is important to its circulation. Probably more important, however, is the sense of bodily well-being that results from this pleasant interlude with the mother. Ribble points out that thoroughbred kittens who are not licked by their mothers develop serious disorders or die and that young anthropoid apes who are not groomed by their parents sometimes sicken and die. Some readers will be familiar with the extraordinary story of the wolf-children of India. The older child had developed an animal nature and showed no responses to affection until the missionary's wife gave her a daily massage. Then she began to show affectional responses and became, to some degree, socialized. Most mothers talk to their babies when giving the bath or the oil massage, and this is a period of fellowship in which the baby acquires a sense of security and has a positive reaction to his new world.

None of these behavior sequences—nursing, toilet training, bathing or sucking—appears to be the single key to the development of emotional responsiveness. The mother who desires to nurse her baby but because of some illness is unable to do so need not think that her child will be only halfway emotionally developed. For a fundamental fact outweighs the importance of any one of these procedures: it is the loving and tender affection accompanying these activities that determines their value. Neither rocking nor breast-feeding assures the child of either emotional growth or physical health. It is the accepting and loving attitude which underlies these ministrations that gives them value. If this attitude is genuine, if the mother has wanted and continues to want the child, if she accepts her own sexual role and is happy in it, we may be reasonably certain that the child will develop positive and construc-

[32] *Ibid.,* p. 150.

tive affectional attitudes. A mother may rock a baby and sing, but unless there is some rhythm in her life and a song in her heart, the experience may not be genuine. That is what Ribble means when she says:

> Obviously feeding, bathing, and all the details of physical care come in, but in addition to these duties which can easily become routine and perfunctory, we mean all the small evidences of tender feeling . . . fondling, caressing, rocking and singing or speaking to the baby. These activities have a deep significance.[33]

These early conditionings have determined in a major manner every adult's attitudes and expectations. The experiences of his own children in this period of their infancy will, likewise, structure much of their adult life, including their basic emotional capacity, their verve for life, their sexual interest and fulfillment. Preparation for marriage begins at birth and, today, we are beginning to know something of the crucial experiences which later will implement or inhibit emotional responsiveness and sociability.

SELF-ANALYSIS

The facts in this chapter will have little meaning for the reader unless they are specifically related to his own background, and little meaning for his children unless they are absorbed and become part of his attitudes. None of us are completely conscious of the experiences we had as infants. For this reason, it is necessary to depend upon conversations with our parents and pediatricians to piece together the story of our early months.

Most parents enjoy talking over with a child the experiences of his infancy. The reader may obtain a fairly accurate story of his early life if he discusses with his parents his birth, their philosophy of child-care, his toilet training and nursing experiences. Even the attitudes of his parents as they review his first days will reveal something of the joy and tenderness or anxiety that characterized their attitude toward him during this period of his life.

When the reader has accumulated as many insights as possible into his early care, he may wish to relate these to his present degree of sociability, emotional responsiveness, and acceptance of his sexual nature. After this, he may desire to talk over this period of his life and its meaning with a counselor.

[33] Ribble, *op. cit.*, p. 9.

VISUAL AIDS

Life with Baby, University of California, Department of Visual Instruction, 405 Hilgard Avenue, Los Angeles 14, California.

Self Discovery In a Mirror, Encyclopedia Britannica Films, 20 North Wacker Drive, Chicago 6, Illinois.

Baby's Day at Forty-eight Weeks, Encyclopedia Britannica Films, 20 North Wacker Drive, Chicago 6, Illinois.

READINGS

MARGARET MEAD, *Male and Female,* New York, William Morrow and Company, 1949, Part II, Chapter III.

MARGARET RIBBLE, *The Rights of Infants,* New York, Columbia University Press, 1943, Chapters II, III, and IV.

BENJAMIN SPOCK, M.D., *The Pocket Book of Baby and Child Care,* New York, Pocket Books, Inc., 1946.

ROBERT F. WINCH, *The Modern Family,* New York, Henry Holt and Company, 1952, Chapter VIII.

CHAPTER 3

Factors in Childhood

INTRODUCTION: CHILDHOOD WILL BE CONSIDERED HERE AS
THAT PERIOD FROM ABOUT EIGHTEEN OR TWENTY MONTHS TO THE
beginning of puberty. The attitudes learned and the behavior patterns
developed in this period are of major importance in determining later
adjustment in marriage. Reuben Hill studied 135 Iowa families living
under the stress of adjusting to a father who had been in the armed
services and reported a positive association between the childhood
happiness of the wife and "good" adjustment to the crisis of separation
from her husband.[1] Terman found happiness in childhood to be the most
important of the background factors associated with marital adjustment.[2]
Locke submitted the following statement:

> My childhood on the whole was: very happy_____; happy_____;
> about averagely happy_____; unhappy_____; very unhappy_____.

He found that a significantly larger percentage of the happily married
than of the divorced, both men and women, reported their childhood
as happy or very happy.[3] Travis and Brauch describe childhood experience and its effect behavioristically:

[1] Reuben Hill, *Families Under Stress*, Harper and Brothers, 1949, p. 111.
[2] Lewis M. Terman, *Psychological Factors in Marital Happiness*, McGraw-Hill Book Company, Inc., 1938, pp. 225–228.
[3] Harvey J. Locke, *Predicting Adjustment in Marriage: A Comparison of a Divorced
and a Happily Married Group*, pp. 107–108. By permission of Henry Holt and Company,
Copyright, 1951.

We have all lived through those long dark problems of childhood. Each and every one of us remembers at least in small proportion. We may say, "I was the world's worst." Or we may murmur, "I was really a good child; my problems were very mild." No matter which, we still remember. We remember, also, how we were handled when these problems were upon us. We remember injustices. We remember righteous anger. We remember cajolings and less persuasive methods. We remember heads hung low, tears under hot lids, dry, set lips held from retort. We remember fury in return for fury. Penance, shame, regret. We remember what we did; what was done to us; what that did to us in turn—at least what it did to us at the moment. But almost never do we realize what it did to us for all time.[4]

"What it did to us for all time." That last arresting clause indicates that ten or twenty years after childhood we shall still be playing the roles we learned then. Life, to the child, may be a paradoxical experience. It is full of wonder and discovery; at the same time it is fraught with immense challenges, constant misunderstandings, and painful adjustments. There is always the admixture of ringing laughter and bitter tears. In each hour there is learning; learning by the tear ducts, the tensor muscles, the aesthetic sensitivities, the fingers, the tongue, and the heart. The mild-worded mother and the "manly, mean, anger'd father," together with brothers, sisters, grandparents, uncles, aunts, and guests, are, during childhood, the dominant influences in molding personality.

But it need not be "for all time." For as we review the critical areas of our growth in our childhood we can see that some of the particular ways we were handled brought about particular results (we can see, too, how we may handle our own children differently and get different results). And, as we review these past hours of conditioning, the conditioning itself is modified. Travis and Baruch themselves suggest this possibility:

And finally, we see that what has happened in the past needs to hurt us no longer. Reviewing the behavior problems of childhood is often akin to digesting food that has long lain heavily against one's diaphragm. We begin to see our own past behavior in a different perspective. We begin to see where present behavior has unsuspectedly been related to the past. We begin to see that how-we-are is related to how-we-were more than we guessed.[5]

[4] Lee Travis and Dorothy Baruch, *Personal Problems of Everyday Life,* New York, Appleton-Century-Crofts, Inc., 1941, p. 129. Reprinted by permission.   [5] *Ibid.,* p. 130.

45

EARLY SOCIALIZATION AS PREPARATION FOR MARRIAGE

At eighteen months or thereabouts the infant begins to be mobile—begins to bump into chairs and into the world. His style of personality and his bent of character are determined by the peculiar way in which he learns to adjust to others. This style and bent are determined partly by his "tempo," which is largely an inherited characteristic, but more importantly by the degree to which he is socialized. Winch defines the tasks presented to the growing psyche as these:

> (a) the incorporation into his behavior of a sufficient proportion of the parental discipline to enable the child to achieve a workable level of adjustment with his parents; (b) as a corollary of this, acceptance of the idea that a considerable number of "immediate" pleasures are to be foregone in the interest of some "future" gain; (c) the creation of the ego-ideal and the beginning of the struggle to realize it; and (d) integration into the appropriate age and sex groups.[6]

We should add to this list a fifth aspect of socialization, namely, the incorporation into his behavior patterns of an awareness of the generalized expectations of others sufficient to enable him to communicate and to share.

The quantity and the quality of communication in the parental home and in the play group have a decisive influence later on, for social sharing is based on verbal and emotional communication. Communication means the sharing of symbols whose meaning is understood by those who participate. The meanings of symbols come to us as children when, through experience, we internalize what these symbols mean to others. Only when the symbol signifies to us an act yet to be completed does its meaning become clear. Until we learn that the muscle tension, the defiant pose, the tight lips, and the clenched fist mean that a blow is intended, we are not prepared to defend ourselves. In social communication our understanding of the meanings of gestures or word symbols enables us to imagine the response of others to our gestures or our words, and thus we anticipate the reaction of the other. This is the meaning of incorporating into ourselves the reactions of others. Upon this fundamental process all interaction with others is based.

It is obvious that the richer the variety of situations in which the child is placed the more adaptable will he be in marriage. The large

[6] Robert F. Winch, *The Modern Family*, p. 242. By permission of Henry Holt and Company, Copyright, 1952.

family, variety of play and gang activities, freedom in emotional inter-action—these are all critical factors in acquainting the child with the range of meanings associated with gestures and word symbols and enabling him, later on, to communicate effectively. The role we play at any given time is essentially the one which we imagine will bring us status among our fellows. Usually we discard a role which brings ridicule or disdain or increases the social distances between us and our playmates or our parents.

Because we learn to conform in order to achieve status or to avoid punishment we tend to internalize, to make our own, the values of our parents and our friends. Thus we acquire a "conscience" as childhood progresses—we learn to distinguish between acceptable and non-ac-ceptable behavior. The content of our conscience, our particular norms of right and wrong, will be related to the general culture and especially to the way our parents have mediated that culture to us. The degree to which we are "at home" in our culture depends on our internalization of its symbols and its values.

Socialization is an important aspect of becoming a marriageable person. Locke found sociability—defined as "the disposition to unite with others for companionship"—crucial in marriage success.[7] Locke noted as the components of sociability making friends easily, liking to belong to organizations, caring what people think about one, and having a sense of humor.[8] A socialized person is one who has a minimum of social inhibitions and a maximum of spontaneous interest in others. The key-note of socialized conduct is mutuality.

Adjustment in marriage depends on the degree to which the partners are "socialized." If they are to be emotionally responsive to one another, life must have taught them to laugh and to cry without fear, to love and to be tender without affectation or inhibition. If they are to under-stand the almost infinite moods, reactions, and needs of their mates, they must not have been isolated, in childhood and youth, from the floodtide of emotional experiences.

The group of children gathered under the tree discussing the problem of where to tie the swing is learning creative ways of group living—a learning that will play its part in the group experience of marriage.

Socialization begins during those early months of transitions from egocentric to group behavior. In this period the child discovers the im-portance of the demands of other individuals, learns that these others

[7] Locke, *op. cit.*, p. 212. [8] *Ibid.*, p. 212.

47

have rights and interests. If the social setting is a happy one, children soon learn that others also make contributions, and that taking turns or sharing toys or cooperating in games increases their own satisfaction. The roles they choose to play are altered as some action on their part brings them either isolation or greater respect. Hence one learns to limit one's demands, to consider the expectations of others, and finally to relate these to the interest of the group. Out of such experience comes social poise and adaptability. These characteristics cannot be taught— they are distilled from successful living and experience.

Thus the play group and the family give the child practice in adjustment. He early learns to gauge his behavior by what that behavior elicits from others in the way of encouragement, reward, or punishment. He knows that Grandfather can be "worked" for an ice-cream cone but that Father objects to that game very quickly. He knows that Father has a rather consistent sense of justice but that Mother may be more vacillating. He learns that there are days when Father comes home exhausted and irritable, when his voice does not have its usual enthusiasm. He also learns that Mother not only can love him tenderly but can sometimes be very distant to him, and to Father as well. The picture of marriage which the child projects into the future is inevitably derived from his experience with his parents. If they are, on the whole, happy together his picture will be modeled on their marriage. If, on the other hand, the days of irritability and the hours characterized by distance are too numerous, if the reactions of mother and father are too harsh and threatening, the marriage the child projects into the future will take on characteristics opposite to that of his parents.

The family is a school of living. Life in the family is without mask or "front." His brother may be quiet and respectful at school and a demon at home. His father may be a model of patience at the office but shout and swear while making repairs on the kitchen stove. His mother, when she is in society and with her friends, may carefully assume in her speech and tone of voice the exact attitudes her friends expect from a mother; but at home, when the confusion and frustration are too great, she may abandon this role. Day by day, hour by hour, the child learns that life is a place of masks, poses, and roles, and he learns to adjust to this as reality. When, in later life, his own wife, now a mother, abandons the socially expected role of tenderness and patience and becomes upset and irritable, he will not be too shocked.

The experience of family life is deeply imbedded in the child's attitudes. If there is good humor and happy bantering, if the solemn moments of discipline are counter-balanced by the abandon of self-forgetting play, the child's expectation will be of a family life of fun and mirth intermingled only occasionally with shadows. For this child the family is fun and on occasion he will prefer the family circle to the gang or stop watching the TV screen to romp with Dad. On the other hand, if the family is dominated by conflict patterns, by repressed emotions or silent tensions, the child must inevitably internalize a less pleasant picture. Terman supports this view in his findings:

> The happiness of both spouses is positively correlated with attachments and also with lack of conflict. The correlations are highly reliable and are consistent in direction. . . . The highest means (happiness scores) are for subjects reporting greatest attachment or least conflict, and they drop with considerable regularity as attachment decreases or conflict increases. The critical ratios of these differences run high. The data justify the assignment of fairly heavy weights in the happiness prediction scale.[9]

Locke's study, on the other hand, does not seem to verify this. While he did not ask an identical question, it is close enough in meaning to allow a comparison. Locke concluded:

> Affection toward parents appears unrelated to marital adjustment, whereas conflict with parents was related in reverse order from that found in the other studies. . . . Thus, the report of "no conflict" with father was associated with marital maladjustment and "a little" conflict with adjustment. This may mean that the divorced felt that the failure of their marriage was not due to their home situations and minimized the conflict with parents; however, they did not report more affection than the married. Another interpretation is that some emancipation from parents is an essential factor in marital adjustment and possibly "a little" conflict goes along with such emancipation. Also, no conflict at all may imply parental domination.[10]

Although Locke indicates that his and Terman's studies elicited some contradictory findings, a closer scrutiny may clarify the seeming contradiction. It is not the categories of "no conflict" or "a little conflict" that are important. For it is in the home characterized by constant and bitter conflict that we should expect to find the poorly adjusted individual. Locke does not tell us, as Terman does, what happens when conflict increases; hence we have no way of really knowing whether

[9] Terman, *op. cit.*, p. 215. Reprinted by permission. [10] Locke, *op. cit.*, pp. 109–110.

his data support or contradict the findings of Terman. Our thesis has been that a great deal of constant conflict will damage the attitudes of children toward marriage, and Locke does not contradict this.

PARENTS' SEXUAL ADJUSTMENT AND CHILDREN'S SEXUAL EXPECTATIONS

Specifically, too, the child has come to anticipate the meaning of marriage in the affectional relationships of Mother and Father. If they are cold and distant, if they rarely hug or kiss each other, if their marriage is polite, formal, and reserved, the meaning of this behavior is clear to the child. For although he may never hear them argue about their sexual life or other basic differences, he will be aware of the lack of tenderness and sense the barrenness of their marriage—and to some extent associate it with marriage in general. Marriage for him can hold no promise of deep and rewarding affectional patterns, for he has never experienced a relationship of tenderness. Parents today are much concerned about being able to talk easily about sexual matters before their children. But this will never take the place of warm response patterns frequently exhibited. Travis and Baruch stress this factor:

> One thing we must take into consideration is that our children will not always hear nice things about sex. All the more must we counteract this. We must let them know that other people have varying ideas on this score, just as they have different ideas about sex—just as they have different ideas on countless other matters. Different religions, different prejudicial slants, different opinions about politics, different ideas on sex— all these fit into the picture. Yet, even more important, we must give to our children a conviction that sex is essentially wholesome. This we will be able to do only as we work out our own conflicts about the part sex plays in our own lives. For proper sex education, then, the parent must see to his own sexual adjustment. After that, what he says, what he does, and how he feels will take care of themselves.[11]

THE EMOTIONALLY IMPOVERISHED HOME AND FUTURE MARITAL ADJUSTMENT OF THE CHILDREN

One of the chief and valid complaints of today's children is that parents spend no time with them. The parents are rarely at home, and when they are, their attention is given to other interests. A little boy

[11] Travis and Baruch, op. cit., p. 302.

was once referred to a counselor by a school because of serious malad-justment. The boy had an acute shoulder tic; he could not communicate; he was listless and depressed. After a series of conferences in which his contribution was only a series of "uh huh's" and "huh uh's," he finally was induced to talk. After many weeks, he began to talk about recurrent dreams in which there appeared an enormous door which seemed very threatening to him. Persistent and patient examination revealed that there was indeed an important door in this boy's life. It proved to be the door to his father's study. When his father came home from his research laboratory, he would enter his study and shut the door. No one was permitted to enter or knock upon the door. Through the years the boy had come to hate that door and all that it symbolized in the way of affec-tional deprivation. Children hate doors, real or symbolic, that shut them out of the lives of their parents.

The mother who washes her children's clothes and cooks their meals, the father who provides for their present comfort and insures their future—such parents often think that they have thereby fulfilled their obligations; but they may have failed to give their children something even more important—time and attention. Without these, children grow up in emotional and spiritual isolation. We shall see later how urban life, with its media of mass communication and its commercial recreation, tends to accentuate this deprivation. Many modern parents do not give enough of themselves to make for even partial identification on the part of children. It is our belief, derived from careful analysis of case studies, that this must result in emotional impoverishment and insecurity.[12]

Child-neglect may be due to what is popularly termed rejection of children. Studies of infancy cited in the last chapter indicate the possibility that rejection of children may result from their arriving when they are definitely not wanted. Plant stresses this point, putting it first among the four reasons he cites for the rejection of children. He thinks that if the first baby arrives before the parents are ready to give up their carefree childlessness that baby is likely to be rejected.[13] Rejection may also occur if one parent is so preoccupied with the child that the other parent feels displaced and jealous. A third motivation for rejection is present if the child possesses some of the traits of one parent which are distasteful to the other. A further cause for rejection is the fact that

[12] William Goldfarb, "Psychological Privation in Infancy and Subsequent Adjustment," *American Journal of Orthopsychiatry*, 15, (1949), pp. 247–255.
[13] J. S. Plant, *Personality and the Cultural Pattern*, New York, The Commonwealth Fund, 1937, pp. 99–100.

pregnancy often focalizes a woman's lifelong resentment at being a woman. Rejection simply means the denying of affection or closeness. The result of rejection is an emotionally impoverished child who has not been able to learn to love. In so far as the child needs recognition, his rejection will damage his security and his ego strength.

A third type of emotional impoverishment is brought about by domination. The dominated child is a puppet who never has the possibility of using his own imagination or of solving his own problems. Since this problem will be dealt with more fully when adolescence is discussed, it is only mentioned here. Suffice to say that parental over-protection, or "smother love," make for such dependency that normal exploration, experiment, discovery, are not possible.

DISCIPLINE AND THE PRODUCTION OF HOSTILITY

Winch has indicated that an interiorization of discipline is the basis for adjustment between parent and child. Whitman mentions "the blow" as one of the decisive patterning forces of childhood. The whole question of discipline has meaning in relation to preparation for marriage. The anxiety and basic hostility that threaten many marriages have their origin partly in the overall relations between parents and children. The growth of anxiety patterns may conveniently be discussed under the question of discipline. Every parent has the obligation to help his child become acculturated. The parent who does not orient the child in terms of safety precautions, manners, laws, customs, and mores sends him forth without the moral and social equipment to adjust to the world. We begin with a recognition of this fact. But no child automatically knows that ac-culturation is necessary for his future. He does not welcome the cultural straitjacket which is the price of admission to human society. He can-not naturally respond to all adult demands. Consequently friction in-evitably develops.

The way in which hostile and aggressive reactions of children to their parents' expectations are handled will affect their emotional security or adjustment. If the parents are understanding and permissive of the rebellion of an immature child and, as a result, consistently forgive the child's natural hostility, the child operates in a secure atmosphere in which he becomes acculturated with a minimum of neurotic results. But if parents are defensive and lack understanding, the child may be afraid to express his antagonistic and angry feelings and keep them to himself. He may feel that if he expresses these negative feelings he will be physically punished. He may fear that his parents will shame him for not having "proper respect," or that he might lose whatever affection his parents manage to give him. He may have tried it and been made to feel "guilty," as if he were a bad person. Thus he stores up repressed hostility, a reservoir of hostility. It may never be expressed toward his parents; it is very likely to be vented in later life on his business associates, his wife, and his own children. The mechanism involved here is laid bare in a case study in which the client said:

> The fact that my father gets so mad so easily and hollers has definitely created in me a feeling of inferiority, because in the past I've always been afraid of doing something which would make him bawl me out. Even though I no longer fear being bawled out, the attitude of being timid and the fear of making mistakes has clung to me to some extent. I'm too concerned with what people think of me and I'm usually worried about doing that which will please others and make others like me.[14]

This young man was afraid of his father. He could not talk back. Baruch reports a different type of father.

> As a final case in point, let's get back to our Heine who wouldn't eat and who had threatened to fling his food all around. . . . Suppose now that Heine actually begins to throw his food around. This obviously won't do. It's destructive to the rug and furniture, and besides, a chicken bone might land in father's eye. Heine's father is now on the spot; how can he continue to accept and mirror Heine's feelings and yet at the same time curb Heine's actions?
>
> Here is father's opportunity to slip back into the good old ways of disciplining. He is, in fact, on the verge of this. He feels anger mounting inside him and he starts to think longingly of every threat in his vocabulary, from lambasting Heine to forbidding him ice-cream cones for a week. But he, too, remembers the new ways of discipline just in time:

> SEE how he feels.
> ACCEPT how he feels.
> REFLECT how he feels.
> Help him GET OUT THE POISON.
> If necessary, help him STEER his ACTIONS.

> "Heine," Father says, his anger dwindling, "You're mad at me. It's not hard to see that. Why don't you tell me about it. You can say anything

[14] From a case study in the author's files.

you feel like saying. It's okay to get out your anger in words. But I can't let you throw food around. Understand?"

Heine looks up challenging, "Suppose I do it anyway?" Heine's father notices quickly that there has already been a change in Heine. He is no longer concentrating on throwing the food. He is focusing on threatening his father. In other words, Heine is now using threats instead of food-flinging as a way of releasing his anger. This is the feeling that his father now mirrors.

"You want to threaten me, Heine?"

"I sure do. You're an old meanie. I'd like you to trip in the garden and get mud in your mouth. Old stinky mud. Old stinky—nice daddy!" And Heine bursts into a wide grin. "Come on, Dad, let's play kick-ball. I'll eat this here stuff up first real fast."

The crisis is past.

"But" you protest, "It doesn't work that way. If I'd forbidden him, my child would have gone right on throwing the food. I'd have had to resort to punishment, I know. The mere forbidding wouldn't have helped."

Heine's father had not, however, used mere forbidding. He had forbidden the action only. He had not forbidden the feeling. He had given Heine's feelings many chances to come out. The curtailment lay in the fact that they could not come out in this particular kind of action. If they had needed to come out further, they would have to be channeled into other kinds of action instead.[15]

If the parent helps the child get the poison out day by day, it does not accumulate to complicate other adjustments. Furthermore, it does not accumulate to prevent normal affectional development. The child who can express open rebellion, anger, and resentment without fear of reprisal is also the child who will show a maximum of spontaneous love for his parents. Neurotic behavior often has its origin in the fact that many parents threaten their children in such a way that hostility and anxiety, and the consequent guilt feelings are never worked off. In a sense, every child must undergo constant frustration. As a result, he will be rather constantly hostile. These feelings must be allowed continuous expression. Can we confirm these generalizations from our studies? There is some confirmation in the questions raised by Terman and Locke in regard to severe discipline. The relationship of a permissive home atmosphere to later marital adjustment is reported by these two investigators. Terman found that "firm but no harsh discipline" was the type associated with marital adjustment.[16] Locke concluded:

[15] Dorothy Baruch, *New Ways in Discipline*, McGraw-Hill Book Company, Inc., 1949, p. 97. Reprinted by permission.   [16] Terman, *op. cit.*, pp. 228–236.

A significantly larger per cent of both divorced men and women reported that they "never had own way" in their parental homes. "Usually had own way" was reported by a significantly larger per cent of both happily married men and women than by the divorced.[17]

Travis and Baruch report another study which bears directly on this point:

> A bit of interesting evidence comes from two hundred graduate students at Columbia University. Those students who, in their childhood, had been severely disciplined, managed to get over their "bad" behavior. But in the process they developed great animosity toward their parents. Quite naturally then, they also developed a tremendously large load of guilt feeling toward themselves. They owned up to having had strong desires to hurt, or even kill their parents. They wished their parents death through accident or disaster. They condemned themselves so mightily for such thoughts that they wished themselves dead. Many of them had seriously contemplated suicide. In contrast, where discipline had not been felt severe, the students were comparatively free from such feelings. Discipline which was resented had left its mark. It was succeeded by worse problems.[18]

PARENTAL PROJECTIONS ONTO THEIR CHILDREN

Parents have special emotional needs which they often expect their children to meet for them. Exploited children are the boys and girls whose parents used them to make up for their own deficiencies, real or imagined. Such parents drive their children to embrace ambitions which they themselves could not realize. One of the most common illustrations of this tendency to relive one's life in that of one's child is to steer the child into the profession or occupation the parent desired but failed to enter. Or parents find their status in the accomplishments of their children. A student reports:

> When I was in the third grade I almost failed math—and this hurt my parents terribly. I had to struggle with math until I was a sophomore in college. I will always remember my parents' friends asking them if I was smart in this subject and they always had to apologize for me.

Another illustration is the mother whose undemonstrative husband has never given her an outlet for her affectional needs; thus she turns all

---

[17] Locke, *op. cit.*, p. 111.   [18] Travis and Baruch, *op. cit.*, pp. 285–286.

of her love upon her little boy and makes him dependent upon her. When the time comes (around eight or nine) when he should identify with his father, she blocks that transfer of affection. Later, when time for marriage approaches, she finds it impossible to surrender him to any other woman.

Unhappy mothers who have failed in several love matches and in marriage itself sometimes want their children to reject marriage. If these children fall in love, the mother always finds something wrong with the intended mate. Or she may become ill so that her child will feel guilty if he leaves her.

Still another type of parent expiates a neurotic sense of guilt by bringing up his children with extreme care lest they sin too. Children of such parents approach life with a perfectionism so rigid that they find marriage very trying. Others with a stronger ego develop patterns of distrust and deception toward their parents since they cannot live up to the high standards set for them.

Plant emphasizes the parents' need for projection when he says:

> There are few matters so common and impelling as the need that the individual has for mending the broken threads of his own life in the growing lives of those over whom he has a feeling of control. It is for this that the adult looks to family experience.[19]

SEXUAL DEVELOPMENT DURING CHILDHOOD

The general conditioning of the sensual self described in Chapter I becomes much more specific during childhood. The sexual interests of children seem to focus during the fifth, sixth, and seventh years, upon their genitalia. After this comes the so-called "latency" period. The handling by parents of this interest in genitalia and sexual experimentation affects personality adjustment as well as sexual adjustment in marriage. Teachers of family-life courses in high schools, in submitting curriculum materials, include such observations as these:

> Because of an unfortunate experience in another high school in our district, the word sex is not used in any of our schools, and consequently is omitted from this unit of study.
>
> As the school board has locked up any films on reproduction and has

---

[19] James S. Plant, "Mental Hygiene Aspects of the Family," reprinted by permission from the April, May, June, issues of *The Family*, p. 14.

frowned on any instruction in the field of sex we confine ourselves to the more sociological factors in marriage.

Students' reports indicate the same type of situation at home:

> I first learned of sex not from my parents but from a little French girl when I was in the fifth grade. What she told me shocked me terribly. I can remember telling her that "My parents never did that." Yet my parents never told me a thing about sex.
>
> The knowledge of sex that I acquired in the later years of grammar school and in the early years of high school was somewhat confusing. My parents, most especially my mother, suppressed sexual information or conversation. The information derived from classmates was not often of a wholesome nature but degraded sex considerably. Sexual information that derived from my parents was very inadequate; and that derived from my classmates was mostly inaccurate.

Inadequate and inaccurate! These are the words that most often occur as young people describe their childhood initiation into sexual knowledge. How important is this to marital adjustment?

It is important to keep the sexual factor in marriage in proper perspective. The statistical studies of Terman, Locke and Burgess, and Wallin are all in agreement that in marital adjustment the sex factor is secondary to personality and interactional factors.[20] Nevertheless, as studies by Davis, Schroeder, and Terman indicate, proper sexual education is significant in later marital adjustment. Bowman calls the attitude of society toward sex "obscurantism," and points out that "marriage is the only human endeavor in which ignorance is considered a virtue.[21]

MASTURBATION

One of the crises for many parents is the discovery that their child or children are getting satisfaction out of manipulating their sexual organs. Masturbation has come to have associations with very severe feelings of clandestine evil. Parents are consequently appalled at this practice and often use harsh discipline to end it. The practice of masturbation itself has no harmful results unless it is practiced to great excess, but the sense

[20] Ernest W. Burgess and Harvey J. Locke, *The Family, From Institution to Companionship*, New York, The American Book Company, Copyright, 1953, p. 437.
[21] Henry A. Bowman, *Marriage for Moderns*, p. 311, Copyright, 1948, by McGraw-Hill Book Company, Inc.

of guilt associated with it and the general feeling of unworthiness that assails the punished offender may cause severe inhibitions in later life. Robie discovered, in interviewing several hundred men and women whom he classified as "being the most moral, the most successful, happy, useful and well-educated members of the community," that all of them had practiced masturbation.[22] Obviously, no serious moral, spiritual, or personality defects had resulted from their experimentation. But if the child is made to feel that he is a criminal and a social outcast because of this experimentation, that feeling itself may impede his later effective sexual relations with his mate. A more important consideration for parents who find that their child masturbates is the question whether or not the practice is a retreat from life, a comfort-finding device used to compensate for a life that has little joy and constant defeats. If masturbation is a compensatory outlet, the parent will do well to consider how the life of the family can be reconstructed so that the child no longer has a need for such physically soothing retreats.

The child sooner or later will hear from someone all of the myths concerning the damage done by masturbation. He will suffer from anxiety about it unless his parents have given him an antidote of correct information and an accepting permissiveness. The practice itself will disappear if a child masturbates only for sensory pleasure. But if he comes to feel guilty and unworthy because he has practiced it, the influence of this anxiety will be lifelong. These feelings of guilt and unworthiness may actually prevent him from marrying; if he does marry, they may debase the sexual side of his marriage and destroy the response he might otherwise have made.

EARLY HETEROSEXUAL EXPERIENCES

Heterosexual experiences come to children in the several guises in which they express their interest in learning more about the other sex and about sexual intercourse. The Ramsey study indicated that the early heterosexual activity of childhood involved most frequently manual exploration, direct observation of reproductive anatomy, exhibitionistic sex-play, attempts at intercourse, oral contacts, and other forms of experimentation. Table II taken from Ramsey's study indicates the number of boys involved and the percentage of these boys who had had some experience:

[22] W. F. Robie, *Sex and Life*, Ithaca, Rational Life Publishing Company, 1924, p. 330.

TABLE 2. Pre-Adolescent Heterosexual Play*

Age	Number of boys involved	Percentage with some experience	Increment at each age
5	286	2.4	2.4
6	286	16.8	14.4
7	286	24.8	8.0
8	286	34.8	10.0
9	286	41.2	6.4
10	286	46.9	5.7
11	280	52.5	5.6
12	235	48.3	5.8
13	122	66.1	7.8

* Glenn V. Ramsey, "The Sexual Development of Boys," the *American Journal of Psychology*, 56, 2, April, 1943, p. 226. Reprinted by permission.

By the age of 13, two-thirds of the boys had been involved in one form or another of sexual play with girls. One student reports this initiation into the "mysteries":

Sex as sex never actually entered my mind, but sort of accumulated. I never bothered to think about it. At one time (which I do not now recall) at the tender age of five or six my mother read a book especially prepared for children about the "birds and bees" which I forgot just as quickly. I specifically remember all the neighborhood boys and girls all assembled together and taking off their clothes. I was too young to know what it was all about although I felt it was "nasty" and it completely repulsed me; however, I never connected it with sex. At the age of ten my school teacher thought I needed to know so she explained everything to me with my full comprehension and I admit that the facts of life revolted me at first, but I do not feel this an unnatural reaction.

A counselor reports the following experience as fairly typical of the problems he must deal with in this field. A mother came to him because she had discovered her children in sexual play with two brothers from a nearby family. She reported what she had done. When she discovered the children, she sent the boys home, 'phoned their mother, and took her own daughters into the house to talk with them. Her voice was full of tension and fear during this talk, which was for her, she said, the most important and the most difficult she had ever had. This troubled her. Because of her own upset emotions she found herself saying things she

59

did not believe. She then forbade the girls ever to play with these boys again and kept her girls in the house for a week. The counselor knew that from that time on those girls would never be able to confide in their mother regarding their sexual curiosities or problems, and that they would find sex somehow ugly and evil.

The boys had fared worse than the girls. Their father had given them a severe whipping and isolated them. Moreover, he felt so chagrined that he put his house up for sale and was planning to move out of the neighborhood. The counselor thought that unless these boys and girls received special help they would never completely overcome this traumatic introduction to their sexual selves. While no scarlet letter had been burned on their skins, an equal hurt had been inflicted on their attitudes. Out of such experiences come lasting repressions and inhibitions. Sex comes to be thought of as naughty, bad, sinful, something one does not discuss or think about. Fortunate, indeed, is the child who grows up in the country. To him, sex is a natural and normal part of life. But for the urban dweller who never observes the processes of reproduction in nature and who is isolated from the births of his siblings, it may be extremely difficult later to play an adequate role. This makes it even more important for parents to instill an accepting and wholesome attitude toward sex.

FAMILY RITUALS

As children grow older certain ways of living and of responding in the family become rather permanently structured and take the form of what may be called rituals. Bossard and Boll have studied the integrative effects of the development of regular and expected modes of family life and have interpreted these in terms of preparation for marriage in *Ritual in Family Living*. Some of their conclusions bear on this point.

1. Many, perhaps most, family rituals develop with the coming of a child. Often they partake of the nature of a family drama, designed to impress the children. Many rituals center about the children, usually they participate in them.
2. Many family rituals cannot but make a vivid impression upon children. . . .
3. Many, if not all, of the family rituals recalled have pleasant associations. Often they center about holidays, birthdays, anniversaries, and other happy occasions. Because of the nature of family rituals—their

recurrence, the sense of rightness which accompanies them, the pleasurable associations . . . they groove themselves deeply and pleasantly into the accumulating layers of the youthful mind, which constitutes the essence of the unconscious.

4. When the individual leaves home, a major part of the readjustment involves the change in ritualistic behavior. Marriage and the formation of a new family is such an occasion, obviously. Both mates bring with them to form the new family their respective experience. Similarity in such experiences seems to be an important factor in making for marital success; lack of it appears to have the opposite effect.[23]

Rituals tend to promote family integration by producing "likemindedness," by emphasizing "cooperation," by instilling a sense of "group participation," and by developing a sense of "rightness" that contributes to pride and interest in family life and achievement. For children ritual means an organization. Perhaps the most important of the rituals are those which center around the festival occasions of life—birthdays, vacations, and holidays. The tensions of ordinary living are relaxed as the family becomes a unified and organic group completely disposed toward making the occasion one of immense satisfaction. Much of life's meaning comes out of these festival periods, and to secure the continuation of the meaningful experience is a strong motivation for marriage.

The interruption of family rituals by divorce has serious consequences for the child. This crisis situation results in the immediate cessation of many of the rituals—and the breakdown of the structures of family living which have given security and meaning to the child's life. Of course, the trauma associated with divorce goes beyond this. The child may be attached to both parents: their separation throws him into conflict. In many cases there is a contest over the child's affection which makes him an unwilling pawn of adult bitterness. He may resent profoundly the coming of other children in a new marriage. He may feel that they "belong" more completely than he does. He will undoubtedly feel the differences between his status and that of children from unbroken homes and the moral castigation that society vents upon those who fail in marriage. All of this may result in a critical rejection of marriage for himself as well as a general neurotic insecurity.

The difficulties entailed when the ritual in family living consists mostly of conflict are equally serious. Bossard thinks that "quarreling parents

[23] James H. S. Bossard and Eleanor S. Boll, *Ritual and Family Living*, Philadelphia. Quoted by permission of the University of Pennsylvania Press, 1950, pp. 198–199.

make quarreling children who grow up to be quarreling mates."[24] Parents who point with scorn at divorced persons are often aggressive people who maintain in their own homes an atmosphere of strain and perpetual conflict which likewise wounds children. An excerpt from a case study indicates this:

> From early childhood I can remember the strained relation between my parents which frequently resulted in quarrels. When I heard my parents quarrel and almost come to blows I had a feeling that was close to terror —when I finished high school I was very insecure and had strong feelings of inferiority.[25]

Children from homes dominated by conflict are apt to be too eager for any kind of tenderness or too suspicious in dealing with others. Children from homes split by divorce or splintered by conflict often grow up as insecure persons and are timid in thinking about marriage.[26]

THE COMMUNITY AND ITS INFLUENCE ON THE CHILD

Today, influences outside the home likewise play a very important part in socializing the child and giving him attitudes which will be useful or demoralizing in a future marriage. As Waller points out:

> The role which the child plays within the family is not wholly a matter of family interaction. The entire family is involved in a number of processes of interaction in the community, in the social class, in the church, and in the economic system, and it is as true of the family as of any other group that its external relations determine its internal structure. The status which the child gains outside the family has its repercussions within it. The boy who distinguishes himself in athletics or in his studies is thought to reflect credit upon the entire family group, and his status in the family is correspondingly enhanced. The girl who disgraces the family may likewise find her family relations endangered. Similarly, the position of the family in the community profoundly affects intrafamily relationships, and intrafamily relationships affect the role of each member in the larger group.[27]

[24] *Ibid.*, pp. 254–255.   [25] From a case study in the author's files.
[26] Andrew G. Truxal and Francis E. Merrill, *Marriage and the Family,* Prentice-Hall, Inc., Copyright, 1953, p. 547.
Ray E. Baber, *Marriage and the Family,* McGraw-Hill Book Company, Inc., Copyright, 1953, pp. 502–508.
[27] Willard Waller (Revised by Reuben Hill), *The Family: A Dynamic Interpretation,* Copyright, 1951, by The Dryden Press, Inc., pp. 90–91. Reprinted by permission.

Today, the scout leader, the school teacher, the athletic director, the Sunday School teacher, and the probation worker exercise important influence on the child. As the family becomes more individualistic, the roles the child plays in groups outside the home become increasingly important in determining his attitudes. These again interact with his role as a child in the home.

Provided the child does not come from an emotionally impoverished home, all of these new experiences and roles add to his ability to adjust. The modern school with its "child-centered" approach, which aims to compensate for and ameliorate ego wounds suffered from the blows of early life, is important. The school's emphasis on communication and socialization contributes substantially to that type of maturity associated with wise marriage choice and optimum marriage adjustment.

CONCLUSION

The child assimilates, consciously or unconsciously, the attitudes, the values, and the roles of those about him—learning prejudices and stereotypes for or against affection and later marriage, maturing or growing fearful—all depending upon the stability and the values and the roles of the people who influence him most powerfully. Out of these many impacts grows a unique type of response, different from the response of anyone else in the world. This unique response pattern will also have its own special way of adjusting to situations, being confident or fearful, easy in interaction or inhibited in approaching interaction. He may accept sex as normal and wholesome or reject it as vulgar and indecent. But whatever the experience gained through childhood, the individual has a history by the time he comes to adolescence, a history that will affect this new and challenging period, and a history which will influence in every significant way his adjustment in marriage.

SELF-ANALYSIS: AUTOBIOGRAPHICAL STATEMENT

The analysis of the conditioning factors that operated during your childhood can be readily made by writing an autobiographical statement about your childhood experiences. Much of the material in this chapter will help the student recall significant areas of past experience that were instrumental in forming current attitudes. As Travis suggested, once these are related to present behavior and present attitudes, they lose

some of their power to control us. For convenience, the following outline is provided for self-analysis. This is a general outline, and each
individual will think of important material that is not allowed for.

In writing this statement, the student should remember that precise-
ness of phrase is not as important as freedom in the expression of feelings. If the student finds himself carried away by some memory, it is
better to continue writing about this experience than to hold strictly to
the outline.

I. Family Background
    A. Describe your family configuration, your father, mother, or step-
       father or stepmother, your brothers and sisters, uncles, aunts, or
       grandparents who lived with you, and analyze their relationship to
       each other. Which siblings were older, which were younger than
       yourself? Give special attention to their emotional characteristics
       and attitudes, and to the "emotional climate" each created in the
       house.
    B. Indicate the relationship of each parent to each child, noting par-
       ticularly any evidences of favoritism, hostility, dominance, rejection,
       and their effects.
    C. Analyze your relations with each of your parents during early and
       middle childhood, with your brothers and sisters; with uncles, aunts,
       grandparents, or others. If you were an only child or stepchild, what
       deprivations resulted, and what close friendships or adjustments
       were made?
    D. What crisis did the family encounter during your early or middle
       childhood that influenced you? Give particular attention to deaths,
       divorces, economic failures, long illnesses, or separations.
    E. Analyze the degree of sociability that prevailed in your home with
       special reference to feelings of isolation or loneliness.
    F. What ritualistic behavior did your family have?
    G. How important were the festival occasions in your family?
    H. Analyze in what ways economic, social, or religious status influenced
       the behavior of the family.

II. Social and Neighborhood Influences
    A. How long did your family live in each house, each neighborhood,
       each city?
    B. Did your parents own their home or rent?
    C. Analyze the various neighborhoods in which you grew up, in terms
       of your relationship with other children and adults.

    D. Which teachers, children, and activities exerted the greatest influence on your personality development and why? When?

    E. Analyze your adjustment in the first six grades in school. Were you generally happy and secure while in school?

    F. Describe the various play groups and gangs in which you participated as a child. What role did you play in them?

III. Pyscho-Sexual Development

    A. At what ages, on what occasions, and from what sources did you acquire information regarding sex during childhood?

    B. How accurate was this information, and what was your reaction to it?

    C. In what way did your relationship with your parents contribute to or retard wholesome development?

    D. In what way did other children contribute to your sexual development or confuse you?

    E. What specific experiences did you have that gave you a sense of guilt or inhibition?

    F. In what way did your early religious education contribute to or detract from a wholesome development?

IV. Socio-Cultural Influences

    A. What clubs and groups did you belong to as a child? What positions of leadership did you hold in them? Were you happy in these groups?

    B. How many churches have you attended? What denominations? How often did you attend as a child? Were you happy in participating?

    C. What physical or social influences handicapped your early social adjustment?

    D. What social class did you belong to in the community?

V. In what ways did these childhood experiences and conditioning factors influence those attitudes that will be important in determining the degree of adjustment of your marriage?

AUTOBIOGRAPHICAL ANALYSIS

Once the autobiographical statement has been completed, it is important to analyze its meaning for marriage adjustment. Therefore, the last segment of the statement asks that this analysis be made. It is important in considering this to remember what sections of the statement were difficult, what areas of childhood memories were hard to recover or were recovered with some pain. For these are the areas in which we have had negative experiences and uncomfortable associations. If there are areas which we cannot remember at all, that may indicate either very traumatic experiences or no experience. In any case, we should give particular attention to them. The feelings that accompanied them writing this analysis are also important. There will be particular value to this effort if the material presented is talked over with the instructor of the course with particular emphasis upon those areas which produced marked emotional reactions. Once insight into present feelings and attitudes has been achieved, perhaps as the result of this study, a more mature attitude will result.

VISUAL AIDS

Films may be used to illustrate clearly some of the points raised in this chapter. The following films are suggested:

Feeling of Hostility, 1948, National Film Board of Canada, 1270 Avenue of the Americas, New York, 20.

Feeling of Rejection, 1948, National Film Board of Canada, 1270 Avenue of the Americas, New York, 20.

Overdependency, 1949, National Film Board of Canada, 1270 Avenue of the Americas, New York, 20.

READINGS

JAMES H. S. BOSSARD, *The Sociology of Child Development*, New York, Harper and Brothers, 1948, Chapters IV, V, and XV.

HARVEY J. LOCKE, *Predicting Adjustment in Marriage: A Comparison of a Divorced and a Happily Married Group*, New York, Henry Holt and Company, 1951, pp. 86–123.

LEE TRAVIS and DOROTHY BARUCH, *Personal Problems of Everyday Life*, New York, Appleton-Century-Crofts, Inc., 1941, Chapter VII.

ROBERT F. WINCH, *The Modern Family*, New York, Henry Holt and Company, 1952, Chapter IX.

CHAPTER 4

Factors in Adolescence

INTRODUCTION: CHILDHOOD ENDS WITH THE RELATIVELY TRANQUIL YEARS OF EIGHT THROUGH TWELVE. THIS LAST PERIOD of childhood is so harmonious that it is often described in literature as the golden period. It is a time of happy group activities in which earlier socialization problems have been largely solved and the spurt of sexual interest manifested earlier has quieted and become latent. Parents find it difficult to give up the rich and rewarding fellowship of these years. But this period must end. Nature itself decrees it. The happy relationships of late childhood are destined to disappear in the storm and stress of those turbulent experiences which mark the years from twelve to twenty.

In America, the adolescent lives in a tumultuous ambivalence. He feels new inner sexual tensions which discharge themselves in emotional outbursts or are dispelled through channels of high religious or moral idealism. The adolescent struggles with his new sensations from within even as he tries to adjust to new and vacillating expectations from without. For now he is expected to conform to adult behavior patterns for which he has no background of experience. While his biological development demands growing independence of action, he often encounters the resistance of his parents who resent his repudiation of the patterns of control which marked his childhood relations with them. The outcome of these years of struggle to achieve adulthood is decisive for marriage.

THE MEANING OF ADOLESCENCE

Adolescence is regarded chronologically as the years between twelve and twenty-one; physiologically as the time between the onset of puberty and the achievement of maximum physical growth; psychologically as the period of transition from childhood dependence to adult independence; socially as the period from the beginning of the loosening of home ties to the establishment of a new family unit.

The onset of puberty presupposes certain marked physiological developments which differentiate the adolescent from the child. Height increases most rapidly in boys from 12½ to 14½; in girls from 10½ to 14. Weight increases most rapidly in girls from 11½ to 14½ and in boys from 13 to 16. Furthermore, this weight is distributed on a changing bony structure. The boy's chest enlarges, his shoulders broaden; his hips become narrower, while his legs and arms grow longer and terminate in what seem to him at the time enormous hands and feet. The girl grows in a somewhat different way. Her hips become wider; and there is an increase in chest, shoulder, hand- and foot-size, but less marked than in the boy. Her weight is also distributed differently. The boy grows harder, more muscular, and straight, while the girl becomes soft and round in contour because of a layer of fat that is deposited under her skin. For this reason the boy comes to have a greater immediate strength while the girl develops greater reserves and has longer endurance.

The physical changes in both sexes are related to glandular developments. During childhood, the endocrine system, except for the thymus and pineal glands, is relatively inactive. Early in adolescence, the pituitary, thyroid, ovaries, testes, and suprarenals show a sharp upturn of activity. These glandular and physiological changes are related to sexual development. Boys and girls who develop faster in bone structure, height, weight, and endocrines also mature more quickly sexually. This onset of maturity is marked by menstruation for girls and sexual emissions for boys. Table 3 taken from Ramsey gives the indices of sexual growth by age groups: puberty and its physical changes appeared generally at ages 12, 13, and 14, but many boys did not mature sexually until age 15 and a few not until 16.

In this study of 291 boys, Ramsey shows that the secondary physical changes such as voice-change and growth of pubic hair parallel the maturation of the sex glands. With sexual maturity inevitably come sexual sensations. To adjust to the inner promptings of these sexual pressures while at the same time adjusting to equally insistent social pressures constitutes one of the main problems of the adolescent.

TABLE 3. Per Cent of Given Age Group Showing Phase of Sexual Development*

Age-group (in yrs.)	Ejaculation	Voice-change	Nocturnal emission	Pubic hair
10	1.8%	.3%	.3%	.3%
11	6.9	5.6	3.7	8.4
12	14.1	20.5	5.3	27.1
13	33.6	40.0	17.4	36.1
14	30.9	26.0	12.9	23.8
15	7.8	5.5	13.9	3.3
16	4.9	2.0	16.0	1.0

* Glenn V. Ramsey, "The Sexual Development of Boys," *The American Journal of Psychology*, 56, 2, April, 1943, p. 217. Reprinted by permission.

ACHIEVING INDEPENDENCE

Achieving independence would not be so difficult if all parents were sensitive to the developmental needs of their children.

Many parents, however, cannot and do not draw aside, happy that their child has grown beyond the need of their constant help. They have learned so well the role of being superior guides and found such satisfaction in it that they continue to demand obedience all through adolescence; moreover, their own lives have been, up to this point, centered on their children, and allowing freedom to the children means for them the loss of the most rewarding function they have ever had. Young people need to understand the emotional investment parents make in them; if they do, they will be more tolerant of what they sometimes regard as mere interference. Children, too, must remember that their parents grew up in a different cultural era; hence, their recollections of their own adolescence do not always give them an adequate base for understanding the new generation. Yet studies indicate that many parents do well in trusting their young people. In a major study of 5,500 high school seniors in Washington, Elias asked them to check each of nine areas of serious disagreement with parents. The percentages are surprisingly low —in only one area did more than 30 per cent disagree with their parents.

Elias also asked about the degree of respect which parents showed for their children's opinions and judgments, which is indirectly a measure-

TABLE 4. Percentage of 5,500 High-School Seniors Who Checked Certain Areas Of Serious Disagreement with Their Parents*

AREAS OF DISAGREEMENT	Boys	Girls
Spending money	27.8	24.9
Friends	7.6	11.9
Choice of clothes	8.9	9.6
Attitude toward parents	13.9	19.0
Outside activities	19.9	20.0
Schoolwork	26.3	12.4
Future plans	16.9	19.2
Share of work	28.6	29.6
Social life	14.4	15.1

* L. J. Elias, *High School Youth Look at Their Problems,* State College of Washington, Washington, January, 1949. Reprinted by permission.

ment of recognition of the adolescent's need to gain independence. The high-school seniors answered this question as follows:

TABLE 5. Responses of 5,500 High-School Seniors Who Checked the Statement: "My parents respect my opinions and judgment."*

RESPONSE	Boys Per cent	Girls Per cent
All of the time	10.0	13.4
Most of the time	52.3	53.7
About half the time	27.5	23.8
Seldom respect their opinion	7.0	6.8
Never do	1.4	1.1

* L. J. Elias, *High School Youth Look at Their Problems,* State College of Washington, Washington, January, 1949. Reprinted by permission.

These figures would indicate that many families are considerate of the opinions of young people. Still, for a sizable percentage of young people, there are problems involved in achieving independence. The following case study indicates some of the dynamics of this problem:

Mary is a girl of 21, a senior in college, of singular mental and artistic abilities. She can sing, dance, paint, play the piano, or write a script for a radio play. She has held many major positions on campus. Her classmates know her as one of the campus "wheels." What her classmates do not know is that this very chic girl does not select her style of hairdo nor has she ever picked out a coat or a dress for herself. Her mother does this. When she makes major decisions regarding any organizational matters it is only after a long distance telephone conversation with her mother. She has majored in telecommunications but her mother made the choice because the mother owns a great deal of stock in a radio station in her city where she wants Mary to work.

Mary is often depressed. In such a mood she does not turn to her roommate or her house mother; she calls home and receives comfort. Mary's career, her looks, her religion, and her plans have all been determined by her mother.

Mary is engaged to a young man with a promising future. He has begun to resent Mary's dependency although he is not fully aware of the reasons for his increasing irritability. He does not know yet that Mary's mother has decreed that they must put off marriage until Mary has worked for two years after graduating. He does not know that when Mary objected to this, her mother immediately became ill and made Mary feel very guilty. He does not know that Mary was told over and over when she was a little girl that not to obey Mother or to think ill of Mother was a very deep sin. He does not know that when Mary's mother decides they may marry she will also decide, as she has already intimated, that Mary and her husband must move to her community and live close to her.

Mary is becoming aware of what her mother is doing to her. While she feels guilty about it, she has begun to save part of her allowance and has purchased her first dress of her own choosing. And, although it depresses her to do so, she has been giving steady attention to the question whether it would be wise to live near home after marriage. Mary says, "I was always taught never to doubt Mother's wisdom. If I ever did when I was younger such a hurt and angry look came over Mother that I retreated and I've retreated ever since."

Mary thinks she understands her fiancé's irritation. She says that when vacation comes she is going to fly home and talk to her mother about waiting two years to get married. She also says that this will be the hardest task she has ever undertaken and probably the most necessary. Mary has been trying to crowd five years of gradual growth towards independence into five months and it has not been easy. Mary now understands the need to work through her emotional feelings whenever she must make a decision or oppose her mother. She still has the feelings but she is on the road to being a person in her own right.[1]

Mary will become a person. She has had help. But there are a great many other adolescents who do not get help. To them, it seems right and

---

[1] From a case study in the author's files.

proper to obey without question the dictates of their parents. These young people often lose opportunities for marriage because their prospective mates do not meet their parents' special expectations. These expectations often include a lifetime supervision of the married children and then of their grandchildren. One psychiatrist who specializes in marriage-counseling estimates that 75 per cent of his cases of marital maladjustments are the result of unbroken dependency patterns. While this psychiatrist's practice represents only a small segment of the population, it is probably true that many marital problems stem from such problems as Mary exhibits.

On the other hand, it is true that parents are often right about the lack of wisdom in their children's marriage plans. Young people are all too often so romantic that they fail to see obstacles to their future happiness. The parents who see these obstacles become alarmed and often drive their sons and daughters further into mismatches by their criticism. These parents lost their opportunity years ago when they failed to shift gradually from dictators to advisors, from guides to companions. Now, when they attempt to give advice, the channel of communication is clogged with past bitterness and misunderstanding. Had the children been allowed to make many minor decisions throughout childhood and early adolescence, they would have matured, and through minor mistakes become prepared to make intelligent major decisions. Furthermore, the parents would have gained their children's confidence because they did not stifle them with anxious care. Young people who are allowed to grow and mature are really closer to their parents than those who are psychologically bound to them; those parents who cling too tightly to their children eventually destroy any possibility of love between them.[2]

Dependence operates in subtle ways. A young woman falls in love and tells her family that she wishes to announce her engagement. Immediately the mother or father becomes agitated. Not wishing to face the need for the daughter's continued emotional servitude, the parent invents any number of rationalizations. "She must finish school." "She must work long enough to have some experience." "He is not frugal or saving, you will never have anything." "He is too frugal, you will never have any fun." "He is not intelligent enough." "His family background is poor." "His mother is a snob." "He may be called into service." All of these objections are repeated every day in one form or another. If reasoning does

[2] Ernest R. Groves, *The Family and Its Social Functions*, Philadelphia, J. B. Lippincott Company, 1940, p. 429.

not work, the parents may feign illness or other special needs, thus inducing guilt feelings in young people. Translated into the truth, all of these phrases and actions say only one thing: "I can't bear to let you go."

Nor can we overlook the consequences of dependence in the marital relationship. The dependent adolescent is unconsciously looking for someone to lean on. He does not search for a companion, but for a foster mother. His life pattern is one in which a mother has always cared for him and made his decisions. He is not prepared to live in a companionship setting with vigorous give and take. He has nothing to give and he has been protected from taking anything. For this reason, he needs and unconsciously searches for someone who will play the role of maternal protector all through life.

On the other hand there is a danger that a reaction to the struggle for independence will swing too far; Cole speaks of the problems of the type of individual who overcompensates because of parental dominance:

> This type of unemancipated adolescent is seen in the boy who gets drunk, uses profanity, or has illicit sex relations as a means of demonstrating his independency to the world. When an over-attached adolescent sets out to break the bonds between himself or herself and the family by unwise and violent methods, it is generally because all ordinary methods have failed. A boy or girl rarely succeeds in growing up by such violent means; all he does is to build up a habit of childish resentment. The adolescent who is free to buy his own clothes (provided he keeps within his budget), free to bring anyone he will to his own house, free—within reasonable degrees of guidance—to choose his own work, and free to plan his own time, has adequate opportunity for self-assertion without going to such extremes. The boy who gets into serious difficulties in order to prove he is grown up is no more independent of his home than the boy who cannot make up his mind which book to read until he has asked his mother for her advice. One is positively conditioned, the other negatively; neither is mature and neither can regard his home objectively.[3]

Such a person generally makes a poor adjustment in marriage. In trying to get out of too tight a social contract at home, he has developed an attitude of contempt for all social obligations and responsibilities. Much of his behavior shows his lack of concern for the feelings or needs of others.

In contrast to the over-dependent and the over-independent, there are the boys and girls who work out good relations with their parents.

[3] Luella Cole, *Psychology of Adolescence*, Fourth Edition, New York, Rinehart and Company, Inc., 1954, p. 340. Reprinted by permission.

The adolescent has the power to help create good relations. Where there is only a minor degree of dominance or conflict, he can often change the situation into a humorous one. Again, if the adolescent attempts to understand the parents' point of view, he can often by his own reasonableness effect a compromise and educate his parents to a better way. Adolescents should realize, too, that often the verbal criticisms of their parents are only symbolic expressions of deep concern for their welfare. On many matters it is better for the boy or girl to accept advice graciously from his parents than to engage continuously in a bitter battle of wills. Finally, if efforts to work out the situation bring no results, the adolescent can suggest to his parent that the two of them talk with a counselor. Young people often take the initiative in improving family relations.

ACHIEVING SEX IDENTIFICATION

It is imperative that during the period of physiological change into womanhood and manhood corresponding changes in social role take place. Menstruation indicates with finality that a girl is now a potential mother; an ejaculation indicates potential fatherhood for the boy. To achieve acceptance of our sexual selves is as important as gaining poise in our relations with the opposite sex. To some extent, these processes are interrelated, for those adolescents who are blocked socially in heterosexual development find it hard to accept their sexual capacities. Many case studies of adolescents with deviant sexual behavior indicate that when social adjustment with the opposite sex had not been achieved, such behavior was used as a substitute to find some response.

MENSTRUATION

Menstruation often comes as a shock to those girls who have not had a normal expectation of puberty. The following case illustrates something of the trauma introduced into a girl's life because her mother, her church, her school, and her community had failed to introduce her to facts she could not overlook or escape:

Helen was the only daughter of Mrs. B. Mrs. B had been divorced when Helen was 8 because of her own sexual inhibitions which had made her marriage a period of physical frustration for her husband and a time of neurotic illness for herself. As a result she had been unable to share any kind of sexual information with her daughter. Due to a sense of failure, she embarked on a program of entrusting Helen to anyone else she could. Helen was kept in boarding schools during the school year and sent to a wealthy aunt's beach home during the summer. The summer when Helen was 12 she began to menstruate. She immediately thought she would die and confided in a girl friend who was slightly older. The girl friend told her about menstruation and took her to a drug store but Helen was alarmed. She called her mother and asked her to come and get her. Mrs. B, not knowing the cause of her illness, immediately drove to the beach.

The aunt inquired of Mrs. B, after she had talked to Helen, what the trouble was. Mrs. B could not discuss it and assured the aunt that Helen had an intestinal upset and would be all right. The aunt, never hesitant to spend money if the cause was adequate, insisted on taking Helen to the doctor. Mrs. B was now put in a ridiculous situation but she eluded it by saying that perhaps Helen would be better off if she saw her own doctor who was familiar with her background. This peculiar conversation contrasted so sharply in Helen's mind with what her girl friend had told her that she now became even more anxious and was very happy about going home to see her physician.

But when they arrived home her mother showed no concern and told her that the trouble would be over shortly. It was, but both Mrs. B and the girl friend had forgotten to tell Helen that the trouble was to be a regular or an irregular regular one. So when Helen returned to the beach the same situation reoccurred with Helen now obsessed with the fear concerning cancer. This time no reassurance would do and a doctor had to be consulted. While this introduction to womanhood was only part of the conditioning process, it definitely contributed to a very frigid sexual reaction on the part of Helen.[4]

Menstruation is a natural evidence of creativity. It is the process which monthly clears the uterus of stored material so that a fresh supply of food and nourishment may be gathered, in case a new life process is begun. As such, it is part of the cycle nature has developed in sharing with men and women the nurturing of another generation of human beings. It is true that in the past the days of the menstrual flow were regarded as "sick" days, but this is looked upon today as a psycho-somatic reaction. Excessive pain or cramps are almost always due to attitudes and posture, not to any physiological condition. There is a description, in Appendix I, of an exercise which has proved to be most helpful in relieving distress in this period. The modern girl has no need for either

---

[4] From a case study in the author's files.

seclusion or special care during her menstrual period. She may swim, dance, and play, provided she does nothing to excess. Menstruation is a burden only if girls make it so. It should be regarded as an intrinsic part of the whole process of motherhood. Adolescents who have learned to regard it in this way rarely have any physical problems, or any psychological difficulties in accepting it.

SEMINAL EMISSIONS

Seminal emissions are nature's way of relieving the excess of stored sperm. They may cause fear reactions on the part of maturing boys. While a few boys may regard nocturnal emissions as a welcome sign of maturity and future fatherhood, very often no thoughtful father or teacher helps them come to this conclusion. Instead, the natural questions motivated by "wet dreams" are answered by uninformed peers whose inadequate explanations may lead to guilt feeling or fear. Seminal emissions are as normal as menstruation and cause no physical damage.

MASTURBATION

Most normal young people experiment with various sexual outlets during adolescence. The most common way of dealing with early sexual tension is through masturbation. Ramsey confirms the belief that masturbation among boys is practically universal. In the study mentioned

TABLE 6. Incidence of Masturbation*

Age-group (in yrs.)	Number of boys involved	Percentage with masturbatory experience	Increment at each age-group
6 or less	284	5.3	5.3
7	284	9.5	4.2
8	284	14.1	4.6
9	284	22.9	8.8
10	284	28.8	5.9
11	283	53.5	24.7
12	278	72.6	19.1
13	230	84.8	12.2
14	161	95.0	10.2
15	105	98.1	3.1

* Glenn V. Ramsey, "The Sexual Development of Boys," *The American Journal of Psychology*, 56, April, 1943, p. 224. Reprinted by permission.

previously he discovered both the onset and the incidence of masturbation. Over 98 per cent had masturbatory experience by the age of 15. All that was said in the last chapter about the harmlessness of this practice in childhood applies, too, during adolescence. However, masturbation comes to be more highly charged with emotion during these years because now both the girl and the boy are capable of an orgasm, which means for the boy an ejaculation and for the girls a series of pleasurable contractions of the muscles of the vagina. Ramsey makes the following significant comment after reviewing his material on masturbation:

> Before or soon after the onset of adolescence over 90 per cent of the boys reported masturbatory experience, which in the majority of cases ranged in frequency from one to four times a week. As socio-sexual forms of outlet were developed, the frequency of masturbation usually declined. Worry over alleged deleterious effects of masturbation was the most common sexual problem presented by these boys. The popular literature of sex-education and lecturers was primarily responsible for the widespread misinformation on this subject.[5]

EROTIC FEELINGS

Certain sensations, erotic in nature, bother the adolescent. The erection of the penis is often a source of shame to an adolescent boy as are feelings of erotic satisfaction that come from physical contact with a girl. Dancing sometimes proves a problem to very healthy young people who find themselves erotically stimulated by body contact. Yet these reactions

TABLE 7. Source of Most Sex Information of 5,500 High-School Seniors[*]

SOURCE OF INFORMATION	Boys per cent	Girls per cent
Parents and adults at home	38.2	64.6
Church, Sunday school, minister	3.2	2.5
Older kids, magazines, movies	52.3	26.7
Class and supervised discussion	10.5	20.8
An adult counselor	8.7	6.4

[*] L. J. Elias, *High School Youth Look At Their Problems,* Permission to quote granted by The College Bookstore, State College of Washington, Washington, January, 1949.

[5] Glenn V. Ramsey, "The Sexual Development of Boys," *The American Journal of Psychology,* 56, April, 1943, p. 232. Reprinted by permission.

are normal signs of developing womanhood and manhood. Common questions such as those that deal with menstruation, seminal emissions, masturbation, and sexual sensations might not cause anxiety if they were anticipated by parents or answered during early adolescence, but, unfortunately, these questions often are not answered. Elias found that for boys the source of information was most frequently their friends, but for girls the primary source was their parents.

Table 7 is interesting but it does not reveal what the scope of the discussion may have been. Parents may describe the reproduction process but fail to deal with the sexual problems that are unique to the early adolescent. Ramsey gives us more detailed information in the following table:

TABLE 8. First Sources of Sex Information of 291 Boys, in Per Cents*

First Source of Information	Origin of babies	Ejaculation	Nocturnal emissions	Contraceptives	Menstruation	Masturbation	Intercourse	Prostitution	Venereal diseases
Conversation, male companions	52.5	67.4	68.0	92.1	57.6	44.2	90.0	93.0	65.5
Conversation, female companions	.7	—	—	.5	4.3	—	1.7	—	—
Mother	27.5	1.3	2.8	2.7	20.2	1.0	.5	.5	4.8
Father	3.5	2.6	2.8	1.6	4.3	—	1.0	1.9	4.8
Printed matter	4.4	2.2	1.6	1.0	5.1	2.1	2.1	1.3	14.3
Adults	3.0	1.3	2.4	.5	4.3	.4	.5	1.3	6.8
Observation	4.1	11.3	—	—	2.1	21.2	.7	—	—
Actual experience	—	10.9	22.4	—	—	30.7	—	—	—
Others (school, movies, radio, etc.)	2.2	—	—	—	—	—	—	—	3.8
Indefinite or unknown	2.1	3.0	—	1.6	2.1	.4	2.6	1.0	—

* Glenn V. Ramsey, "The Sex Information of Younger Boys," *American Journal of Orthopsychiatry*, XIII, April, 1943, p. 349. Reprinted by permission.

Ramsey confirms our hypothesis that many of the more tangential and yet critical areas of sexual information are not discussed with their boys by mothers and fathers. We do not have similar information for girls but we should suppose that parents do not differ markedly in their ability to discern important areas of anxiety for young people. These facts mean that students need to assess their adolescent histories for any indications that inhibiting feelings of guilt or sex rejection occurred during this period. If the acceptance of our sexual selves is normal and wholesome during this first period of adulthood, that normality forms a basis for good adjustment during adulthood.

ACHIEVING HETEROSEXUAL POISE DURING ADOLESCENCE

Independence and sexual adjustment have so far been discussed as important goals of adolescence. The third major area of growth for this

TABLE 9. Per Cent of 5,500 High-School Seniors Who Checked Certain Problems in Boy-Girl Relationships*

PROBLEM IN BOY-GIRL RELATIONSHIP	Boys	Girls
What makes a good marriage	13.9	32.6
Making a successful marriage	9.1	25.5
Going steady	12.9	13.3
Can't date the right person	12.7	12.5
Not enough dates	11.5	11.6
Break with girl, boy friend	9.0	13.4
How much intimacy to permit	6.9	14.7
Getting along with other sex	12.2	9.5
Not having (girl/boy) friend	9.0	8.4
Understanding about love	4.4	10.5
Should I get engaged	3.1	11.5
Not attractive to other sex	7.8	7.5
Right attitude about sex	7.9	7.3
Insufficient sex knowledge	7.6	6.9
"Going too far"	8.5	5.9
Sex problems	7.6	6.5
Uncomfortable with other sex	8.9	5.2
Wonder if anybody will want me	5.1	7.6
Learning about sex	6.4	6.4
(Girls/boys) on mind too much	7.5	5.2
Concerned about sex disease	6.4	4.1
"Necking, smooching"	4.8	5.4
Proper sex relations	5.5	4.3
"Petting"	3.5	3.9
Thinking too much about sex	5.9	1.6
Embarrassed about sex	2.8	3.6
(Boy/girl) friend stepping out	3.8	2.2
Too many dates	3.1	2.5
Self-abuse, masturbation	4.8	0.8
Not able to get married soon	3.3	1.2
Quitting school to get married	0.3	0.7

* L. J. Elias, *High School Youth Look At Their Problems*, State College of Washington, Washington, January, 1949. Reprinted by permission.

age group that is specifically related to marriage is the achievement of poise and ease in interacting with members of the other sex. During early childhood we fix our affectional patterns around our parents as love objects. In later childhood, we are members of a one-sex gang and we often focus our affectional life upon a "pal." Crushes and identifications with the same sex are normal in early adolescence or late childhood, but such fixations during later adolescence are very unhealthy. Individuals who fail in their attempts to relate to the other sex sometimes become homosexuals.

The period of middle and late adolescence is characterized by many affectional trials, by infatuations and quick love affairs. These are the trial runs of courtship. They serve a profound purpose in maturing our ability to get along with the other sex. And success in developing apt and secure relational abilities in this period has a strong bearing on success in marriage.

How important it is to achieve poise and ease—and an ethical attitude in meeting and sharing with the other sex—is further indicated in Elias' study of the problems of 5,500 high-school seniors in Washington.[6] These seniors were very much concerned with the attributes of a good marriage as well as with their interaction with each other. The largest percentage of boys (13.9) and the largest percentage of girls (32.6) indicated that what constitutes a good marriage was their most important problem. "Going steady," "Can't date the right person," and "Not enough dates" all ranked about even as next in importance. Roughly, 12 per cent of both the girls and the boys indicated that dating was a major concern. Ethical concerns such as "Proper sex relations," "Petting," "Right attitudes about sex" were not as important as problems but they did trouble many.

While many of the topics in Table 9 receive specific consideration in the next chapter on dating, Elias' findings indicate how important many of these points of stress are to adolescents. It is interesting to compare this list of problems with those of the next age group, students in junior college. A list is prepared from a summary prepared by junior-college teachers of Southern California, as shown in Table 10.

It is obvious from this table that problems of conversation, of shyness, of what to do and where to go have not been finally settled even by late adolescence. The adolescent is concerned with these prob-

---

[6] L. J. Elias, *High School Youth Look at Their Problems*, State College of Washington, Washington, January, 1949.

TABLE 10. Fifteen Dating Problems of Junior College Students of Southern California by Rank Order for Men and for Women by Per Cent*

Rank Order	MEN'S PROBLEMS	Per cent	WOMEN'S PROBLEMS	Per cent
1.	Finances	34	Petting	36
2.	What to do (where to go)	29	What to do (where to go)	26
3.	Finding suitable girl	17	Conversation	12
4.	Conversation	15	Finances	12
5.	Petting	11	Getting the "wanted" man	8
6.	Asking for date (opportunity for)	10	Drinking	6
7.	Shyness	7	Time to come home	6
8.	Lack of time	6	Behavior—lack courtesy	6
9.	Getting too serious	6	Parent problems	5
10.	Transportation (distance too far; no car)	4	Getting too serious	5
11.	How late to stay	4	How to refuse or discourage	5
12.	Getting along with parent	4	Lack of opportunity	4
13.	Etiquette on date	3	No problems	4
14.	Girls spoiled (not punctual)	3	Shyness, or lack social skill	3
15.	Arguing, criticizing	2	Last minute dates	3

* Material arranged from data supplied by Junior College Teachers of Southern California. Material gathered in a joint research project in mariage-education classes.

lems of developing into a person others will like. Consequently his speech, dress, manners, attitudes, and even morals are bent toward this goal. Some adolescents think that to be accepted is more important than to use good grammar, to wear clean clothes, or be dignified in bearing. These later will be the goal of young adulthood but in the phase of seeking status they are sacrificed to the great god of conformity. Conformity means acceptance. Hence the precocious or withdrawn boy or girl who develops hobbies or pays too much attention to studies does so at the cost of ostracism. On the other hand, the most popular students are the friendly, enthusiastic, happy individuals who make others feel secure in their presence.

Whether these heterosexual contacts are initiated early or late, the ability to make them is crucial as training for marriage. To accept a member of the other sex as a stimulating companion, to be able to communicate without hesitation, to feel free and easy in his company are preliminary steps to the later achievement of the permanent companionship of marriage, of the ability to differ, to discuss, to plan, and to love without hesitations. Locke has studied the importance to marital adjustment of the solution to this problem of heterosexual poise. He measured the relationship of the number of friends before marriage to marital adjustment:

> A sociable woman, as measured by the number of both women and men friends, is a good marital risk. About 1 in 4 divorced women as compared to 1 in 7 married women reported "almost no" and "a few" women friends (per cents: 26.0 and 15.5, CR 2.1). This, of course, means that more happily-married than divorced reported "several" and "many" women friends. Likewise "almost no" men friends were reported more frequently by divorced than by married women (per cents: 19.6 and 7.9, CR 2.8), with happily married more frequently reporting "several" men friends before marriage.[7]

Adolescents in an urban setting and, generally, members of small families find the development of sociability or heterosexual relations difficult. Nevertheless, to face the problem successfully is an important step toward later happy marriage.

CONCLUSION

In this chapter, three major developmental tasks which face every adolescent have been analyzed: the problem of becoming an independent, secure adult, the problem of accepting wholesome adult sex roles, and the problem of achieving heterosexual sociability. Involved in facing these problems is adjustment to the institution of dating. This is the subject of the next chapter.

It is important to assess individual growth or retardation in the process of orientation to male and female roles, in developing poise in heterosexual interaction, in skill in communication, and in pleasure in companionship. This is the purpose of the self-analysis schedule which follows.

SELF-ANALYSIS

The following outline, like the one at the end of the chapter on childhood, tries to discover important areas of growth that are correlated

[7] Harvey J. Locke, *Predicting Adjustment in Marriage: A Comparison of a Divorced and a Happily Married Group*, p. 348. By permission of Henry Holt and Company, Copyright, 1951.

with marital adjustment. The student will want to add any experiences or facets of his life during adolescence which seem important to him but which are here omitted.

I. Family Background
   A. Describe the following areas of interaction with your father during your adolescence:
      1. Use of car or home.
      2. Male or female friends.
      3. Hours for study, hour to "get in."
      4. Clothes, make-up, or mannerisms.
      5. Discipline.
      6. Your developing independence.
   B. Describe the above areas of interaction with your mother during adolescence.
   C. Describe any areas of conflict during this period with your siblings.
   D. What particular crises did the family encounter during these years and how did you react to them?
   E. What was the degree of happiness of your parents' marriage during this period?

II. School and Neighborhood Influences
   A. Describe your problems in school in terms of adjustments in studying, use of time, relations with other students, reading or writing problems.
   B. Describe your relationship with your teachers during this period.
   C. Analyze your social adjustments during these years in terms of friendships and groups. Did you feel accepted or rejected?
   D. Were there any particular families or institutions in your neighborhood that influenced you?

III. Psycho-Sexual Development
   A. Describe your various infatuations during this period.
   B. Did you have a problem with inadequacy of sexual knowledge during these years?
   C. Did evidence of puberty (seminal emissions or menstruation) come as shock or embarrassment to you? What preparation had you had for these experiences?
   D. Did you worry about masturbation or have a fear of homosexuality?
   E. What early petting or sexual experience, if any, gave you guilt feelings during these years?
   F. What dating behavior did you develop that troubled you?

IV. Mood Reactions
  A. Did you tend to be cheerful, worried, fearful, depressive, optimistic?
  B. Were you burdened by feelings of insecurity, inferiority, or doubt?
  C. Did you feel shy and self-conscious?
  D. Were you satisfied with your use of your time?
  E. Did you quarrel excessively with friends, siblings, or parents?

V. Social Values
  A. Did you have problems in deciding on your stand on sexual matters, smoking, drinking, gambling? What were your values in these fields?
  B. Did you struggle over religious ideas and ideals?
  C. Were you concerned about your choice of and success in an occupation?
  D. Analyze any conflicts in values you had with your parents.

VISUAL AIDS

The Story of Menstruation, International Cellucotton Products Company, 919 N. Michigan Avenue, Chicago 11, Illinois.

You and Your Family, Association Films, Y.M.C.A. Motion Picture Bureau, 347 Madison Avenue, New York 17, New York.

The Quiet One, Athena Films, New York.

Angry Boy, Mental Health Film Board.

Farewell to Childhood, International Film Bureau, Inc., 57 East Jackson Boulevard, Chicago 4, Illinois.

Children's Emotions, McGraw-Hill Book Company, Text Film Department, 330 West 42nd Street, New York 18, New York.

READINGS

PETER BLAS, *The Adolescent Personality*, New York, Appleton-Century-Crofts, Inc., 1941.

LUELLA COLE, *Psychology of Adolescence*, Fourth Edition, New York, Rinehart and Company, Inc., 1954.

PAUL LANDIS, *Adolescence and Youth*, New York, McGraw-Hill Book Company, Inc., 1952, Chapters 5 and 7.

ROBERT F. WINCH, *The Modern Family*, New York, Henry Holt and Company, 1952, Chapter 10.

C. B. ZACHARY and M. LIGHTLY, *Emotion and Conduct in Adolescence*, New York, Appleton-Century-Crofts, Inc., 1940.

Dating as a Factor

INTRODUCTION: DATING PROVIDES THE OPPORTUNITY FOR THE MOST IMPORTANT SOCIAL RELATIONSHIP WHICH A YOUNG person can have. The importance of dating lies in its contribution to socialization, to the maturing of personality, to the selection of a mate, and to subsequent marital adjustment. In this chapter, we study dating in terms of its function at different age levels and for different classes. We shall consider some of the problems associated with the present system of dating and some possible solutions to these problems. As Lowrie[1] has suggested, dating is a neglected field of study. There is little research material available on the subject.[2] This chapter summarizes existing research and uses interviews and papers of young people as the basis for its generalizations.

THE BACKGROUND FOR DATING

Dating generally begins with puberty. But this statement neglects the important training for dating that ordinarily precedes it. The last stage of childhood is marked by widespread participation in one-sex groups. In this pre-adolescent stage, the other sex is either despised or ignored. With the advent of puberty comes another type of gang in which

[1] Samuel H. Lowrie, "Dating, a Neglected Field of Study," *Marriage and Family Living*, 10, 1948, pp. 90–91, 95.
[2] Ernest W. Burgess and Paul Wallin, *Engagement and Marriage*, Philadelphia, J. B. Lippincott Company, Copyright, 1953, p. 63.

boys and girls mix but do not pair off. Crist, in a study of 120 high-school students in the ninth through the twelfth grades of a university laboratory school,[3] concluded that successful early heterosexual social relationship was associated with enjoyment of the first dating experiences.[4] He also found that individuals who had not had previous conditioning in a mixed group were apt to be more anxious, fearful, and shy than those who had had frequent heterosexual contacts.[5] Hollingshead, in his study of many of the adolescents of Elmtown, found that early dating experience was characterized by over-cautiousness in physical contact, shyness, difficulty in saying the right thing, and anxiety about proper behavior.[6] Duvall and Hill stress the fact that few schools or communities make adequate provisions for "this mingling of the sexes of different age groups, thus making dating more difficult."[7] Crist's study indicated the importance of the status achieved in other areas of interaction to the enjoyment on the first date.[8] There is agreement that successful heterosexual group activities are an important prelude to successful dating.

DATING IN JUNIOR HIGH SCHOOL

Duvall and Hill characterize dating in junior high as "fleeting affinities" and describe such dates as coke dates, being walked home from school, or other types of temporary try-outs of pairs.[9] The extent of dating in this age group varies with regional mores and with individual physical maturity. There is a difference of five years in the physical maturation of the sexes with girls maturing earlier on the average than boys. Hollingshead reported that, by the time they enter high school, 43 per cent of the boys and 58 per cent of the girls have had at least one date. Crist found that dating in its earliest stages developed "primarily because the group expected it, not because of any particular interest in the girl or the boy in dating as such. . . . "[10] Mead thinks that this very early dating accentuates tensions and hostilities because boys, particularly, are not ready for such activity:

> During the very age when most of our comparative material suggests that boys are least ready to engage in sex activity in which they have to take

[3] John R. Crist, "High School Dating as a Behavior System," *Marriage and Family Living,* 15, Copyright, 1953, pp. 23–28.   [4] *Ibid.,* p. 25.   [5] *Ibid.,* p. 25.
[6] A. B. Hollingshead, *Elmtown's Youth: The Impact of Social Class on Adolescence,* New York, John Wiley and Sons, 1949, p. 224.
[7] Evelyn M. Duvall and Reuben Hill, *When You Marry,* Revised Edition, Boston, D. C. Heath and Company, Copyright, 1953, p. 54.
[8] Crist, *op. cit.,* p. 24.   [9] Duvall and Hill, *op. cit.,* p. 55.   [10] Crist, *op. cit.,* p. 25.

the initiative, they are being drawn into a life that mimics the sex activities of late adolescence.[11]

Despite the differential in physical and psychological maturity, Crist found that 87.9 per cent of this age group dated their classmates, while in high school only 54.7 per cent would select companions from their own grade.[12] These data indicate that much early dating is motivated by status considerations and may make for problems later by forcing individuals into situations for which they are not yet sufficiently mature. Early discouragement may be a factor in later withdrawal. McGuire reports an interview which illustrates the importance of a good beginning.

> Maybe I ought not to tell you—but, when I was a Freshman and a Sophomore [in High School], I didn't dress very nice or pay any attention to my figure. The kids didn't talk to me. I wasn't in any clique. Cliques are natural; you like some people better than others. So I turned to the skating rink. Because I didn't belong to any clique here at school I tried hard to make friends at the skating rink. Then I began to pay more attention to my clothes and my appearance. I worked into the crowd. Then— at school, when I looked better—the kids began to be more friendly to me. But you never really get in the top crowd if you don't start early.[13]

Status for dating may depend on an early acceptance by the "top crowd." It is not difficult to understand failures in development if considerations of social status force boys and girls to play roles for which they are not ready and for which they have had little preparation.

HIGH-SCHOOL DATING

The structure of dating in high school is very complex because it is related to clique formation, community class structure, and psychological maturity. Hollingshead identified 106 cliques in Elmtown, and concludes: "The adolescent clique and dating patterns are a reflection in large part of adult social structure."[14] McGuire emphasizes the following categories of cliques which seem to supersede community stratification:

> For convenience, the following terms are being used by research workers to designate the reference groups which mark the several categories of peer acceptance.

[11] Margaret Mead, *Male and Female*, New York, William Morrow and Company, 1948, p. 280.   [12] Crist, *op. cit.*, p. 25.

[13] Carson McGuire, "Family and Age-Mates in Personality Formation," *Marriage and Family Living*, 14, 1953, p. 20. Reprinted by permission.

[14] Hollingshead, *op. cit.*, p. 242.

1. Wheels . . . "the active ones," "the top crowd."
2. Brains . . . "Students," "good kids, but they don't know the score."
3. Outsiders . . . "skaters," "not in the crowd," but "they get around."
4. Mice . . . "quiet ones," "inoffensive," and "seldom heard."
5. Outcast . . . "you don't want to be with them."[15]

There are a number of subdivisions of outcasts. McGuire describes these:

> Apparently, according to the interview data, there are at least two kinds of outcasts. A "drip" is a would-be wheel who "doesn't know how to run around." A "dope" is a would-be brain who arouses antagonism by parading his knowledge and by not knowing how to act appropriately when certain role behaviors are expected.[16]

The clue of "appropriate behavior" is important because it indicates that those who are psychologically inhibited or whose behavior patterns reflect class backgrounds that are out of harmony with the peer group cannot make the grade. Hollingshead confirms this in his study of cliques; for he found that the cliques in Elmtown reflected the social class structure.

We may now summarize the high-school dating structure. One is prepared or not, depending upon the opportunity to participate in heterosexual groups before dating. Dating takes place in cliques. Ability to participate in these cliques depends on psychological adjustment, upon membership in the social class structure, and upon the ability to fit into the peer pattern. Once a rating is established it is difficult but not impossible to move from one group to another. Our next task is to define dating in terms of patterns for different social classes.

HIGH-SCHOOL DATING AND SOCIAL CLASS

The life pattern of young people determines their dating behavior. How early they must accept adult status, find a job, and establish their own home has much to do with their dating attitudes. Hollingshead describes the lower-class youth of Elmtown as definitely looking forward to early marriage and early employment.[17] They leave school very early for casual employment in low-paid jobs. This fact is reflected in an emphasis on freedom of action and freedom from parental control at a much earlier age than at the middle or upper-class levels.

Lower-Class Dating. This emphasis on freedom is reflected in the

[15] McGuire, *op. cit.*, p. 20.   [16] *Ibid.*, p. 20.   [17] Hollingshead, *op. cit.*

ways of securing dates, dating behavior, and marital choice. Dates are "picked up" after cruising around in a car or visiting various ice-cream parlors or taverns which are known as centers for these youth. The boys may discuss the girls and make an agreement as to how they will pair off. The invitation is quite casual and may simply consist of a promise of a ride home or to a park. But implied in the ride home are many other things such as refreshments, necking, or sex activities.

Sexual activities among adolescents are more prevalent in the lower-class group than in any other. A Southern California teacher who daily counsels young people in this group explains something of their pattern and of the reasons for the pattern:

> The home is truly patriarchal in domination, especially those of the Slavs, Italians, Mexicans and Japanese. It is not uncommon for the girls to be forbidden to go on unescorted dates. If the girl wishes to see a boy, she must meet him at the dance, on the street corner, at a girl friend's house, or in a movie. Very few parents will allow their daughter to go on a date as we know it. A large number of girls and boys have intercourse before they reach high school or soon after reaching high school. These are some of the superficial reasons: the close living conditions of the lower economic classes, the low morals of their parents, the poor family life education in junior high school.[18]

It is apparent that the dating-sexual pattern of the lower-class reflects the more casual sexual patterns of the parents. Going steady means engagement for these young people, and pregnancy is often the prelude to marriage.

Middle-Class Dating. Most of the literature on dating really deals with middle-class dating. Dating for this group can be divided into three stages: Cavan calls the first stage "the Ritual of Making a Date."[19] The boy must take the initiative although the girl has many opportunities of subtly indicating her interest in him. In contrast to the lower-class patterns, dates must be arranged somewhat formally to conform to middle-class standards. It is often easier for the insecure adolescent to "break the ice" and ask for a date on the telephone than in a face-to-face encounter, and consequently the telephone is a most important adjunct to dating. The telephone conservation is often prolonged and serves as a preliminary getting-acquainted period. The telephone is also

---

[18] Document in the author's files.
[19] Ruth S. Cavan, *The American Family*, New York, Thomas Y. Crowell Company, 1953, p. 309.

very useful in the development of the relationship, and for discussing the date afterward with various girl or boy friends. This often leads to friction with parents, who generally do not understand the function of the telephone in developing these relationships. Dates must be arranged some time in advance, for last-minute dates are regarded as fill-ins and are demoralizing to a girl's sense of prestige.

The second stage of the date is the sharing of some common activity such as a movie, a dance, a party, or a sports event. These events occur generally on Friday and Saturday nights and last considerably longer than week-day events. There seems to be an almost universal compromise between children and parents regarding hours. The hour to be home is one of the major points of conflict between adolescents and parents. Boys and girls feel that they will lose status if they cannot stay out as long as their peers do, and their parents feel that extremely late hours are injurious to the morals, education, and health of their growing sons and daughters. This often leads to bitter and incessant quarreling because two different sets of values are involved. The problem is most generally solved by a compromise—the young people agree to stay at home during school nights but are given considerable freedom on weekends when they do not have to get up early the next morning.

The boys who excell in sports, dancing, sophistication, and personality are the most popular, while girls with good clothes, a sparkling manner, and at least a minimum of prudery are most popular with the other sex. During the social activity of the date, both boys and girls, if they are not going steady, will try to meet and favorably impress those who rank high on the prestige scale. This is because of the insecurity engendered by the whole dating system. It leads to such bitter complaints as, for instance, that "the boy or the boys are fickle, they are always making a play for another girl or girls even when on a date with you." This competitive aspect of dating gives it an insecurity which is not always conducive to harmonious relationships.

In order to escape the competitive aspects of dating, many give up rather early in their dating career and escape by means of going steady. Cavan has summarized some of the mores which control going steady:

1. No boy other than the chosen one will ask the girl for a date; this rule is highly respected and rigidly followed. The girl, for her part, may not entice any other boy or show him favors.
2. The couple are always invited together to social functions; if one cannot attend, the other may not attend. They have become a social unit.
3. Symbols are exchanged, such as rings, class pins, club pins, bracelets

with the owner's name inscribed, or sweaters. These symbols are not gifts; ownership remains with the original owner, the symbols are returned when the arrangement of going steady breaks up. In fact, the absence of the pin or ring signifies to the high school crowd that the two are no longer going steady.

4. Nonmaterial symbols are cultivated between the two. They may have a favorite song, a favorite seat in the motion-picture house, or a favorite place to park. They thrill to the sound of "our song," and resent innocent intrusion of another couple who happen to occupy the favorite seat or parking spot.

5. More intimacy is permissible and expected than on a casual date.[20]

Going steady is motivated by a sense of insecurity, by the prestige that comes to those who have a "steady," by new opportunities for parties, dinners, and other social events, and by its effect in enchancing the self-esteem of the individual involved.[21] But with these advantages come several disadvantages. Going steady involves tensions with parents who lament the limitations of experience inherent in going steady, a sexual tension because of the greater intimacy involved,[22] and a social tension in so far as many of these young people soon tire of their companions and wish to dissolve the relationship.

Upper-Class Dating. In the upper class, dating does not have the same motivation as in either of the classes already discussed. As prestige inheres in the social class itself, these young people are not ordinarily troubled about prestige or status. Furthermore, parental control operates in the selection of a mate, so that freedom of choice in dating and freedom of dating activity are much more circumscribed. Going steady is not part of the mores of this group. Many of the girls in this class attend girls' schools, and dating is restricted to highly controlled social occasions arranged by the school. Sexual experimentation is frowned upon because prestige is much associated with personal morality. Much of the dating in this group is carried on at clubs and resorts where parents are present and a part of the social group.

COLLEGE DATING

Dating for college students involves a great many opportunities and some problems. It gives further opportunity for the growth of personality, for wider heterosexual contacts, for development of greater poise when with the other sex, for greater discrimination in marriage

---

[20] *Ibid.*, p. 314. Reprinted by permission.   [21] *Ibid.*, p. 315.   [22] *Ibid.*, p. 315.

choice, and for broad recreational experience. On the other hand, it produces insecurity for those who fail, it confronts almost every college student with sexual tensions, and it sometimes produces competitiveness between men and women. We shall discuss the problems of sexual tension first.

THE DATING DILEMMA

Dating operates on an improvised basis with few mores thus far developed to regulate the behavior of young people. The result is that they must develop their own standards. They find themselves in the dilemma of being strongly stimulated sexually and yet expected to behave as though they were without sexual feelings. This means that they must exercise an unprecedented amount of self-control and make difficult personal decisions.

These decisions are not easily made today. We live in a social atmosphere heavily charged with sexual allusions and sexual stimuli. Lazarsfeld and Stanton conclude in their study of the lyrics of songs on the hit parade between January 1, 1941, and July 1, 1942, that of 90 songs, 83 had lyrics with sex interest and only 7 had no sex interest.[23] So the songs which young people sing, and which contribute to their expectations, directly or indirectly, motivate sexual activity. Movies universally stress the theme of sex. No advertiser is unaware of the advantage of an attractive pair of woman's legs in selling cars, refrigerators, or beer. Radio has its "lonely gal" with her insinuating, low, and husky voice, while the "Continental," who adjured his audience "not to be afraid because it's only a man's apartment," and then a little later whispers, "I ought not to do the things I do," was elevated to a national network on television. Novels are more and more concerned with sex.

The inference from these facts is that many consider sex to be the basic need and interest in life. Young people approaching later adolescence (which Kinsey claims is the most potent period of the sexual drive in men) are bombarded with sexual allusions, suggestions, and stimuli. It is impossible for young couples today to escape making some decisions regarding sexual conduct.

These decisions are complicated by a number of factors. The first

[23] P. F. Lazarsfeld and F. N. Stanton, *Radio Research*, 1942, 1943, New York, Duell, Sloan and Pearce, 1944, p. 365.

factor of importance is that for the first time in our society young people are relatively unchaperoned. They are permitted more freedom and are more mobile than at any time in history. A recent magazine article referred to the automobile as the "passion wagon." Young people may drive into the mountains, to the beach, to a resort, and may be completely alone for many hours without anyone noticing them, checking on them, or caring much about them. What happens in the car or in the mountains is not determined now by parents or by society but by the young people themselves. Hence, at the very time in their lives when young men are exceptionally virile and passionate, society has put them on their own.

If chaperonage is gone, so too are some of the other controls that formerly operated for restraint. Very few young people today are much concerned about venereal disease. The threat of these diseases, therefore, does not inhibit sexual behavior. Again, the fear of pregnancy is not as strong as it once was. Contraceptives have taken away some of the fear formerly associated with sexual intimacy. Social controls have also become less positive. Religion is not the force in inspiring prudent conduct that it was fifty or seventy-five years ago. Parents do not provide their children with either an understanding of their sexual feelings or a set of values to regulate those feelings.

A study in 1952 of the background of 1,000 students of 5 college campuses of South Carolina indicated that only 385 or 38.5 per cent of the students were given any sex education by their mothers and only 19.7 per cent by their fathers.[24] Thus, young people are open to stimulation and provided with opportunities for sexual experimentation; social controls that formerly guided them in this area are not supplied by either parents or society; and yet they are expected to conform to adult standards. This is the dilemma of dating.

In college, the dating dilemma is sharpened by still other factors. Sexual prowess or sexual experimentation seems to give status to individuals in groups such as fraternities or college cliques. A fraternity man, reporting on the impact of fraternity life on attitudes toward dating, says:

> Once the preliminaries are over and the fraternity man starts dating, he is likely to find that a flashy car and sporty clothes will increase his rating. However, this is greatly over-rated by critics of the system as well as by

[24] R. Grann Lloyd, "Parent-Youth Conflicts of College Students," *Sociology and Social Research*, 36, 1952, p. 229.

those members who are less fortunate. A degree of determination and some help from the brothers who have automobiles is all that is required to get over these obstacles. On the other hand, the new member will find that as time goes by, his standing among the brothers *within* his own fraternity will depend more and more on the frequency of his dates and the date-rating of the young women he does take out (that is to say, how attractive they are, and whether they belong to a big sorority). Furthermore, the number of sexual experiences he has had will definitely increase his standing. If there are no such experiences, as is the case in about two out of three college men [as shown in the chart below], the tendency is for the individual to fabricate some or at least leave the implication that he "is the lover."[25]

Thus there is some tendency within groups to regard the sexually experienced as possessing some merit that the less sophisticated do not have. Consequently, there is some pressure to achieve status through actual sexual experimentation or fabricated reports of sexual activity.

How do college young people meet this situation? In the following table Landis and Landis compare two studies, one at Cornell and one at Michigan:

TABLE 11. Per Cents of Students Checking Each of Four Statements Representing Attitudes on Pre-Martial Sex Standards, 2000 Michigan State College Students, 1947, 173 Cornell University Students, 1940–41*

APPROVED STANDARDS	MEN		WOMEN		BOTH	
	M.S.C.	Cornell	M.S.C.	Cornell	M.S.C.	Cornell
	PER CENT	PER CENT	PER CENT	PER CENT	PER CENT	PER CENT
Sexual relations for both	16	15	2	6	12	9
None for either	59	49	76	76	63	65
For men only	10	23	15	11	12	16
Between engaged persons only	15	11	7	6	13	8

* Judson T. Landis and Mary Landis, *Building a Successful Marriage,* New York. Permission to quote granted by Prentice-Hall, Inc., 1948, p. 121.

In contrast to these figures are those of Kinsey. He reported that of his college interviewees some 44 per cent had had pre-marital inter-

[25] From a case study in the author's files.

course by the age of twenty.[26] Burgess and Wallin's sample included only 22.4 men and 36.5 women who had a high-school education or less, so that their findings are generally comparable to those of Landis and Kinsey. The men in this sample were divided into 32.2 per cent who had not had pre-marital intercourse and 67.7 per cent who had; 53 per cent of the women had not had intercourse before marriage and 47 per cent had had such experiences.[27] Kinsey reported that about 83 per cent of men at the grade-school level and 75 per cent of men at the high-school level had had intercourse by the age of twenty.[28] Conflict and confusion are inevitable when ethical decisions are demanded in an area of stress where a large group carries on an activity and a large group condemns that activity. Expectations necessarily vary and individuals are at a loss regarding personal standards.

DATING AND THE DEVELOPMENT OF ETHICAL STANDARDS

Seen in this broad perspective of changing and confused standards, dating becomes a process of establishing norms for lifelong ethical conduct. Young people must make up their minds about a wide variety of moral matters. The following excerpt from a girl's analysis of her own ethical growth indicates something of the scope of decisions facing contemporary youth:

When I first got to school I just took everything in my stride; nothing shocked me because I was expecting completely new experiences. I had been there ten days the first time someone offered me dope. Never in my life have I had the slightest inclination to try it, nor at that time I hadn't even any inclination to try liquor or cigarettes, but the casual way in which it and other things drifted through my environment left me with the feeling that though I certainly would not drop my standards, I was never shocked at anything anyone else did. For this reason my friends have always brought their troubles to me—at least half of my close friends had to get married.[29]

For that large part of the population which has had no instruction in sex either in the church, in the school, or in the home, dating be-

---

[26] Alfred C. Kinsey, W. B. Pomeroy, and C. E. Martin, *Sexual Behavior in the Human Male*, Philadelphia, W. B. Saunders and Company, 1948, p. 550.

[27] Ernest W. Burgess and Paul Wallin, *Engagement and Marriage*, Philadelphia, J. B. Lippincott Company, 1953, p. 28.

[28] Kinsey, *et al., op. cit.*, p. 550.   [29] From a document in the author's files.

95

comes an experience of groping for permanent answers to the meaning of sex in life and its function in contributing to happy living. If one talks with young people on an intimate basis he soon learns that this drive to establish standards is almost as great as the sexual drive itself. Leland E. Glover held interviews or received questionnaires from 1,289 college students who listed for him their chief problems. The result of this survey indicated that the largest number of students were concerned with values, ethics, and morals.[30] The sorority house discussion and the fraternity "bull session" have been much maligned for their preoccupation with sex. Those who listen to these discussions with an attentive ear are aware that the motivation for them falls under two headings: (1) the need for accurate information which the young people never had an opportunity to acquire, and (2) their eagerness for some norms for their own conduct. Society has freed the sexual impulse, but it has not given guidance which would assist young people in using their freedom with either accurate knowledge or well-defined values.

In so far as the first expressions of sexual feelings or the first experiences of sexual contact are basic in establishing later attitudes toward the sexual phase of life, what happens during dating is of great significance for marital adjustment. These dating experiences may result in such disgust as to bring on frigidity or impotence, or they may result in standards adequate for later adjustment in marriage. Dating may make a person a physical wreck, burden him with intolerable doubts and crippling guilt feelings. Most young people in college face weekly decisions as to how they will behave in the dating situation, and many of them have no background of parental guidance to help them. It is crucial, then, to recognize the importance of dating as preparation for marriage.

THE RATING-DATING COMPLEX

There are many factors which influence the development of sexual standards. One of these is the so-called Rating-Dating Complex as it was analyzed by Waller and discussed earlier in this chapter. In observing groups of young people Waller noted that their dating conduct was often motivated by a desire to achieve high status on campus. The individual's desire to build up personal self-esteem through dating the

[30] Leland E. Glover, *The Teacher of Marriage and the Family as Counselor*, unpublished Ph.D. Dissertation, the University of Southern California Library, 1950, p. 87.

most desirable persons is reinforced by the desire of his group to rate on campus. One student confirms this:

> This pressure is so great that when I entered a fraternity and was dating a girl from my high school who was not going to college it was suggested to me that I drop her and begin to date girls from _____ sorority. I liked the girl and wanted to go with her so I continued. But the pressure got so great from the fraternity that I finally had to give her up.[31]

This student thinks there is a discernible cycle in dating which starts out with a girl's being very popular, then descending in popularity, and finally, weary of the competition, wishing to find a more permanent status.

DATING, RATING, AND SEXUAL STANDARDS

Perhaps the struggle for prestige is so intense that many boys and girls are subtly aware that the entire dating relationship is exploitative in the sense that its ultimate purpose is not friendship or fun but achievement of status. How difficult it is to adjust to status demands is indicated in the following excerpt from a student's analysis of her reactions to the struggle for prestige:

> However, though I had made tremendous adjustments, I was not accepted by the rest of the school for being any different than I had been in the seventh grade. I made up my mind that in high school it would be different, because new students would judge me on the present, not the past. By the second day of high school I had bids to five social clubs, and before the month was over I was going steady with one of the leading football players. I was no longer a nonentity. I joined two social clubs in the tenth grade and was in the height of my glory; but after six months I became very disgusted with the two-faced back stabbing that one had to engage in to maintain prestige, and spent a couple of months being antisocial and not dating at all.[32]

Or, on a date, one is not motivated to contribute to the enjoyment of one's partner so much as to impress the other with a view to what each will say about the other later in the fraternity, sorority, or other group. Obviously those who lead the race for prestige are not under pressure to win favor by excessive petting or by permitting sexual intimacies. But those who do not measure up to the cited requirements for high rating,

[31] Statement by a student in the author's files.   [32] From a document in the author's files.

and who feel desperate because of lack of status, or who are very insecure because of their inability to attract dates, may feel that dating is so important that they will use sexual means to attain a type of temporary popularity. Hence, the rating-dating complex has serious repercussions on those who are not so popular. This is particularly true of those individuals who have never had an adequate love response from parents. They may engage in sexual intimacies not only to gain status but also because it seems the only avenue open to the experience of kindness, closeness, and tenderness. The dangers of such conduct will be discussed later.

THE ROMANTIC FALLACY AND SEXUAL STANDARDS

It is possible, too, that the romantic nature of the dating ideals of today has much to do with accentuating the dilemma. Many young people find it difficult to escape romantic interpretations of affectional relationships. Consequently they expect that dating or heterosexual relationships will be based on romance. Sexual attraction is camouflaged under intense romantic feelings which many young people assume to be love. Hence, young people concentrate on a "line" or an "atmosphere" which does not stress happy recreation, stimulating conversation, interpersonality exploration but, instead, moods associated with moonlight and roses and thrills. They become more and more embroiled in relationships which have sexual connotations and involve sexual stimulation but which they think of in terms of romantic love. When their caresses and kisses reach the stage of producing compelling emotions they have no way to cope with them. Indeed, they often rationalize these unusual feelings as the normal flowering of a beautiful and supposedly lasting love. Some young people have indicated that while they consider promiscuous sexual relations completely immoral, they believe that when a couple are "deeply in love" sex relations are natural and good. But what they are experiencing is not love involving the whole personality but an infatuation based only on sex attraction. Thus a lack of knowledge of the basic differences between love and infatuation often leads to overt acts they do not understand.

One antidote to domination by either the drive for status or the romantic fallacy is a private but frank appraisal of one's own values. If one chooses an occupation one plots the necessary steps to achieve one's goal. Likewise, if one focuses his attention upon marriage he should be concerned with the steps necessary to achieve a happy union. When one has thought over his personal life very carefully and has arrived at a decision regarding his behavior in potentially dangerous areas, he is then prepared to handle with courage and imagination any situation which may arise. If he is confused about what he believes, he is very likely to be carried away by powerful emotions.

PHYSICAL ASPECTS OF DATING

Because of what we have labeled the dating dilemma, it is well to consider the various solutions of the problem in terms of their later influence on marital adjustment. Dating behavior varies in intimacy from a verbal "good-night" to coitus. In between are the steps known as necking, petting, petting to climax. By necking is generally meant rather casual embraces and kissing. By petting is meant more passionate embraces, deep kissing (soul kissing), and caressing most of the body. By petting to climax is meant stimulation of the erotic zones of the body until orgasm occurs. Coitus is sexual intercourse. Various individuals set different limits for affectionate behavior. There is no sharp distinction between any of these stages, and all affectional responses lead to more passionate ones. Nature endowed us with a powerful drive to procreate and accomplishes this by making the effect of physical contact progressive and cumulative.

The demarcation between necking and petting is particularly hard to make, for couples going steady find it easy to pass from casual embraces and kissing to more passionate involvements. As we shall explain later, petting is normally the foreplay before intercourse. In marriage, petting is essential to mutuality and is a part of the satisfaction of the normal sex act. But before marriage, when love play does not result in intercourse, petting represents an incomplete emotional adventure. Petting may be compared to the hypothetical experience of the couple who love good swing music and have purchased tickets to hear Duke Ellington give a concert. They look forward to the concert and build up their expectations. Excitement mounts as they enter the concert hall. They look at the program and see that some of their favorite numbers are to be played. The band walks in. There is a hushed silence and the great moment is at hand. Then an attendant comes on stage and announces that Duke Ellington has suddenly become ill and that the concert must be postponed. They go home frustrated and unhappy. But the next week comes the announcement that Duke Ellington is well again and tickets will be honored at this performance. Again they go to the concert with expectations even higher than on the first evening. They take their seats, the band marches in, there is silence as they await the appearance of the leader. Then the attendant comes on stage and announces that the orchestra leader has had an accident on the way to the theater and that there will be no concert. Again they go home, filled with chagrin and consternation. Suppose this happens a dozen times. The final conclusion of the couple is that the experience of going to hear Duke Ellington is a dismal one, that all they have got out of it is disappointment, and that they will have nothing to do with his concerts from now on.

Something similar but more devastating often happens when a couple pets continuously. Petting brings them to a high pitch of excitement in which every nerve cell is urging them to finish what they have begun. But they say "no." There is no normal outlet for their emotions, so they learn that sexual play of this kind is a frustrating and dismal experience. Often such play so upsets girls that they cry and cannot sleep. If petting continues throughout high school and throughout college, the whole conditioned response of the woman's body and to some extent of the man's, is to say "no" whenever strong sexual feelings or sensations arise. How is it possible, then, that they should on their wedding night be able to reverse this situation and say "yes"? The answer is that many cannot.[33] Under such conditions a certain degree of frigidity is unescapable, at least for some years.

PETTING TO CLIMAX

If, however, the emotional pressure becomes too great and the couple determine that there must be some other answer they may pet to climax. Petting to climax may release dammed up emotional feelings but it may also cause numerous psychological problems. Recently, a girl who was about to cancel her "pinning" to a boy honestly faced this situation. She had a rigid set of morals which did not permit her to have coitus but under emotional pressure allowed her to pet to climax. During the next three months the couple practiced this intermittently. In the meantime she began to raise a great many rather minor questions regarding her fiancé. She was not now altogether sure that he was careful enough about his dress. She was not sure that he could hold a steady job. She

[33] Margaret Mead, *Male and Female*, New York, William Morrow and Company, 1949, pp. 294–295.

resented the fact that at home he paid too much attention to her folks and seemed to neglect her. At every conference with the counselor she brought up an increasing list of objections to marrying him. But all of these objections appeared to have originated at the time they had begun to pet to climax. Previously none of these faults had troubled her. The fact was that she felt intensely guilty and unhappy about this type of love play. She enjoyed petting physically but could not tolerate it ethically. Hence, she projected blame upon her boy friend but camouflaged the reason for it by stressing minor objections. She did not realize the degree to which her petting to climax was interfering with a growing love relationship.

PRE-MARITAL COITUS AND PREPARATION FOR MARRIAGE

Pre-marital coitus involves similar difficulties. Coitus, to be successful, requires a sense of security in the future relationship of the personalities involved. Coitus involves some sensitive adjustments, and these can rarely be made before a couple lives together. Many who have undertaken a trial period of intercourse have been so unsuccessful that a relationship that had held great promise was destroyed by disgust.

The second factor involved in pre-marital sexual relations is the absence of many of the conditions which make of intercourse a binding experience of love. The couple rarely has a sense of privacy. They fear they may be discovered in one way or another. They seldom have enough time to become completely relaxed and to share enough things together to make intercourse a normal outcome of other experiences. Then, too, there is the fear of pregnancy. The only tested medical methods of birth-control—the diaphragm and contraceptive jelly—are not readily available to the unmarried. And in any case some danger of pregnancy always exists—a danger which produces both fear and resentment. Again, emancipated as educated young people sometimes are today, they still are the products of a culture which has put a taboo on pre-marital sexual relations. Thus they must carry on their sexual activities covertly and with much scheming. All of these factors go to create a situation which is so disturbing that coitus, instead of being a climax to love, becomes a difficult and distasteful experience. Because of these factors and because sexual relations are not automatically successful at first, even in the security of marriage, it is difficult to achieve desirable learning experiences from pre-marital coitus.

The aggressor in sex play may also be primarily concerned with his or her pleasure and not at all with the mutuality of the experience. Those who have been sexually exploited under the guise of love are likely to be very suspicious of the motives of other partners and somewhat insecure about their capacity to adjust sexually in marriage. They also may have doubts as to whether or not they should tell their future mates about such experiences and, if they do not, whether they will nevertheless be found out. For these reasons, pre-marital sexual experimentation is correlated with somewhat poorer adjustment in marriage. An analysis of the statistical studies of the impact of pre-marital sexual intercourse will be presented in the chapter on engagement, and so is not included here.

Values in sex behavior differ for different classes and for different generations. Values are today much in flux. After a great many class discussions and individual consultations with students, the author has only admiration for the courage and insight with which most young people face the dating dilemma. Couples who feel confused or who feel that their dating experience is having some unfortunate results should talk with a counselor so that their future relationship will not be destroyed by guilt feelings or unconscious hostilities. Personalities are plastic, and difficulties that seem insurmountable may actually be overcome with the understanding help of a counselor.

DATING AND ITS CONTRIBUTION TO WISE MARRIAGE CHOICE

Dating is an extremely useful experience if it is used for the development of heterosexual poise and ease in communication. Those who concentrate entirely on necking and petting lose the chance of the personality development inherent in dating. For dating may be a school for marriage, and dating failure may mean marriage failure. During the dating period, young people may come to appreciate differences in masculine and feminine points of view. They may come to know as many different types of people as are represented in their college group. If they become acquainted with a diverse assortment of individuals, they will learn which types complement their own personalities. They will know with what type they feel most comfortable and which most stimulates growth. Conversely, those who concentrate on the physical relationship may be quite blind to the other areas of adjustment needed in a good marriage. The objective of dating, then, ought to be different from that of courtship wherein an individual is consciously trying to pick a marriage partner. Dating is most useful when it functions in maturing a person in the social aspects of his relationship to the opposite sex. If it is to do this, dating must result in several positive achievements: (1) the growth of ability to communicate, (2) the growth of new social and cultural interests, (3) the growth in personal attractiveness.

DATING AND COMMUNICATION

Through dating in high school and college young people should learn how to communicate with the other sex. Communication is a very basic process in marriage. Those who can make articulate their emotions, their tenderness, their enthusiasms, their ideals, their values, and their points of view are generally good marital risks because they have developed means of facing conflicts intelligently when they arise. Dating which is focused on companionship enables a couple to explore each other's points of view, to begin to appreciate the many differences of approach, and to learn to deal with differences constructively. In order to develop mutuality of thought and basic communication, it is best if both have an opportunity to express themselves regarding their intentions and feelings. In so far as a couple frankly discusses the limits they will set in meeting the dating dilemma, they are developing the ability to be free in marriage when dealing with sexual problems. As was indicated at the beginning of the discussion of dating, shyness and awkwardness characterize first dating attempts. When the time for courtship arrives, ease and verve in communication should have superseded shyness.

DATING AND THE GROWTH OF INTERESTS

Dating ought to include activities that interest both parties and some things neither has explored before. Young people who have always listened to Beethoven's symphonies may also find modern music interesting. Those whose preparation for occupational life has been scientific do not detract from their lifetime goal if they develop an interest in one or more of the various art forms they may find at any good museum or art institute. Dancing the rhumba well does not preclude the possibility of enjoying some of the more intricate folk or square dances. The same thing is true of various sports. If a girl cannot play tennis, she may prove to be a very good competitor on the golf course or in the swimming pool. Imaginative dating may become an adventure. Many individuals tend to

103

be inordinately provincial in their tastes in food—and in life. Likewise the fact that one has never engaged in folk dancing is no reason for not discovering whether or not it may add a new pleasure to life. Life may be a sweep of exciting experiences or it may be a routine of dull, repeated exercises.

DEVELOPING DATING DESIRABILITY

How do you rate as a date? Several studies have recorded those qualities which others desire in a date. Christensen made a study of 674 unmarried and unengaged university students who rated twenty-four items on a six-point scale according to what they considered most desirable qualities.

Figure 3 clearly indicates the premium put on companionship in dating. The 674 unmarried and unengaged Purdue University students who rated these items on a six-point scale stress those qualities which will make communication easy and stimulating. Some differences are interesting. Females obviously stress conventional sex standards, good financial prospects, ambition and industriousness, religious nature, considerateness and sociability, while the men stressed the affectionate and romantic aspects of a date, physical attractiveness, and "not smoking." However, in general, they agree. The student may well ask himself or herself the degree to which these qualities reflect his or her unconscious needs in a date.

One girl who sees the dating process with clarity and who very spontaneously and effectively outlines her own standards says:

> Most girls eighteen to twenty-one put a boy up to some kind of qualification standard they have developed through dating many boys. Even if the girl knows she isn't ready to think seriously because she wants to go three more years to college or wants a career, she is bound to set up standards. She spends many leisure hours in dreaming, formulating opinions on character, and comparing boys, so that the subject of dating is always in the back of her mind and affects many things she does.
>
> When a girl meets a boy, the first thing that is noticed is appearance. She likes someone who is neat, clean, and pleasant looking. The second thing would be friendliness since by this quality we meet, talk, and arrange dates. When a girl is on the date, the first thing she notices is: "How does he treat me?" She knows whether or not he has her best interests at heart, whether he wants to please her, or whether he just wanted "a date" for some occasion. He should be considerate, kind,

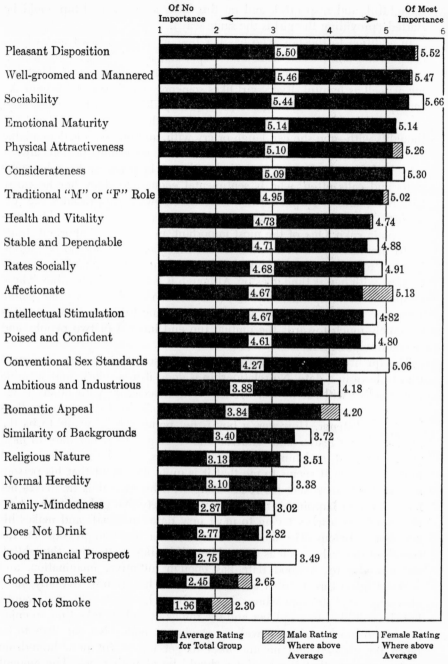

FIGURE 3. Preference Patterns in Date Selection*

	Of No Importance ← → Of Most Importance
	1　　2　　3　　4　　5　　6
Pleasant Disposition	5.50 / 5.52
Well-groomed and Mannered	5.46 / 5.47
Sociability	5.44 / 5.66
Emotional Maturity	5.14 / 5.14
Physical Attractiveness	5.10 / 5.26
Considerateness	5.09 / 5.30
Traditional "M" or "F" Role	4.95 / 5.02
Health and Vitality	4.73 / 4.74
Stable and Dependable	4.71 / 4.88
Rates Socially	4.68 / 4.91
Affectionate	4.67 / 5.13
Intellectual Stimulation	4.67 / 4.82
Poised and Confident	4.61 / 4.80
Conventional Sex Standards	4.27 / 5.06
Ambitious and Industrious	3.88 / 4.18
Romantic Appeal	3.84 / 4.20
Similarity of Backgrounds	3.40 / 3.72
Religious Nature	3.13 / 3.51
Normal Heredity	3.10 / 3.38
Family-Mindedness	2.87 / 3.02
Does Not Drink	2.77 / 2.82
Good Financial Prospect	2.75 / 3.49
Good Homemaker	2.45 / 2.65
Does Not Smoke	1.96 / 2.30

Average Rating for Total Group　　Male Rating Where above Average　　Female Rating Where above Average

* Harold T. Christensen, *Marriage Analysis*, New York, The Ronald Press Company, 1950, pp. 212, 213. Reproduced by permission.

thoughtful, and respectful, and on this basis a true friendship could be started (providing the girl is the same way).

In addition to the boy who has her best interests at heart and who is considerate, kind, thoughtful, and respectful, a girl likes a boy who is sweet and fundamentally gentle—a boy who is patient and understanding as well as helpful. Every girl likes someone who is sincere—whom she can believe, without getting too worried or jealous. Girls like a boy who is a true friend—one she can talk freely with, one she can share her thoughts with—one she can laugh or cry with, and one who is dependable and faithful, and the natural, wholesome and refreshing person, always rates high because he acts natural. A girl can't help but go for a boy who visits and calls often, who is sentimental enough to show her he cares, who is capable of surprising her, and who shows he appreciates the "extra little things in life"—in other words, he puts the frosting on the otherwise plain cake. One of the most important, in fact very important, traits a girl should look for in a boy is his intelligence. A girl should be able to look up to a boy and he should be interesting and stimulating enough to grow with her as time goes by. Although it is good to have a boy whose temperament complements yours, it is not too good to have one whose views are radically different from yours. Having things in common does extremely much towards the mutual fun and interest of two people, and is absolutely necessary.

The quality of being able to get along in society is a very important trait to have in a date. No relationship is good if it is selfish, and since no one can live without others, the aspect of association with others is extremely important. Girls like boys who can talk intelligently as well as be a good listener. However, a boy is not popular if he wants to be the big social ring leader and "run the show." A girl likes her date to have personality, wit, and humor and good manners, and she must feel proud to be with him. It seems to me that it is quite important that his personality and actions reflect his relationship with his girl; thus he makes her feel a sense of happiness—not jealousy or anxiety. No girl goes for a type of boy who is always trying to meet new date "material" and makes his intentions obvious. He should try to make a good impression on the friends of the girl as well as the girl herself by being attentive, thoughtful, and considerate. A good date has enough initiative, imagination, and sense of adventure to plan amusements with his friends. Actually, most girls agree that it is not where she goes but who she is with that counts, but she still likes to go places and see things as well as take time to enjoy her friendship by taking a walk or staying at home. No one likes to be taken for granted and no one likes to get into a rut or a hum-drum routine, and so that is why dates should be of both types. The amount

106

of money spent is not the important thing. Girls naturally like the boys who have the same views on morals that they do and who are individual enough to do what is right instead of tagging along with the group.

To me the highest trait a boy can have is his realization of life on a spiritual basis. A girl respects a boy who has high ideals and the courage to live by his convictions and admit that sometimes he is wrong. A God-fearing boy knows how to be humble, forgiving, and kind to others, and he knows the value of faith and hope. His life reflects his beliefs and he has a much deeper relationship and bond to offer a girl—for his love is on the spiritual, not only the physical basis.

I realize that I have put up a pretty big order and I don't expect my best friends to be this perfect. But it does not hurt to know what is liked in a person. I don't feel that we always sit down and rate a boy, but we unconsciously love or "like" a person if he fits our major requirements without always realizing what happens.[34]

CONCLUSION

This chapter has presented the developmental nature of dating experiences, showing how dating behavior patterns are determined by peer and class groups. It has indicated something of the problems and opportunities in the dating system. The problems have to do with finding an answer to the sexual dilemma of dating and with the problem of status or rating in groups or cliques. Solutions to both of these problems involve the growth of communication and understanding between the sexes. Such achievements carry on into marriage to form a positive basis for good adjustment.[35] Failure in dating is likewise reflected in marriage, and is correlated with poor adjustment.

SELF-ANALYSIS

The following outline will help the student assess his own past for the way his dating behavior has prepared him or her for a happy or an unhappy marriage. Those who discover areas in their past dating experience which seem to have set up inhibitions or left them without enthusiasm for married life will probably want to discuss this with the instructor or the marriage counselor. No past event necessarily predetermines failure in marriage, but certain events may make marriage adjustment dif-

[34] From a statement in the author's files.
[35] Robert F. Winch, *The Modern Family*, New York, Henry Holt and Company, 1952, p. 437.

ficult; the way may often be eased by frank discussion of the problem with an expert in the field.

I. Dating Behavior
  A. High School Experiences
    1. Discuss your problems of dating while a freshman and sophomore in high school. Were you shy? Were you lacking in confidence? Were you insecure regarding dancing, talking, or other heterosexual activities?
    2. Discuss your problems of dating while a junior and senior in high school. Did you have enough dates? Had you at this time solved the problems mentioned above? Did you go steady? Were you infatuated with one or more individuals? What did you learn in these experiences?
  B. College Experiences
    1. Discuss your college experiences. In what ways do these experiences differ from those in high school?
    2. What pressures do you feel from your group, clique, or house in dating? What pressures are there to go steady? To be pinned? To be engaged?
  C. Your Dating Problems
    1. Have you ever or have you often become so involved emotionally that sexual tension was a problem? How did you meet the problem? What permanent results did your behavior leave with you that might influence your marriage?
    2. Do you feel that you have definite inhibitions or guilt feelings that were the result of that behavior? Have you discussed it with anyone?

II. Values for Dating
  A. What values do you have with respect to:
    1. Necking
    2. Petting
    3. Petting to climax
    4. Pre-marital coitus
  B. Have you ever discussed these norms of conduct with another with whom you found a problem developing? Why? What resulted?

III. Goals for Dating
  A. What particular contribution do you expect from dating? Analyze yourself in terms of your ability to:
    1. Feel secure and confident when with a member of the opposite sex.

2. Carry on an intelligent and animated conversation.
3. Understand the other sex.

B. Analyze the types of personality represented by those you have dated. Have you had contact with many different types? What type seems to be most stimulating to you? Do you need to date other types for further exploration?

C. What is your pattern of dating? Do you always dance? Do you always go to a movie? Is dating contributing to your skills, culture, and interests?

VISUAL AIDS

Wrong Way Out, Teaching Films Custodian, 25 West 43rd Street, New York 18.

Youth in Crisis, Association Films, Y.M.C.A. Motion Picture Bureau, 347 Madison Avenue, New York 17.

SPECIAL PROJECTS

1. Let every member of the class write a brief but complete summary of his or her standards for dating.
2. Appoint a committee to determine whether or not the "rating and dating complex" is a true picture of your campus.

READINGS

ERNEST W. BURGESS and PAUL WALLIN, *Engagement and Marriage,* Philadelphia, J. B. Lippincott Company, 1953, Chapter 3.

RUTH SHANLE CAVAN, *The American Family,* New York, Thomas Y. Crowell Company, 1953, Chapter 12.

JUDSON T. LANDIS and MARY LANDIS, *Building a Successful Marriage,* New York, Prentice-Hall, Inc., 1948, Chapters 4 and 6.

ANDREW G. TRUXAL and FRANCIS E. MERRILL, *Marriage and the Family in American Culture,* New York, Prentice-Hall, Inc., 1953, Chapter 8.

RECORDING

Problems of Modern Dating, by James A Peterson, is a twenty minute sociodrama illustrating problems of modern dating. It is prepared to stimulate discussion of these problems as well as to throw light upon them. Educational Recording Services, 5922 Abernathy Drive, Los Angeles 45, California.

PART TWO

MAKING A WISE

MARRIAGE CHOICE

C H A P T E R 6

Psychological Factors*

DATING AND COURTSHIP

THERE IS LITTLE TO DISTINGUISH THE COURTSHIP PROCESS FROM DATING IN OUR SOCIETY. THE MAJORITY OF COLLEGE WOMEN ADMIT that for them college dating is courtship, if courtship be defined as activity directed toward the goal of marriage. It is true that there is a subtle difference between such purposive activity and dating with no other goal than that of having a good time. However, the dynamics of infatuation and sexual attraction are such that dating often turns out to be more goal-directed than is supposed, and couples who start off with a very casual relationship are surprised at the extent to which they rather soon find themselves emotionally interdependent. Likewise, the mores associated with going steady complicate the distinction between dating and courtship. Going steady, as we have seen, involves considerably more intimacy than casual dating. The goal of going steady might only have been adopted for the sake of convenience, but the emotional commitments associated with this relationship often lead to a courtship pattern. There is no way to mark decisively the step from dating to courtship, other than to say that courtship begins when one consciously begins to think of the partner as a possible life mate and to order one's emotional relationships with this in mind. This may happen in high school, in

* This chapter was written with Henry J. Wegrocki, M.D., Ph.D., Associate Professor of Psychiatry, University of Southern California Medical School.

college, or in post-college life; whenever it happens the transition from pure dating to courtship occurs.

The present analysis of courtship is primarily concerned with wise marriage choice. Four sets of factors seem most important: (1) psychological factors, (2) socio-cultural factors, (3) economic factors, and (4) engagement behavior patterns as associated with later adjustment in marriage.

NEUROTIC MOTIVATIONS FOR MARRIAGE

When the motivation for marriage is unhealthy or inadequate, when the choice of a partner is made on an unrealistic, accidental, or neurotic basis, when one or the other or both of the partners are emotionally immature, marriage maladjustment is likely.

Explorations of these areas must be made with a full realization that many major determinants of personality are unconscious and that varying degrees of depth analysis are necessary to gain a true picture of a personality structure. The character of the motivation for marriage often reflects this; the needs a marriage meets may be quite different from the rationalizations the partners offer in explaining their marriage.

Thus a young woman, who, from childhood on, had been consistently rejected by her father, was unconsciously driven to marry because her husband's father represented the approving, accepting, loving image which she had wanted during her earlier life.[1] She had met her future father-in-law after her discharge from Army service as a WAC, when she went to work for the firm of which he was an executive. He was an elderly, kind, and gracious individual who immediately assumed a very protective role toward the shy and gentle girl. As a Christmas gesture, he invited her to dinner, where she met his wife and son. She soon became very friendly with the son but this relationship did not progress beyond friendship despite the high degree of interest displayed by the son. Then her elderly protector retired; and within a few months after his resignation she married his son. She later admitted, "I was marrying the family and not particularly marrying my husband." Soon after the marriage, her father-in-law died, whereupon the young woman developed multiple nervous symptoms and became incapable of adjusting to her husband. What she did not realize was that she had married not be-

---

[1] All case material in this chapter, unless otherwise noted, comes from the case studies of Dr. Wegrocki.

cause she was in love with her husband but because his father fulfilled for her a need she had felt all her life.

EGOCENTRIC MOTIVATION FOR MARRIAGE

When neurotic factors affect marital motivation, emotional immaturity is indicated, but there is another type of personality limitation which might best be described as egocentric. A successful young professional man in his late twenties, for example, was much baffled by the fact that his wife, who as his fiancée had been well integrated, developed multiple, crippling anxiety reactions and irritability after their marriage. A study of the case revealed that during their courtship he had been extremely attentive and had shared his experiences with her. Soon after marriage, however, he had redefined her role as that of a housekeeper who was to minister to his physical comforts and sexual needs. The entire pattern of their family life was organized about his professional activity, with the wife functioning as a kind of interested observer rather than as a partner. What the husband considered to be a love relationship with his wife was basically a relationship in which she happened to be the individual who could uniquely satisfy those of his emotional and physical needs which previously had not been satisfied. He was made to realize that his attitude was fundamentally egocentric and not representative of a true love orientation; fortunately he was capable of growth. He was able to achieve a satisfactory adjustment with his wife—whereupon her crippling nervous reactions disappeared.

MATURE MOTIVATION FOR MARRIAGE

The husband in the case given above was able to evolve from a basically egocentric orientation to a more mature viewpoint. Where motivation in marriage is mature, rather than neurotic or egocentric, the chances for happiness in marriage are much greater. A truly mature type of motivation for marriage is associated with a need to share and give so as to achieve a sense of togetherness and growth.

MOTIVATION TO MARRY AS NEUROTIC ESCAPE

The neurotic factors which may color motivation for marriage may be anchored at varying depths of the personality. Some of these factors have to do with the need for escape from unpleasant or domineering home situations. A young, intelligent woman of nineteen, who had married at seventeen, soon became aware, in psychotherapy, that the reason for her marital dissatisfaction was her neurotic expectation that, once she was away from her very rigid and strict parents, she would have complete freedom of movement and would not have to be responsible to anyone. The situation was further complicated by the fact that her husband had married her precisely because she came from a strict environment. As a result, her behavior and attitude caused him much distress. Fortunately for both, they were capable of recognizing where their difficulties lay and subsequently achieved a good relationship. To this young woman, marriage represented an escape from an intolerable situation. The choice of a particular partner did not enter into the decision too much. It was her picture of marriage, projected as freedom from an oppressive home atmosphere rather than as an opportunity for giving and sharing, that had motivated her.

NEUROTIC FACTORS AND THE IDEAL IMAGE

In the choice of a particular marriage partner, whatever neurotic proclivities an individual has are likely to express themselves. To a certain extent every individual carries within his mind an unconscious, or at least unverbalized, blueprint of the type of individual he would like to marry. This blueprint might have lines which are so deeply drawn in the unconscious that they are not modified by experience or time. On the other hand, the blueprint may vary with the time, circumstances and stage of an individual's development. Thus a brilliant but insecure girl college student became depressed when her fiancé, a prominent athlete, broke his engagement with her to marry an outstanding girl on the campus. Her association with him had represented to her the achievement of a status that she did not feel within herself. A few years later, when her standard of values had changed, she made a satisfactory marriage with a man whom she had likewise known during her college days, but who had not appealed to her then because of his lack of status on the campus.

The broad range of cultural expectancies, such as age, race, religion, social level, physical appearance, size, and similar elements which also play a role in setting limits on the choice of a partner, will be considered in the next chapter. These elements, however, may be colored by neurotic factors. A New England spinster, for example, deprived herself of more than one opportunity for what might have been a satisfactory marriage, by reason of her particular social standards. These were neurotically exaggerated as a consequence of her deep sense of insecurity about her own personal value. Another lady from New England, on the other hand, made a point of marrying a man from a racial minority group, partly as an act of defiance against her very rigid, socially conscious parents, and partly because she felt identified with an individual who was discriminated against. She had been an only, but unwanted, child, and all her life had felt keenly a sense of parental rejection. Her marriage did not turn out satisfactorily because her husband had many neurotic tendencies and unconsciously resented the fact that she had married him out of sympathy. Paradoxically, his marriage to her, instead of increasing his own self-esteem, had merely lowered her status in his eyes. At the time of their marriage, the husband was a symbol of persecution and rejection to his wife—the unconscious image of her own inner rejected self.

This tendency to choose a partner who is, in a sense, a reflection of one's unconscious image of one's self is rather common. In another instance, a brilliant but only moderately attractive young lady was married almost immediately after she was graduated from college to a man who was intellectually and socially her inferior. Obsessed with the idea that she was homely and undesirable so far as men were concerned, she became panicky at the idea of remaining unmarried. Because of her acute self-depreciation, she could not picture herself as being acceptable to anyone who was superior to her socially or intellectually. Shortly after her marriage, the gross disharmony between herself and her husband became apparent in a variety of difficulties. Divorce was the final resolution of the problem.

THE PARENTAL IMAGE IN MARRIAGE CHOICE

A mother or a father very frequently functions as the basic image for the blueprint of a future mate. Since parents play such an integral role in the personal development of an individual, it is not surprising that this should be so. An attractive, twenty-year-old mother was referred as a patient after the birth of her first baby because she developed a very severe depression with crying spells and a feeling of revulsion against her child. Psychiatric exploration revealed that she was an only child; she had been overprotected by her parents and she had idolized her father. She had married, at eighteen, a man more than twenty years her senior and, like her father, a very successful business man. Until her pregnancy, the marriage was superficially successful, largely because her husband functioned so well as the friendly and considerate father-image. In her marriage she was thus still the little girl living with her father. This factor did not become apparent during her pregnancy, because the social circumstances of cultural expectancy contributed to give her a feeling that having a child was something particularly wonderful. She was much amazed at her emotional reaction at the birth of her son. A dream, which she had soon afterward, illumined as well as anything could the basic anxiety factor involved in giving up the dependent little-girl role. She dreamed that she was holding her son in her arms and that suddenly he began to increase in size while she began to decrease in height. Within a few seconds her child was standing, holding *her* in *his* arms. This patient unconsciously wanted to continue to be the child, to prolong indefinitely the dependency relationship that she had with her father and the father-image.

In view of the extensive popular psychological literature about dependency, it might be well to point out that dependency is a normal need, that it is not, in itself, neurotic. Marriage provides an opportunity for an individual to satisfy legitimately his normal dependency needs. This issue was highlighted by the very intelligent mother of a young man who was having marital difficulties. John had always been very deeply attached to his mother and was very affectionate and demonstrative with her. The mother was a mature, well-balanced, extremely successful professional woman. She had been widowed early in life and for this reason had been driven all the closer to her son. Because of the son's attachment to his mother, he was called a "sissy" by his childhood friends. During adolescence, John attempted to compensate for this by particularly vigorous athletic activity. Throughout adolescence, however, his dependency upon his mother continued, although at a very subtle level. The son did not realize how very restrained he was in his emotional expression toward his wife because he had brought into marriage some of his earlier complexes about being considered masculine. With the intelligent help and cooperation of his mother, John was made aware of the factors responsible for his dependency upon her as well as with his inability to play a dependent role in relationship to his wife. There was a marked improvement in his marriage when he was able to allow his normal dependency needs to be satisfied by his wife rather than to interpret them as signs of a lack of masculinity on his part.

A counter-image can also exist. In such cases the individual looks precisely for the person who is entirely unlike the mother or the father. A young woman who believed herself to be rejected and unloved by her very rigid and puritanical minister-father married an emotionally expressive Latin—whose extreme possessiveness and jealousy became almost as intolerable as her father's unloving behavior.

THE MADONNA-PROSTITUTE PATTERN

The madonna-prostitute pattern is frequently met with in the unconscious blueprints of men. Women are frequently judged as marriage material on the basis of their sexual accessibility. A middle-aged man fell deeply in love with a woman who refused his sexual advances despite the fact that she showed some response to his feeling for her. This refusal, along with her disapproval of his tendency to vulgarity and cursing, and her devotion to church and social work activities, corresponded with his picture of the ideal woman whom he had been seeking. They were married. Then, as so often happens in such cases, at the onset of sexual relations her image changed in his eyes because she reacted so intensely during sexual intercourse. This led him unconsciously to depreciate her, and he returned to his verbal habits of vulgarity and cursing which had been his lifelong pattern. This produced so much stress and incompatibility that a separation resulted. A few months later, having realized how unreal his expectations had been, he wished to resume relations with his wife. She refused to return to him, whereupon he plunged into a depression and again over-idealized her.

The cases that have been presented show that the blueprint of a potential marriage partner which an individual carries with him includes many elements which are conscious and many which are unconscious. The unconscious elements, surprisingly enough, are often relatively obvious to the friends of the particular individual. The fact, for instance, that a girl has chosen to marry a father substitute is clear to her friends, yet quite unknown to her. In other instances a couple seems ideally matched, yet in the marital relationship unconscious factors emerge which indicate that the choice of a particular partner was neurotically determined. The question rises of what can be done to prevent a neurotic choice of a partner. There is no easy solution. Some of the unconscious elements can be brought to light through interviews in pre-marital counseling. Hence, pre-marital counseling is extremely valuable. Specific ways of dealing with such problems in pre-marital counseling will be discussed later.

TEMPERAMENTAL FACTORS IN WISE MARRIAGE CHOICE

The factors responsible for an individual's motivation in getting married and for his choice of a particular partner are bound up with the total personality structure. We have indicated how two individuals entering into the continuous interpersonal relationship of marriage bring into it the psychological baggage of all their conscious and unconscious conditioning experiences since infancy. We must now discuss certain predominant temperamental inclinations and their meaning for wise marriage choice. These inclinations are often so interwoven into the fabric of an individual's personality that they cannot be readily separated out. In some instances, however, temperamental factors play such an outstanding role that they may be considered in isolation for purposes of analysis.

INTROVERSION AND EXTROVERSION

Wide temperamental differences in introversion and extroversion, like all biologically derived personality differences, make for a very poor marital adjustment, unless they are compensated for by mutuality in many other areas. Minor differences, on the other hand, seem to act in a stimulating manner, such differences being complementary rather than conflictual. The introvert is pushed to play a role for which he is temperamentally unsuited and which causes him distress and a sense of tension, while the extrovert feels inhibited and chained in having to control his spontaneous, outgoing impulses. Thus, an introvert husband in his early thirties was able to have a happy marital life as long as he lived in close proximity to his parents and friends in whose company his wife could find a continuous satisfaction of her extrovert needs. When the husband's job required a transfer to California, and he was alone with his wife and child, many difficulties arose because the new pattern of life was not adequate for his wife. Her desire for external social life met with opposition on his part. The husband was angry at her disloyalty in preferring the company of others to his.

A middle-aged couple had made a relatively good adjustment while their two daughters were at home; later, when the daughters married and left town, the couple found themselves in conflict. Because of the husband's introvertive habits, the wife had actually lived through her daughters and now found that adjusting to her husband's pattern was practically impossible because of her strong gregarious and social needs.

It is difficult to imagine how opposite are the attitudes of the extrovert and introvert. Waller discusses these differences in terms of fantasies:

> There are great differences in personalities in regard to types of fantasy and the importance of fantasy in the individual's life. In the so-called introverted personality, fantasy has great importance and is likely to be both clear-cut and unified. The extroverted person is likely to deny that he indulges in any fantasy at all, and certainly he sees little value in it. Boredom arises in the introvert from that which interrupts the flow of fantasy. The introvert is never bored when he is alone, but rather when the outer reality fractures the inner reality. The extrovert is bored and ill at ease when he has nothing outside himself to attend to.[2]

The problem that temperamental difference presents for wise marriage choice is very difficult.[*] Some differences are stimulating and cohesive but wide differences produce conflict. The problem is aggravated because during courtship basic temperamental moods are apt to be modified in the interest of pleasing the loved one.

AGGRESSIVENESS AND PASSIVITY

Although they are associated with temperamental factors, the patterns of aggressiveness and passivity are far more colored by experiential elements. If aggressiveness is characteristic of the male partner, then the possibility of a good adjustment is present because of the cultural expectancy that the male will be the aggressive leader in the family. Modifications of this generalization will be considered in the next chapter. When the situation is reversed and the wife leads, there is much possibility for psychological mischief. For example, a young married couple in their twenties had a sizable problem. Despite having two children, the wife was extremely active in social and church work and was constantly serving as president or chairman of various organizations. This provoked

[2] Willard Waller (Revised by Reuben Hill), *The Family: A Dynamic Interpretation,* Copyright, 1951, by The Dryden Press, Inc., pp. 63–64. Reprinted by permission.
[*] Specific discussion of how this problem may be practically managed will be found in Chapter 10.

much joshing of the husband by his friends and was a source of constant marital disharmony since the wife's activity was interpreted by the husband as a reflection on his male leadership role.

DOMINANCE AND COMPLIANCE

The problem of dominance and compliance in the marital relationship differs somewhat from the problem of aggressiveness versus passivity, in that temperamental factors play a role in the latter situation. In exploring particular personality backgrounds of aggressive and passive persons, one usually finds that the individual has played a consistently passive or aggressive role since infancy. Problems relevant to dominance and compliance, on the other hand, may be referred to experiential factors which provoke these specific kinds of integration. The cultural factor of expecting the male to play the dominant role complicates the dominance-compliance relationship. The brilliant woman, who is aware of her intellectual superiority over her husband in matters of judgment, will find herself in a difficult situation if she has to permit the husband to make important decisions. Many women believe it to be psychologically wise for a bright woman to "play down" her intelligence and to give her husband a feeling of superiority, but this sometimes is done at a great cost if there are no adequate compensations. In a truly harmonious marriage the problem of dominance and compliance is no problem because it is resolved by a mature distribution of responsibility, with each partner acceding to the other.

In some marriages the struggle for dominance finds resolution only in an armed truce. This type of neurotic competitiveness occurs more frequently in those instances in which the wife is incapable of playing any other than a dominant role. The popular or beautiful girl, for example, finds it difficult to adjust herself to a situation in which she is no longer receiving constant assurances of the really great value others put upon her. In one instance a very active and successful girl, a leader of the university campus, married an equally successful male leader and found it impossible to relinquish her dominant role. Unconsciously her revolt against what she conceived to be unwarranted male dominance reflected itself in sexual frigidity as a protest against her husband. This was extremely puzzling to her because of the fact that she had been able to achieve a high pitch of sexual excitement in situations associated with necking and petting. In exploring the background factors responsible

122

for her marital maladjustment, it became obvious that her initial motivation for marriage was very egocentric and that she had chosen as a marriage partner a man who might be expected to enhance her personal prestige. When the wedding took place it was considered an ideal marriage. Very soon after the honeymoon, her unconscious rivalry with males became overt—as a struggle with her husband over the question of dominance and compliance.

SADISM AND MASOCHISM

The pattern of dominance and compliance sometimes reaches profound neurotic depths when it expresses itself as sadism and masochism —as either a strong, inner, compulsive need to gain satisfaction by completely dominating and humiliating the other partner or, on the other hand, by inducing situations in which one will allow one's self to be dominated or humiliated. Psychological exploration often reveals that individuals with tales of prolonged suffering in a marital relationship have a subtle, unconscious, neurotic need for suffering.

DEPENDENCY AND INDEPENDENCE

The polarities of aggressiveness and passivity, dominance and compliance, are related to still another polarity, that of dependency and independence. Although the compliant individual is apt to be also a dependent one, this does not mean that the aggressive or dominant person is independent. Because dependency has been so much associated with neuroticism, there has been a tendency to regard its opposite, independence, as having the highest value. Actually, however, independence as well as dependency can reach neurotic proportions. The well-integrated, flexible individual is one who is capable of satisfying, in appropriate situations, his independent as well as his dependent needs. One thirty-year-old bachelor experienced severe anxiety-panic reactions in contemplating his engagement. The unconscious determinants of this anxiety during courtship had to do with his very strong dependency upon his parents and especially upon his mother. The assumption of a new role as a person upon whom someone else could lean was an unconscious threat to him involving the loss of a protective mother figure. Another bachelor of similar age, although highly desirous of getting married, had a great deal of difficulty in achieving any close interpersonal

123

relationship with women because he consistently played an "I don't care" role toward them and, consequently, never gave them a chance to get close to him. In his particular case several experiences of rejection within his family and during adolescence had caused him to build a strong protective armor about himself. He protected his self-esteem by not allowing himself to become involved emotionally, despite the fact that deep within himself he felt the need for it. In courtship this type of person is often most attractive to the other sex because he seems to be hard to marry. Yet this aloofness is really an indication of a neurotic defense. No matter how attractive this type of personality configuration may appear to be, such an individual is a poor risk in marriage.

Of all the personality integrations which are productive of marital difficulty, dependency of a neurotic type is undoubtedly the most troublesome. Neurotic dependency patterns date back to early life and are associated with one of two extremes; the extreme of overprotection or the extreme of rejection. Overprotection is a subtle factor which may manifest itself as merely overconcern on the part of parents, especially the mother, creating an unhealthy atmosphere in which the individual unconsciously leans on the parents. Rejection, too, can occur in not too apparent ways. A mother in describing her daughter said, "We have given her everything all her life," without realizing that she had given the daughter no affectionate display or basic emotional acceptance. The daughter, a very attractive looking girl, unconsciously played the role of the striving "popular" girl during her adolescence and in her twenties in order to gain the approval of others and bind them to her. When she married at twenty-five, her pattern did not change, in fact it expanded. The husband, a very busy business man, was content to allow her to play this role since she was an excellent housekeeper and hostess. When she had reached her middle thirties, however, she began to experience a sense of emptiness in her pattern of living, realizing that her "social success" was rather hollow compensation for an inner feeling of sterility. Symptoms began to appear in the form of intense resentment toward her husband, as well as depressive episodes, which basically represented aggression turned toward herself. The case study revealed that her parents had never allowed her to develop any feeling of dependency upon them. She compensated by trying to bind others to her but found that they did not reciprocate when she wanted to lean on them. Some degree of symptomatic improvement was achieved when her husband began to play a more dominant role and allowed her to satisfy her dependency needs. Farber has made a significant analysis of dependence by defining two modes of the dependency-independency relationship.[3] He calls behavioral dependence the material services which members of the family perform for one another: the wife as a homemaker and the husband as a provider. Emotional dependence involves the reliance upon the mate for much reassurance, approval, and security. Obviously, the outcome of marriage will differ for these differing types and degrees of dependency. Neurotic dependence may be flattering during courtship but it is lethal in marriage.

NEUROTIC SYMPTOMS AND WISE MARRIAGE CHOICE

In addition to prolonged or neurotic dependency, the emotionally immature individual may manifest immaturity in other ways which may be observed during courtship, at least in part. The emotionally insecure individual who, consciously or unconsciously, depreciates himself is in a very vulnerable situation in a marital relationship because the intimacy of the relationship exposes him to threats to his shaky security. Under circumstances like this, such attitudes as suspiciousness, possessiveness, jealousy, and general defensiveness may develop. These are all reflections of the individual's own personal sense of inadequacy. A possessive, jealous individual is practically saying to the world, "I think so little of myself that I resent it when, in any way, you show that you likewise think little of me." Some individuals who are flattered by the jealousy of their companions during courtship or engagement might better analyze the basic psychological determinants of this behavior. A young woman who gained the approval of numerous friends by extending herself showed how much she was motivated by a feeling of her own self-depreciation when, after marrying a very popular young man, she continued to flirt with other men. She was then trying to prove her attractiveness to herself. The same girl responded with profound jealousy and hysteria to any gestures of friendliness that her husband made toward other attractive women.

Such individuals are critical of everyone else, but anything remotely critical of their own behavior is regarded as extremely offensive. This type of reaction indicates the individual's neurotic need for reassurance and emotional security. Besides suspiciousness, jealousy, possessiveness,

[3] Bernard Farber, A Study of Dependence and Decision-Making in Marriage, Chicago, University of Chicago Libraries, M.A. Dissertation, 1949.

and defensiveness, hostility may also appear in varying forms. One form of hostility is that of nagging or chronic irritability and dissatisfaction with the other partner. When this hostility, instead of being turned outward is for various reasons turned inward, it may take the form of moodiness and sulking. This type of hostility reaction can occur wherever frustration is involved; that is, in any situation where an individual is either prevented from satisfying a need or a drive or where he is forced to do something or behave in a way in which he has no spontaneous desire to do. Marriage as a relation in which two people attempt to adjust to one another and to satisfy one another's needs is replete with situations involving potential frustrations. It is a mark of emotional maturity if the marital partners can tolerate and handle the frustrations they experience. In those instances in which the needs which are frustrated are neurotically colored, the possibility of having a frustrating situation is, of course, tremendously increased and the problem can rarely be resolved. An instance in point is the character integration known as perfectionism. A patient in her late twenties was referred by her lawyer for psychiatric examination because he believed that the marital problem between her and her husband was psychological and might be resolved. The husband in the case was a business man whose income had rather quickly changed from approximately $5,000 a year to around $75,000. His new status required him to entertain important clients. He did his entertaining for the most part in a hotel—until he acquired a splendid new home. He then wanted his wife to entertain and be his hostess. Many dinner parties were planned but practically all were cancelled because on the very last day the wife would insist that she simply couldn't get everything ready, that some small thing wasn't exactly perfect, that she couldn't quite decide what they should have, etc. Her behavior provoked intense resentment on the part of her husband and a great deal of alienation in their relationship. Finally he decided to consult a lawyer about a divorce. Inquiry into the wife's background revealed that, as a young girl, she had had a tendency to be quite fat. Because of her poor grooming she had been constantly called "sloppy Joe" and told that when she grew up no man could possibly be interested in her. When she reached adolescence, she overcompensated; she went on a rigid diet until she had slimmed down; she was extremely over-careful about herself in every way and attempted so to dress and carry herself that no one would, in any sense, be justified in calling her "sloppy." With marriage and two children this pattern continued but it

126

caused no difficulty because no challenge was offered to her sense of security. When, however, her husband had provided the family with a large home and she was exposed to individuals toward whom she felt inadequate, her perfectionistic, neurotic trends came to the surface. Having gained an awareness of the roots of her perfectionistic orientation, she was able to modify it and to meet the social obligations of her husband's position.

Obsessive perfectionism is a mode of reaction to the inner anxiety associated with unconscious threats to the personality. Anxiety itself, in the emotionally immature individual, can assume the status of an obsessive, compulsive state. Hence the "worry warts" who are nervously over-alerted as if every move and every day represented a possible threat to their security. One young wife suffered constant agonies because her husband, a real estate speculator, was so free about the manner in which he bought and sold property. For herself this represented a chronic threat to security and she thought that he did not love her because he refused to change his occupation. Equally immature, of course, can be the opposite of overanxiety, the characteristic of irresponsibility or at least the failure to assume responsibility implicit in the marital relationship. This sometimes takes place when both the husband and the wife work. The adjustment of one couple changed markedly soon after the wife became pregnant since the husband then became the sole support of the family and resented this fact.

The lack of a truly mature love relationship often underlies the emergence of the above symptoms of anxiety of perfectionism. The inability to forego an egocentric selfishness and to achieve a truly mature love relationship, in which concern for and consideration of the other person are the important things, lies at the root of much marital disharmony. Many patients defend themselves stoutly against any implication that they aren't really showing much love for their partners. One such young man of twenty-four, whose wife was reacting nervously because he insisted on carrying on his bachelor mode of life with its freedom of movement and secretiveness, responded by saying, "Gosh, Doc, I don't see how you can say I don't love my wife. Why, when I was married just over a year ago, I couldn't sleep or eat well for two months before we were married. Naturally after a while we sort of got used to one another and I wanted to get together with my old gang again. I don't see why she should want to deprive me of my freedom entirely." The confusion of this young man is the confusion of many who have married while in a disturbed emotional state. There is a distinct difference between the almost acute, obsessional anxiety which characterizes romantic love and the attitudes attendant upon a love which is directed primarily toward satisfying the needs and increasing the happiness of one's mate. When this primary orientation is not present there is fertile soil for the development of multiple marital difficulties.

Lewis M. Terman is noted for his study of psychological factors in marital adjustment. While these traits, to be described, existed in marriage (and were not observed before marriage), it is reasonable to assume that such deeply set behavior patterns as are indicated in his summary must have been present at the time of marriage. As we have pointed out, neurotic tendencies may be brought out or accentuated by marriage but they are generally present by the time of courtship. Terman's summary of psychological factors in marriage may be used during courtship to insure wise marriage choice. Terman studied 792 couples. We present the material first for women and then for men.

> Happily married women, as a group, are characterized by kindly attitudes toward others and by the expectations of kindly attitudes in return. They do not easily take offense and are not unduly concerned about the impressions they make upon others. They do not look upon social relationships as rivalry situations. They are cooperative, do not object to subordinate roles, and are not annoyed by advice from others. Missionary and ministering attitudes are frequently evidenced in their responses. They enjoy activities that bring educational or pleasurable opportunities to others and like to do things for the dependent and underprivileged. They are methodical and painstaking in their work, attentive to details, and careful in regard to money. In religion, morals, and politics they tend to be conservative and conventional. Their expressed attitudes imply a quiet self-assurance and a decidedly optimistic outlook on life.
>
> Unhappily married women, on the other hand, are characterized by emotional tenseness and by ups and downs of moods. They give evidence of deep-seated inferiority feelings to which they react by aggressive attitudes rather than timidity. They are inclined to be irritable and dictatorial. Compensatory mechanisms resulting in restive striving are common. These are seen in the tendency of the unhappy wives to be active "joiners," aggressive in business, and overanxious in social life. They strive for wide circles of acquaintances but are more concerned with being important than with being liked. They are egocentric and little interested in benevolent or welfare activities, except in so far as these offer opportunities for personal recognition. They also like activities which are

fraught with opportunities for romance. They are more inclined to be conciliatory in their attitudes toward men than toward women and show little of the sex antagonism that unhappily married men exhibit. They are impatient and fitful workers, dislike cautious or methodical and pains-taking effort. In politics, religion, and social ethics they are more often radical than happily married women.[4]

The men, happy and unhappy, showed some of the same characteristics as the women, but there is sufficient difference to justify presenting Terman's findings.

Happily married men show evidence of an even and stable emotional tone. Their most characteristic reaction to others is that of cooperation. This is reflected in their attitudes toward business superiors, with whom they work well; in their attitude toward women, which reflects equal-itarian ideals; and in their benevolent attitudes toward inferiors and underprivileged. In a gathering of people they tend to be unself-conscious and somewhat extroverted. As compared with unhappy husbands, they show superior initiative, a greater tendency to take responsibility, and greater willingness to give close attention to detail in their daily work. They like methodical procedures and methodical people. In money mat-ters they are saving and cautious. Conservative attitudes are strongly characteristic of them. They usually have a favorable attitude toward religion and strongly uphold the sex mores and other social conventions.

Unhappy husbands, on the other hand, are inclined to be moody and somewhat neurotic. They are prone to feelings of social inferiority, dislike being conspicuous in public, and are highly reactive to social opinion. This sense of social insecurity is often compensated by domineering atti-tudes in relationships where they feel superior. They take pleasure in the commanding roles over business dependents and women, but they withdraw from a situation which would require them to play an inferior role or to compete with superiors. They often compensate this withdrawal by daydreams and power fantasies. More often than happy husbands, they are sporadic and irregular in their habits of work, dislike detail and the methodical attitude, dislike saving money, and like to wager. They more often express irreligious attitudes and are more inclined to radical-ism in sex morals and politics.[5]

In addition to the basic polarities outlined above there are certain generalized health and psychological needs in life which must be con-

[4] Lewis M. Terman, *Psychological Factors in Marital Happiness*, New York. Permission to quote granted by McGraw-Hill Book Company, Inc., 1938, pp. 145–146.
[5] *Ibid.*, p. 155.

sidered in relationship to marriage.[6] Most of these cluster around the wish for response and the wish for recognition. Marriage is important to personality fulfillment in so far as it enables each individual to complete himself through marriage. The particular way in which each individual feels such needs is unique *for himself but he shares in the general group of wishes* which characterize almost every acculturated person. Straus in his doctoral dissertation, "A Study of Three Psychological Factors Affecting Choice of Mate," at the University of Chicago, analyzes the Ideal Mate, the Parental Image, and Personality

TABLE 12. Per Cents of Men and Women Indicating Various Needs They Wanted Satisfied in Marriage*

PERSONALITY NEED FOR SOMEONE TO:	*Men*	*Women*
Love me	36.4	53.5
Confide in	30.6	42.0
Show me affection	20.8	38.0
Respect my ideals	26.0	26.0
Appreciate my goals of achievement	28.3	24.0
Understand my moods	23.1	27.5
Help me make important decisions	15.0	32.5
Stimulate my ambition	26.6	21.0
Look up to	16.2	29.0
Give me self-confidence	19.6	24.0
Stand back of me in difficulty	16.2	25.5
Appreciate me just as I am	20.2	20.5
Admire my ability	18.5	19.5
Make me count for something	20.8	17.0
Relieve my loneliness	18.5	18.5

* Ernest W. Burgess and Harvey J. Locke, *The Family, from Institution to Companionship*, New York, The American Book Company, 1953, p. 368. Reprinted by permission.

[6] Problems in the physical aspects of wise marital choice occasionally arise as a predominant issue. These are referable to certain areas; 1. The general health of the potential partner; 2. The presence in the other person (or his/her blood relations) of disorders which might be regarded as hereditary; 3. Doubts with reference to the dimensions of the sex organs. A complete pre-marital physical examination and laboratory study would be a wise precaution to detect and control any disturbances in general health. A low thyroid condition or persistent anemia can be as provocative of marital maladjustment as over-protective in-laws. The number of mental, nervous, or physical disorders which are directly hereditary is extremely small. In a far greater percentage, the genetic factor operates as a *predisposition*. The relative chance of either a partner or a child inheriting the predisposition to a disorder depends on the genetic family history. Specific individual study of a person's family history is required. Recourse to competent psychologists, psychiatrists, or appropriate medical specialists would help resolve the issue. The problem of sex-organ dimensions, in their relation to a satisfactory sexual relationship or childbirth, can most readily be handled by a gynecologist or a urologist. Sex-organ dimensions are very rarely a problem.

Needs. Burgess and Locke report an interesting response that Straus obtained when he asked engaged men and women to indicate various needs they felt marriage would satisfy. Analysis of the material in the preceding table indicates that, for the individuals studied, marriage meant basic personality fulfillment. Mate choice, then, partially involves satisfying by that choice individual personality needs. Burgess and Locke report on Straus' study as shown in Table 12.

Wise marriage choice always involves the establishment of the emotional interdependence that results from mutuality in answering needs. Wise marriage choice therefore involves some awareness of one's own needs as well as of the needs of the beloved.

CONCLUSION

Courtship is marriage-goal-directed activity. The two basic factors involved in wise marriage choice during courtship are psychological and socio-cultural. This chapter has been concerned with a description of various types of personality configuration and needs which are the product of the psychogenic processes reviewed in the previous chapters and which determine the type of adjustment achieved in marriage. The fundamental needs of an individual, such as the need of being accepted, of feeling that one belongs, of experiencing and expressing affection in its various forms, of achieving approval and a sense of personal signifi-cance—all these are values to be incorporated into the goal of personal maturity and to be sought in a future mate. When the motivation for marriage and for courtship is egocentric or neurotic, when the choice of a partner is neurotically based, when an individual's personality integra-tion is such that he is inhibited in achieving a true love relationship, then his or her prospects for a proper relationship diminish greatly. This chapter has attempted to mark out dynamic areas of personality func-tioning which are significant not only in marriage choice but in marriage itself. As such it has meaning for personality growth of the self and of the individual's awareness of the basic needs of his intended mate.

SELF-ANALYSIS

There are many inventories and projective tests of ascertaining the degree of personality maturity an individual has attained. The outline given by Henry Bowman in his book on marriage is used here because of its distinctive reference to maturity in and for marriage. The points utilized here are the paragraph headings in Bowman's long and valuable description of the criteria of mature behavior.[7] In only a few places have new items been inserted. Individuals will use this outline to study their own degree of maturity and the degree of maturity of their intended mates.

I. A mature person not only has intelligence comparable to his calendar age, but he uses this intelligence on a mature level in his daily life.
   A. He develops a reasonably objective point of view toward both himself and things and persons other than himself, determining a considerable part of his behavior on this objective basis.
   B. He profits by his own experience and the experience of others.
   C. He integrates what he knows and lives by that integrated knowledge.
   D. He sees various sides of a problem, studies it carefully, seeks a thorough solution.

II. A mature person sees himself as part of a larger whole.
   A. He has an appreciation of man's relation to the universe and has worked out a philosophy of life which includes things cosmic and eternal as well as things earthly, temporary and immediate.
   B. He has some knowledge of social life, how it is organized, what the requirements are for living in society.
   C. He understands the finesse of social relations.
   D. He makes concessions to others but at the same time he does not become too dependent upon them.
   E. He has a reasonable respect for authority and tradition.

III. A mature person lives in a world of reality.
   A. In so far as he is able to discover reality, he faces it.
   B. He does not escape from problem-facing through fantasy.
   C. He does not escape from problem-facing through illness.
   D. He is adaptable.
   E. He lives in a world in which past, present, and future are balanced and integrated.
   F. He faces an unalterable situation, in which he has a deep interest, with poise and a minimum of conflict.
   G. He depends upon adult accomplishments for prestige.

[7] Henry A. Bowman, *Marriage for Moderns,* New York, McGraw-Hill Book Company, Inc., 1948, Chapter V. Used by permission of McGraw-Hill Book Company, Inc.

H. He uses the present rather than the past as a point of departure.

I. He accepts his chronological age for what it is.

IV. The mature person is independent.

    A. He can fulfill his economic role in life.

    B. He is relatively independent of his parents.

    C. A mature person does not depend too much upon flattery, praise, and compliments.

    D. He does not take offense at slights or what he interprets as slights.

    E. He accepts responsibility for his own acts.

    F. He is not generally anxious or hostile.

    G. He applies adult criteria to his personal traits.

V. A mature person controls his behavior.

    A. He acknowledges possible undesirable urges and appetites within himself but he tries to rise above them and to exert conscious and intelligent control.

    B. He will endure present discomfort and sacrifice for future gain.

    C. His behavior is determined in part on the basis of principles rather than pleasure or pain.

    D. He exhibits adult restrictions upon his behavior.

        1. He does not always demand attention.

        2. He does not exaggerate the expression of emotion.

        3. He is not always either way up or very depressed.

        4. He exerts some control on his temper.

        5. He is not cruel, and does not enjoy others' cruelty.

        6. He can take leadership and yet be democratic.

    E. He has an integrated personality; he is not always in inner conflict.

VI. A mature person has an attitude toward sex, love, and marriage compatible with adulthood.

    A. He is heterosexual.

    B. He has a healthy, well-balanced, informed attitude toward sex and marriage.

    C. He is adequately prepared for marriage.

VISUAL AIDS

Are You Ready for Marriage? Cornet Instructional Films, Chicago.

Choosing for Happiness (Bowman Series), McGraw-Hill Book Company, Inc., Text Film Dept., 330 West 42nd Street, New York 36.

It Takes All Kinds (Bowman Series), McGraw-Hill Book Company, Inc., New York.

READINGS

HENRY A. BOWMAN, *Marriage for Moderns,* New York, McGraw-Hill Book Company, Inc., 1948, Chapter VI.

ERNEST W. BURGESS and HARVEY J. LOCKE, *The Family, from Institution to Companionship,* New York, The American Book Company, 1953, Chapter XIII.

EVELYN DUVALL and REUBEN HILL, *When You Marry,* Revised Edition, Boston, D. C. Heath and Company, 1953, Chapter IV.

CHAPTER 7

Socio-Cultural Factors

INTRODUCTION: HAPPINESS IN MARRIAGE DEPENDS PARTLY ON THE MATURITY OF THE INDIVIDUALS CONCERNED AND THE WAY the configuration of personality of each partner meets the needs of the other in intimate communication. Adjustment in marriage also depends upon the way the attitudes, values, and roles of each matches those of the mate. This chapter describes the areas of agreement which, research indicates, are related to happy adjustment as well as the areas of disagreement which are related to unhappiness. In Chapter I, some emphasis was put upon the transitional nature of contemporary family life. It was indicated there that two persons who expected different kinds of behavior from their mates would meet much conflict. Our society is very heterogeneous. Young people with dissimilar backgrounds and expectations are often in such close contact that they develop romantic attachments. The purpose of this chapter is to help young people orient themselves in terms of their sometimes unconscious role expectations and in terms of sociological insights which will enable them to choose a marriage partner wisely. It does not attempt to contribute to the adjustment of the problems indicated; that will be done in a later chapter. Here, consideration is given to patterns of marital choice which would insure happiness or result in a failure to adjust.

The problem of the changing role of women as it relates to wise marital choice has several facets: the psychological tendencies of superi-

135

ority, dominance, and competition discussed in the last chapter; the changing economic roles of women, which will be discussed in the next chapter; the way she and her husband define her place or her function in relation to her home, her community, and her children. This last, unlike the other two, may be regarded as sociological and is considered in this chapter.

MENTAL SEX DIFFERENCES

In the past the education of women was so different from that of men that mental sex differences were never a problem. (Men and women were expected to be dissimilar.) Today men and women receive essentially the same schooling from kindergarten through college, but the stereotypes which control the relationship of the sexes derive from the earlier period. Komarovsky says that, "Today the survival of some of these stereotypes is a psychological straitjacket for both sexes."[1] Two different studies show that 40 per cent of women and undergraduates are so aware of men's need to feel superior in ability that the women "play dumb" on dates, simulate ignorance about school subjects, and fail to win when they have the ability to win.[2]

The girls soon learn in the school of dating how to submerge any innate efficiency in sports or any native intellectual ability. Sixty-five per cent of the girls in one large Western school thought that to be outstanding in academic work diminished a girl's chances for dates.[3] To illustrate this problem, Komarovsky quotes a letter from a girl to her brother, the brother's answer, and the girl's reaction to his comment.

> What a wonderful evening at _____ fraternity house. You would be proud of me, Johnny! I won all the ping-pong games but one!

> "For heaven's sake," came the reply, "when will you grow up? Don't you know that a boy likes to think he is better than a girl? Give him a little competition, sure, but miss a few serves in the end. Should you join the Debate Club? By all means, but don't practice too much on the boys."

The girl's reaction was as follows:

[1] Mirra Komarovsky, *Women in the Modern World*, Boston, Little, Brown and Company, Copyright, 1953, by Mirra Heyman, p. 77. This discussion closely follows Komarovsky's analysis of this problem.
[2] Mirra Komarovsky, "Cultural Contradictions and Sex Roles," *American Journal of Sociology*, November, 1946, p. 187. [3] Komarovsky, *op. cit.*, p. 82.

Believe me I was stunned by this letter, but then I saw that he was right. To be a success in the dorms one must date, to date one must not win too many ping-pong games. At first I resented this bitterly, but now I am more or less used to it and live in hope of one day meeting a man who is my superior so that I may be my natural self.[4]

In discussions in marriage classes, girls have reiterated this point of view over and over. They have also revealed the bitterness they feel about this contradiction. They are expected to develop skills and leadership ability but when they succeed, as their parents and schools expect them to, their very success threatens their relationship with men. Komarovsky suggests one solution for this problem:

> It may be conceded that in so far as the sexes are not protected from rivalry by the sharp demarcation in the ideals of feminine and masculine aptitudes, such rivalry may be on the increase. But the way to alleviate excessive competition is to attack its profound roots in the isolation, the insecurities, and the hostilities of men and women. Excessive competitiveness is also destructive between members of the same sex. Since it seems neither realistic nor idealistic to attempt to reverse the trends which have increased women's competence in traditionally "masculine" spheres, there remains only one thing to do: give the man fairer odds, by relieving him of the need to demonstrate superiority over women in intellectual aptitudes.[5]

The same problem exists in decision-making in courtship and in marriage. The emerging role of the wife as a partner assumes an equality in making decisions about money, home management, the use of leisure time, and other matters. Many men like to believe that they want their wives to be their social and intellectual equals, but when it comes to "running things," old stereotypes stand in the way of their behaving in a consistent manner. And so conflict develops.

The solution suggested by Komarovsky undoubtedly is for the long term, involving as it does a basic modification of the attitudes of both men and women. It has little relevance to the immediate problem of marriage choice. A more practical solution is suggested. Men and women, realizing they are living in a period of transition, will do well to explore in rather great detail their own and their partners' attitudes toward the woman's role. There is no pat solution to this problem but a be-

[4] *Ibid.*, pp. 81–82. Reprinted by permission.   [5] *Ibid.*, pp. 86–87.

ginning can be made by bringing to the surface one's stereotypes and expectations about the role of the mate.

SOCIAL CLASS AND WISE MARRIAGE CHOICE

The following case illustrates some of the problems involved in cross-class marriages:

> The problem which brought Henry and Marion into the counselor's office was a bitter conflict over the type of home to be purchased prior to their marriage. Marion was shocked because Henry did not know the period styles of architecture or furniture and hurt because he did not match her interest in these. Henry was shocked because of the importance Marion placed on such "unimportant details" and hurt because she was insisting upon teaching him all about architecture, furniture, decoration and other home concerns. Henry furthermore resented Marion's gentle admonitions regarding his manners and his vocabulary. Marion was troubled because of her parents' reaction to the way Henry always dressed. These two had been brought together because both were champion skiers and enjoyed this sport during every leisure hour they did not have to be in school. Their courtship had taken place in winter practically entirely on the ski lift and their marriage had been arranged for spring. It was not until they began to make specific plans for their home life that important differences began to appear in almost every area of values. They belonged to widely different socio-cultural classes and this difference accounted for Marion's lack of satisfaction with her fiancé's manners, speech, background, dress and interests. After exploring still other areas of values Henry and Marion decided to break their engagement. Outside of skiing they literally did not speak the same language.[6]

Much of the literature about marriage choice deals with the controversy as to whether "like attracts like" (homogamy) or "opposites attract each other" (heterogamy). Hollingshead found that in 587 of 1,008 marriages, or 58.2 per cent, the partners came from the same class of residential area and presumably from the same social class. The table also indicates that when class lines were crossed, the man chose a woman from a lower class much more frequently than the reverse. Obviously, homogamy operated in about 60 per cent of the cases, heterogamy in about 40 per cent. These 1,008 couples, 50 per cent chosen at random, were interviewed by Hollingshead after their marriages in New Haven in 1948:

[6] A case study in the author's files.

138

TABLE 13. Residential Class of Husband and Wife for Residents of New Haven*

CLASS OF HUSBAND	CLASS OF WIFE						
	I	II	III	IV	V	VI	TOTAL
I	13	7	1	0	3	1	25
II	8	56	8	12	13	8	105
III	1	4	15	5	7	7	39
IV	0	8	4	55	35	38	140
V	0	12	8	30	252	87	389
VI	0	5	9	40	60	196	310

* August B. Hollingshead, "Cultural Factors in the Selection of Marriage Mates," *American Sociological Review,* 15, 1950, p. 625, Table 4. Reprinted by permission.

A comparable indication of the degree of cross-class marriage is found in the study of Centers who analyzed occupational levels and marital selection. The following table gives in percentages the mobility of various classes of men in terms of mate selection. The higher the occupational status of the husband, the more likely he is to choose a wife from a lower social class.

TABLE 14. Distribution of Marriages by Occupational Strata*

OCCUPATIONAL STRATA OF HUSBANDS	PERCENTAGE OF MEN WHO MARRIED WIVES		
	Above Own Level	*At Own Level*	*Below Own Level*
Business executives	0	15	85
Professional	7	25	68
Small business	11	40	49
White collar	37	23	40
Skilled manual	24	46	30
Semiskilled	49	41	10
Unskilled	60	40	0

* Richard Centers, "Marital Selection and Occupational Strata," *American Journal of Sociology*, 44, 1949, p. 533. Reprinted by permission.

The crucial question in these inter-class marriages is the degree to which the incorporation in a marriage of different sets of values, attitudes, and expectations causes conflict and tension. Roth and Peck have analyzed the original schedules of the Burgess-Cottrell marriage-adjustment study and worked out the social-class placement from their data. Cavan has given graphic summary to their findings.

139

FIGURE 4. Marital Adjustment and Social Class*

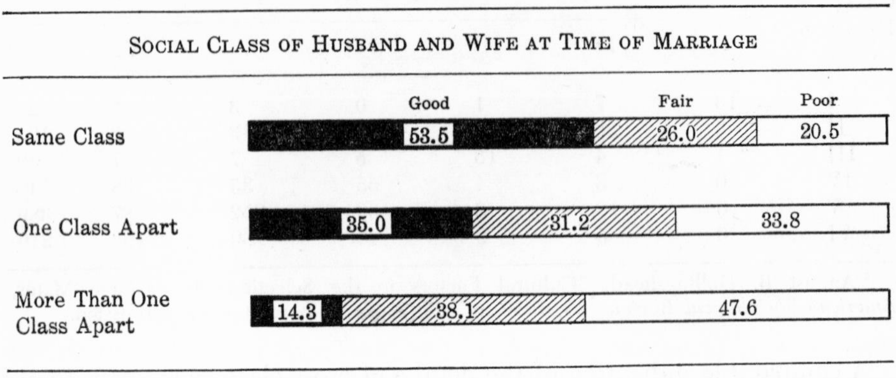

SOCIAL CLASS OF HUSBAND AND WIFE AT TIME OF MARRIAGE

	Good	Fair	Poor
Same Class	53.5	26.0	20.5
One Class Apart	35.0	31.2	33.8
More Than One Class Apart	14.3	38.1	47.6

* Ruth S. Cavan, *The American Family*, Thomas Y. Crowell Company, New York, 1953, p. 232. Reproduced by permission.

Cavan follows the graph with this observation:

> This figure shows that intra-class marriages are preponderantly characterized by fair or good adjustment; marriages with one class difference between husband and wife are about equally divided between good, fair and poor adjustment; and marriages with husband and wife more widely separated in social-class placement have almost half showing poor adjustment and a very low percentage with good adjustment.[7]

Burgess and Wallin's study indicated that cross-cultural differences are not only an important factor in broken engagements but that they inevitably cause conflict in greater or lesser degree. While they think that some husbands and wives have the adjustive capacity to be tolerant of such difficulties, they also think that divergent cultures are apt to become minor or even major sources of irritation and resentment. They feel that such cultural differences as those in the areas of family background, religion, nationality background, educational background, and social class contribute to maladjustments.[8]

This discussion of social class and marriage choice indicates that a great many heterogamous marriages take place, but that they are often replete with irritation and conflict, and that in general the adjustment

[7] Ruth S. Cavan, *The American Family*, Thomas Y. Crowell Company, New York, 1953, p. 232. Reprinted by permission.
[8] Ernest W. Burgess and Paul Wallin, *Engagement and Marriage*, Philadelphia, J. B. Lippincott Company, 1953, pp. 438–439.

in such marriages is not as satisfactory as in those in which class lines are not crossed.

AGE DIFFERENCES AND WISE MARRIAGE CHOICE

The effects of our cultural standards on marital choice are well illustrated in the stereotypes regarding the proper relationship of the ages of a man and his wife. As has been indicated in the chapters on adolescence and on psychological factors, the variable of age is almost meaningless when compared to the differentials in physical and psychological growth of men and women. Some men and some women at eighteen are more mature than others in the same group who are three or four years older. There is a general tendency in society to feel that the man must be older than his wife. The following table from Hollingshead's study in New Haven illustrates how well this cultural pattern operates, particularly for the younger age group:

TABLE 15. Age of Husband and Wife by Five-Year Intervals for New Haven Marriages, 1948*

Age of Husband	Age of Wife								
	15–19	20–24	25–29	30–34	35–39	40–44	45–49	50 & up	TOTAL
15–19	42	10	3						55
20–24	153	504	51	10	1				719
25–29	52	271	184	22	7	2			538
30–34	5	52	87	69	13	5			231
35–39	1	12	27	29	21	2	3		105
40–44		1	9	18	17	8	2	1	56
45–49	1		3	6	16	16	7	1	49
50 & up			1	4	11	15	21	43	95
Total	254	850	365	168	86	47	33	45	1848
X^2 2574.8905	P	.01	C	.76	C	.80			

* August B. Hollingshead, "Cultural Factors in the Selection of Marriage Mates," *American Sociological Review*, 15, 1950, p. 622. Reprinted by permission.

The factor of age in relation to marriage adjustment has been considered in previous research studies. Burgess and Cottrell found that age might be considered an index of maturity; they reported that wives under 16 and husbands under 22 tend toward poor adjustment and "in the great majority of cases there seems to be no doubt regarding the unfortunate effects of early marriages."[9] They found that the best marital adjustment was present when ages were equal or the husband was one to three years older than his wife. Locke found that for those married only once, the differences between the mean age at marriage of married and divorced was very significant, 21.5 and 19.1 years.[10] Married and divorced men showed an equally significant difference in mean age at marriage, 24.1 and 23.2 years. He found that approximate equality of age was correlated with marital adjustment, and that, if men were three or four years older than their wives, the prospects of adjustment were unfavorable.[11] Terman, on the other hand, found the top happiness scores for husbands when they were older by three to five years and for wives when they were younger by three to five years.[12] In summarizing all of the data available Locke concludes that "this seems to indicate that marital adjustment is better when wives are not too much younger than their husbands at the time of marriage."[13]

The significance of this conclusion is that a cultural stereotype gives young people a pattern of expectation which may not be in accord with contemporary realities. If modern education enables young women to mature at about the same rate as young men, then Locke's finding that they should be nearly the same age at marriage is valid.

There is more agreement among the studies on the fact that early marriages are often disastrous. This may be due to a number of reasons. Some people marry at an early age in order to escape intolerable home conditions. But the environmental factors that push them into marriage have also given them certain instabilities which will mar their adjustment. Thus early marriage may be symptomatic of social and psychological problems. Again, a girl in her teens marries a man in his thirties. Obviously that girl has failed in her adjustment to her own group or she is a very dependent person looking for a father-substitute. Yet if the man and the girl are otherwise well suited, such marriages are sometimes extremely happy. Perhaps the most apt generalization about the age to marry is that marrying either very young or very late and marrying when there is a large age difference may be quite hazardous and therefore should be considered with that much more care.

[9] Ernest W. Burgess and Leonard S. Cottrell, *Predicting Success or Failure in Marriage*, New York, Prentice-Hall, Inc., 1939, p. 115.

[10] Harvey J. Locke, *Predicting Adjustment in Marriage: A Comparison of a Divorced and a Happily Married Group*, New York, Henry Holt and Company, 1951, p. 101.

[11] *Ibid.*, p. 103.

[12] Lewis M. Terman, *Psychological Factors in Marital Happiness*, New York, McGraw-Hill Book Company, Inc., 1938, pp. 183–187.   [13] Locke, *op. cit.*, p. 104.

142

INTER-RACIAL MARRIAGE AND MARRIAGE HAPPINESS

The problems associated with inter-racial marriage are social in nature. Biologists are in almost universal agreement that there is no genetic or organic problem associated with cross-racial marriages. However, in this country racial antagonisms and stereotypes infiltrate the cultural milieu so deeply that partners in an inter-racial marriage must face problems of segregation and great resentment. These prejudices operate to strip the couple of membership in their own groups and to isolate their children. This causes difficulty in the adjustment of the partners to each other, and to their groups.

Baber investigated inter-racial marriages over a period of several years. He studied 48 marriages and classified them according to sex and race as follows:

T A B L E 16. Combinations of Inter-Racial Marriages*

Yellow X white	18	White—yellow	20**
White X yellow	2		
Black X white	18	Black—white	25
White X black	7		
Yellow X black	3	Yellow—black	3
	48		48

* Ray E. Baber, "A study of 325 Mixed Marriages," *American Sociological Review*, 2, pp. 705–716. Reprinted by permission.

** The symbol X is used to designate a marriage classified by sex, the male always being first. The symbol—is used to designate marriage not classified by sex. For example, the 25 black—white marriages include both the black men marrying white women (B X W) and the white men marrying black women (W X B).

Baber attempted to measure the happiness of this group of marriages by scaling it from 0 to 100—with 100 representing very happy; 75, moderately happy; 50, neutral; 25, very unhappy; and 0, very very unhappy—and arrived at the ratings for this group shown in Table 17. In general, he found that as dissimilarity in color and feature increased, the degree of marital adjustment or happiness decreased.

Baber compared this result with happiness ratings for inter-marriages involving both nationality and religion and those involving only religion. The rating of inter-racial marriages is somewhat lower than that of

TABLE 17. Happiness Ratings of 48 Inter-Racial Marriages*

	Number of Cases	TYPE OF MIXTURE	Happiness Rating
	18	Black X White	57
	7	White X Black	39
Both combinations	25	Black—White	52
	18	Yellow X White	67
	2	White X Yellow	100
Both combinations	20	Yellow—White	71
	3	Yellow X Black	75
All combinations	48	Black—White—Yellow	62

* Ray E. Baber, "A Study of 325 Mixed Marriages," *American Sociological Review*, 2, pp. 705–716. Reprinted by permission.

nationality-religion cross marriages and lower yet than those involving religion only. For those involving religion only Baber found an over-all happiness score of 73.[14]

Baber comments on the motivation for such marriages:

> In some cases, especially among college students, a mixed marriage springs partly from a protest against the prevailing pattern of race prejudice, the idealistic young people getting a certain satisfaction from defying public opinion. Or it may be a protest against the parental domination of a daughter who has been warned to have nothing to do with a cultured Oriental in whom she has become interested. Or again the unpopularity of a girl among her own kind may drive her to accept the attentions of attractive young men of another color. Certainly such a course is attention getting and is some compensation to the never-noticed person who thereby gains the spotlight. In cases where the "protest" motive is absent, the very fact that two persons of different race are willing to brave the unyielding opposition of all about them in order to wed may be evidence of an unusually strong personal attraction, and they may achieve happiness. Furthermore, such opposition makes them fully aware of the difficult adjustments ahead and may result in early and determined efforts to justify their decision. Such factors are favorable to adjustment, and occasionally they outweigh the heavy hand of prejudice.[15]

[14] Ray E. Baber, "A Study of 325 Mixed Marriages," *American Sociological Review*, 2, pp. 705–716.

[15] Ray E. Baber, *Marriage and the Family*. Permission to quote granted by McGraw-Hill Book Company, Inc., New York, 1953, p. 97.

One of the factors frequently overlooked in thinking about inter-racial marriages is the reaction of parents and other relatives. Both often resent out-group marriages of any kind but most particularly inter-racial marriages which they may feel bring disgrace upon themselves. The following excerpt from a case study indicates something of this problem; the case involved a Negro girl and an Oriental boy:

> "I love Bob very much," the girl said, "but his mother has threatened to commit suicide if we get married. And I know of a similar case where a mother did just that. I don't want that on my conscience the rest of my life. Can't you see the mother and explain to her how much in love we are?"[16]

Baber cites a case which indicates that the problem for the children of such a union is not only ostracism at school but sometimes trouble between the siblings themselves:

> In one case (W X B) the boy is white and his two sisters are dark. They quarrel a great deal, his most effective technique being to call them "nigger," which infuriates the girls and stirs up both the parents. In another (Y X W) the six-year-old daughter is called "chink" by her playmates at school. Her parents are ostracized by whites, and her Chinese father is "beaten up" periodically by her mother's brothers. The mother in another case (W X B) hates the daughter because she is light like her father yet will not let the girl marry a dark person. In one instance (Y X B) the wife had a daughter by her first marriage with a white man, and now in this second marriage the white daughter resents having a Chinese stepfather and half brother. Misery attends the mother in another union (B X W) because her little daughter hates her for being white and loves her father because he is black, as she is. Her little brother, however, loves his mother and hates his sister for hating and striking his mother. The mother "has no friends." Still another mother in a mixed marriage (W X B) is hurt because her daughters avoid introducing her to their friends but are eager to introduce their father and show him off.[17]

Inter-racial marriages cause difficulties in (1) alienating the parents, relatives, and past friends of the man and wife, (2) inviting the resentment and prejudice of communities and neighborhoods where racial caste systems are rigid, (3) causing the offspring of such unions extreme problems in adjusting to their peers and to their siblings. Baber rightly

[16] From a case study in the author's files.   [17] Baber, op. cit., pp. 95–96.

145

comments that such marriages are sometimes successful but that they are fraught with the problems outlined above in addition to normal problems of marital adjustment.

INTER-FAITH MARRIAGES AND WISE MARRIAGE CHOICE

Inter-faith marriages are marriages between any two people from such diverse religious backgrounds that their difference in religious values are possible causes of conflict. This may be a Catholic-Protestant, a Catholic-Jewish, a Liberal-Protestant—Fundamentalist-Protestant union, or the union of one who has a wide interest in religion and one who has none. There are a great many variations in loyalty to religious groups as well as in types of beliefs. Our analysis is confined to Catholic-Protestant inter-faith marriages (1) because they are the most numerous and (2) because more research has been done on this type. However, the type of approach used here applies to all forms of inter-faith unions and may be applied by those couples who have questions regarding the outcome of their marriage.

What is the extent of such inter-faith marriages? Clement S. Mihano-vich, writing in a Catholic periodical in July, 1949, said: "Over 40 per cent of all Catholic marriages in 1946 were mixed marriages."[18] Paul Blanshard thinks that there are over one hundred thousand Catholic-Protestant marriages in the nation every year.

> There are more than 100,000 priestly mixed marriages a year in the United States and recently studies by priests show not only that such marriages are increasing rapidly in spite of ecclesiastical pressure, but also that a very large proportion of mixed families are lost permanently to the church.
>
> The corresponding number of such dioceses in the 1948 Catholic Direc-tory was thirteen, and the statistics in that directory recorded 97,497 priestly mixed marriages in the United States in the previous year, not counting the great diocese of Boston which, for some reason, does not disclose its mixed marriage statistics.[19]

To the mixed marriages performed by priests must be added all those mixed marriages performed by Protestant ministers and justices of the peace. This would probably mean that 50 per cent of Catholic youth are

---

[18] Clement S. Mihanovich, *The American Ecclesiastical Review*, July, 1948.
[19] Paul Blanchard, *American Freedom and Catholic Power*, Boston, The Beacon Press, 1949, pp. 165–166.

marrying non-Catholic mates. Leiffer[20] made a special study of 6,236 families and found among them 743 families of divided religious loyalties at the time of marriage. Of these families some 444 were Protestant-Catholic unions.

A national study of the extent of mixed marriage has been made by Mihanovich, Schnepp, and Thomas:

TABLE 18. Mixed-Marriage Statistics for 7 Archdioceses and 43 Dioceses, 1934–1941 *

Year	TOTAL MARRIAGES	CATHOLIC MARRIAGES	MIXED MARRIAGES	
			Number	Per Cent
1932	59,329	42,196	17,133	28
1933	66,198	46,869	19,329	28
1934	91,179	67,844	23,825	25
1935	83,397	58,377	25,020	29
1936	90,712	63,651	27,061	29
1937	94,582	65,759	28,823	30
1938	92,198	64,044	28,154	30
1939	102,831	71,865	30,966	29
1940	114,985	79,153	35,832	30
1941	117,440	79,583	37,857	31

* From: Bishop's Committee on Mixed Marriages, "A Factual Study of Mixed Marriages" (Washington, D. C.: National Catholic Welfare Conference, 1943), p. 5. Reprinted by permission.

Intensive studies of individual parishes seem to show that the mixed marriage rate may vary rather widely from one area to the next. Thus, in a study of a parish on the Atlantic seaboard, mixed marriages constituted about 50 per cent of all marriages; another parish, also in the East, gave a figure of 20 per cent. By diocese Thomas found rates ranging from 70 per cent to 10 per cent and noted a negative correlation between the proportion of Catholics in an area and the percentage of mixed marriages. Further, mixed marriage rates seem to be higher in the upper socio-economic classes and lower in areas occupied by cohesive ethnic groups. Thomas believes that the over-all rate is increasing and offers five factors to support that position: (1) national groups gradually fusing with the host culture; (2) Catholic and non-Catholic interaction is increasing; (3) mixed marriages seem to have a cumulative effect; (4) there is increasing individualism in the selection of a marriage partner;

[20] Murray H. Leiffer, "Mixed Marriages and Church Loyalties," *Christian Century*, January 19, 1949, pp. 87–90.

147

and (5) the attitude of both Catholic and non-Catholic young people seems to be becoming more tolerant to mixed marriages.[21]

HAZARDS OF MIXED MARRIAGE

Some of the results of inter-faith marriages are analyzed by these authors. They depend for their data on a study of a single parish made previously by one of them, Schnepp.[22] This study can be summarized by saying that while 6.1 per cent of Catholic marriages ended in divorce, some 12.5 per cent of mixed and 15.1 per cent of invalid marriages ended in divorce; from 30 to 40 per cent of non-Catholics were converted and from 20 to 30 per cent of the Catholics involved gave up their faith; only 51 per cent of the children of these mixed families attended Catholic schools. Even more important for future trends is the summary dealing with the marriages of children from mixed marriages:

> Of 702 children whose parents were united in Catholic marriage, 425 or 60 per cent contracted a Catholic marriage; 206 or 31 per cent a mixed marriage, and 61 or 9 per cent an invalid marriage—Of 200 children whose parents married mixed, 44 per cent contracted a Catholic marriage; 44.5 per cent contracted a mixed marriage and 11.5 per cent an invalid marriage—It seems fairly correct to say, then, that mixed marriages have bred mixed marriages in this parish. The proportion of Catholics to mixed marriages is approximately two to one when the parents' marriage was Catholic, and one to one when the parents' marriage was mixed.[23]

Three other studies which analyze the fate of these mixed marriages are summarized by Skidmore and Cannon, as shown in Table 19.

Peterson studied the impact of religion upon family adjustment of 440 persons selected on a cross-sectional basis from the County of Los Angeles. Religious histories were taken and the questions in the Burgess-Terman-Locke adjustment-scale were asked. From the answers to these questions basic adjustment scores were derived. When the individuals were grouped according to their religious backgrounds, mean adjustment scores were computed. It was evident from the study that religious groups differ significantly in the way couples belonging to those groups adjust in marriage. One finding was that inter-faith couples have the

[21] Mihanovich, Schnepp, and Thomas, *Marriage and the Family*, The Bruce Publishing Company, Milwaukee, Wisconsin, 1942, pp. 202–203. Reprinted by permission.

[22] Gerald J. Schnepp, S. M., *Leakage from a Catholic Parish*, Washington, D. C., the Catholic University of America Press, 1942.

[23] *Ibid.*, p. 209. Reprinted by permission.

T A B L E 19. Per Cent of Marriages of Mixed and Non-Mixed Religious Faiths Ending in Divorce or Separation in Given Studies*

RELIGIOUS CATEGORIES	LANDIS STUDY IN MICHIGAN		BELL STUDY IN MARYLAND	WEEKS STUDY IN WASHINGTON
	No.	Per Cent	Per Cent	Per Cent
Both Catholic	573	4.4	6.4	3.8
Both Jewish	96	5.2	4.6	
Both Protestant	2794	6.0	6.8	10.0
Mixed Catholic-Protestant	192	14.1	15.2	17.4
Both none	39	17.9	16.7	23.9
Protestant changed to Catholic	56	10.7		
Catholic changed to Protestant	57	10.6		
Protestant Father Catholic Mother	90	6.7		
Catholic Father Protestant Mother	102	20.6		
Father none Mother Catholic		9.8		
Father none Mother Protestant	84	19.0		

* Rex Skidmore and Anthon S. Cannon, *Building Your Marriage*, New York, Harper and Brothers, 1951, p. 166. Reprinted by permission.

lowest mean adjustment score of any group in the study. The following table indicates the mean Catholic-Protestant adjustment score as compared to the mean score of Catholics married to Catholics and Protestants married to Protestants.

These studies indicate that Catholic-Protestant marriages are very hazardous unions. For this reason most Protestant denominations and all Catholic groups strongly urge their members to marry within their

T A B L E 20. Inter-Faith Marriages Compared as to Adjustment Score with Catholic, Protestant, and Non-Religious Marriages*

ADJUSTMENT SCORE	CATHOLIC-PROTESTANT	CATHOLIC	PROTESTANT	NON-CHURCH
	Per cent	Per cent	Per cent	Per cent
Low adjustment	50	39	20	29
High adjustment	50	61	80	71

* James A. Peterson, *The Impact of Objective and Subjective Religious Factors on Adjustment in Marriage*, unpublished Ph.D. Dissertation. Permission to quote granted by the University of Southern California Libraries, 1950, p. 196.

own faith. Four general individual problems characterize this type of marriage:

1. *The Problem of Family Participation.* Where will the family of an inter-faith marriage worship? This question was raised by Leiffer who came to the conclusion that in general children go to the church of the mother, despite the fact that a couple married by a priest signs a pledge promising to bring up the children as Catholics. This may be one reason for the very high rate of divorce of Catholic men and Protestant women shown in the Landis study. In his study of 444 husbands in Catholic-Protestant marriages he found that 110 were no longer connected with their church and 124 had not attended in the previous year. Almost the same thing happened on a smaller scale with wives. Of 449 Catholic-Protestant wives, 60 had no denominational affiliation and 91 had not attended in the previous year. Three generalizations are possible: (1) a few individuals are converted to the spouse's faith, (2) many drop out of religious groups altogether, and (3) children tend to go with the mother to the church of her choice.

2. *The Problem of Family Planning.* Spacing children is an important concept which many Protestants accept but which Catholics, according to their church dogmas, may not. If a Catholic, under pressure from his or her Protestant mate, does accede to the use of mechanical or chemical methods of birth control, it is often with deep remorse and guilt.[24] A couple married in the Catholic Church solemnly promise not to use any artificial form of birth-control. Birth-control is regarded as a serious sin in the Catholic philosophy. The highest aim for the Catholic family is the procreation of children, a privilege God shared with man, and this privilege may not be disregarded for the pleasure of individuals.

3. *The Problem of the Religious Pressures of In-Laws.* Some wives and husbands in inter-faith marriages might adjust if left to themselves. In-laws have an interest in the life of their son or daughter and because their religious interests are so intense are often factors for disunity. A Catholic-Protestant couple contemplating marriage should assess what importance their parents' attitude will have in the religious lives of themselves and their children.

4. *Culture and Style of Life.* Religion is more than a special way of genuflecting or subscribing to creeds. It involves a whole cluster of

---

[24] A copy of the agreement that must be signed by a Protestant when married to a Catholic in a Catholic church by a priest is included in Appendix II.

attitudes and values. One church may use raffles and dice games to raise money and a church not far from it may preach against gambling. The Protestant church may have a large dinner serving turkey or a roast on Friday night but the Catholic partner cannot attend that dinner. During Lent some Protestants deny themselves some luxury, while others do not. Almost all Catholics fast and make some denial or sacrifice during the period. In these and hundreds of other ways religion is a strong cultural force in determining not only religious beliefs but specific family and personality rituals and attitudes. Inter-faith couples need to be aware of the many ways in which their religious background reflects a way of life.

How can couples who feel that they are in love determine to what extent their religious differences will cause difficulties when they are married? These four areas of concern do not affect all individuals. For some with a Catholic or a Protestant background may have so little real interest in their religion that it will not affect their adjustment in marriage.

Not everyone who is a member of or who participates in a religious group does so with the same degree of zeal or intensity. A rough scale of this follows:

Our Interest in Religion

Almost No Vital Interest	Some Interest	Much Interest	A Very Great Interest

Where one places oneself on this scale and where the intended mate is placed on the scale may suggest the degree to which the couple may be troubled about religious differences. If both fall at the end of the scale marked "Almost No Vital Interest" there would obviously be very little trouble no matter how great the differences between their alleged religions. On the other hand, if both had "A Very Great Interest" and then differed significantly in their religious beliefs, the matter would call for greater exploration.

A second scale has to do with the degree of interest of the immediate relatives, for parents will have a deep and constant concern for the welfare of their married children and for the religious education of their grandchildren. Therefore it is well to place the families on a similar scale:

151

Our Families' Interest in Religion

My Family	Almost No Vital Interest	Some Interest	Much Interest	A Very Great Interest
Intended Mate's Family				

By using these two scales and studying the type of their religious affiliation young people can objectify the degree to which religion may be a problem in later adjustment, both for themselves and their families. A Catholic-Protestant couple contemplating marriage will do well to assess what importance their parents' attitude will have in their religious lives and those of their children.

The best safeguard against future difficulties is a full and frank discussion of religious beliefs and differences. Such a discussion will include the frank acknowledgment of any basic disagreements about the place where the marriage will take place, about birth-control, the religious education of children, and the family's future religious life. The interest scales proposed above may help them determine to what extent differences will be major obstacles to their happiness. In so far as possible they must think clearly about the future and project themselves into the role of parents and try to determine how they will feel then. There are many happy Catholic-Protestant couples who find that their fundamental beliefs are fairly similar and that their different religious traditions enrich rather than destroy their marital happiness.

RECREATION AND WISE MARRIAGE CHOICE

The use of leisure time is generally believed to be important in American life. Burgess and Wallin think that many of the conflicts about leisure-time pursuits reflect traditional sex differences in our culture as expressed in different degrees of interest and participation by men and women. Even as children, the American boy is encouraged to participate in sports because to do so is a typically masculine pattern in this country, while the girl is discouraged from such pursuits. Women like the gentler pursuits of the theater, or visiting friends, or dancing, while men appreciate prize fights and baseball games.[25]

In marriage young people face the necessity of giving up some of their

[25] Burgess and Wallin, *op. cit.,* pp. 258–260.

independent recreational behavior because, previous to marriage, recreation is ordinarily a same-sex pursuit. Adjustment to a new type of leisure-time activity may be difficult. Two significant studies have attempted to analyze the result of difference in recreational habits on marriage adjustment. Locke in his study asked the following question:

> In leisure time both husband and wife prefer to be "on the go," both prefer to stay at home, one prefers to be "on the go" and the other to stay home?[26]

Another question dealt with agreement on recreation: the couple were asked to check on a six-point scale the degree to which they felt they agreed. Locke put the answers to all his adjustment questions in rank order of their importance in differentiating happily married and divorced. There were thirty-four items on this scale, and the question regarding leisure time quoted above rated in sixth place, while the agreement question rated in twenty-sixth place. It appears that differences in preferences in the use of leisure time are highly important in determining the adjustment of a man and wife. Williamson confirms this study, finding that agreement on recreation was one of the most significant factors in marital adjustment:

T A B L E 21. Agreement in the Following Areas*

Item	Critical Husband	Ratio Wife
Sex relations	10.5	9.0
Recreation	10.2	6.4
Dealing with in-laws	8.9	7.5
Finance	7.8	6.9
Amount of time spent together	7.3	6.6
Aims, goals and things believed important in life	7.2	5.6
Choice of friends	7.1	6.7
Conventionality	3.9	7.6

* Robert Williamson, *Economic Factors in Marital Adjustment*, unpublished Ph.D. Dissertation, University of Southern California Library, 1952, p. 136. Reprinted by permission.

Williamson's study corroborates our conclusion that recreation is one of the major factors producing happiness and cohesion in marriage.

It is obvious that stereotypes derived from past cultural traditions seriously hamper men and women in preparing for marital adjustment.

[26] Locke, *op. cit.*, p. 374.

In the face of such contradictions, young people need to assess very carefully their recreational backgrounds and activities to be sure of common interests after marriage.

CONCLUSION

This chapter has presented material dealing with cultural definitions and expectations relating to the woman's role, inter-class marriages, age difference in marriage, inter-racial marriages, inter-faith marriages, and recreation. Cultural stereotypes place burdens on marital adjustment. The roles prescribed by the stereotypes lag behind actual educational preparation for marriage. This produces tension in marriage. On the other hand, in inter-racial and inter-faith marriages cultural values and expectations are so diverse that adjustment is difficult. Young people need to orient themselves in view of their own cultural backgrounds so that they can predict what their reaction will be in relation to others of either similar or dissimilar backgrounds. Because of the heterogeneity of our culture a large segment of the population becomes involved in cross-class, or cross-religious unions. These place a special burden on the adjustment processes of marriage.

SELF-ANALYSIS

Obviously this analysis must be made not only for you but for your intended mate. The value of understanding your own value structure is that it enables you to compare it with that of the person with whom you must adjust in marriage. For those not contemplating marriage the self-analysis will help them realize more adequately their own expectations and goals. When woman's role is analyzed, the man will think of his own attitudes toward woman's role, but the woman will try to make articulate her own concept of her own goals and wishes.

    I. Woman's Role in Marriage:
        A. Should a woman assume an inferior role in
            1. Sports and recreational pursuits?
            2. Intellectual activities?
            3. Community leadership roles?
        B. In terms of decision-making should a woman have
            1. Equality with men?
            2. A subordinate role to men?

II. Social-Class Membership
   A. To what social class do you belong?
   B. What particular characteristics of your behavior pattern do you ascribe to membership in that social class?
   C. Do you aspire to move into another social class?
   D. What problems would moving into another social class bring to you?

III. Recreational Interests and Background
   A. During middle and later adolescence or young adulthood what specific skills and interests have you developed in the following areas of leisure-time activities:
      1. Sports
      2. Intellectual pursuits
      3. Aesthetic fields
      4. Hobbies
   B. During middle and later adolescence or young adulthood what specific skills and interests have you developed in these four areas that would appeal to a member of the opposite sex?
   C. During middle and later adolescence or young adulthood what skills and interests have you developed in these four areas that would appeal not only to your mate but to children?
   D. List the most rewarding activities you have shared in a mixed group during the last six months.
   E. Remember, if you can, most of your dates for the past six months, and describe the types of activities they entailed. Are you satisfied with this report?
   F. In general, are most of your leisure hours devoted to things you do yourself, or do you depend on the skill of others to amuse you?
   G. Analyze your reactions when participating in a game.
      1. Are you primarily interested in winning or in sharing a good time?
      2. Are you a "good loser" or do you feel a little depressed at losing?
      3. Do you select activities to give you status or do you select them simply because they appeal to you?
      4. Can you spontaneously forget yourself in play? or are you somewhat serious even in recreation?
   H. Analyze your general reactions with a group
      1. Can you engage in happy "small talk"?
      2. Can you take a joke?
      3. Do you "banter" or "tease" in an easy way?
      4. Do you laugh easily, and often?

155

I. Analyze your present state of health in terms of your recreational life. Is your feeling one of physical buoyancy? Do you have energy and "bounce"? Are you keeping fit through sufficient exercise?

IV. Religious Participation and Interest
    A. On the scale provided on page 151 rate yourself on the intensity of your religious interest.
    B. On the scale provided on page 152 rate your family on their religious interest.
    C. Write out a simple statement outlining your expectations in marriage in terms of:
        1. The importance of worship, grace at meals, prayer for your incipient family.
        2. Your feeling regarding birth-control.
        3. Your feeling regarding the importance of religious education of your children; your desire as to the type of religious training they would receive.
        4. Your religious beliefs.
    D. Write out briefly the ways in which the religious atmosphere of your childhood and youth makes important contributions to your cultural pattern of life.

VISUAL AIDS

It Takes All Kinds, McGraw-Hill Book Company, Inc., Text Film Department, 330 West 42nd Street, New York 36, New York.

READINGS

RAY E. BABER, *Marriage and the Family*, New York, McGraw-Hill Book Company, Inc., 1953, Chapter 4.

ERNEST W. BURGESS and PAUL WALLIN, *Engagement and Marriage*, Philadelphia, J. B. Lippincott Company, 1953, Chapter 6.

MIRRA KOMAROVSKY, *Women in the Modern World*, Boston, Little, Brown and Company, 1953, Chapter 3.

HARVEY J. LOCKE, *Predicting Adjustment in Marriage: A Comparison of a Divorced and a Happily Married Group*, New York, Henry Holt and Company, 1952, Chapter 5.

JAMES A. PETERSON, *The Impact of Objective and Subjective Religious Factors on Adjustment in Marriage*, unpublished Ph. D. Thesis, University of Southern California Libraries, 1950.

Economic Factors

INTRODUCTION: WORK, MONEY, AND OCCUPATION ARE IM-
PORTANT OF COURSE FOR THOSE WHO CONTEMPLATE MARRIAGE.
This chapter will deal with the question: (*1*) the way socio-economic
factors are related to marital happiness; (*2*) the impact of occupational
choice on marital adjustment; (*3*)the economic role of the wife. These
are all important to marital choice because when one chooses a mate,
he also chooses for life his security level and the specific pattern of life
imposed by an occupation. Equally important for future marital adjustment is the attitude of husband and wife toward the wife's gainful employment.

ECONOMIC SECURITY AND MARITAL ADJUSTMENT

Economic factors have received much attention in marital studies.
Terman studied 792 couples of early middle age from the upper middle
class.[1] He found that insufficient income was frequently mentioned as a
negative factor in marriage. This factor was rated as one of the sources
of trouble of 70.5 per cent of the husbands and 68.8 per cent of the
wives. He found, however, that it was the way income was handled
rather than the actual amount that was important.

Burgess and Cottrell's study was of a middle-class sample of 526

[1] Lewis M. Terman, *Psychological Factors in Marital Happiness*, New York, McGraw-
Hill Book Company, Inc., 1938.

couples who had been married 5 years or less when studied.[2] By using the statistical device of partial correlation they were able to hold other major factors constant and so measure the importance of any one single item. When they did this for economic items they found that the economic factor had little importance by itself but was a symbol of cultural and education factors. Locke studied a fairly evenly divided sample of happily married and divorced families in Indiana.[3] His study represents the average population more adequately than any other major study. By asking the happily married sample to name couples who were divorced, and then interviewing these, he obtained a matched sample. He asked these married and divorced families whether or not they believed their total income met their needs as families. He also asked them to judge the adequacy of income on the following scale: very adequate, adequate, inadequate, or very inadequate.

The happy group said, in general, that they considered their income adequate and the unhappy described their income as inadequate. Locke also found that certain indices of security—namely, possession of life insurance, savings at marriage, and accumulated savings at the time of the interview—were associated with good adjustment. He found, too, that those families that rated higher on rent, life insurance, utilities, and luxuries had better adjustment than those that rated lower on these items. Williamson's findings give moderate support to Locke's conclusion that security is associated with marital happiness.[4]

Three conclusions with reference to factors determining wise marriage choice emerge from these studies. The first is the very obvious conclusion that the security factor is important to the well-adjusted family. Steadiness of income is more important than size, but both Locke and Williamson indicate that adjustment is somewhat better as security increases. The second conclusion (from Terman) is the importance of management of income. Young people contemplating marriage need to know the skill with which the intended mate meets his or her obligations. It is important that at least one of the couple has some ability to manage well. The following excerpt from a pre-marital interview indicates an awareness of this factor:

[2] Ernest W. Burgess and Leonard Cottrell, *Predicting Success or Failure in Marriage*, New York, Prentice-Hall, Inc., 1939.

[3] Harvey J. Locke, *Predicting Adjustment in Marriage: A Comparison of a Divorced and a Happily Married Group*, New York, Henry Holt and Company, 1952.

[4] Robert Williamson, *Economic Factors in Marital Adjustment*, unpublished Doctoral Dissertation, University of Southern California Library, June, 1951.

I suppose she wrote down on her form that I couldn't handle money. That's right. Money slips through my pockets like quicksilver through your fingers. I never have been able to save anything. I have a great time the first of the month and I starve the last week. That's one reason I'm marrying her. She will get my check and pay the bills.[5]

The third conclusion is that the economic backgrounds of the couple are more important than the actual security rating at marriage. Couples are apt to have problems if there are wide differences in their past economic experience. For our expectations regarding the normality and use of comfort-providing items and luxury items are all contingent on family patterns. Baber comments on this problem:

> One common source of economic conflict is in the unequal economic status and habits of the husband and wife prior to marriage. When a young man with a small income marries a girl from a family of somewhat higher economic rank (not necessarily wealthy) who has been used to a higher standard of living than the young husband can afford, she is likely either to spend beyond his income or to become irked at the necessity of restraint. Before marriage, in the rosy haze of romance, it looks easy to economize, and she promises to be the most thrifty of wives. But habits of a lifetime are not easily changed, and what looked simple turns out to be a long, hard process of learning self-denial. It can be done, but the record of success is certainly below the one-hundred mark.[6]

OCCUPATIONAL LIFE AND WISE MARRIAGE CHOICE

Does it make any difference whether your husband-to-be is a plumber, a doctor, a school-teacher, or a minister? Can the factors associated with his vocation seriously affect your life as his mate? These questions are frequently asked by young people when they become aware of the importance of occupational determinism in behavior patterns.

Three factors relating to occupational roles appear to be important to marital adjustment. One is the degree of stress associated with the vocation, since such stress may be reflected in tension in the home; another is the requirements of the vocation in hours and mobility; the third is attitudes associated with specific occupations which may seriously affect marital adjustment. Adams reports on Lang's study that

[5] From case study in the author's files.
[6] Ray E. Baber, *Marriage and the Family*, New York. Permission to quote granted by McGraw-Hill Book Company, Inc., 1953, p. 229.

"in one study of more than 17,000 marriages, ratings on marital happiness were contrasted with fifty different occupations." The ten occupations associated with the greatest happiness and those associated with the least happiness are given below:[7]

Highest	Lowest
1. Chemical engineers	1. Gas station employees
2. Ministers	2. Truck drivers
3. College professors	3. Musicians
4. Teachers	4. Real estate salesmen
5. Engineers	5. Plumbers
6. Wholesale salesmen	6. Auto mechanics
7. Chemists	7. Carpenters
8. Accountants	8. General mechanics
9. Civil engineers	9. Traveling salesmen
10. Office workers	10. Laborers

Locke's study partially confirms this finding; he found that professional and semi-professional vocations are associated with marital adjustment.[8] Weeks' study involved high-school students filling out questionnaires in Spokane, Washington. He related divorce to occupation as follows:

TABLE 22. Number of Divorces per 100 Families, by Occupation*

Professional	6.8
Proprietary	8.4
Clerical	10.4
Skilled	11.6
Semi-skilled	13.4
Unskilled	7.3

* H. Ashley Weeks, "Differential Divorce Rates by Occupations," *Social Forces*, 21, pp. 332–337. Reprinted by permission.

Williamson's study is the most comprehensive attempt yet made to measure the economic and occupational factor in relation to marital adjustment. He studied a representative sample obtained on the basis of the Shevky-Williams analysis of the social areas of Los Angeles by securing a random sample within selected social areas. His sample consisted of about 140 wives and husbands from each of three areas. The Burgess-Terman-Locke adjustment scale was employed to obtain his

[7] Clifford Adams, *Preparing for Marriage*, New York. Permission to quote granted by E. P. Dutton and Company, 1951, pp. 151–152. [8] Locke, *op. cit.*, p. 271.

judgment of the relative adjustment of the couples. This correlated occupational and income groups with adjustment scores.

Williamson's findings as shown in Table 23 confirm those of Lang and Weeks. In Table 23 the first item deals with occupation at the time of the interview; the second item deals with occupation at time of marriage. Both indicate that belonging to the white-collar, professional, and executive groups was significantly associated with marital happiness. In addition, the table indicates that wives of these men belonged largely in the adjusted group.

The third item deals with the number of hours required by the vocation. Those that required 47 hours or more are associated with unhappiness, indicating that occupations which require too much time away from home are associated with maladjustment of the marriage.

T A B L E 23. Per Cent of Happy and Unhappy Husbands and Wives with Given Economic Activities*

Item	Per Cent of Husbands' Responses			Per Cent of Wives' Responses		
	Happy	Unhappy	CR	Happy	Unhappy	CR
Occupation at present: white-collar, professional, and executive	65.1	52.3	1.6	68.3	48.4	2.3
Occupation at time of marriage: white-collar, professional and executive	77.1	59.3	+2.8	62.0	35.1	3.1
Average number of hours worked per week: 47 or more	63.5	73.3	−1.2	78.3	69.8	−1.1
Degree of husband's interest in his work:						
High	58.8	46.2	1.5	64.6	55.9	1.9
Intermediate	32.4	35.3	−0.3	25.3	28.8	0.0
Low	8.8	18.5	−1.7	10.1	15.3	−1.9
Low degree of interest in fellow employees	10.4	22.9	−2.2	8.3	21.5	−1.7
Little or no opportunity for responsibility and initiative in his work	6.5	10.8	−1.0	1.5	9.1	−1.8
Marked fatigue at the end of the day	57.1	72.1	−1.5	60.9	71.4	−1.1

* Robert Williamson, *Economic Factors in Marital Adjustment*, unpublished Doctoral Dissertation, University of Southern California Library, June, 1951, p. 159. Reprinted by permission.

After reviewing all of his findings, Williamson states:

> From the findings it can be concluded that a positive relationship exists between martial happiness and occupational adjustment.[9]

May's summary of the experience of psychologists and counselors in dealing with marital maladjustment and vocation problems also indicates that frustration in one's occupation leads to some maladjustment at home.[10]

THE STRESS-POTENTIAL OF OCCUPATIONS

The stress-potential denotes the degree of tension-producing strains in various occupations. The stress-potential of various occupations has never been accurately measured. Obviously, individual temperaments make such a measurement difficult. A phlegmatic person will not be as anxious in tension-producing situations as a more volatile one. It is certain that the man in a highly competitive business situation is confronted with a great many worries. This is true whether he is a small entrepreneur trying to make a small profit in a small store or an executive responsible to many stockholders for dividends. Many of these men think that their status depends entirely upon their economic success, and sometimes their wives are much concerned with "keeping up with the Joneses" in physical luxuries. Aristophanes once said that "Whirl is king," and he might have said it of our economic competition and its resultant personality tensions.

These tensions bring conflict and quarrels into the home. It is not possible for a business man to express his frustrations or hostilities toward his business associates, customers, or employees. This would lower the very status he is attempting to establish. He therefore tends to contain himself until he is in a more intimate situation where an explosion will not mar his opportunity for worldly success. As a result his general hostility may be vented over small matters in the home and directed against the wife or the children. The marriage consultant often hears this phrase: "I cannot understand my husband, he is such a different person at work than he is at home." On the other hand, the wife may identify herself with her husband's economic problems so that his recital of difficulties falls on sympathetic ears and they face the problems together.

[9] Williamson, *op. cit.*, p. 162.
[10] Mark A. May, *A Social Psychology of War and Peace*, New Haven, Yale University Press, 1943, p. 153.

The business man is not the only person in a tension-producing vocation. The doctor must share sorrow, shame, and despair with his patients and is faced with daily decisions which involve life or death. The minister shares a great many of the same anxieties with members of his congregation. Policemen have a vocation in which danger is a constant companion.

OCCUPATIONAL MOBILITY AND MARITAL ADJUSTMENT

The separation of the bread-winner from his wife and children may have a serious impact upon the family.

> In the few situations where the man's work involved a good deal of traveling this became an additional hazard to the marriage in terms of aggravation of a problem already existing for other reasons. One young husband, for instance, complained bitterly that his wife was unwilling to leave her parent's home. He was a professional hockey player who had to travel considerably during the hockey season. Now it is certainly true that all wives whose husbands travel do not feel that they cannot establish a home of their own and must instead stay with their mothers; there must be some unusual parental ties involved when this occurs without other obvious reasons. But it also seems likely that this fact that the husband in this case was traveling a good deal of the time made it somewhat more difficult for the wife to break her tie with her parents' home and set up an independent establishment.[11]

In every economic group there seems to be a segment that is highly mobile; thus the tenant farmer moves on an average of once every three years and many industrial workers must constantly shift to those areas where work is plentiful. Each move tends to have a disorganizing effect on the personality of individuals and on the family itself. For these reasons high job mobility may be said to be correlated with marital maladjustment.

On the other hand, Burgess and Locke contend that in certain circumstances mobility may be associated with an organizing and not a disorganizing effect on family relations.[12] They believe that travel such as honeymoons, vacations, or long trips may have a cohesive effect if the trip satisfies both partners. In the opinion of Burgess and Locke tem-

[11] Florence Hollis, *Women in Marital Conflict*, New York. Permission to quote granted by the Family Service Association of America, 1948, p. 135.
[12] Ernest W. Burgess and Harvey J. Locke, *The Family, from Institution to Companionship*, New York, The American Book Company, 1953, p. 500.

porary separations seem to have no disturbing effect on family relations and actually, in some cases, the return of the absent member enhances the pleasure of the association. Certain mobile families like gypsies and families in trailers seem to be highly organized. Finally, a family or members of a family which may have been highly disorganized in one locality, sometimes, in moving to a new location, find an opportunity for readjustment. Nevertheless mobility is disorganizing, as Burgess and Locke point out:

> The chief disorganizing effect of mobility is that it individualizes the person by detaching him from his family and other personal associations. This takes place (1) by the interruption of communication with family and friends, (2) by bringing the person into communication with those engaging in divergent practices, (3) by freeing him from primary social controls over his conduct, (4) by weakening personal attachments and loyalties to his family and friends, and (5) by increasing the opportunity of choice between various patterns of behavior.[13]

OCCUPATIONAL ATTITUDES AND MARITAL ADJUSTMENT

The third impact of an occupation upon marriage is that of attitude formation. Bogardus first called attention to the impact of occupations on attitudes and personality configurations. He found that the vocabulary, the frame of reference, the polarity of thought are all greatly influenced by one's vocational group. One tends to have his social, his recreational, and his educational experiences within his own occupational group. Thus each vocational group develops its characteristic speech mannerisms, its own sources of authority, its own ethics, and its method of problem-solving. Unfortunately, we know almost nothing about the way occupational determinism affects marital adjustment. Some case studies have indicated that it plays a part in marital adjustment.[14] An engineer, in discussing the problem of his children, said:

> In engineering after we have studied the problem we seek out the principle that is involved in the solution of that problem. When we have found the principle then we can easily deduce the solution. The same must be true about kids; there must be true principles. Once I have discovered them I think the rest will be easy.[15]

---

[13] *Ibid.*, p. 505. Reprinted by permission.

[14] See particularly the notable series of marriage counseling cases presented by Dr. Maurice Karpt in *Marriage and Family Living*, 14, Nos. 3 and 4 in which occupational attitudes are shown to be definitely involved in the conflicts presented.

[15] From a case study in the author's files.

This engineer has had eminent success in hydraulics. His children, unfortunately, do not respond to the principles used in hydraulics and his shifting search for the one scientific solution to their problems is rather hard on them.

Young men, in choosing their vocation, might well give some attention to the way various occupations will affect their family life. So, too, in selecting her marriage partner a girl must realize that economic factors play a part in marital adjustment. The level of economic security implied in her fiance's vocational choice and the occupational patterns peculiar to that choice should have some consideration. A minister's wife must be made of tough fibre, and her dedication to the church must be virtually as great as that of her husband if they are not to have serious difficulties in their marriage. The same is true of a doctor's wife. Perhaps the most important question to be asked is whether or not the occupation is stable, promising a fairly secure employment with consequent steadiness in income. When a man chooses a vocation he chooses a way of life. The wife, too, must of necessity elect his way of life when she chooses a given man.

THE CHANGING ECONOMIC ROLE OF WOMEN AND ITS MEANING FOR WISE MARRIAGE CHOICE

Hollis reports a case which displays some of the problems occasioned by women working or men's reaction to their working:

> This couple has been married for four years and there were two children —3 and 2 years old. However, at the beginning of marriage Mr. F. was earning a small salary and Mrs. F. had continued to work until the previous May, employing a housekeeper to care for the children and home. At that time Mr. F. had secured a better paying job and the couple had agreed that it would be better for the children if Mrs. F. stayed at home. Now Mrs. F. complained that her husband was gambling and that they were much in debt and that there was constant quarreling; Mr. F. had threatened to leave. Mrs. F. was devoted to her husband and greatly distressed at this possibility. As the caseworker listened to Mrs. F.'s spontaneous story she noted that Mr. F. did not show any great change during the marriage. She noted, too, that Mrs. F. traced her anxiety about this back to the previous May. Mrs. F. did not make any connection between this and the fact that this was the very month she had stopped working. The case worker pointed out the coincidence and asked if Mrs. F. thought there might be a connection. It developed that Mrs. F. hated housework and that she had really been making something of a

drudge of herself in an attempt to do a thoroughly good job even though she disliked it. It was also clear that this left her in a constant state of irritation and thus with less ability to tolerate her husband's carelessness about financial matters. Also, she seemed to miss the security of having some money she considered her own because she had earned it. Since Mr. F. had earlier no objection to Mrs. F. working it seemed possible that the previous harmonious balance in the family might be restored if Mrs. F. returned to her former plan of employing a housekeeper and working outside the home itself.[16]

One of the most frequent questions raised in marriage classes is the perplexing one of whether or not women's working interferes with their chances of happiness in marriage. While modern young people are com-

FIGURE 5. Per Cent of Women, 14 Years of Age and Over, in Labor Force, by Marital Status for 1890, 1940, 1950*

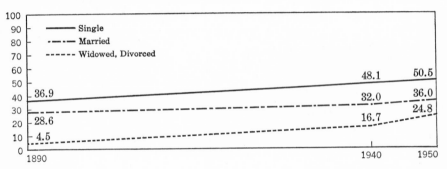

* J. D. Durand, *The Labor Force in the United States, 1890–1950,* and the current *Population Reports–Labor Force–*U. S. Census.

mitted to the equality of women and men, they are not quite sure what this means in terms of careers for wives and mothers. The first important answer to this question is the prevalence of women's working.

Figure 5, based on current population reports, shows that the percentage of married women who work rose from 4.5 in 1890 to 16.7 in 1940 and finally to 24.8 per cent in 1950. A third of the women in the population of the United States are gainfully employed. In 1952, a report from the Women's Bureau of the United States Department of Labor indicated that some 19 million women were in the civilian labor force.[17] Two significant trends appear in the report: (1) the growing proportion

[16] Hollis, *op. cit.,* pp. 137–138.

[17] *Status of Women in the United States,* Women's Bureau, U. S. Department of Labor Publication, D-55, p. 5.

of married women in the labor force and (2) the growing number of older women employed.[18] While Figure 5 indicates that in 1950 some 24.8 per cent of working women were married, the Women's Bureau report shows that by 1952 this group constituted 27 per cent of all women gainfully employed.[19] This represents a 19 per cent gain over 1940.

Women's earnings remain lower than those of men in comparable employment. For example, in certain manufacturing industries in New York in 1951 the average weekly pay for male production workers was $77.61 but for women it was $47.06 or about 60 per cent of what men received.[20] In 1950, the median annual income of men was $2,659 and for women $1,230. Equal-pay legislation has been enacted by thirteen states. This is an expansion of a trend already widely apparent in teaching and in government service.

These figures certainly do not mean that only one wife out of four is ever gainfully employed. While only 25 per cent were employed at the time of the census in 1950, a different 25 per cent might be working five years later. This seems likely because with length of marriage there is a differential in economic need. Many wives work for the first four or five years of marriage and then retire to begin their families. This means that the problem of the wife's working arises in a much larger percentage of marriage than might be indicated if we took the 27 per cent as an absolute measure. The problem of working has assumed new seriousness because of two contemporary developments: (1) the inflationary spiral which has made it difficult for a couple to start a family on the average wage of a young husband and (2) the postponement of marriage because of military service.

THE MARITAL ADJUSTMENT OF WORKING WIVES

There is not much statistical information on the adjustment of working wives. Locke has collected data in two different studies, one in Indiana and a second (with Muriel Mackeprang) at the University of Southern California.[21] The second was devoted to measuring the adjustment of wives who worked and wives who did not. Both studies failed to show any statistically significant differences between the married women who worked and those who did not work. Locke is not convinced, however,

[18] *Ibid.*, p. 6.   [19] *Ibid.*, p. 7.   [20] *Ibid.*, p. 9.
[21] Harvey J. Locke and Muriel Mackeprang, "Marital Adjustment and the Employed Wife," *American Journal of Sociology*, 54, 1949, pp. 536–538.

167

that his findings reflect the true situation, for some persons when interviewed indicated that the wife's employment was a primary factor in the divorce:

> The first ten years of our marriage, my wife and me got along fine. I earned good money and managed it right. Then I lost my job and couldn't get another, and she got out and made money. She got independent. She wanted to run everything, and she was no manager at all. If she wanted anything, she would run up town and charge it.
>
> She would go to work and the kids would go to school, and I would be all alone. She wanted me to stay right at home, cook the meals, and do all the work. She would call up home to see if I was there. She wanted to boss everything.[22]

Locke found one interesting difference in opinion between the married and divorced samples in regard to the employment of women. In answer to the question directed to husbands, "If the wife worked during marriage, did the husband approve or disapprove?" a significantly larger percentage of divorced than of married men expressed disapproval. This introduces one of the basic components of the problem. In American culture it has been assumed that there is a wide difference in the economic roles of men and women, that it is the man's duty to provide well for his family and the woman's function to assume domestic duties. When these prototypes determine the attitudes of husbands or wives, a wife's working may be in conflict with the husband's expectations of what her role should be. If the man is somewhat sensitive about his own male role, this encroachment of the wife on a formerly masculine area may cause him to react violently. If she earns more than he earns it may be especially traumatic for him. This point is illustrated by the following statement by Tead in a Washington address:

> It is of course trite and oversimplified to state the conflict as that between motherhood and a career. The dilemma is rather to be stated more profoundly as centering in decisions as to where, when, and how the drive to creativity, love, and self-growth is to express itself. In each individual case how are creative urges—psychological, intellectual, moral, and spiritual—all to get reasonably balanced and adequate expression? For many women in today's United States I venture that this dilemma is harder to resolve than for many men. One is prompted to say on their behalf as Antonio said of himself in Merchant of Venice:

[22] *Ibid.*, p. 295. Reprinted by permission.

"And such a want-wit sadness makes of me
That I have much ado to know myself."

I hasten to agree that the dilemma of this irrepressible conflict about the focus and flowering of creativity is not helped but hindered by the typical marital situation, if one can identify any situation as typical. I refer to the fact that men, broadly speaking, immersed in their own aggressive drives for creativity and for ego-maximizing in a competitive society, do not seem yet ready on as wide a scale as necessary to realize the deep roots of the woman's dilemma. Hence, they do not do what they might as husbands and as citizens to alleviate the contributing causes. There are still vast accumulations of male pride, possessiveness, false social standards, self-centeredness, and fearfulness of job competition, which aggravate the over-all social picture that women confront. These are a part of the social pattern she encounters. There is no solution, as affecting these negative forces, which can come about without frank collaboration and a truer equal fellowship between the sexes both in the home and in the market place.[23]

On the other hand, if a wife marries to be "taken care of" and discovers that because of economic insecurity she must herself contribute to the support of the family, trouble may ensue. The important question is the attitudes the husband and wife have toward the proper role of married women in our society. Some agreement on this question ought to be reached before an engagement takes place.

This problem becomes even more acute for the girl who establishes herself in a career she enjoys and after some time gives it up for motherhood. She had the satisfaction of accomplishment, the security of her own pay-check, and the stimulation of those she worked with. All this she exchanges for the routine of keeping house and caring for children. This involves readjustment of attitudes, reorganization of life patterns, loss of economic independence, disruption of daily patterns, loss of at least the intimacy of former friendships, and perhaps the development of a sense of injustice because being a woman means abandoning this rewarding and sometimes exhilarating work pattern. It is not that she does not want children. She does want them. It is not that she does not appreciate homemaking. Her home may mean a good deal to her. But having experienced the satisfactions of a man's world, it is most difficult to be wholly content with a mother's lot. This problem is growing more

---

[23] Ordway Tead, "Social Patterns for Women: The Present and the Prospects," Address, February 18, 1948, Washington, D. C. Mimeographed copy in files of author.

and more acute because an increasing number of college girls are continuing to work after college and during the early years of marriage.

If the woman decides to combine motherhood and a career she likewise faces much strain. Society still has a strong opinion about the right place for the wife and mother. Furthermore, society is very vocal about it, so that it is easy for all but the most calloused woman to have some guilt about the limitations work imposes on her care of her children. The problems associated with managing a successful home and being a mother while at the same time developing a career are many and complex, and there are no pat solutions for them. Girls of ability are inspired to look forward to performing a creative function, to achievement, to social status and responsibility, but the conditions they must meet in the responses of other persons and in situational stress create a dilemma only the most creative can solve. The tensions associated either with working for a time and then giving it up or with trying to combine motherhood and a career need to be honestly and cogently discussed by future partners so that dissension between the two will not add to the stresses already present in these situations. In all situations, modern young people will be concerned to protect the personality resources of the future wife as well as the needs of the future marriage.

Many of the complicated problems involved in the collision between the values of the woman who wants to work and the husband who thinks her place is in the home are illustrated in the following case adapted from Komarovsky:

> Mrs. Clark is a pretty and vivacious woman of twenty-nine, a mother of three children. She comes from a well-to-do Latin-American family. Her mother had two years of college and Mrs. Clark was sent to college in the United States. She married Mr. Clark, who still had four years of medical school ahead of him. Upon her graduation from college she went on to work for her M.A. and the young couple was supported by Mr. Clark's father.
>
> Serious sickness caused Mr. Clark to interrupt his studies for three years. In the meantime, their first child was born. When Mrs. Clark was offered a teaching job at a private school, Mr. Clark did not object to her accepting the offer, because he wished to lighten his father's financial burden. The practical problems were solved by the arrival of Mrs. Clark's mother, who, though residing elsewhere, arrived at the Clark's apartment at 8:30 A.M. daily and stayed till 6:00, at which time both parents returned, one from the medical college and the other from her job. The

birth of the second child did not change the arrangements. Mrs. Clark's mother gladly took over the additional duties, with the help of a maid.

For Mrs. Clark her teaching job was not a regrettable necessity but the culmination of a lifelong ambition. As a child, her nickname was "the studious one" and the whole family was proud of her achievements in school. It was understood that she would go to college and she herself always planned to have a profession. Because she was quick and efficient she managed to be a good student and at the same time look and act like a "party girl" and have plenty of beaux. Even at present she gets a kick out of the amazed look on the faces of strangers when they learn that she is a mother of three children and a high-school teacher. She loves to teach and is working towards her Ph.D. in order to advance to college teaching.

Mr. Clark, on the other hand, soon came to the conclusion that, even with the serious financial problems, he would rather go into debt than have his wife continue teaching. Mrs. Clark assured the interviewer that her husband suffered no practical inconvenience as a result of her working, neither did he have any worries about the children. He admired her mother and liked her way with the children. He returned to a clean home, happy children, and a good meal. He himself had to work evenings and his wife's extracurricular duties on the job never interfered with his leisure. He needed her earnings and yet he wanted her to quit her job. It was "the principle of the thing."

"Why did you get married," he asked, "if you didn't expect to do your own housework and to take care of your children?" He is especially indignant on occasions when she returns too late to feed the children and put them to bed, even if she spent the morning with them, which her flexible hours allow on some days. "I can buy the help of a servant," she replies, "and do more interesting things. You should respect me all the more for it. As to putting the children to bed, how many of the women in your southern home town had 'mammies' who practically brought up their children. Why don't you accuse those mothers of shirking their duties?"

Mrs. Clark is bewildered by his attitude. Throughout her life, praise came to her through certain attainments, and now he "despises" what to her are her proudest accomplishments—"He never refers to my work as a profession, always as a job." When she jubilantly informed him of her promotion all he said was, "Now I suppose you will be even busier." His mother also looks at her as a "museum piece" or a "freak." Mrs. Clark always looked down upon women whose chatter was limited to a recipe for apple pie and gossip about maids. But her mother-in-law would drop a contemptuous remark about "a Ph.D. who doesn't know how to cook."

The marriage relationship of the Clarks is strained. Their conflicting values are doubly hard to reconcile because each has an emotional stake in his own version of marriage responsibilities.[24]

In the later chapter on marital adjustment some suggestions are made as to how men and women can solve some of the problems that accompany the employment of women. In the present chapter we have presented some of the problems rising from the conflicts of values and expectations when the wife works or desires to work which need to be taken into account in a wise marital choice.

CONCLUSION

Three economic factors are important in wise marriage choice: the economic security required for marital happiness, the style of life associated with various occupations, and the wide difference in attitudes toward women working and the conflicts and problems that result from those different attitudes. On all three counts, young people need to assess their future relationship wisely and become aware of the attitudes of their mate and of the type of life and economic security his or her working will insure. The self-analysis schedule should help us clarify our latent feelings about these important matters.

SELF-ANALYSIS

    I. Our Socio-Economic Expectations

        A. Analyze your socio-economic expectations in life in terms of the ways of living that have characterized your background.

            1. In what socio-economic group were you raised? Have you always had access to all the luxuries you wanted?

            2. In what kind of a house do you live? What kind of a car do you drive? How much spending money have you had for your own the last two years?

            3. How important do you feel these "things" have come to be for you? Do you feel you could live on a much lower scale for five years, for ten years, for life?

            4. What social-status values have come to you because of your socio-economic background? Is this important to you?

            5. If you are a girl, would you mind doing your own house cleaning,

[24] Mirra Komarovsky, *Women in the Modern World*, Boston, Little, Brown and Company, Copyright, 1953, by Mirra Heyman, pp. 173–176. Reprinted by permission.

cooking, ironing, washing, if this is necessary? If a man, would you mind your wife doing this?

B. Analyze the way you "dream" about your home, its furnishings, your own function in the home when you think about the future.

II. Your Occupational Expectations

A. Analyze your thoughts about the general type of occupation you wish for yourself and your mate.
1. What was your father's occupation?
2. What values do you expect an occupation to provide?
3. Do you have prejudices toward some types of occupation?

B. If you are a male, note the contributions your chosen occupation will bring to your family in terms of
1. Security
2. Time schedule
3. Stimulation of the job

C. List the disadvantages your occupation will bring to your family in terms of
1. Security
2. Time schedule, trips, long hours, etc.
3. Business pressure

III. The Changing Role of Women

A. Analyze your reactions to the following possible "roles" of women:
1. Those who make "homemaking" a career
2. Those who work two or three years to get the family "well started"
3. Those who work all the time except for certain months taken off for child-bearing
4. Those who are most interested in a career

B. Do you believe that talented women should contribute those talents to society? Or do you think a woman's place is in the home?

C. If a man, would you feel comfortable helping in the home if your wife worked? If a woman, would you feel comfortable if your husband did part of the housework if you contributed to the family income?

VISUAL AIDS

Managing the Family Income, Y.M.C.A. 38 minutes–sound.

Men in White (deals with problem of wife supporting husband in school and of marriage between individuals of different cultural backgrounds).

Captains Courageous (family problems attendant upon a father's too great absorption in his business).

READINGS

NORMAN HIMES, *Your Marriage*, New York, Farrar and Rinehart, Inc., 1940, Chapter 14.

MIRRA KOMAROVSKY, *Women in the Modern World*, Boston, Little, Brown and Company, 1953, Chapter 5.

JUDSON T. LANDIS and MARY G. LANDIS, *Building a Successful Marriage*, New York, Prentice-Hall, Inc., 1948, Chapters 14, 15, 16.

HARVEY J. LOCKE, *Predicting Adjustment in Marriage: A Comparison of a Divorced and a Happily Married Group*, New York, Henry Holt and Company, 1951, Chapter 13.

NANCY MAVITY, "The Two Income Family," *Harper's Magazine*, December, 1951.

JOHN LEVY and RUTH MONROE, *The Happy Family*, New York, Alfred A. Knopf, Inc., 1946, Chapter 6.

C H A P T E R   9

Military Service

as a Factor

INTRODUCTION: MILITARY SERVICE COMPLICATES BOTH PLAN-
NING FOR MARRIAGE AND ADJUSTING TO IT. PERHAPS THE MOST
serious complication is the impact military service has upon wise marriage choice. The ways in which men and women reacted to war conditions during World War II provide ample illustration of this.

WARTIME ANXIETY ABOUT FINDING A MATE

The feeling of desperation is one of the prime factors in the disorganization of the family in time of war. A new sense of time pervades society.
The "now" is all important. As men continue to go into the service the
girls become more and more aware of the possibility of remaining unmarried, and consequently take the initiative in speeding up courtship.[1]
In college, as the junior and senior men face and discuss their future in
the service, their girl friends may become very anxious about marriage.
This anxiety is a major factor in promoting many marriages which would
never have been contracted under peacetime conditions. One student
summarized her feelings as follows:

> Though strictly speaking our time should not be called a time of war,
> still, it is an undeniable fact that since the beginning of World War II we

[1] Evelyn M. Duvall and Reuben Hill, *When You Marry*, Revised Edition, Boston, D. C.
Heath and Company, 1953.

have been in a continual state of emergency, which, if not actual war, at least produced the same effect. Certainly it can be said that for my generation the distinction is slight. It is true that some men are not called into service at all. It is true that some men serve their military duty stateside, never leave home and the girl they want to marry, and practice, while in the service, the profession of their choice. It is true that, for a fortunate few, military services offer the opportunity to receive free an education in just the technical skills needed to enable the young man to get ahead, and a salary while learning, but these are, I am afraid, in the minority. Men are still being conscripted into service; they still are sent suddenly overseas (even from the National Guard); they are still giving their lives on the battlefields; many of them are still going to come back and find adjustment difficult; careers are still being halted and opportunities hopelessly lost; girls are still having to adjust to no husband at all, a husband now and then, or a husband away. . . .

Strangely enough, women are more fundamentally disturbed by war than men. Their loneliness, their sacrifice, and their fears may seem more obscure but they are very real to them. Women between 18 and 25 are hoping and dreaming of marriage opportunities. They know that chances dwindle after twenty-five. They realize that war diminishes man power and causes husband shortages. This causes a feeling of desperation.[2]

EMOTIONAL DISTORTIONS ASSOCIATED WITH WARTIME

But there are other explanations for the hasty marriages of wartime. Our control of our emotional impulses seems to be reduced during such a time. As Overton says:

> Elemental urges are released in wartime; all our ways of behaving are disturbed. Exposure to danger, uncertainty, and suffering bring a kind of bond of kinship between men and women. Men want a woman for whom to fight, and women want a man for whom to work and for whom to wait —always war quickens the desire to live while there is yet time. To most people, "to live" means fundamentally to love and to be loved and to experience parenthood.[3]

THE ACCENTUATION OF THE ROMANTIC COMPLEX

Moreover, the pressures of the time accentuate the romantic complex. Some girls give themselves sexually out of deep sympathy for men who

[2] From a personal document in the author's files.
[3] Grace Overton, *Marriage in War and Peace*, New York, Abington-Cokesbury Press, 1945, p. 147. Reprinted by permission.

are giving their all for their country. Some girls marry servicemen as a way of doing their bit for the morale of the boys. Others are overwhelmed by the glamour of the uniform. Others succumb to the pressure to do what everybody else is doing. This accentuates the desire for marriage. These factors resulted in types of marriage which are regarded as peculiar to wartime but which have continued during the cold war. Goldstein differentiates the types:

> The adolescent marriage is the marriage in which one or both of the young people are too young, too immature to marry. . . . A tremendous change takes place in young people, and especially in young women, between the ages of seventeen and twenty-two or twenty-three. There is a change in interest, a change in outlook, a change in standards and ideals and certainly a change in the concept and meaning of marriage.
>
> The hasty marriage is the marriage in which two young people do not allow themselves sufficient time to know each other as they should. . . . Both the young people are caught up in the emotional whirl of hysteria. The future is so uncertain and dangerous . . . who knows what the morrow may bring? [Young people] are not in a normal social setting; they do not, as a result, act as they would in a normal environment and in a normal frame of mind.
>
> The foreign marriage is the marriage of an American soldier, for example, with a young woman in Iceland, Ireland, Australia, or India, or even China. These foreign marriages are really intermarriages, national, religious and sometimes racial. They have all the disadvantages and involve all the dangers of intermarriages contracted in peace-time, with this difference, that they are contracted with less thought and more impulsiveness. In some few cases these intermarriages will survive; but if experience is a guide, in most cases they will not.
>
> The ante-dated marriage is the marriage that would normally take place in peace-time but that takes place earlier because of the draft or the exigencies of war.[4]

EXTENT OF WARTIME MARRIAGES

The extent of "adolescent" and "hasty" marriage can be roughly estimated from analyzing the 1935–1946 marriage statistics. The Bureau of Census Release indicates that between 1940 and 1943 a grand total of 6,579,000 marriages took place. By comparing this total with what might have been expected, a "wartime marriage surplus" of 1,118,000

[4] Sidney Goldstein, *Marriage and Family Counseling*, New York, McGraw-Hill Book Company, Inc., 1945, pp. 173–179. Reprinted by permission.

unions appears to have resulted from the special stimuli of that period.[5] The following table indicates the increase during the first part of the war, the decline when so many men were away in the service, and the great acceleration in the number of marriages when the soldiers returned.

T A B L E 24. Marriage Rates, per 1000 Population, 1935–46*

1935	.	.	.	.	10.4	1941	.	.	.	.	12.6
1936	.	.	.	.	10.7	1942	.	.	.	.	13.1
1937	.	.	.	.	11.2	1943	.	.	.	.	11.8
1938	.	.	.	.	10.2	1944	.	.	.	.	10.9
1939	.	.	.	.	10.5	1945	.	.	.	.	12.3
1940	.	.	.	.	11.9	1946	.	.	.	.	16.3

* *Marriage and Divorce in the United States*, 1937–1945, National Office of Vital Statistics. Permission to quote granted by the Federal Security Agency, Vol. XXIII, No. 9, 1946 and No. 10, 1947.

SPECIAL PROBLEMS OF WARTIME MARRIAGES

It is important to understand the conditions under which these marriages were entered into and the outcome for the partners who participated in them. The results were, of course, diverse, depending upon the nature of the marriage and the maturity of the persons involved. The following case presented by Cuber as "not entirely typical, but certainly not completely atypical" illustrates many of the problems involved:

We were college "steadies" for six months with no mention of marriage ever made between us. We were not prudish in our erotic behavior though I did remain a virgin. . . . Then he was drafted. I promised to write him twice a week and he promised to write as often as he could. Gradually his letters became more and more ardent. And soon he proposed. Before I could collect my wits for a reply he was home for a furlough. We weren't alone for an hour before he was pressing the marriage issue with all the high pressure tactics I had ever heard of, plus a few more. . . . I liked him very much. We did seem to have much in common. I doubted that I was in love but I couldn't prove it. We were both emotionally tense after months of separation. I don't know just how it happened but I suddenly realized that I was no longer virginal. The seven day furlough was almost over and and the pressure to get married was now greater than ever. . . . We were married on the sixth day of the furlough. He then went back to camp. I didn't see him for three months. Then I received a letter

[5] Bureau of the Census Release, "The Wartime Marriage Surplus," Series Pm-I. November 12, 1944.

from him stating that he had made arrangements with his commanding officer to have his weekends free. I could surely find a job there. So overnight I packed a few belongings and boarded a train for another part of America where I had never been before. And there I lived for three months, a semi-prisoner.

One and a half days each week were deliriously happy; five and a half days were dismally lonely, like a prisoner in a foreign land. Then he received orders to move and I went back to my home community because in his new situation it was impossible for him to live with his wife. At first I was lonely, but soon the exhilaration of being "among my own" again readjusted me. I moved in my old circle of friends. . . . One day someone suggested that I go on a "date"—a purely platonic date, of course, with a fraternity brother of my husband. And the date was platonic to the point of brutality. Both of us were anxious that it remain platonic and that there be no infidelity that the whole affair was funny or tragic depending on how you look at it. There being no harm on that date, there was another and another and suddenly they weren't so platonic. Gradually, I began to realize that I was falling in love with this man and he with me. And accordingly we broke off the relationship, abruptly.

Soon thereafter I discovered that I was pregnant, by my husband, of course (the other affair never having gone that far). When I wrote the news to my husband he was very disturbed. Though solicitous of my welfare he couldn't help revealing the fact that the role of a father was incomprehensible to him under the circumstances. I could understand him because I felt the same way. We had never been truly married and both of us knew it. If we had had a normal home life we could perhaps have fallen into some kind of normal love relationship even after marriage. But the sum total of our married life was seven week-ends in the not-too-pleasant room in a foreign culture. Meanwhile I was haunted by my recently discovered relationship with the second man. I cannot justify it ethically but I feel it emotionally. A week ago I learned that my husband had gone overseas. I shall not see him now for the duration, at least. The second man, like me, finds it difficult to call our relationship off, even though he knows that I am pregnant and I strongly wish to remain loyal to my marriage. . . . I haven't the slightest idea how it will all turn out, but I must confess, being as rational as I can, that I can see many possible outcomes but none that is satisfactory.[6]

The ever recurring theme of the "pressure" to get married is well indicated here. This girl was not sure that she was in love, in fact doubted

[6] John F. Cuber, "Changing Courtship and Marriage Customs," *Annals of the American Academy of Political and Social Science,* September 1943, Volume 229, pp. 35–36. Reprinted by permission.

it, but still she allowed the marriage to take place. The case illustrates, too, the brevity or complete absence of any period of adjustment in a honeymoon. The plans for the marriage were so abruptly made, the wedding was so hurried, that it lost the beauty, the significance, and impact it might otherwise have had. So that in terms of a wise marriage choice, in terms of a meaningful marriage ceremony, and in terms of that important first period of adjustment during the honeymoon, the marriage was severely handicapped.

HOUSING AND WAR MARRIAGES

This case illustrates another constant problem. This girl lived in a "not-too-pleasant room in a foreign culture." The conditions under which a great many war brides lived were "not-too-pleasant." Certainly they had few of the aspects of the shining apartment or the little house in which a couple normally set up housekeeping. Even if this girl had been able to follow her husband from camp to camp, their housing facilities would not have improved nor would they have been able to spend more time together. Consequently, even if the bride had not returned home when she did, she and her husband would have had neither favorable facilities nor time to make a good adjustment.

Bossard speaks of the importance of the time factor in his article on "War and The Family":

> Now the essential danger in such marriages is that the couple do not have the customary opportunity to make the gradual, unbroken transition from romantic bliss to prosaic adjustment which is the basis of continued domestic accord. Happiness in marriage, according to the experts, is an achievement, not a discovery. It comes as a byproduct to successful experience in living together. Beginning their life together on the romantic level, and with the help of the romantic aura, married couples learn to compromise as they cohabit. It is this normal process which is lacking in marry-and-run marriages. The romantic glow may fade, or be dimmed, during separation, while each shares different life experiences.[7]

ANXIETY IN SERVICE-CONNECTED MARRIAGES

Cuber's case also portrays the great anxiety of the girl regarding the outcome of the marriage. Because the couple have not been able to

[7] H. S. Bossard, "War and the Family," *American Sociological Review*, 6, 1941, p. 234. Reprinted by permission.

become organized as interacting members of a unified family there must necessarily be concern as to what the future holds for them. If, as Levy and Monroe suggest, there is real stability in a marriage then attraction to another person is easily fended off by the individual. In this case, however, no such stability had been developed. There were many so-called "Dear John" letters in the last war telling the husband that the wife had found a new romantic attraction. Cuber has paid particular attention to this problem. In analyzing over one hundred personal letters from men in the service and interviews with soldiers on furlough, men's women friends, fiancés, and wives he concludes:

> The newly married man in service lives in a one-sex community, is deprived of wholesome female companionship, has no legitimate outlet for his sexual energies, finds himself associated with a great many coarse and hedonistic men who scoff at standards, suffers uneasiness about what "the woman" is doing and where she is. The bride, like her betrothed sister, faces the temptation to "step out" a bit, hears the sensational stories about the morals of the men in service and finds it impossible to participate in the newly discovered pattern of affectional interaction. Though both men and women are quick to claim that the fact of marriage has given them a "sacred bond of union" and other trite phrases they are as a rule willing to admit that the feeling is not as real as they would like to have it. They have not yet learned the husband-wife role, and, though they dare not admit it openly, because they must save face, they will confess privately that they have serious misgivings about the wisdom of their choice.[8]

PREGNANCY IN WARTIME MARRIAGES

Pregnancy often complicates these marriages. This girl rightly related her feeling about the child to the fact that "we had never really been truly married." A child needs the security of a home and the early support of well-developed bonds of affection. The father was missing and the mother was in doubt about her feelings for him. What should be a time of mutual planning and expectation turned into a period of greater loneliness and of doubt. There was also the problem of financial support. Most servicemen's wives take it for granted that they must partially support themselves while their husbands are away. But with the coming of a baby there is a time when they cannot work. After the

[8] John F. Cuber, "The College Youth Goes to War," *Marriage and Family Living*, 5, 1943, p. 7. Reprinted by permission.

birth of the baby, the child must be cared for by someone else if the mother works. The problem may be complicated by the fact that although it may be a distinct liability for the girl, the husband may want a baby very badly. Not knowing whether he will return or not, he often feels that in a baby he leaves something living of himself, a token of immortality, if he is not to return. Hence, many servicemen press their wives into having children and these children later prove very burdensome to the wife. She may not care for them or love them as she might have done in other circumstances.

Because of these and other factors many wartime marriages end in divorce. While it is not possible to make a direct correlation between the statistics of hasty war marriages and the great rise in divorce immediately after the war, it is reasonable to assume that it was this type of marriage which failed.

A special problem in war marriages is the different rates and directions of growth in maturity of the man and the wife while they are separated. This plagues even those marriages resulting from long and unhurried courtships. Goldstein points out that a girl changes very radically from seventeen or eighteen to twenty-two or twenty-three. But the man changes, too. In the service he is experiencing traumatic and crucial impacts on his own personality. Consequently, when the two come together again, marriage may have to begin as though it had never been. If there are children the wife may have developed an affectional pattern of transferring to the children some of the emotional drive previously directed toward the husband. The returning father may be rejected by these children who have never seen him or at any event may not remember him. If the father has been disabled physically or psychologically, there will be additional problems of adjustment between him and his wife.

THE WORKING WIVES OF SERVICEMEN

When "Molly the Riveter" had earned a check, she became a different person as far as her marital expectations were concerned. No longer did she believe she had to stay in a marriage which had been unsatisfying to her. Her new-found freedom meant freedom in many other ways. Before working status was as acceptable as it is now, if a girl had married too hastily or was unhappy, her economic need constrained her to put up with much in order that she and her children might be secure. After large numbers of women entered the working force with relative success, women no longer were forced to put up with a husband who came home bitter, or irritable, or neurotic.

THE PROBLEM TODAY

The problem for a young couple today is essentially not very different from that of a couple during the last world war. One girl explains:

> This is an unsettled time in the world. It doesn't look like it is going to improve very soon. I am twenty-two and my fiancé is twenty-three. He is in the air reserve and when he graduates he will go into training to become a cadet and after that there will be three or more years of service. This was more than we could take. We could not expect to put our marriage on ice for over three years. What to do?[9]

The following eight suggestions are in answer to that girl and to others who find themselves in similar situations. These suggestions are derived from experience in dealing with the problems of a great many young people who have had to make decisions about marrying when confronted with military service.

Beware of extraneous motivations. Because so many young men are being inducted into the various services many girls and many young men feel panicky over their chances of marriage. One girl said recently:

> But I'm twenty-three. All the men my age are in or are going into the service. When they get out they will be interested in younger girls. If I am ever going to be married it is now or never.

This girl came for counsel because she was contemplating marrying a person about whom she had grave doubts. She may be married because of the pressure she feels simply to "get married now or never" but it will not be because she has built up a community of interest with the young man or because she can confidently expect a long and happy future, but only because she feels desperate. Hers may be called an extraneous motivation. A second motivation, sympathy for the man going into service, is not as strong as it was during World War II because the social feeling about the present situation is not as strong. But that it does exist is evidenced every time young people discuss marriage today. Feelings of compassion and feelings of desperation bias the selection of a life partner.

[9] From a personal document in the author's files.

Insist upon a longer and not a shorter courtship. The knowledge that so many hasty World War II marriages failed should be an object lesson. Because of the possibility that some inadequate motivations may be present in the developing love of a man and woman, they should test their affection over a longer period than might be necessary in a different situation. The selective service requirements are stable enough today so that most couples should be able to avoid hasty courtships and "quickie" marriages.

Be realistic about the problems involved in marriage today. Couples who are to be married when the man is going into the service will further their adjustment immeasurably if they enter the situation realistically. There are many ways of insuring this. Young couples generally have friends who have been in the same predicament and have had to make similar decisions. A talk with such a couple should help them avoid unhappy "surprises" later on. Older couples who were in the same dilemma during World War II can also tell them, in realistic terms, of the difficulties that are likely to rise after marriage. Having learned what the problems are, the couple should have a thorough discussion of possible solutions—the problems include housing, the wife and work, the possibility of a child, and the readjustment after separation. If they meet these problems directly and courageously they are not apt to suffer as much as those who never think about the negative aspects of the days ahead. It should help later adjustment, too, if they will face honestly the problem of meeting their affectional needs while they are separated. This is not an easy problem, but mutual agreement will help them face their days apart and help their readjustment when they are reunited.

Be realistic about yourself and your mate. Some persons are not capable of making the adjustment involved in a service marriage. No one can arbitrarily say that one person will or will not make a success of a trying situation. If a girl dislikes being uncomfortable, hates travel, is unwilling to uproot herself from her home community, objects to the unexpected, she needs to think twice about marrying a person who will be in the service for a number of years. On the other hand, the girl who is very adaptable, likes change, new experience and new surroundings, and finds joy in making new friends will probably not have too much trouble in adjusting to a marital situation that involves moving about. Comfort and order are very important to some people, but mean nothing to others. There are girls who look forward to "three years of gypsy life"—to the continual leaving and saying goodbye, the surprise visits, the unexpected leave—as a period in which "we shall achieve such security and oneness that it will see us through any adjustment problem that comes when we must settle down." Such girls have anticipated realistically the problems that are to come but welcome them as opportunities to test their mettle and to build a permanent structure of togetherness. Anyone who has serious misgivings about his ability to live this way ought to face such misgivings honestly.

Build a pair-solidarity before marriage. There is no way of avoiding the problems that arise from living together. But problems can be anticipated and the unity of a couple strengthened before the wedding vows are spoken. If a couple can engage in different types of recreation before marriage, if they can spend much time discussing their future home and its requirements, if they can focus upon the problem of children and begin to plan the way in which they will guide those children, if they can search out the long-range values they will try to attain, if they can achieve a certain amount of adjustment of temperamental and personality differences, they will then have some background of unified interests and plans. There will then be some security and some stability in their marriage to hold them together when they are separated.

Use available pre-marital counseling facilities. Because of all the complications which have been mentioned, it is essential for a couple to obtain as much pre-marital help as possible so that certain of the adjustments of marriage can be made with as much dispatch as possible. It may be a cause of deep anxiety to the wife to spend the months or years her mate is away wondering if they will ever achieve sexual compatibility. It is possible to make great strides if one works through such problems with a counselor. For example, if there is sexual inhibition as the result of earlier experience or home conditioning this may be modified before the ceremony ever takes place. The couple will better understand, too, that if certain adjustments are not made before they separate this is normal and no cause for prolonged worry.

Choose with care the time for marriage. The problem of adjusting to "boot camp" or to the early months in any of the services is difficult enough without the further problem of adjusting to a new marriage. Moreover, these first months of training are such that a couple can generally be together only a very small part of the time. It thus seems wise for the couple to marry either some months before or some months after induction. Even if they are in college and both are finishing their senior year, they might use the last semester or the last year for adjustment, and for building solidarity. If this is not feasible, it may be better to postpone marriage until after the period of basic training so that two adjustments do not come at once. Whether the wife should plan to work during the time immediately after marriage must be decided by the needs of the situation. Some branches and ranks of the service pay better than others. In all cases, the couple must abide by the regulations of the different services regarding marriage.

Consciously pursue togetherness even when separated. If the man must go overseas or into some area where his wife may not follow him, they should work out ways of continuing their efforts to achieve unity. If the wife is working, she may save a little each week and put it aside as a sinking fund. The husband, too, may take pride in sending small sums to add to the fund. This growing nest egg may be earmarked for a home, or a start in business, or even a trip together. It does not matter much what the purpose of the fund is; the important thing is that it is an activity that both share during their separation. Again, they may read a number of books they have selected and write comments back and forth. They may decide that further enlightenment on marriage is in order, and elect to read books about marriage. Their letters should be frequent and filled with references to happy times in the past and the happy times they expect to have in the future.

The attitude each partner has toward the service itself is important. If they regard military service as an intolerable imposition by an arbitrary force, both will find the interval very difficult. On the other hand, if they believe that both of them are engaged in building a world in which their children can be free and family life can be more secure from the social and economic ravages of war, they will have common unity in a great cause. If the free forces prevail because of the dedication of young people, a new and richer world may emerge for all families of tomorrow.

Finally, it must be recognized that the present unsettled period may continue for some time. There is no use trying to escape the fact. Young people may be faced for years with the need to adjust to marriage while in the service. The problem it raises must be met courageously and creatively. There is no perfect solution. But if a couple determines to work out an answer in terms of their own personalities, using all of the resources offered by counseling facilities, a surprisingly well-adjusted marriage may result. Every age has its traumatic experiences. The parents of this generation faced two depressions as well as two wars. Life must go on during disaster, depression, or war and young people need not lament their lot. A period of difficulty may be a prelude to a period of profound happiness.

PROJECTS

1. The class may discover a member who has had experience in working out a marital situation during service and be willing to discuss some of the problems which occur in marriage in wartime. If there is not such a person in the class, outsiders may be invited to discuss possible problems and their solutions.
2. If there is a military representative on campus, invite him to come before the class and explain the rules on marriage of servicemen and make any recommendations from his experience.
3. Discuss the degree to which the prospect of service after marriage has made men and women anxious about marriage possibilities.

READINGS

"The American Family in World War II," *Annals of the American Academy of Political and Social Science,* Volume 229, September, 1943.

JAMES H. S. BOSSARD and ELEANOR S. BOLL, *The Sociology of Child Development,* New York, Harper and Brothers, 1948, Chapter 23.

JAMES H. S. BOSSARD, "War and the Family," *American Sociological Review,* 6, 1941.

ERNEST W. BURGESS and HARVEY J. LOCKE, *The Family, from Institution to Companionship,* New York, The American Book Company, 1953, Chapter 21.

HAROLD T. CHRISTENSEN, *Marriage Analysis,* New York, The Ronald Press Company, 1950, Chapter 7.

JOHN F. CUBER, "The College Youth Goes to War," *Marriage and Family Living,* Volume V, No. I, February, 1943.

WILLARD WALLER (Revised by Reuben Hill), *The Family: A Dynamic Interpretation,* New York, The Dryden Press, Inc., 1951, Part III.

187

... ...

PART THREE

PREPARATION
FOR MARITAL
TOGETHERNESS

CHAPTER 10

The Engagement Period

INTRODUCTION: CHANGE CHARACTERIZES NOT ONLY MAR-
RIAGE IN OUR SOCIETY, BUT ALSO THE PERIOD OF ENGAGEMENT
which precedes it. In the past it served as a preparatory period for a
marriage that was almost certain to take place. Today engagement serves
two needs, according to Waller:[1] "(1) the need of cushioning the sharp
transition from youth to adulthood, from the state of single irresponsibility to that of married responsibility, and (2) the need for group sanc-
tion for the shifts in activity and changes in role which accompany the
assumption of mature adult responsibilities." Hornell Hart thinks that
the most important function of this period today is to test out the relationship between future husband and wife:[2] "The engagement might
well be characterized, then, as the period during which the idea of marriage with this particular mate is being explored as a working hypothesis."
Waller stresses the contribution of the engagement period to marital adjustment but Hart lays his emphasis upon the importance of the period
for wise marriage choice. Waller in a later passage also mentions the
tentativeness of contemporary engagements:

> It is quite apparent from the foregoing functional analysis that the en-
> gagement activities which would serve the social structure best in our
> society are poorly communicated in the "promise to marry" and "engaged

[1] Willard Waller (Revised by Reuben Hill), *The Family: A Dynamic Interpretation*, New
York, The Dryden Press, Copyright, 1952, p. 220. Reprinted by permission.
[2] Hornell Hart and Ella Hart, *Personality and the Family*, Boston, D. C. Heath and
Company, Copyright, 1935, p. 142.

191

to be married" ideas. The mergent idea of engagement is of an arrangement that is constantly being re-evaluated with the possibility of being broken. It is a tentative agreement to marry if in the experiences of play acting premaritally the permissible marital roles prove promising for future relations.[3]

The accuracy of this analysis has been substantiated by the Burgess-Wallin study of engagement. This study followed 1,000 couples through engagement and the first five years of marriage. Of the sample only 22.4 per cent of the men and 36.5 per cent of the women had a high-school education or less.[4] Consequently it represents a highly educated college group. Protestants predominated with 42.5 per cent of the men and 57.5 per cent of the women coming from that group; 14.9 per cent of the men and 13.9 per cent of the women were Catholic; 18.8 per cent of the men and 19.7 per cent of the women were Jewish; the remainder stated that they had no religious affiliations.[5] The 666 couples who eventually married and were included in the follow-up study of their early marital adjustment had known each other, on the average, for 45.0 months, had been keeping company 31.5 months, and had been engaged 13.2 months.[6] Their unions had not been "runaway, overnight" affairs. In summarizing their findings regarding the function of the engagement period, Burgess and Wallin prove their contention by citing engagement fatalities; 24 per cent of the men and 36 of the women reported prior broken engagements. In addition, 15 per cent of the couples broke their engagements while the study was going on.[7] The engagement period thus may be regarded as the final factor in wise marriage choice.

LENGTH OF ENGAGEMENT

If the engagement period is regarded as the final testing period for marriage, it should be long enough for this process to take place. Furthermore, if the thesis that engagement is a "working hypothesis" is correct, it will follow that long engagements are correlated with later marital success. Burgess and Cottrell found that as the length of the engagement increased the average adjustment score was higher.[8] Terman's study

[3] Waller (Revised by Hill), *op. cit.*, pp. 226–227.
[4] Ernest W. Burgess and Paul Wallin, *Engagement and Marriage*, Philadelphia, J. P. Lippincott Company, Copyright, 1953, p. 54.
[5] *Ibid.*, p. 55.　[6] *Ibid.*, p. 56.　[7] *Ibid.*, pp. 272–273.
[8] Ernest W. Burgess and Leonard S. Cottrell, *Predicting Success or Failure in Marriage*, New York, Prentice-Hall, Inc., 1939, pp. 167–168.

likewise showed that very short engagements were unfavorable and long engagements favorable to marital adjustments.[9]

Bowman objects, however, to a too dogmatic conclusion regarding long engagements:

> We may, however, set up some very rough criteria and say that an engagement is too long if there is an excessive amount of nervous tension generated; if the couple experience a sense of frustration; if they become more than usually tired of waiting; if they grow discouraged; if they become indifferent to one another; if they begin to accept the status quo as a substitute for marriage and lose interest in the latter; if the engagement constitutes more than a relatively small fraction of the total period from meeting to wedding. This is a dogmatic statement and we have no substantial evidence on which to justify it. We wish to counteract the opinion so commonly expressed among students to the effect that on the basis of a few months' courtship a couple may without risk enter upon an engagement of several years' duration.[10]

It must always be remembered that the conclusions of research studies are based on averages. It is certainly possible that a young couple who are more apt than others at communication and more relaxed in sharing affectional relationships may accomplish this "dress rehearsal" for marriage in a shorter time. There is a rhythm in growth of cohesion for couples and this rhythm may vary from couple to couple. There is no need to assume that what is essential for one or for most relationships is necessarily best for all. Duvall and Hill give some functional criteria which may be helpful to young people thinking about the duration of their engagement:

> Engagements need to be long enough to act as a screening device to alienate and separate incompatible couples who would otherwise marry, only to separate more painfully after some years of marriage. The answer to the question of length of engagement is given best, not as a number of months or years, but in terms of the indefinite "long enough." The engagement, then, should be long enough to perform the many functions of testing, discussing, learning, fighting, and loving which underlie successful marriage.[11]

[9] Lewis M. Terman, *Psychological Factors in Marital Happiness*, New York, McGraw-Hill Book Company, Inc., 1938, pp. 198–199.

[10] Henry A. Bowman, *Marriage for Moderns*, New York, McGraw-Hill Book Company, Inc., 1948, p. 249.

[11] Evelyn M. Duvall and Reuben Hill, *When You Marry*, Revised Edition. Reprinted by permission of D. C. Heath and Company, Boston, 1953, p. 89.

193

ESSENTIALS IN PRE-MARITAL ROLE BEHAVIOR

The assumption underlying the approach to engagement as a working hypothesis of marriage is that the intimacy and new status accorded a couple during engagement enable them to test their relationship in ways that were not possible previously. There are other essential factors which are tested in an engagement and which do not play such a part in early courtship. The clue to the nature of these factors appears in Waller's term, pre-marital play-acting. This play-acting has to do with the actual planning for and solving of situations which will be faced in matrimony. Previously, during courtship, the attention of a couple has been centered upon the personality and background factors which operate to draw them together in a developing love situation. But during engagement, the focus is upon whether or not that love relationship has the resources and the strength to weather the problems of marriage. In this respect new elements related to the future become more important. The new elements that are specially tested during engagement are the adaptability of the individuals, their facility in communication, their adjustment to reality, and their abilty to solve problems.

ADAPTABILITY

The transitional nature of contemporary family life plus the heterogeneous nature of a social group often brings together individuals with diverse religious, cultural, social, and economic backgrounds. Individuals in love often bring to their engagement conflicting expectations of the roles they will play as husband and wife, as parents, and as members of the larger community. When such a couple are engaged and face the reality of their coming marriage, they tend to focus their attention on the way they will act after marriage. The extent to which they can adjust to differences will determine the success of their engagement and is a measure of later marriage success. The extent to which they can adjust is largely a function of their flexibility or adaptability. This quality is not much tested when they are making love or seeking to impress each other. But when they face actual planning for the future, their adaptability comes to the fore.

Burgess and Wallin analyzed the way engaged couples face disagreement and stress. They measured the extent of agreement and disagreement on such questions as dates with one another, demonstration of affection, arrangements for marriage, religious matters, table manners, attitudes toward conventionality, recreation, philosophy of life, money, ways of dealing with in-laws and friends.[12]

Some 1.7 per cent reported that they "always agreed" on all items, 18.5 per cent reported that one "always agreed" and the other "almost always agreed," but nearly four-fifths of the couples state that they disagreed on one or more items and one-half reported disagreements in one to four areas of their relationships. This means that adjustment between these partners must involve the modification of individual expectations and adaptation to the other's role.[13]

Important differences in attitudes and values face the majority of engaged couples in our day. If these differences cannot be solved or resolved the relationship will not endure. On the other hand, couples with seemingly great divergencies of background and interests may be successful if they are highly adaptable. Burgess and Wallin account for the successful adjustment in marriage of some couples who rated low on their engagement-adjustment scores by suggesting that one or both members may have had a general personality pattern of adaptability.[14]

Locke found, too, that adaptability was associated with marital adjustment.[15] He measured adaptability by the capacity for "giving in" in arguments, not being dominating, slowness in getting angry, and quickness in getting over anger.

Burgess and Wallin list the conditions of adaptability as empathy, flexibility, command of appropriate attitudes and roles, and the motivation to adjust. They define empathy as "the ability to recognize and appreciate the motivation of the actions of others."[16] Flexibility is the capacity to vary one's responses in interpersonal relations; a capacity which is partly psychogenic.[17] Motivation to adapt means the drive that impels the marriage partners to work at adapting their behavior to that of the other person. By command of appropriate responses is meant the possession of responses which can be integrated with the understanding of the behavior of the mate. Adaptability can be increased most by improving awareness of appropriate responses.[18] This can be accomplished in marriage by learning by experience the roles, attitudes, and responses appropriate to the spouse's behavior, and it can be enhanced in mar-

[12] Burgess and Wallin, *op. cit.*, p. 246.
[13] Burgess and Wallin, *op. cit.*, p. 247.   [14] *Ibid.*, p. 520.
[15] Harvey J. Locke, *Predicting Adjustment in Marriage: A Comparison of a Divorced and a Happily Married Group*, New York, Henry Holt and Company, Copyright, 1951, p. 205.
[16] *Ibid.*, p. 624.   [17] *Ibid.*, p. 626.   [18] *Ibid.*, pp. 639–640.

riage classes by stressing the significance of adaptability in situations which can be productive of future misunderstanding and conflict. Engagement is important not only in testing but also in developing adaptability.

COMMUNICATION

Being able to adapt to another person depends largely on understanding that person's needs and expectations. Unless role expectations are communicated in engagement neither person will learn how the other needs to adjust.[19] The basic need for affection in marriage will not be met unless the marriage partners are able to communicate their sentiments of devotion and tenderness. Karlsson thinks that communication is basic to marital adjustment. He says: "In order to perform the marital operation efficiently it is necessary for the spouses to be able to predict what the other one will do next. Such prediction requires communication of intentions."[20]

Before engagement, communication regarding role expectations is generally not adequate. Often it is not satisfactory during the engagement period either. During this period, if it is to be a testing period, a couple must discuss all of the important areas of married life. The following excerpt from a case study indicates the importance of communication in engagement adjustment:

> *Girl:* I listed, in the things I wanted changed, a more masculine support from Herb. We are going to be married in a month and we haven't yet found a place to live. Last Saturday I had to get a paper, I had to find the ads for apartments to rent, and I had to suggest we go looking. He is supposed to take the lead in those things and I resent having to do it.

> *Man:* I thought about looking for an apartment but I didn't know what she wanted me to do about it. I resented her hauling out the paper and suggesting that we had better find an apartment. There are a lot of things I'd like to do but I don't know what to expect from her. I did suggest some things about the wedding and she seemed to resent that.[21]

In this case the role expectations were quite similar but a lack of communication caused friction and resentment. Often the counselor

---

[19] George Karlsson, *Adaptability and Communication in Marriage,* Upsala, Almquist and Wiksells, 1951, p. 33.

[20] *Ibid.,* p. 33.   [21] Excerpt from a case in the author's files.

functions in such a case to clear the channel so ideas flow more freely between the partners.

Karlsson developed an index to measure the degree of communication. He brought together a number of items such as talking about children, work or finances, appreciating the work of the mate, criticizing the mate, praising the mate, or playing with children. He then asked whether a change in the behavior of each mate was wished for by the other. He measured the amount of communication in the marriage by comparing the answers of the husband and wife and noting the degree to which each understood the wishes of the other.[22] The communication index thus constructed showed a high correlation with marital adjustment. Karlsson believes that this indicates an association between communication and marital satisfaction, and that the communication index can be used in predicting marital adjustment.

Locke also measured the relationship of intimacy of communication to marital adjustment. He investigated items dealing with face-to-face communication, loss of unity through decline of communication, sympathetic understanding, frequency of kissing, talking things over together and engaging in outside interests together. His index of items includes that of affectional communication as well as verbal. His conclusion supports that of Karlsson.[23]

> Intimate, friendly, and prolonged communication between a husband and a wife tends to weld them together, whereas a decided decline in this type of communication tends to break up existing attachments. This conclusion was supported, in part, by items in the questionnaire, but was supported to a much greater extent by the case materials secured in the interviews.[23]

Waller thinks that communication is a stabilizer of interaction for the engaged pair:

> Since there is so much to learn, so many differences of background to be accepted, understood, and accommodated, and since pluralistic ignorance (the uncertainty of each concerning the real attitudes of the other) has so completely characterized dating and courtship relations, communication becomes a major process of stabilization in engagement.[24]

Couples that develop ease of communication in engagement are beginning the adjustment process which will be important in their later marriage.

[22] *Ibid.*, pp. 132–133. [23] Locke, *op. cit.*, p. 246.
[24] Waller (Revised by Hill), *op. cit.*, pp. 236–237.

ADJUSTMENT TO REALITY

Courtship is apt to be a time of over-idealization. It is important during the engagement period that a realistic appraisal of the future mate take place so that there will be few "surprises" when marriage actually begins. During courtship, idealization, whether due to the frustration of sexual drives as suggested by Waller or the need for self-esteem as suggested by Burgess and Wallin, has tended to distort and obscure the real self of the future mate. Furthermore, each party in courtship tends to obscure his or her negative qualities in order not to threaten the developing affectional relationship. The love relationship thus tends to develop between two masked individuals. Each person actually wears a double mask, one self-imposed and the other created by the lover. It is obvious that, if marriage choice is to be adequate, it must involve stripping away these masks.

This adjustment to reality takes place in many situations. During courtship both partners present themselves with as much glamour and appeal as possible. Life cannot be lived on this plane. During engagement, society sanctions more intimate contacts so that each may see the other, as Waller says, "without makeup." During courtship such matters as religious differences are largely ignored but in the engagement period some settlement must be made regarding the use of birth-control, the religious education of children, religious rituals in the home, and philosophies of life.

To adjust to reality involves conscious planning on the social, economic, religious, ethical, and recreational planes. The decisions that are reached need not be final. But in discussing such problems, the masks come off, communication begins on a level of reality, and practice in adapting takes place.

PROBLEM-SOLVING

In companionship marriage, the way a couple goes about problem-solving often determines the success or failure of the marital union. As society today does not furnish cultural answers to problems, most young couples must improvise their own solution. Communication is essential, so is adaptability, and facing reality helps the couple make wise decisions. The manner in which a young man and woman face problems involves establishing an approach, a way of meeting difficulties. The pattern worked out during engagement is most likely to be the pattern to be followed during marriage.

There are many alternatives as far as decision-making is concerned. None of them is superior to the other. This is because of the difference in background expectations of individuals. A girl coming from a first-generation German home in which the family stability pattern involved the dominance of the father is not prepared to enter a democratic structure. She has had a happy home experience in which the father was the master. In her own home she will expect the husband to take the lead. In some cases the boy who has been brought up by a mother with a very strong personality will be more comfortable in a home in which his wife takes the lead. In general, however, the well-adjusted American family follows democratic procedures and shares decision-making, depending on consensus rather than on autocratic rule. This generalization is supported by the following data from Locke: Some 62.3 per cent of the married men and 66.9 per cent of the married women,

TABLE 25. Per Cent of Happily-Married and Divorced Reporting Democratic Relationships in Given Situations, with Critical Ratios of the Difference of Per Cents*

| | MEN | | | WOMEN | | |
SITUATIONS	Married	Divorced	CR	Married	Divorced	CR
1. Making family decisions Own family	62.3	35.9	3.2	66.9	36.3	4.7
2. Disciplining the children Own family	55.2	40.5	1.9	58.3	22.0	4.8
3. Handling money Own family	50.9	38.1	—	58.1	34.8	3.7
4. Affectionate behavior Own family	59.9	41.0	2.5	59.0	33.3	3.7
5. Religious behavior Own family	52.9	38.9	—	59.7	25.0	5.0
6. Recreation Own family	57.6	42.6	2.0	54.2	36.4	2.7
7. Meeting people Own family	40.4	32.3	—	42.6	33.7	—

* Harvey J. Locke, *Predicting Adjustment in Marriage,* New York, Henry Holt and Company, 1951, p. 263. Reprinted by permission.

but only 35.9 per cent of the divorced men and 36.3 per cent of the divorced women, reported democratic methods of making decisions. Equally significant differences between the married and divorced samples were found in the areas of disciplining children, affectional behavior, religious behavior, and recreation for both men and women. Thus democratic relationships are clearly associated with success in contemporary family life.

Locke concludes that: "democratic relationships, as measured by reported equality in taking the lead, were decidedly more prevalent among happily-married than divorced couples."[25, *]

While the method of making family decisions may vary from family to family, the most important consideration is that decisions be made. If matters that cause disagreement are shunted out of consciousness because they threaten the affectional relationships, the relationship itself is weak. If partners become angry whenever a problem arises, they will have little or no basis for wise decision-making during their marital experience. It is imperative that in facing reality during the engagement period, the man and woman explore their problem-solving abilities and seek to establish the type of approach to decision-making which corresponds to their role expectations and in which both feel comfortable.

The couple that builds problem-solving patterns efficiently during the engagement period is laying a firm foundation for the growth of togetherness during marriage. Honest facing of differences involves compromises, but the compromises result in cohesion. In most cases the achievement of the democratic approach during engagement will insure good marital adjustment. At the end of this chapter there is a simple inventory which may help couples to determine the degree of their communication, their relationship to real problems, and their problem-solving techniques. It may be useful to some couples to test the quality of their engagement behavior as preparation for marriage.

BROKEN ENGAGEMENTS

According to Burgess and Wallin, about one-third of the young men and one-half of the young women in their sample had had one or more broken engagements. More and more young people are willing to break

---

[25] Locke, *op. cit.*, p. 262.
* The relationship of democracy to successful marital adjustment is described more fully in Chapter XX.

an engagement rather than face a broken marriage later in life. Sometimes it is difficult for a girl who has made a formal announcement of her intention to wed, who has been feted by her friends, and who has organized her future plans around a particular man, to break off relations with him. But if she finds that they cannot adapt to each other, that communication is difficult, that role expectations are very diverse, and that their problem-solving techniques do not work, it is better to suffer the trauma of sending back engagement presents than to pack them away after a divorce.

Burgess and Wallin found that broken engagements were due to the following disruptive factors: (1) slight emotional attachment, (2) separation, (3) parental opposition, (4) cultural divergencies, and (5) personality problems.[26] In the first case the strength of and the degree of communication of affection is related to engagement success. The importance of face-to-face communication (as Locke indicates) is vital to the development of engagement success. Burgess and Wallin's evidence both from interviews and from statistical analyses indicates that parental opposition is an important factor in engagements that fail. Locke's data confirm the importance of this factor. He found that parental approval or disapproval of the prospective mate differs considerably between the married and the divorced persons in his Indiana study.[27] The following table compares the Burgess-Cottrell study with Locke's Indiana and Swedish studies in regard to parental approval of the future mate.

Adjusted men and women in all three studies reported significantly

TABLE 26. Per Cent of Adjusted and Unadjusted Reporting Parental Approval of Mate before Marriage: Three Studies*

STUDY	MEN			WOMEN		
	Adjusted	Unadjusted	CR	Adjusted	Unadjusted	CR
Chicago study (Burgess-Cottrell)	87.3	68.2	4.3	80.8	62.2	3.8
Indiana study (Locke)	76.8	51.9	4.6	82.3	45.6	7.1
Swedish study (Locke)	85.8	60.0	4.0	90.5	66.1	4.4

* This table was prepared by Harvey J. Locke for the annual Research Lecture at the University of Southern California, May, 1953.

[26] Burgess and Wallin, op. cit., p. 273.   [27] Locke, op. cit., p. 119.

greater parental approval of mates than did the unadjusted men and women.

FACTORS IN ENGAGEMENT FAILURE

Burgess and Wallin measured cultural divergencies by studying differences in religion and differences in leisure-time interests. They found that couples with the same religious affiliations showed fewer unbroken engagements (73.1 per cent) than those of mixed faith (58.8 per cent).[28] Likewise differences in leisure-time interests, indicating different cultural backgrounds, show the same kind of percentages of disrupted engagements.

Burgess and Wallin conclude that people with important personality problems tend to break engagements: men who are dependent, promiscuous, insecure, or contented with the less-demanding bachelor state; young women who have over-idealized or have been over-attached to their fathers, who are afraid of sex or childbirth, and who have such high standards for a mate that their fiancés cannot meet them.[29]

Other personality problems that make for engagement failure listed by Burgess and Wallin are incompatibility of temperament, unsatisfied personality need, and the career interest of either man or girl. As these have been discussed in the chapters on psychological and economic factors in wise mate choice, they will not be described further here.

When it appears that prolongation of the engagement is not wise because the couple cannot adjust well to each other the engagement must be broken. This may be done by one or the other or by mutual consent. It may be done by breaking completely and at once or by "tapering off" the relationship. There is much diversity of opinion at this point. Bowman feels that, even if a broken engagement results in the suicide of one partner, it is better to break sharply and be free of a burdensome situation. Burgess and Wallin give the values of both procedures but stress the diminution of emotional turmoil for the rejected person when the slower procedure is followed. Every situation should be viewed as creatively as possible by the individuals involved and the method chosen which will be least painful. Young people need to anticipate the feelings of remorse and chagrin that follow a broken engagement. However, if the act of breaking an engagement can be regarded as a learning process, as a step in wise marital choice, it may serve to promote more discriminating

[28] Burgess and Wallin, *op. cit.*, p. 289.   [29] *Ibid.*, pp. 278–279.

202

choices in the future. Burgess and Wallin suggest that an increase in the rate of broken engagements may well result in a decrease later in the divorce rate.

IMPORTANT CONSIDERATIONS FOR ENGAGEMENT BEHAVIOR

There are a number of other areas of behavior and planning which are important for a couple to consider. The first of these is sexual behavior during engagement.

Sexual Behavior During the Engagement Period. Sexual behavior during courtship has already been considered so that this discussion is limited to the effect of sexual activity on engagement success and on later marital success. Burgess and Wallin found that those who did not have intercourse with their future mates tend to have the highest engagement-success scores. Men who had never had pre-marital intercourse had a mean engagement-success score of 155.5 as compared to a mean score of 145.5 for those who often participated in pre-marital coitus. For women the scores were: never, 154.3 and often, 147.4. Never having pre-marital intercourse is associated with engagement success.[30]

The next question deals with the relation of pre-marital sexual intercourse to marriage adjustment. Burgess and Wallin related sex histories to four criteria of success in marriage: (1) marital happiness, (2) general marital satisfaction, (3) love, and (4) marriage-permanence scores. Detailed statistics are given only in regard to the relation of love scores in marriage to pre-marital intercourse. The love score was scaled as 0 to 13. Under 9 was considered a low score and from 12 to 13 was regarded as a high score. Forty-nine per cent of the husbands who had never had pre-marital intercourse with their mates fell into the high category of love scores as compared with 25.8 per cent of those who had.[31] The statistics indicate that those men who had had intercourse seemed more likely to fall into the low love-score class and much less likely to be included in the high-score group. The same characteristic pattern is revealed in the case of women. Sixty-two per cent of the women who had never had pre-marital coitus fell into the high category of love scores as compared with 49 per cent of those who had frequently had pre-marital intercourse.[32]

Burgess and Wallin summarize the relationship of pre-marital relationship between spouses and the other adjustment indices as follows:

[30] Burgess and Wallin, *op. cit.*   [31] *Ibid.*, pp. 368–369.   [32] *Ibid.*, p. 369.

203

"In general the other measures of marital success have the same relation as the love scores to frequency of pre-marital intercourse with spouse. . . ."[33]

Burgess and Wallin conclude from these data that: "Summarizing roughly, the result of different studies, although not decisive, supports the conclusion that husbands and wives with no experience of pre-marital intercourse have the higher probability of marital success. . . ."[34]

Kinsey also analyzed the pre-marital experience of 5,774 females in relationship to marriage. His findings are the most detailed to date, but they are limited by the nature of his sample for (a) his subjects are all volunteers, (b) 3,138 are below the age of 25 and 1,927 are below the age of 20, (c) 3,313 or 58.2 per cent are not or never have been married, (d) only 445 of the 4,922 or 9 per cent under forty have ever been divorced, separated, or widowed, (e) 75 per cent had some college or post-graduate study and only 17 per cent were limited in education to high school. This means that Kinsey's conclusions regarding the effect of pre-marital sexual intercourse on marriage is based on about 40 per cent of his volunteer sample, or those married.

Kinsey found that nearly 50 per cent of the females in his married group had had coitus before they were married.[35] Of these, 46 per cent had coitus only with their future husbands, 13 per cent had it only with other males, and 41 per cent had coitus with both fiancé and other males.[36] Only 30 per cent of the grade-school group had had pre-marital coitus as compared to 47 per cent of the high-school and 60 per cent of the college group.[37]

The following adapted table from Kinsey indicates the relationship of orgasm in marital coitus and pre-marital coitus.

On analyzing these figures we find that 468 did not have orgasm in pre-marital intercourse and 614 did have orgasm from 1 to 25-plus times in pre-marital intercourse. The lowest rate of orgasm in marriage is not for those who never had pre-marital intercourse but for those who had coitus which did not result in orgasm. The physiological or psychological factors involved in the reactions of these women were not analyzed.

A considerable number of pre-marital sexual experiences results in pregnancy. Kinsey's sample included 2,094 single, white females who had

---

[33] *Ibid.*, p. 369.   [34] *Ibid.*, p. 370.
[35] Alfred C. Kinsey, W. B. Pomeroy, and C. E. Martin, *Sexual Behavior in the Human Female*, Philadelphia, W. B. Saunders Company, Copyright, 1953, p. 286.
[36] *Ibid.*, p. 336.   [37] *Ibid.*, p. 293.

T A B L E 27. Pre-Marital Coital Experience vs. Percentage of Marital Coitus Leading to Orgasm*

| Percentage of marital coitus with orgasm | WITHOUT PREMARITAL COITUS | | WITH PREMARITAL COITUS | | | |
| | | | No orgasm in pre-marital coitus | | With orgasm in pre-marital coitus | |
	No orgasm from any source	Orgasm from other source	No orgasm any source	Orgasm from other source	Orgasm with coitus 1–24 times	Orgasm with coitus 25 plus times
FIRST YEAR OF MARRIAGE (percentage of females)						
None	40	15	56	38	8	3
1–29	10	12	10	12	16	8
30–59	11	14	10	13	14	15
60–89	10	15	7	8	12	11
90–100	29	44	17	29	50	57
NUMBER OF CASES	563	566	223	245	258	356
IN FIFTH YEAR OF MARRIAGE (percentage of females)						
None	28	6	43	14	8	1
1–29	14	11	14	22	14	11
30–59	16	15	9	17	14	16
60–89	11	19	11	14	12	19
90–100	31	49	23	33	52	53
NUMBER OF CASES	399	385	129	154	146	217

* Adapted from Alfred C. Kinsey, *et al.*, *Sexual Behavior in the Human Female*, Philadelphia, W. B. Saunders Company, 1953. This table is adapted from Table 109, "Premarital Coital Experience vs. Percentage of Marital Coitus Leading to Orgasm," p. 406.

had coitus for whom he had data on pregnancy. The number of pregnancies was 476, or 18 per cent.

It is important to point out here that these findings are all averages. Some couples who had had very frequent sexual relations were included in the most successful engagement and marriage groups; some couples who were continent fell into the lowest engagement and marriage-adjustment groups. Each couple has different cultural and ethical backgrounds.

205

Perhaps the safest rule to follow here is to suggest frequent and honest communication about the problem, to try to find the appropriate response to assure the long-time happiness of the engagement partner, and to adapt to the needs of the other. On the other hand, in doing so, it is well to remember that for the average person intercourse in engagement is not correlated with engagement success or marital success.

Looking Forward to Marriage. Burgess and Wallin discovered that there were a number of important values which need to be ascertained during the period of engagement in order to prepare properly for marriage. These entailed the following considerations: (1) is love necessary for marriage? (2) should married couples who cease to be in love divorce, separate, or continue living together? (3) is divorce ever justifiable for reasons other than unfaithfulness? (4) are extra-marital relations ever justifiable and if so under what circumstances? (5) after marriage is it objectionable for a man or woman to keep their friends of the opposite sex and to go out with them? (6) is the husband expected to help with the housework? (7) what are the attitudes of the engaged man and woman to having children and how many would they like to have? (8) how soon after marriage would they like to have a child and how soon do they plan on having one? (9) should the wife work? (10) what are the main factors making for success in marriage? (11) do men and women consider their knowledge of sex adequate for marriage?[38]

In answering these questions, Burgess and Wallin asked their interviewees to list in order of importance the three main factors which they thought made for success in marriage. Those chosen in order of rank importance were listed by men as (1) compatibility of agreement and congeniality, 22.9 per cent, (2) love and affection, 21.1 per cent, (3) common interests, 12.6 per cent, (4) understanding, 9 per cent, (5) sexual compatibility and attraction, 6.7 per cent, (6) financial security, 4.5 per cent, (7) cooperation, 3.1 per cent, (8) respect, 2.2 per cent, (9) children and home, 0.9 per cent, (10) other factors, 11.2 per cent.[39] Women had a different choice as to the most important factors: (1) love and affection, 30.6 per cent, (2) compatibility of agreement and congeniality, 16.2 per cent (3) common interests, 10.4 per cent, (4) understanding, 8.6 per cent, (5) companionship, 5.9 per cent, (6) cooperation, 4.5 per cent, (7) sexual compatibility and attraction, 3.6 per cent, (8) respect, 3.2 per cent, (9) financial security, 2.7 per cent (10) children and the home, 0.5 per cent.[40]

[38] Burgess and Wallin, *op. cit.*, p. 393.   [39] *Ibid.*, p. 403.   [40] *Ibid.*, p. 403.

It is interesting that only a small percentage mentioned children as an important factor in marriage. Also worth noting is the relatively low ranking of sexual compatibility and attraction. The greatest attention was given to love and affection, compatibility, and common interests. This indicates that couples today are most concerned about the quality of their future interpersonal relationship.

CONCLUSION

The most useful function of the engagement period is the final and essential test it permits of the relationship of the future husband and wife. During the engagement period, the euphoric nature of the love relationship can be set aside, and the partners can explore and measure their capacity for communication, adaptability, and problem-solving. If a couple finds that the divergences are too great, it is well to break the engagement—in the most constructive way possible. On the other hand, achievements in communication, accommodation, adaptation, and problem-solving during engagement create a solid foundation for the initiation of married life. The general engagement inventory that follows is designed to help a couple test their development in cohesion and problem-solving as well as their agreement on values and attitudes. It summarizes points considered so far as essential to courtship, wise marriage choice, and engagement adjustment.

Analysis of Your Interaction with Future Mate

1. Agreement on economic matters with future mate.
   A. Approximately how many times have you discussed your future financial plans and problems?_____
   B. What has been the result of these discussions: (1)_____new insights for both; (2)_____happy agreement; (3)_____temporary disagreement; (4)_____bitter disagreement.
   C. Have you discussed   Have you reached agreement on

1. A budget;	Yes___No___;	Yes___No___.
2. Savings;	Yes___No___;	Yes___No___.
3. Wife's working;	Yes___No___;	Yes___No___.
4. Buying a home;	Yes___No___;	Yes___No___.
5. Who will manage the money;	Yes___No___;	Yes___No___.
6. Your occupational plans.	Yes___No___;	Yes___No___.

207

Which of these caused conflict?_____

Which of these would you like to discuss?_____

2. Agreement on matters of recreation with future mate.

   A. Approximately how many times have you discussed your future recreational plans and problems?_____

   B. What has been the result of these discussions: (*1*)_____new insights for both; (*2*)_____happy agreement; (*3*)_____temporary disagreement; (*4*)_____bitter disagreement.

   C. List the recreational activities of your future mate that you do not participate in:

                                            1. _____

      2. _____   3. _____

      4. _____   5. _____

   D. List the recreational activities that are important to you that your future mate does not participate in:

      1. _____   2. _____

      3. _____   4. _____

   E. List the different recreational activities in which you and your intended mate have participated as a couple more than once in the last six months:

                                        1. _____

      2. _____   3. _____

      4. _____   5. _____

      6. _____   7. _____

   What conflicts do you have over recreation?_____

_____

   Which of these would you like to discuss?_____

3. Agreement on religious matters.

   A. In what church did you receive your childhood religious training? _____. How intensive was it?_____

   B. At present to which religious group do you belong?_____

   C. Approximately how many times have you discussed your future religious plans?_____.

   D. What has been the result of these discussions? (*1*)_____new insights for both; (*2*)_____happy agreement; (*3*)_____temporary disagreement; (*4*)_____bitter disagreement.

   E. Have you discussed   Have you reached agreement or

      1. Religious education

         of children;   Yes____No____; Yes____No____

      2. Grace at meals;   Yes____No____; Yes____No____

      3. Attendance at

         church;   Yes____No____; Yes____No____

4. Birth control;   Yes____No____;   Yes____No____.
5. Who will marry you;   Yes____No____;   Yes____No____.
6. Your basic religious
      ideas.   Yes____No____;   Yes____No____.

Which of these caused conflict?_____

Which of these do you wish to discuss?_____

How often have you worshiped together in the last six months?___

F. Rate on the scale below your religious interest:

Intense interest	Average interest	Little interest

G. Rate your future mate's interest on the scale above.

4. Agreement on children.
   A. Approximately how many times have you discussed children and how they will be raised?_____.
   B. What has been the result of those discussions: (1)____new insights for both; (2)____happy agreement; (3)____temporary disagreement; (4)____bitter disagreement.
   C. Have you discussed   Have you reached agreement on
      1. Methods of discipline;   Yes____No____;   Yes____No____.
      2. Number of children;   Yes____No____;   Yes____No____.
      3. Sex education;   Yes____No____;   Yes____No____.
      4. Allowances.   Yes____No____;   Yes____No____.

      Which of the above caused conflict?_____

      Which would you like to discuss?_____

5. Agreement on demonstrations of affection.
   A. Approximately how many times have you seriously discussed the degree of sexual intimacy you should permit while going steady, being pinned, or being engaged:_____.
   B. What has been the result of those discussions: (1)____new insights for both; (2)____happy agreement; (3)____temporary disagreement; (4)____bitter disagreement.
   C. Have you discussed   Have you reached agreement on
      1. Petting;   Yes____No____;   Yes____No____.
      2. Petting to climax;   Yes____No____;   Yes____No____.
      3. Pre-marital intercourse;   Yes____No____;   Yes____No____.
      4. Birth-control;   Yes____No____;   Yes____No____.

     5. Achieving good sex
        relations in marriage; Yes____No____; Yes____No____.

     6. Demonstrations of
        affection.   Yes____No____; Yes____No____.

  D. How free have you been as a couple in demonstrating affection:
     (1)____very inhibited; (2)____somewhat inhibited; (3)____
     quite free; (4)____very free.

  E. How free have you been as individuals in demonstrating affection
     by your verbalizations of love: (1)____very inhibited; (2)
     ____somewhat inhibited; (3)____quite free; (4)____very
     free.

  F. Which of these caused conflict?_____

  G. Which of these would you like to discuss?_____

6. Agreement on matters relating to in-laws.
  A. Approximately how many times have you seriously discussed your
     relations, now and in the future, with your in-laws:_____.

  B. What has been the result of those discussions: (1)____new
     insights for both; (2)____happy agreement; (3)____tem-
     porary disagreement; (4)____bitter disagreement.

  C. Have you discussed   Have you reached agreement on
     1. Proximity of your home
        to in-laws;   Yes____No____; Yes____No____.
     2. Your dependence on
        parents;   Yes____No____; Yes____No____.
     3. Degree in-laws may
        interfere in marriage; Yes____No____; Yes____No____.
     4. How to achieve happy
        relations with in-laws. Yes____No____; Yes____No____.

  D. Which of these caused conflict?_____

  E. Which of these would you like to discuss?_____

7. When you discuss a problem can you talk: (1)____very easily;
  (2)____easily; (3)____with some difficulty; (4)____with great
  difficulty.

8. As you think about the conflict noted previously how would you
  characterize your method of settling disputes: (1)____future wife
  gives in; (2)____future husband gives in; (3)____matter is never
  settled; (4)____matter is settled by give and take; (5)____some
  matters are avoided which tend to cause unhappiness.

In these disputes what is the result: (*1*)_____quick forgiveness; (*2*) _____period of feeling estranged; (*3*)_____an agreement to forget the matter; (*4*)_____an attempt later to solve the problem.

In these disputes can you: (*1*)_____easily express resentment; (*2*) _____sometimes express resentment; (*3*)_____rarely express resentment.

9. Indicate your degree of agreement on the following items:

	Always agree	Almost always agree	Occa-sionally disagree	Almost always disagree	Seldom disagree
1. Drinking					
2. Petting					
3. Gambling					
4. Smoking					
5. Friends					
6. Politics					
7. Money					
8. Amount of time spent together					

10. Please list the things which have troubled you regarding your coming marriage:

Please list the irritations or annoyances which occur when you and your intended mate are together:

11. If you could make your mate "to order" what things would you change about him or her:

If you could relive your courtship with your intended mate, what things would you not do or do differently from what actually occurred?

211

12. Please rate yourself and your future mate in terms of the following items; make a "Y" for yourself and an "M" for future mate in the column which most nearly indicates the degree to which you and your mate possess each trait:

Items	Very Much So	Consid- erably	Some- what	Not at all
1. Dominating				
2. Submissive				
3. Anxious				
4. Irritable at times				
5. Moody				
6. Depressed at times				
7. Angers quickly				
8. Nervous				
9. Jealous				
10. Conventional				
11. Dependent				
12. Hostile				
13. Ambitious				
14. Sympathetic				
15. Forgiving				
16. Affectionate				
17. Tender				
18. Considerate				
19. Companionable				
20. Flexible				
21. Takes responsibility readily				
22. Creative				
23. Domestic				
24. Adaptable				

PROJECTS

1. Interview your married friends and bring back a report to the class regarding wise steps to be taken during the engagement period.
2. If you are engaged, ask your instructor to give you the Burgess-Wallin Pre-Marital Prediction schedule or the Preston Pre-Marital Counseling schedule and discuss with him areas of necessary growth in wholeness of interaction.
3. Let the class take the Sex Inventory and discuss any questions that result from taking the test.
4. Ask a gynecologist to come and speak to the class on the values of a premarital examination.

VISUAL AIDS

Are You Ready for Marriage? Coronet Instructional Films, Chicago.

READINGS

HENRY A. BOWMAN, *Marriage for Moderns,* New York, McGraw-Hill Book Company, Inc., 1948, Chapters 8 and 9.
ERNEST W. BURGESS and PAUL WALLIN, *Engagement and Marriage,* Philadelphia, J. B. Lippincott Company, 1953, Chapters 5, 8, and 12.
HAROLD T. CHRISTENSEN, *Marriage Analysis,* New York, The Ronald Press Company, 1950, Chapter 9.
HARVEY J. LOCKE, *Predicting Adjustment in Marriage: A Comparison of a Divorced and a Happily Married Group,* New York, Henry Holt and Company, 1952, Chapter 12.
REX SKIDMORE and ANTON CANNON, *Building Your Marriage,* New York, Harper and Brothers, 1951, Chapters 11 and 13.
WILLARD WALLER (Revised by Reuben Hill), *The Family: A Dynamic Interpretation,* New York, The Dryden Press, 1951, Chapters 12 and 13.

C H A P T E R   1 1

Preparation for Marriage

INTRODUCTION: RESEARCH STUDIES OF MARITAL SUCCESS HAVE BEEN UTILIZED BY PSYCHOLOGISTS, MINISTERS, AND MARRIAGE counselors to gain insight into ways of helping young people prepare for marriage through pre-marital counseling. This chapter deals with steps the couple may take during the two or three months prior to marriage to insure the adequacy of their wedding, their honeymoon, and their early marital adjustment.

PRE-MARITAL COUNSELING

Pre-marital counseling is a relatively new step in preparing for marriage. The Roman Catholic Church has instituted a Pre-Cana conference during which those who are soon to be married receive specific instruction regarding marital adjustment. Many Protestant ministers have been trained in clinical psychology and in the sociology of the family and are prepared to assess carefully any problem areas the couple recognize in their relationship. Many colleges have instituted courses in marriage. The instructors of these courses serve formally or informally as marriage counselors on their respective campuses. Some private agencies have developed pre-marital counseling programs. One of the oldest of these is the American Institute of Family Relations in Los Angeles. The Marriage Council of Philadelphia has developed a notable program of pre-marital counseling under the direction of Emily Mudd

214

The work of Burgess and Wallin proved that it is possible to predict the probability of happiness in marriage from a marriage-prediction schedule consisting of five parts: background factors, personality traits, engagement relations, engagement adjustment, and anticipated contingency factors. This text is being widely used to help locate areas in which growth is essential before marriage takes place. A couple should seek counsel with their minister or priest, a marriage counselor, and a gynecologist. The contributions of the three will now be discussed. It is not assumed that the average couple has great problems that will ruin their marriage if they do not seek help. It is assumed that pre-marital counseling can help every couple to clarify their conceptions of what to expect in marriage and improve their adjustment.

THE MARRIAGE COUNSELOR

The marriage counselor may use a group of tests such as the Burgess-Wallin predictive test mentioned above to determine degrees of compatibility and readiness for marriage. Certainly he will consider background factors, psychological and cultural factors, the problem-solving patterns of the partners as well as any specific difficulties they themselves bring to him. In addition he may explore with the couple attitudes which lead to cohesion in marriage and, on the other hand, situations which are commonly disruptive unless they are met with intelligence and understanding. The engagement-adjustment test used by the author in pre-marital counseling is appended to the engagement chapter. It measures communication, agreement on role, and values and decision-making.

PRE-MARITAL TEMPERAMENTAL TESTS

Two temperament tests widely used by marriage counselors are the Johnson Temperament test and the Guilford-Zimmerman Temperament Survey. Both reveal basic temperament trends of which it is important to be aware before marriage. The tests are given to the two partners and the profiles are then superimposed one upon the other. The results reveal areas of divergence, and degrees of divergency, that might be troublesome in marriage if not anticipated and dealt with. The Guilford-Zimmerman test reveals personality patterns associated with polarities—activity-inactivity, restraint-impulsiveness, ascendancy-submissiveness, sociability-shyness, emotional stability-emotional instability, objectivity-subjectivity, friendliness-hostility, thoughtfulness-thoughtlessness, cooperativeness-criticalness, and masculinity-femininity. If the difference is not too great the counselor will interpret it as complementary. Such a difference will add to the interest and strength of the marriage. If the difference is very great, however, possible friction is indicated, and the couple will want to develop ways of dealing with it. The use of the temperament survey often helps couples to face problems which previously they had felt emotionally but were unable to define intellectually. This is particularly true of the masculinity-femininity index. Society is passing through a period of changing roles, of confused meanings of dominance, submission or equality, of inferiority and superiority. Consequently such a survey often serves to bring latent problems into the open. To take such a test and talk through the meaning of any problems revealed by the test often quiets doubts and helps the couple achieve new patterns of understanding.

The accompanying chart is an actual picture of the way in which one couple relates temperamentally. The prognosis for that marriage is in general very good. The differences in traits are not marked but neither are the similarities so great as to indicate that the partners will be bored with each other. Both are emotionally stable, sociable, friendly, and thoughtful. They are cooperative, and have enough energy to match one another rather well. However, the chart indicates—in the last column—that the woman rated very high on masculinity, the man correspondingly low. Exploration of this contrast indicated a latent but potential conflict. The girl had been a leader in high school, in college, and in groups, and she was used to taking the lead. The man, while moderately successful in his undertakings, had not developed into a leader. He had often resented her taking the lead but had refrained from discussing it for fear of marring their otherwise admirable relationship. When the survey brought the issue to the surface, the man poured out his feelings. His resentment was quite apparent. Surprisingly, she too, had been secretly troubled by what she thought was his lack of purpose. Having spent several hours discussing the problem with the counselor, they made a specific plan for a more democratic approach to difficulties, and the danger of what might, in marriage, have developed into a major conflict in role-playing was ameliorated by communication before the wedding. Sometimes, the temperament survey will reveal profound submissiveness, emotional instability, or much hostility and intolerance. In such cases it is well for

216

FIGURE 6. Profile Chart for the Guilford-Zimmerman Temperament Survey Showing Differences in Temperament between Men and Women*

C SCORE	G General Activity Energy	R Restraint Seriousness	A Ascendance Social Boldness	S Social Interest Sociability	E Emotional Stability	O Objectivity	F Friendliness Agreeableness	T Thoughtfulness Reflectiveness	P Personal Relations Cooperativeness	M Masculinity (of emotions and interests)	CENTILE RANK	NEAREST T SCORE
10	30 / 29	30 / 29 / 28 / 27	30 / 29	30	30 / 29	30 / 29	29 / 28 / 27 / 26	30 / 29 / 28	30 / 29 / 28	30 / 29 / 28	99	75
9	28 / 27	26 / 25	28 / 27 / 26	29 / 28	28 / 27	28 / 27	25 / 24 / 23	27 / 26	27 / 26	27		70
8	26 / 25	24 / 23	25 / 24 / 23	27 / 26	26 / 25	26 / 25	22 / 21	25 / 24	25 / 24 / 23	26 / 25	95 / 90	65
7	24 / 23 / 22	22 / 21	22 / 21	25 / 24	24 / 23 / 22	24 / 23	20 / 19 / 18	23 / 22	22 / 21	24	80	60
6	21 / 20 / 19	20 / 19 / 18	20 / 19 / 18	23 / 22 / 21	21 / 20 / 19	22 / 21 / 20	17 / 16	21 / 20	20 / 19 / 18	23 / 22	70 / 60	55
5	18 / 17 / 16	17 / 16	17 / 16 / 15	20 / 19 / 18	18 / 17 / 16	19 / 18 / 17	15 / 14 / 13	19 / 18	17 / 16	21 / 20	50 / 40	50
4	15 / 14 / 13	15 / 14	14 / 13 / 12	17 / 16 / 15 / 14	15 / 14 / 13 / 12	16 / 15 / 14	12 / 11 / 10	17 / 16 / 15	15 / 14	19 / 18	30	45
3	12 / 11 / 10	13 / 12 / 11	11 / 10 / 9	13 / 12 / 11 / 10	11 / 10 / 9	13 / 12 / 11	9 / 8	14 / 13 / 12	13 / 12 / 11	17 / 16 / 15	20	40
2	9 / 8 / 7	10 / 9	8 / 7 / 6	9 / 8 / 7 / 6	8 / 7 / 6	10 / 9 / 8	7 / 6 / 5	11 / 10 / 9 / 8	10 / 9	14 / 13	10 / 5	35
1	6 / 7 / 5	8 / 7 / 6	5 / 4	5 / 4 / 3	5 / 4	7 / 6 / 5	4 / 3	7 / 6 / 5	8 / 7 / 6	12 / 11 / 10		30
0	4 / 3 / 2 / 1	5 / 4 / 3 / 2	3 / 2 / 1 / 0	2 / 1 / 0	3 / 2 / 1 / 0	4 / 3 / 2 / 1	2 / 1 / 0	4 / 3 / 2 / 1	5 / 4 / 3 / 2	9 / 7 / 5 / 3	1	25

Bottom labels: Inactivity Slowness | Impulsiveness Rhathymia | Submissiveness | Shyness Seclusiveness | Emotional Instability Depression | Subjectivity Hypersensitiveness | Hostility Belligerence | Thoughtlessness Extraversion | Criticalness Intolerance | Femininity (of emotions and interests)

- - - - - - Woman   ———— Man

the individuals involved to discuss their future with a person capable of helping them develop more adequate personality resources for marriage. They will probably be referred, for a more comprehensive counseling, to a psychiatrist or a clinical psychologist.

SEXUAL FACTORS

The marriage counselor will want to discuss quite specifically with the couple the adequacy of their knowledge about sexual intercourse and reproduction. Although sexual matters are discussed rather freely in a few academic circles, we cannot assume that the average young person has escaped traumatic experience or that he is well informed. The chapter on adolescence indicates that this fact has been demonstrated by a number of studies. Therefore, previous to marriage, the couple will need to discuss with a counselor many of the more intimate details of sexual relations which have not been covered in family conferences (if any) and in peer "bull sessions." The counselor may share with the couple a number of books which deal adequately with the subject as well as outlining for them the major prerequisites of sexual enjoyment. These points are fully discussed in a subsequent chapter on sexual adjustment in marriage.

Some aids have been produced which help young people evaluate their information and their attitudes about sex. The Sex Inventory X and Y prepared by the Marriage and Family Council of Chapel Hill, North Carolina, has been put to use by a great many ministers, doctors, and marriage counselors. Form Y of this test is a four-page booklet with vocabulary tests and an ingenious device for determining whether or not the testee understands what happens in intercourse and in childbirth. Form X is longer and more comprehensive.

This test consists of eighty multiple-choice questions which are designed not only to show the couple's familiarity with sexual terms but to enable them to grow toward a fuller understanding. Two questions picked at random indicate the quality of the sexual inventory and its usefulness in assisting a couple to measure the degree of their knowledge and to become even more familiar with important facts.

24. Of the following, which is most closely related to a happy sexual adjustment in marriage?

A. The amount of sex relations wanted by both husband and wife.

    B. The intensity and the length of the sexual climax.

    C. The wish to be together after sex needs are satisfied.

    D. The length of time spent in sex relations and the amount of sleep afterward.

60. How does being unresponsive in sex relations affect a woman's ability to become pregnant?

    A. Makes pregnancy impossible.

    B. Greatly reduces ability.

    C. Has no effect on ability.

    D. Makes pregnancy more likely.

    E. The effect depends on the kind of man she marries.

The counselee is asked not only to pick out the right answer to the question submitted but to circle questions which puzzle him or her. Many counselors give this test to all couples who come for pre-marital consultation and then use it as the basis for discussion of any areas in which doubts or questions exist. While this test is very useful, it does not take the place of the study of basic physiological material or of consultation with someone skilled in sexual counseling.

While the counselor will pay attention to the degree to which the couple understands sexual facts, he will be more concerned with the overtones of the conversation. He will listen for indications of inhibition or fear. If he finds such indications, he will then structure his relationship with the couple to help them overcome such obstacles to happy marriage.

The marriage counselor will also inquire about the practical side of the coming marriage—financial plans, housing plans, budgets, time budgets, and other forms of planning that make adjustment more fruitful and reduce anxiety. Finally, he will ask the couple to return after they have been married for a few months to discuss any obstacles to happiness which may have arisen during the early adjustment period.

The Gynecologist. All marriage counselors recommend that every couple have a thorough physical examination and have several sessions with a gynecologist prior to their marriage. In some cases the couple may raise questions regarding their capacity to bear healthy children which can only be answered by a doctor skilled in genetics. In all cases the couple will wish to discover any abnormalities which might temporarily interfere with the consummation of their marriage, as well as

219

those which would endanger their chances of having children or be obstacles to full sexual togetherness. Both the man and the wife will wish to enter marriage in optimum health, and such an examination will assure them that they have no physical condition which needs correction. Included in the examination will be the routine blood test which is almost universally required today. This test checks for venereal diseases, but young couples may request that it be extended so as to isolate any special problems such as the RH factor if incompatibility exists.

Duvall and Hill have listed desirable steps to be included in a pre-marital physical examination of the future husband and wife:

Pre-Marital Physical Examination

1. Medical history including the previous sex history of both the man and the woman, possible hereditary problems in either line, and the menstrual history of the woman.
2. Clarification of any item or questions one or both members of the couple bring in, along with any that arise during the consultation. Selected books may be recommended as helpful.
3. Brief review of the anatomy and physiology of both male and female genital systems in the human (with charts or films if desired).
4. General physical examination, including blood and urine studies, heart, lung, and pelvic conditions, and search for any possible pathologies in both the man and the woman.
5. Pelvic examination of the woman with special attention to the condition of the vaginal orifice and the adequacy of the vagina for sexual intercourse.
6. Possible instruction in hymen dilation, where indicated and compatible with the attitudes of the couple.
7. Examination of the clitoris, and plan for freeing the clitoris as indicated.
8. Laboratory study of cultures from vagina and cervix with especial concern for the presence of gonorrheal infection, with immediate program of treatment if tests are positive.
9. Examination of the male genitalia with laboratory tests and a program of treatment for possible infection. (Sperm count and motility may be included if desired.)
10. Blood tests for the detection of syphilis in both individuals. Positive findings are followed at once by adequate treatment. No evidence of the disease is the clean bill of health required in most states before the license is issued.
11. Discussion of plans for contraception, as requested, with particular

reference to the initial period of the marriage and the religious factors that may be pertinent: (a) plan for plotting the "safe period" if rhythm method is to be used, or (b) fitting a diaphragm if religious and personal factors allow it.

12. Specific advice on vagina lubricants and coital procedures as requested and indicated.[1]

Such a thorough examination takes care of all physical factors as well as helping the couple deal with doubts which may have been troubling them.

The Minister, Priest, or Rabbi. It is thoughtful to consult the minister, priest, or rabbi some time previous to the actual date of the wedding. Religious leaders are busy people, and they need to know the dates of wedding rehearsals and ceremonies in sufficient time to fit them into their schedules. The minister, priest, or rabbi will arrange for one or more consultations with the couple previous to the rehearsal.

During these consultations the clergyman will talk with the couple about their preparation for marriage, their religious problems or outlook, and the meaning of the ceremony itself. If the minister functions as a marriage counselor he may give the couple some of the tests that have been reviewed earlier in this chapter. He will also help the couple review arrangements for the wedding and the honeymoon.

GROUP PRE-MARITAL COUNSELING

One of the promising movements to aid young people to prepare more adequately for marriage is pre-marital group counseling. The author has conducted five such groups in which the stress was put on sharing needed information and on discussing problems which were distressing the group. Levine and Brodsky have recently evaluated their experience of conducting eight such groups.[2] They ranged in size from two to six couples, but the therapists found that the optimum number for good results is four couples. They held a series of three sessions and dealt with love, sex, and parenthood. At the beginning of each session a brief presentation was made. This was followed by discussion. The author conducted his groups in similar fashion but devoted more time to the

[1] Evelyn M. Duvall and Reuben Hill, *When You Marry*, Revised Edition. Reprinted by permission of D. C. Heath and Company, Boston, 1953, p. 123.
[2] Lena Levine and Jeanne Brodsky, "Group Pre-Marital Counseling," *Mental Hygiene*, Vol. XXXII, No. 4, Published by Planned Parenthood Federation of America, April 1953.

221

presentation of pertinent information and had ten sessions with each group. Levine and Brodsky as well as the author discovered that there is a very grave lack of factual information among engaged couples, and that often their information is distorted. This leads to anxiety since the couple looks forward to marriage as an unknown and sometimes threatening situation. In group therapy, individuals can voice their fears and ask questions about things they do not understand. The value of the group seems to be that to some extent it reduces fear, guilt, and conflict as well as helping individuals to set somewhat more adequate goals for marriage.

THE PLACE OF THE WEDDING

The place of the wedding has been given considerable attention in studies of marital adjustment. In so far as this factor is symbolic of others more positively associated with marriage adjustment, it is probably not of causal importance. Locke has given it some attention and his study is summarized in the following table:

TABLE 28. Per Cent of Happily-Married and Divorced-Married in a Given Place or by a Given Person*

PERSON OR PLACE	MEN		WOMEN	
	Married N 173	Divorced N 161	Married N 171	Divorced N 183
At home	27.7	15.5	29.2	14.8
At church	12.7	9.3	11.1	8.2
By judge	1.2	2.6	1.2	0.5
At minister's home	38.7	39.1	40.4	46.5
By justice of peace	13.3	29.2	11.7	27.3
Elsewhere	6.4	4.3	6.4	2.7
	100.0	100.0	100.0	100.0

* Harvey J. Locke, *Predicting Adjustment in Marriage*, New York, Henry Holt and Company, 1951, p. 238. Reprinted by permission.

Being married by a justice of the peace is unquestionably associated with maladjustment. Marriage at home, in a church, or at the minister's home is associated with marital adjustment. The high incidence of marriages performed in the minister's home in Locke's table is probably referable to the region in which his study was made and would not apply in many localities.

THE DATE OF THE WEDDING

Ordinarily the date of the wedding is determined by the menstrual cycle of the bride, and the date is set so that it will not coincide with her menstrual period. Sometimes, however, other considerations are important such as the attendance of family and friends, or the work schedule of the groom. Then, too, there is the question of the honeymoon. In our society it is customary for the groom and bride to go away for a period of early adjustment. If the man is working, the wedding must take place at a time when it is feasible for him to be absent from his job.

The date ought to be determined far enough in advance so that all arrangements can be made easily and without undue haste, so that all participants can plan their attendance, and so that invitations can be sent out in time.

CUSTOMS AND LAWS OF MARRIAGE

Long centuries of custom have gone into the marriage service. In some cases it may mean more to young couples if they understand some of the symbolism involved in the service.

Prehistoric man probably captured his wife from a neighbor with a show of brute strength. Later when man learned to live in clans the individual still went out to capture a wife, but now he had to go farther away to find her—probably in another clan. The practice of having a "best man" to stand up with the groom is undoubtedly an anachronistic survival of the time when the friends of the bridegroom stood by to fight off the unhappy relatives of the captured bride. As late as the first decade of the twentieth century, the wedding party in South Russia engaged in a mock fight in which friends of the bride gave battle to friends of the groom. When this symbolic fight was over, the whole wedding party was reunited in friendship and the entire company proceded with the service.

The ring had a very important use in prehistoric times. It certainly was not placed around the finger but around the ankle or the wrist because its purpose was to secure the girl until she was ready to remain with her captor as his wife. Sometimes today the ring is placed around the neck, as in Africa; sometimes it is placed in the nose. Wherever it is placed, the ring is supposed to insure the continued loyalty of the bride. The emancipation of women as well as the changing concept of marriage

223

roles is reflected in the growing custom in this country for both husband and wife to wear rings.

The engagement ring has an equally interesting history. In Teutonic countries, marriage was originally arranged by a form of barter in which the father was given a certain amount of money or property for his daughter. The contract was made secure by a pledge or part payment which came to be known as the *vadium*. In time the vadium came to be presented to the bride and was given to her at the time of the betrothal. It eventually took the form of an ornament of some value and was the predecessor of the modern engagement ring. At the time the bargain was made the father symbolized the completion of the cermony by placing the girl's hand in the hand of the man she was going to marry. He thus "gave her away."

Modern marriage law is a product of early Teutonic, Roman, and Hebraic customs as changed by Christianity and modern social and industrial conditions. The changing role of the emancipated woman and the evolving status of children account for sharp differences between ancient and modern marriage laws. A summary of these laws follows:

AGE LIMITS FOR MARRIAGE

In America, the marriage statutes have generally raised the age limit of 14 for boys and 12 for girls which characterized both Roman law and the English common law. Only Idaho, Mississippi, New Jersey, and Washington allow children of these ages to marry. The most common law sets the minimum age of marriage without consent of parents at 18 for girls and 21 for boys. Some states require both the girl and boy to be 21. Even if parents consent, many states do not permit boys below 18 or girls below 16 to marry.

PROHIBITIONS ON MARRIAGE

Consanguineous marriages (or marriages of blood relatives) have been prohibited since ancient times due to the chance that relatives carry similar hereditary traits in their germ plasm. All states prohibit the marriage of close blood relations, including marriage between brothers and sisters, mothers and sons, fathers and daughters, aunts and nephews, uncles and nieces, grandmothers and grandsons, grandfathers and granddaughters—with the exception of Rhode Island which permits the marriage of Jewish uncles and nieces. Twenty-nine states prohibit the marriage of cousins or of brothers and sisters of half-blood.

In the past two decades many health regulations have been introduced into marriage requirements. Seven states prohibit the marriage of those with transmittable disease in the infectious state. Five states require examinations for venereal diseases, twenty-nine states specify such an examination for syphilis, and other states have similar laws although eight states still do not prohibit the marriage of those who have not presented evidence of being free from venereal diseases. All states regulate the marriage of the mentally ill, seventeen will not issue licenses to epileptics, and three prohibit the marriage of the feeble-minded unless they have been sterilized.

The third area of prohibitions has to do with racial regulations. Thirty states prohibit inter-racial marriages. The southern states have been most concerned to prohibit the marriages of Caucasians and Negroes while the western states have statutes prohibiting the union of Orientals and Caucasians. The recent Supreme Court decision in California which declared such laws unconstitutional may affect the constitutionality of all other laws which prohibit inter-racial marriages.

COMMON-LAW MARRIAGES

Common-law marriages are recognized in twenty-one states. A common-law marriage is one in which any agreement to marry is followed by cohabitation as man and wife. In these marriages no license or ceremony is required. Arizona, Illinois, Missouri, and New York have now declared such marriages "null and void" and it is likely that other states will follow suit because the state can have little or no control over such unions.

THE WEDDING

If a couple survives the testing period of being engaged, the inevitable next step is to plan the wedding. Sometimes the couple has relatively little to do with it for the bride's mother may enter the picture here with authority and enthusiasm. Although traditionally the bride is supposed to have the final say regarding wedding plans, many resignedly report that this is a fiction because the mother takes over. And in some cases the end result of this is not unhappy, for it saves the bride and bridegroom much bother and anxiety.

Often, however, the wedding is so pretentious and the arrangements so complex that the whole wedding party is exhausted in carrying out preliminary plans. The huge wedding and reception add further fatigue so that the honeymoon, instead of being an initiation into marriage, is actually a recuperation from a public spectacle. If the wedding is to be a large one, and if at least part of the responsibility for its success falls on the bride and groom, it should be planned well in advance so that all details are taken care of long before the wedding day, and this day should be spent in relaxation, not in telephone calls and automobile dashes hither and yon. The wedding ordinarily should be commensurate with the social and economic circumstances of the bride and groom, but the emphasis should always be upon its meaning and its promise and not upon its details.

The wedding has several purposes. One is to comply with society's regulation that a couple legitimatize their marriage in legal fashion. Another is to secure the blessing of friends and church upon what is regarded as a supremely important event. Still another is to undergird the transition into marriage with symbolic and meaningful ritual. The wedding ceremonializes the final step from singleness to married living. Religiously, the wedding brings the blessings of God through the church to the couple. It is generally believed that weddings performed in the home or in the church have an aesthetic quality which is missing when a couple elopes or is married by a justice of the peace.

THE WEDDING SERVICE

Churches have different types of wedding ceremonies. While the Nuptial Mass of the Roman Catholic Church is markedly different from the silent, or nearly silent, marriage of Quakers, both have some symbolism in common. In an effort to interpret some of the symbolisms, a wedding service is reproduced below with interpolations explaining the background of some of its parts.

The Marriage Service. At the time appointed for the marriage ceremony (*the time appointed means following the seating of the bride's mother, the singing of one or two special songs such as "Oh, Promise Me," and the wedding procession which consists first of the minister and the men of the bridal party and then of the women of the bridal party*) the persons united shall stand, the man on the right, and the woman on the left, and the minister shall say:

DEARLY BELOVED: We are gathered in the sight of God and in the face of this company to join together this man and this woman in holy matrimony which is ordained of God and is to be honored by all men. Therefore it is not by any to be entered into unadvisedly, or lightly, but reverently, discreetly and in the fear of God. Into this holy estate_____ and_____come now to be joined.

Then the minister shall say to the man:

Will you take this woman to be your wedded wife, to live together in the holy estate of matrimony? Will you love her, comfort her, honor and keep her, and forsaking all others, keep you only unto her so long as ye both shall live?

The man shall answer: I will.
Then the minister shall say to the woman:

Will you take this man to be your wedded husband, to live together in the holy estate of matrimony? Will you love him, comfort him, honor and keep him, and forsaking all others, keep you only unto him so long as ye both shall live?

The woman shall answer: I will.
Then the minister shall say: Who giveth this woman to be married to this man?

Then the father (*or uncle, brother, or friend*) shall say: I do; or by a sign, or by putting the hand of the bride into that of the groom shall give her away. (*In ancient times this was the whole of the marriage service. The father placed their hands together reverently and they were married. This symbolizes the surrender of authority from one family to another. It means that the father now commits the happiness of his child whom he has reared from infancy into the keeping of another. In recent years the words used have been changed, so that in some services the father says: "Her mother and I," thus recognizing the part her mother has played in her development.*)

Then the minister shall require the couple to repeat the vows as follows:

I, _____, take thee, _____, to be my wedded wife, to have and to hold, from this time forward, for better or for worse, for richer or poorer, in sickness and in health, to love and to cherish till death do us part, and thereto I plight thee my troth. (*Some couples prefer the word "faith" here.*)

227

> I, _____, take thee, _____, to be my wedded husband, to have and to hold, from this time forward, for better or for worse, for richer or poorer, in sickness and in health, to love and to cherish till death do us part, and thereto I plight thee my troth. (Or "faith".)

At this time the best man shall give the groom the ring, the groom shall give it to the minister, the minister shall give it to the bride and the bride shall return it to the groom who then places it on the finger of the bride. (*This symbolic ring service unites friends, God, family, and the couple in a circle of blessing of love. The ring which is itself a circle makes a wider circle joining all of these in the new configuration of the new family. This most beautiful symbolism is often not known by those who participate in the service.*)

The man shall say as he holds the hand upon which he has placed the ring:

> With this ring I thee wed, and to thee I will be true, in name of the Father, and of the Son, and of the Holy Spirit. Amen.

If there is a second ring in a double-ring service, the same service is repeated. (*A variation consists of the minister taking the ring to the altar and blessing it before he gives it back to the man to put on the finger of the girl; or in a double-ring service, before it is given back to the girl to put on the finger of the man.*)

After this the minister shall say: Let us pray. (*In the unified type of service the bride and groom remain before the minister and simply bow their heads, but in the divided service they go to the kneeling bench provided for this purpose and kneel in front of the minister. In recent years many couples have asked that the "Lord's Prayer" by Malotte be sung before the wedding prayer is said by the minister.*)

Following the prayer the minister shall say:

> For inasmuch as _____ and _____ have consented together in the holy wedlock, and have witnessed the same before God and this company, and have pledged their faith each to the other, by the authority committed unto me, I pronounce that they are man and wife. Whom God hath joined together, let no man put asunder.

After this the minister shall say the closing benediction and the couple close the ceremony with a kiss which is followed by the recessional in which the bride and groom go down the aisle together followed by the entire wedding party.

There are many other details involved in planning a wedding and these should be thought of merely as details. The important part of the marriage is the dedication of one individual to another in a reverent and beautiful way. But when the romantic dreams of the "march in the gown" or the social prestige factors involved in the "great ceremony" occupy the attention, a wedding loses much of its special value to the couple.

The details of wedding courtesy such as the giving of gifts, the arrangement of the reception line, etc. need give us little concern here. The minister who performs the ceremony is well equipped to guide a couple through these details. Many large department stores now maintain special wedding counselors who can advise skilfully concerning what is regarded as proper at a wedding. Yet one fact needs to be mentioned. The bride is right no matter what she desires. If she wants to rewrite the marriage service or dispense with the reception, that is her prerogative. The reactions of her friends may not be positive, but if she wishes to add to the meaning of the occasion in any way, she may rightfully do this. The guiding principle is that the wedding should be as meaningful as possible.

THE HONEYMOON

The purpose of the honeymoon is to facilitate the transition from individual patterns of behavior to group behavior. It is a special period in which in privacy and isolation the couple take the first steps in adjustment to shared living, not only sexually, but in every other way. For this reason a honeymoon should be planned to produce a maximum of growth toward solidarity. It is a period of major importance in every couple's life for it represents the culmination of years of expectations and hopes. What are the conditions which will facilitate these adjustments?

If the honeymoon is meaningful, it is a period in which each of the partners concentrates upon the other; thus mutuality in marriage gets an early emphasis. Hence honeymoons planned in conjunction with long business trips or research projects fail in purpose because they divide the attention of one or both partners. Honeymoons involving extensive travel or busy schedules likewise do not give the partners sufficient opportunity for quiet explorations of each other's personality. This is one period in life which should be completely free of every obligation. The couple should focus on togetherness sexually; and on companionship socially. It is a time when nothing else matters.

This early adjustment involves the place of the honeymoon. Obviously it should be a place that both enjoy. Students seem always to disagree regarding the selection of the honeymoon spot. About a fourth of the girls want to be completely surprised and know nothing about the place the man has selected. Another fourth want to know in general whether it is at the beach, in the city, or in the mountains so that they can bring appropriate clothes. The other half would like to have a voice in planning where to go. Whatever the wishes of the girl, she should be consulted as to her preferences regarding the share she wants to play in selecting the place. If the man selects the place it should be with a full realization of the general attitudes of his bride. And wherever the couple go they should leave word with some trusted relative or friend so that in case of emergency they may be quickly reached.

In planning for the honeymoon the place chosen should be commensurate with the couple's resources. Some couples splurge to the extent that they are impoverished for the next six months and have no money for continued fun after the honeymoon. One of the early accomplishments in the wise use of resources may be the agreement that is reached about an appropriate place for the honeymoon and its length. There is no "good" rule for these matters because they will vary in terms of a couple's background and resources.

It is better for a honeymoon to start immediately after the wedding. Honeymoons which are postponed for a month or six months do not perform the same function as those which enable the couple to begin marriage alone. If a man's work interferes with the possibility of an immediate honeymoon, it is better to shift the date of the wedding so that it corresponds with his vacation.

More important than the details of time and place are the attitudes with which a couple begin married life. Even though they have been most thorough in preparing for marriage, there is apt to be some anxiety about the initial steps in achieving sexual happiness. If, however, they have fully discussed this, and if they have prepared themselves with as much knowledge as possible, they need not be too concerned. Many couples are happy on their honeymoons even if they do not find complete sexual success at first. The attitude of mutuality, the attitude of tenderness, the attitude of patience—these are as reassuring as actual sexual attainment. Any type of adjustment as complex as sexual compatibility

230

takes time. Patience will enable the couple to take any problems in their stride with confidence that they will be worked out later.

Furthermore, a considerate and extensive effort on the part of each of the partners to bring pleasure to the other in all phases of the honeymoon will make their sexual experiments meaningful even though not as completely satisfying as they will be a year later. The excitement of the wedding and the reception sometimes brings on the menstrual cycle two weeks early and this of course interferes with the initiation of sexual togetherness. But if the couple have a sense of humor and if their love is firmly rooted, this will not mar their honeymoon too much.

The initiation of togetherness during the engagement period, during the planning for the wedding, during the epochal moments of the wedding itself, and during the honeymoon is an important step toward further enlarging the degree to which the couple share each other. There will be problems in each of these periods but if the problems are faced frankly and openly their discussion and solution will be steps to unity.

CONCLUSION

Four specific means of promoting growth for marriage have been suggested in this chapter: use of the growing facilities of the marriage counselor; several consultations with a gynecologist; counseling with the minister, priest, rabbi, or other person who is to perform the ceremony; and, finally, planning the wedding and honeymoon so carefully that they contribute to the growing unity of the couple.

READINGS

HENRY A. BOWMAN, *Marriage for Moderns*, New York, McGraw-Hill Book Company, Inc., 1948, Chapter 9.

EVELYN M. DUVALL and REUBEN HILL, *When You Marry*, Revised Edition, Boston, D. C. Heath and Company, 1953, Chapters 8 and 9.

JUDSON T. LANDIS and MARY G. LANDIS, *Readings in Marriage and the Family*, New York, Prentice-Hall, 1952, Chapter 6.

HARVEY J. LOCKE, *Predicting Adjustment in Marriage: A Comparison of a Divorced and a Happily Married Group*, New York, Henry Holt and Company, 1951, Chapter 11.

PART FOUR

THE ACHIEVEMENT
OF TOGETHERNESS

Then Almitra spoke again and said, And what
of Marriage, master?
And he answered saying:
You were born together, and together you shall
be forever.
You shall be together when the white wings of
death scatter your days.
Aye, you shall be together even in the silent
memory of God.
But let there be spaces in your togetherness,
And let the winds of the heavens dance between
you.
Love one another, but make not a bond of love:
Let it rather be a moving sea between the
shores of your souls.
Fill each other's cup but drink not from one
cup.
Give one another of your bread but eat not from
the same loaf.
Sing and dance together and be joyous, but let
each of you be alone.
Even as the strings of a lute are alone though
they quiver with the same music.
Give your heart but not into each other's keep-
ing.
For only the hand of Life can contain your
hearts.
And stand together yet not too near together:
For the pillars of the temple stand apart,
And the oak tree and the cypress grow not in
each other's shadow.[1]

[1] Reprinted from *The Prophet* by Kahlil Gibran by
permission of the publisher, Alfred A. Knopf, Inc.
Copyright 1923 by Kahlil Gibran. Renewal copyright
1951 by Administrators C.T.A. of Kahlil Gibran Estate
and Mary Gibran.

CHAPTER 12

Achieving Individuation
and Togetherness

THE REMAINDER OF THIS BOOK FOCUSES UPON THE WAYS A
COUPLE MAY ACHIEVE TOGETHERNESS. NO MARRIAGE IS ADEQUATE
when both concentrate so completely upon individual interests that there
is no common growth in sharing and companionship. Yet no marriage is
adequate, either, when the basic personality potentialities of either
partner are completely submerged in the demands of the family. Maximum life satisfaction, indeed maximum marriage success, comes when
both partners develop optimum individual and group creativeness. Because this is a book concerned primarily with marriage and not with
personality fulfillment, our main emphasis is upon growth in mutuality
and cohesiveness. Yet rewarding mutuality is predicated upon the degree to which the individuals involved have something to share.

That which does not exist cannot very well be shared. The counselor
hears over and over again that marriage is boring and family life is
meaningless. But how it could be anything else, given the character
structure of the individuals involved, is puzzling. A couple whose major
aim in life is to find only new and more spectacular thrills may expect
life sooner or later to fizzle out; a sparkler does not last forever. Young
people preoccupied with the more superficial aspects of our culture with

its emphasis upon materialistic things must one day discover, as Midas did, that such attitudes turn the rest of life into something hard and unlovely. Again those young people who approach love and marriage on the basis of romantic expectations cannot escape the day when they must summon the doctor for their mate or their baby; when their dreams of the little house are rudely shattered because of a down payment they cannot meet; or when divergent personality needs compel them to face fundamental conflicts. The abundant life does not come to those who have no abundance to share.

In this sense all of human experience is a preparation for marriage. A class in education for family living may focus attention upon special areas such as economic or sexual adjustment but it does little to alter the fundamental richness or poverty of the personalities involved. Hence all college courses, including those in literature, art, music, recreation, anthropology, history, science, et al., are preparatory to any inter-personal relationship because they add to character the dimension of depth. Likewise all experiences which sensitize individuals to beauty, to fun, or inculcate appreciations, or further intellectual interest are adding dimensions to the individual which later will add substance to his marriage. In this sense no one can hope to teach another individual how to find success in marriage for all of his past is involved.

The past continues to be important after marriage. "The oak tree and the cypress grow not in each other's shadow." One is reminded of the farmer who stood sorrowfully outside the state mental hospital shaking his head because he had just committed his wife. "How she could of caught this, I dunno. I kept her in the kitchen for forty years." Each individual must have freedom and time and opportunity to devote to his or her areas of creativity. There must be a respect for significant differences if the differences are to contribute to the enrichment of the union. If the wife loves the piano she cannot indulge her joy in playing without an instrument or time to practice. If the husband realizes that music is an integral aspect of the personality of his wife, he will sacrifice so that she has an instrument and so that she has the time to play upon it. If he does this graciously and even enthusiastically, his wife's music will eventually add happy overtones to their relationship. She may paint, and in time the picture of their marriage will have deeper hues and better perspective. Individual achievement means individual contentedness which cannot keep being reflected in a deeper unity. A union in which interests must be given up by one because of the demands

236

of the other or of children deprives the marriage of elements which can be ill neglected.

We are thus not discounting the basic need for each individual to drink from his own individual cup. This is necessary to avoid standardization and mediocrity. Procrustes saved money on beds but his friends lost their lives when he made them fit his bed. Counselors have the task of helping individuals face their despair when they realize that their marriage partners seek to lop off attitudes, values, or interests which do not correspond to their own. This is not togetherness; this is surgery of a radical nature, and it strips the partner of individuality.

To achieve sympathetic understanding of one another, cooperation in planning, companionship in play and in sexual achievement, togetherness in family life is not easy in today's complex, urban world. The radical differences in cultural backgrounds and consequently of expectations; the half-knowledge and hesitations in the realm of sex and reproduction; the impact of mass media with their insistent demands for conformity to hackneyed values and stereotypes; the constant threat of war and the surging rise of prices—all these combine to place the couple in a social environment of change and anxiety. To establish common interests and ways of solving problems is thus more difficult than it was a hundred years ago.

While modern marriage poses sharper problems it also involves greater challenges to creativity. Young people today who achieve a happy marriage have attained something different in kind from marriages in the past. Neither economic necessity nor social control forces them to remain together when the gears do not mesh. Undoubtedly this new freedom results in more divorces but such freedom also results in more sensitive interrelationships in those marriages (and they are the vast majority) which succeed. These problems then are challenges and opportunities which may result in greater progress.

At the same time the confused state of values and social expectations in themselves render marriage somewhat more precarious than in past generations. Young people need to develop more mature personalities fitted for the acceptance of the responsibilities of marriage and parenthood, and they need to be more skillful in meeting particular problems of marital adjustment that will arise after the marriage service. Hence our concern with the development of those attitudes and increased knowledge of those facts which will be basic tools in achieving togetherness once the marriage bonds have been established.

Marriage means interaction and communication and sharing. If these processes are at a maximum a couple may be said to be truly married. But if they are at a minimum and both partners use the marriage relationship to satisfy only personal aims such as sexual fulfillment or economic support, there is little to keep the marriage together when adversity or conflict threaten it. Thus a pivotal point in understanding success in marriage is to understand means of achieving this togetherness in all aspects of the relationship.

Early Adjustments
in Marriage

INTRODUCTION: THE EARLY MONTHS AND YEARS ARE VERY
IMPORTANT FOR MARRIAGE ADJUSTMENT. A LARGER PER CENT OF
divorces occurs during this period than during any subsequent period
of marriage. Patterns of adjustment are established that tend to be
permanent throughout married life. Many diverse views have been
stated regarding the experience during the first year of marriage and
some of these will be recorded in this chapter. However, the main
theme of the chapter is the establishment of response patterns which will
assure the couple of growing cohesion.

THE VALUE OF MARITAL EXPECTATIONS
FOR EARLY ADJUSTMENT IN MARRIAGE

Baber deplores the one-sided emphasis upon the problems of adjustment at the beginning of marriage. He stresses the prophylactic
power of the expectation of success.[1] For a long time the bride and groom
have been looking forward to their marriage, to living in a home of their
own, to their happiness together. There is a rush of enthusiasm which is

[1] Ray E. Baber, *Marriage and the Family,* New York, McGraw-Hill Book Company, Inc.,
Copyright, 1953, p. 173.

strong enough to carry a couple through the accommodation process of early marriage. There will be disagreements but their joy in their new status is a power for the maintenance of early marital stability.

While such an estimate of the euphoria of marriage as positive force may be correct, it cannot obscure the fact that many couples do fail to make the early adjustments of marriage. The following table indicates the divorce rate by years of marriage:

T A B L E 29. Per Cent of Divorce by Duration of Marriage*

YEARS MARRIED	*Per cent of total divorces*
Under 5	36.0
5–9	29.0
10–14	17.0
15–19	8.0
20 and over	10.0
Total	100.0

* Adapted from Metropolitan Life Insurance Company, Statistical Bulletin, 19:1, p. 9.

Landis studied 409 couples to discover the length of time it took these couples to work out various adjustments in marriage. Husbands and wives responded individually so that a check could be made upon their answers. The remarkable aspect of Figure 7 is the high percentage of couples who reported agreement from the start. Agreement on mutual friends was the least troublesome item and sexual adjustment was achieved last.[2]

Baber believes that the difficulties of early adjustments in marriage are partially due to the way each partner has oversold himself in an effort to impress the other during courtship.[3] Waller and Hill hold that the type of solidarity peculiar to the honeymoon and early months of marriage must break down because no one can continue to live at such a high emotional pitch. When this happens conflict inevitably appears.[4] No matter how successful the engagement process of exploring the reality of the other person, marriage is an undefined situation and each person has a new status which involves playing a new role.[5] Even if

[2] Judson T. Landis and Mary Landis, *Building a Successful Marriage*, New York, Prentice-Hall, Inc., Copyright, 1948, p. 243.   [3] Baber, *op. cit.*, p. 172.
[4] Willard Waller (Revised by Reuben Hill), *The Family: A Dynamic Interpretation* New York, The Dryden Press, Copyright, 1951, p. 253.   [5] *Ibid.*, p. 254.

each person knew the other well before marriage, each was still a single individual. In marriage each is forced to adjust to a person he could not know completely before the wedding and adjust to that person in a new situation. For the marriage partner is also trying to discover the limits and the most satisfactory directions of role playing in this new way of

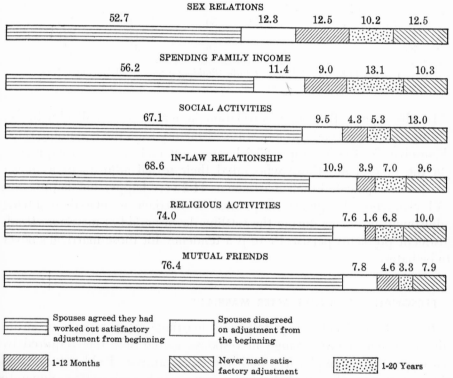

F I G U R E 7. Length of Time Required for Adjustment in Six Areas of Marriage*

* Adapted from Judson T. Landis' study, "Length of Time Required to Achieve Adjustment in Marriage," *American Sociological Review*, 11:666–77, December, 1946. Reproduced by permission.

life. If this redefining of the situation and the role of the self in relation to the emergent role of the mate is not worked out during the first months of marriage, it may never be worked out.

The Landis study indicates that couples who had not worked out adjustment in the early part of marriage had a lower adjustment score than those who had. The following table indicates the relation between the length of time needed to make adjustments in six areas of marriage and marital happiness:

TABLE 30. Self-Rated Happiness of 409 Couples Reporting Various Lengths of Time Required to Make Adjustments in Six Areas*

LENGTH OF TIME REQUIRED	Very happy	Happy	Average
Satisfactory from beginning	53	35	12
1–12 months	50	34	16
1–20 years	35	44	21
Never	19	35	46

* Judson T. Landis and Mary Landis, *Building a Successful Marriage*, New York. Permission to quote granted by Prentice-Hall, Inc., 1948, p. 246.

Landis reports the same correlation in terms of sexual adjustment. Those whose sexual adjustment was satisfactory from the beginning rated themselves 53.3 very happy, 35.3 happy, and 11.4 average in happiness. On the other hand those who rated their sexual adjustment as never satisfactory indicated their marriage as 11.2 very happy, 36.7 happy, and 53.1 average in happiness. Happiness in marriage is related to solving adjustment problems during the settling down period of marriage. If adjustment problems persist, there is a tendency for those marriages never to be happy.

PERSONALITY CHANGES AFTER MARRIAGE

In the transitional period following marriage many aspects of an individual's personality change in response to the new role required by marriage. Waller emphasizes both the reappearance of old patterns and the emergence of new behavior responses.[6] As one settles down to marriage the tenderness and ecstasy of voice and manner give way to more casual approaches. Likewise, if one has been egocentric, or dependent, or introvertive these tendencies, suppressed during courtship, reappear. The husband and wife tend to approximate in their new relationship the roles they learned in their childhood from interaction with their parents. Their parents are the only models they have ever known

In assuming the role of husband and wife, each partner also takes on

[6] Waller (Revised by Hill), *op. cit.*, p. 261.

new tasks, or a constellation of new tasks. These demand a different type of attention and attitude than did the ways of behaving before the wedding. ~~Waller mentions~~ the wife who becomes concerned over the material things in the household and who is upset by the first scratches on her furniture.[7] If she concentrates very much upon her role as a housewife she will inadvertently lose some of the charm that she had for her husband when she played more consistently the role of a companion.

Values change after marriage. One of the surprises after marriage is the constant awareness that now neither person can plan his recreation, his diet, his religious life, his hourly routine, or anything else as he once did. The other person must always be considered. Waller illustrates the shift in values by analyzing changes in leisure-time activities of bachelors and married men.[8] Bachelors pursue thrills, they drink and stay out late. The married man works in his garden, washes his car, and tends to his economic commitments. The married man finds new interests and new satisfactions. Some of these satisfactions come from curbing the egocentric self-indulgences which characterize single life. Day after day he gives up interests, time, money, pleasures, for the sake of the whole family. The immediate rewards of this self-denial are not great.[9] Yet out of such sacrifices family unity is born.

There is a change in the newly married's interest in other people. If the married man no longer needs the thrill-seeking of his bachelor days, he will not have as much in common with his bachelor friends. Anyway, having a wife precludes his taking much part in bachelor activities. Or in bachelor talk, particularly the carefree talk about erotic experiences that single men indulge in, for after marriage there is a rather sudden shift toward regarding as privileged material the same type of experiences at home. Again, he considers his status, and individuals faced with the early adjustments of marriage are not apt to talk very freely about their difficulties to people outside the intimate family circle. This comes about, too, because when one is married one has a stake in the preservation of the moral order. The young married adult who has paid little heed to conventional standards of sexual conduct before marriage begins to have more concern for these standards.[10]

There is also a shift from a picture of the self as a glamorous, exciting lover to that of a husband who must earn a living and face a lifetime of unromantic episodes. This is part of the disillusionment of early

[7] Ibid., pp. 262–263.   [8] Ibid., p. 262.   [9] Ibid., p. 264.   [10] Ibid., p. 267.

marriage. This disillusionment evolves, however, not only from the more realistic picture that one has of his lifetime partner but also from a clearer view of the self. For the same self that existed before it was idealized by the devotion of the other in courtship is recognized again.[11] Psychiatrists find that the motivation for those who cannot accept the ordinary pace of marriage, and who must suffer a perpetual sense of frustration in their marriage or compensate for it by a series of extramarital affairs, comes largely from a sense of inferiority or dissatisfaction with the self.[12] Divorce rarely helps this type of person.

THE DYNAMICS OF EARLY MARRIAGE[13]

We here summarize the conclusions reached by Burgess and Wallin in their study of dynamics of early interaction. Previous to this study, no research material was available that dealt in detail with the interaction during the early years of matrimony. Burgess and Wallin limited their study of marriage to 666 couples who had been married from 3 to 5 years. This material is exceptionally valuable, for Burgess and Wallin have outlined, on the basis of statistical analysis and interview material, those factors they believe to be most important in determining early adjustment in marriage. They summarize their findings at follows:

Those factors which are essential to happiness in the initial years of marriage were found to be: (1) love and affection, (2) satisfactory sexual relations, (3) emotional interdependence, and (4) temperamental interaction. When there was mutual love and affection the marriage was integrated and developed, but when there was indifference or hostility the conjugal relation was frustrated and disrupted. When sexual relations were enjoyable the result was integration, but when there was sexual dissatisfaction the partnership was disrupted. Mutual dependence was developmental, emotional independence was disruptive. Compatibility of temperamental interaction was an integrative factor while temperamental incompatibility was frustrating to the couple.[14]

[11] John Levy and Ruth Monroe, *The Happy Family*, New York, Alfred A. Knopf, Inc. Copyright, 1946, p. 67.   [12] *Ibid.*, pp. 67–68.
[13] This heading is a modification of the chapter heading entitled, "The Dynamics of Marriage" from Ernest W. Burgess and Paul Wallin, *Engagement and Marriage*, Philadelphia, J. B. Lippincott Company, 1953. The nature of the sample raises some question about the accuracy of generalizing upon their findings in terms of marriage as a whole They are certainly applicable to a study of early marriage interaction. Quotations from this book are used by permission of J. B. Lippincott Company.
[14] *Ibid.*, p. 418.

244

INTIMACY OF ASSOCIATION

Material already presented from Karlsson and Locke has pointed up the importance of communication of ideas and affection in marriage. This is another way of saying that companionship (in America, at least) is the most essential requisite for happy marriage. Burgess and Wallin propose the theory that "love, mutual enjoyment of sexual relations and emotional interdependence are typically the strongest social-psychological factors holding the married couple together and making for happiness and satisfaction in that relation."[15]

Love. Love is defined by Burgess and Wallin as "the inner feeling of affection, rapport, and attachment."[16] They hold that the type of love which makes for mutual success in middle-class America is not romantic infatuation but rather "friendship deepening into love." This has its origin in the companionship of courtship and engagement, and deepens during the early years of marriage. The following quotations from interviews indicate something of the change that comes into the love relationship during the early years of marriage:

> *Husband:* I am more in love now. At that time it was a romantic love. Now it is something deeper. It is a mutual understanding of each other; a faith in each other; a companionship. When we are apart we yearn to be together. She has said she is more in love now than ever.

> *Wife:* I think my love has grown stronger. I think it is a different kind. In the first place, I think it is a much more sensible kind. I think it is truer and more understanding.[17]

These interviews and others which Burgess and Wallin record seem to indicate that as romantic love diminishes, companionship and affectional love increase. These authors measured on a scale the degree of companionship in marriage and thus determined a companionship score for each couple. They then correlated this companionship score with the couple's love score. In this way they attempted to discover any association between the growth of love after marriage and the degree of companionship which existed. They found the correlation between the companionship score and love to be +.39 for husbands and +.40 for wives.[18] Statistically, this indicates that there is an association between these two factors which cannot be accounted for by chance. In our society, ac-

[15] *Ibid.,* p. 419.   [16] *Ibid.,* p. 419.   [17] *Ibid.,* p. 420.   [18] *Ibid.,* p. 421.

cording to this study, satisfactory love relationships are related to the development of companionship. Newly married couples concerned about a solid beginning will certainly strive for growing companionship.

Sex Relations. It is the thesis of Burgess and Wallin that sexual adjustment is a function of growing adjustment and relatedness in other aspects of marriage. They also believe that satisfying sexual relations "markedly reinforce" love. The following interviews indicate that passion may draw a couple together but becomes less important after marriage; then the sexual relation is a way of expressing affectional feelings. The following excerpts from interviews express this well:

> *Wife:* My idea of love goes much deeper than even companionship and understanding. I have found love to be not merely an attraction, but something live and growing that makes you forget yourself in an effort to bring complete happiness to your husband—to do things with him and for him that will make his whole being glow with the warmth of satisfaction. We have so many times said to each other that the love we had when we were first married seems so small compared to the love we have come to know now. Sex life is not merely the physical satisfaction that I thought it was going to be, but is an expression of love—a much needed outlet for deep-rooted emotion.

> *Wife:* Sexual intercourse is the only complete way of demonstrating your affection for a person. I would feel pretty deprived if I could not express my affection for my husband in that way, because I would feel that any other expression would be inadequate.

> *Husband:* My love for my wife has changed from the physical attraction to an increase in appreciation for her personality as a whole.[19]

Burgess and Wallin remark that for "practically all couples" sex is secondary to companionship and other aspects of marriage. The following brings out this fact even more strongly. It compares the association of love and of sexual adjustment to happiness scores in the marriage.

Love is associated with happiness in marriage for men by the Pearsonian Correlation figure of .65 and for women by the figure of .63. Sexual adjustment is correlated with happiness for husbands by a score of .45 and for wives by a score of .29. The nearer the Pearsonian Correlation approaches 1.0 the greater is the association of the factors under investigation.[20] Burgess and Wallin state that these are statistically

[19] *Ibid.*, pp. 421–422.   [20] *Ibid.*, p. 423.

significant differences which tend to support the theory that companionship love is more important than sex for marital adjustment.

In the early years of marriage, passion and physical satisfaction recede into the background, and sex as an expression of developing companionship takes its place. This conclusion is justified by the many cases in which sexual adjustment is indifferent or inadequate but in which other binding factors make the love relationship a strong one. Whether or not sexual deprivation would alter marital adjustment over a longer period of years is not known and could not be known from this study. But companionship love is evidently a more dynamic factor than sex in the early interaction of married couples. Nevertheless, young couples need to utilize every resource to develop a mutually satisfying sexual relationship.

Demonstrations of Affection. Two aspects of the demonstration of affection illustrated by the interview material given by Burgess and Wallin are interesting because they seem to underline material presented previously in this chapter. The first has to do with carrying out in marriage roles played in the parental family. It was suggested by Waller that there is a strong tendency to approximate these roles because they are the only models that the young husband or the wife know. The following interviews seem to confirm this explanation of some behavior in marriage:

> *Woman:* Our families are not particularly demonstrative. If anything, the opposite. Neither of us has gone for anything like demonstration of affection.

> *Woman:* I am inclined to be indifferent about demonstrations of affection. This seems to run in our family; we never were. He is demonstrative. I like it, but I don't give it. He likes to get it very much.[21]

The second important insight gained about demonstration of affection is that it changes significantly after the honeymoon or early months of marriage. This is part of the settling-down process. However, if this tendency goes too far, and the relationship becomes too casual the partners, and particularly the wife, may come to resent the lack of demonstration of affection:

> For the first one or two years after our marriage we used to go out the twentieth of every month, our wedding anniversary. One month we both

[21] *Ibid.*, p. 424.

forgot but it made no difference. We now usually congratulate each other and sometimes do, and sometimes don't, make an occasion of it—I bake a cake or we have wine with our dinner.

Woman: Demonstration of affection is not nearly as important as it was when we were first married. It is natural for us to show affection. If he leaves for a few hours and he does not kiss me I don't notice that.[22]

Burgess and Wallin conclude that "a display of love does not in itself insure the growth of a warm feeling between husband and wife."[23] They also think that demonstration of affection is "integrative but not dynamic." This is evidently an impressionistic conclusion because they present no statistical evidence comparing the importance of demonstrations of affection with that of love or sexual adjustment. Their case-study material indicates that demonstrations of affection are much prized in early marriage—particularly by the wife. The development of a pattern of emotional response should be a goal of early adjustment.

Emotional Interdependence. Emotional interdependence is defined as the expectation and reception of sympathetic understanding, encouragement, and expressions of appreciation.[24] Three patterns are possible: (1) both emotionally dependent upon each other, (2) one emotionally dependent, and (3) both more or less emotionally independent. Of these three patterns the first is the most integrative as far as marriage is concerned. This conclusion is based on impressions as no statistical measure of the three patterns of interdependence is offered.[25] An excerpt from an interview indicates how in early marriage the partners come to meet each other's needs.

Wife: I need sympathy and encouragement. I think he gives it very well. Better now than when we were first married because we understand each other better. That goes for him too. He needs encouragement. When we were first married I didn't realize I should encourage him about little things such as writing a paper or speaking in public. . . .[26]

In this case the development of "appropriate response patterns" to fit the need of the partner occurred when mutual understanding increased. This somewhat modifies the theory of disillusionment, for in many cases it is only after the removal of masks that partners come to understand the real needs of each other and to react constructively to them. In other cases the husband and the wife may wish for sympathy or encour-

[22] *Ibid.,* p. 424.   [23] *Ibid.,* p. 425.   [24] *Ibid.,* p. 425.   [25] *Ibid.,* p. 425.   [26] *Ibid.,* p. 426.

248

agement and not receive it because the other mate cannot temperamentally or emotionally meet the need. Again, an emotionally dependent spouse may be married to one who is entirely self-sufficient. Another situation occurs when both members of the union are self-sufficient. Burgess and Wallin conclude that when this is so, one condition for integrating the marriage is lacking because the unification which comes from mutual encouragement and the sharing of sympathetic understanding is absent.[27] Certainly all that has been said in the chapter on Psychological Factors in Wise Marriage Choice would apply here. A great deal more specific attention needs to be given to the ways in which individuals with different personality configurations adjust in early marriage. Burgess and Wallin's study concludes that failure to obtain emotional support in marriage is frustrating.[28] Specific concentration on discovering the deepest needs of the mate in the early months of marriage will be correspondingly rewarding.

Temperamental Interaction. The term "temperamental interaction" is not defined by the writers but is said to be employed in the broad sense of "popular usage." The descriptions subsumed under this title are really temperamental and emotional interactions for they deal not only with such items as introversion and moods but also with hostility, anger, resentments, and other emotional responses. An analysis of a case with adaptations made by interviewees in adjusting to temperamental or emotional disharmonies in engagement and early marriages was presented in Chapter XI.[29]

In some cases temperamental differences prove to be integrating because they are complementary. Burgess and Wallin conclude that marital clashes should be appraised in terms of their long-run effect.[30] So appraised, they indicate that many husbands and wives wish to solve marital clashes for "they realize that they are subject to control." These interviews serve to underline what has been said earlier in the chapter about the new problems of personality and interpersonal relations that appear after marriage. Here the will to understand and adjust appears important to early marital adjustment.

Cultural Accommodation and Assimilation. The four factors already considered are regarded by Burgess and Wallin as being essential and indispensable for marital adjustment.[31] The factors to be considered next,

[27] *Ibid.*, p. 429. [28] *Ibid.*, p. 429.
[29] See Chapters VI and XI for analyses of temperamental interaction.
[30] *Ibid.*, p. 436. [31] *Ibid.*, p. 437.

cultural interaction, stimulation of interests, domesticity, and expectation of the continuity of the union, must also be present to assure marital unity. They are not, however, of such great consequence as the four items already considered and will not therefore receive as much attention. Husband and wife must adjust differences in culture during their early marital life. After marriage the process of conflict, accommodation, and assimilation develop as an effort to adjust to differences in cultural backgrounds. In accommodation the husband or the wife agrees to tolerate differences. In assimilation one member of the couple becomes converted to the attitudes and habits of the other. A third possible solution is for the couple to discover a new pattern which is more imaginative and satisfying than either of the old ones. In conclusion Burgess and Wallin say that the best test for measuring the cultural interaction of husband and wife is to discover whether their interests and values are mutually stimulating and promote their individual personality development.[32]

Stimulating Interests. Burgess and Wallin found that common interests may be classified in terms of the degree to which they bind couples together. They suggest the following classification:

(1) Little or no binding effect: *sports and games*
(2) Some binding effect: *friends, reading and dancing*
(3) Considerable binding effect: *music, theater, church*
(4) Great binding effect: *same or similar professional interests, active community service, devotion to a common cause.*[33]

It is interesting to raise the point as to whether a sample containing individuals who had been married twenty or more years would not result in the transposition of some of these ratings. However, during early marriage it appears that music, the theater, religion, similar professional interests, active community service, and devotion to a common cause are the more dynamic types of common interest. Burgess and Wallin stress the point that in some cases any common interest such as bridge or golf may be as integrating as these mentioned. It is probable that this rating of the binding effect of common interests reflects the high educational status of the Burgess-Wallin interviews. In marriage the development of a group of common interests to expand the areas in which the couple is interdependent is important. The newly married couple need to make explorations during their early adjustment in order to locate a maximum number of jointly enjoyed pursuits.

[32] *Ibid.*, p. 467.   [33] *Ibid.*, p. 462.

Domesticity. In discussing domesticity Burgess and Wallin state that while a chief factor in the success of marriage is the extent to which domesticity reinforces the other factors which are components of companionship, nevertheless, home-centered activities should not be carried to the point where they would mean the complete exclusion of interests outside the home.[34] Thus the ideal situation for the development of the marriage is one in which the vital domestic interests are primary but in which there is time and energy left for participation in one or more educational or cultural activities significant for the personality development of husband and wife.[35]

Burgess and Wallin found that domesticity could be described in six pattern types. These six patterns may be put on a continuum from the most to the least preoccupation with family services.[36] In analyzing the relationship of these six patterns to marital success, they conclude that "the extremes of domesticity and nondomesticity may be inimical to success in marriage and the golden mean which integrated domestic and vital outside interests appears most favorable to marital adjustment. . . . "[37]

It is not easy for a young couple to emerge from a period of almost complete concentration upon courtship and create a new domestic life. In so doing they must balance domesticity with social life, recreational life, aesthetic life, and many other forms of stimulating activity. Burgess and Wallin's emphasis on the "golden mean" stresses the importance of both personality fulfillment and family cohesion.

Expectation of Continuity. The factor of expectation of continuity is related to Baber's emphasis upon the expectation of success in marriage. However, Burgess and Wallin relate their expectation to conventionality and identification while Baber refers to the emotional thrust of premarital hopes. Conventionality refers to the degree to which a person identifies his values with the standards and values of society. The religious factor is an important aspect of conventionality for the couple who happen to belong to the Roman Catholic, Episcopal, or any other church group that puts powerful sanctions on couples for the continuity of marriage. But if too great emphasis is put on living up to conventional standards, companionship goals may suffer.[38] Conventionality is certainly not the potent force it was in past generations in holding an incompatible couple together. At best, expectation of continuity is a static and stabilizing factor when it is based on the degree of conventionality of the couple, their sensitivity to what people say, or their conformity to ideals

[34] *Ibid.*, p. 445. [35] *Ibid.*, pp. 445–446. [36] *Ibid.*, p. 446.
[37] *Ibid.*, pp. 450–467. [38] *Ibid.*, p. 451.

251

of duty learned in the parental home or other character-building institutions.[39] On the other hand, in marriages that grow in cohesion each comes to identify his interests, his goals, his future with his mate. In the Burgess-Wallin interview material this finds expression in the consciousness of the merging of personalities, reaffirmation of love, and in planning for the future.[40] If the expectation of continuity is based on shared experience, on the identification of the husband with the wife, then it is not a static but a dynamic factor in integration.

CONCLUSION

Early marital adjustment is a complex process which results in interactional patterns which tend to persist throughout marriage. Such adjustments are inevitable and involve modifications of personality values and expectation. The achievement of companionship, sexual adjustment, emotional interdependence, and temperamental compatibility are crucial for the development of the union or the disruption of the relationship. The important areas in which a young couple should strive for maximum growth have been outlined. Certainly, considering the totality of personality and interpersonality changes that occur in these early years of marriage, they may be considered most significant for later marital adjustment.

VISUAL AIDS

Who's Right, McGraw-Hill Marriage Series, McGraw-Hill Book Company.

READINGS

ERNEST W. BURGESS and PAUL WALLIN, *Engagement and Marriage,* Philadelphia, J. B. Lippincott Company, 1953, Chapter XIV.

RAY E. BABER, *Marriage and the Family,* New York, McGraw-Hill Book Company, Inc., 1953, Chapter VI.

JUDSON T. LANDIS and MARY LANDIS, *Readings in Marriage and the Family,* New York, Prentice-Hall, Inc., 1952, Chapter VII.

WILLARD WALLER (Revised by Reuben Hill), *The Family: A Dynamic Interpretation,* New York, The Dryden Press, 1952, Chapter XIII.

[39] *Ibid.,* p. 467. [40] *Ibid.,* p. 454.

Planning for Children in the Home

INTRODUCTION: SOME EIGHTY PER CENT OF ALL MARRIAGES
RESULT IN CHILDREN. WOOD AND DICKINSON GENERALIZE ABOUT
the coming of children into the home in this way:

> The joys and responsibilities of parenthood enrich family experience and bring the particular couple into the endless process of renewal and ongoing of all the interests and values of the race. The world is constantly being fashioned and re-fashioned in its homes. To say that the social virtues of tenderness, responsibility, sympathy and devotion have their spots in parental experience is true and important, but pale compared with the radiant joy that parents have in the renewal of themselves and their love in children. In the family plan therefore children should have a central place. It is better to spend money for children than for "nice things" or an expensive manner of living.[1]

The average laymen would react favorably to this quotation. Practically all religious groups have stressed the duty and the joy involved in bearing and bringing up the next generation. The Catholic Church specifically states that the purpose of marriage is to produce new souls for the glory of God. Most Protestant churches echo this sentiment. The

[1] Leland Foster Wood and Robert L. Dickinson, *Harmony in Marriage*, New York, The Round Table Press, 1948, p. 86. Reprinted by permission.

ideal image of marriage includes the crib and the baby buggy. Members of every segment of society believe that children insure the happiness and fulfill the meaning of marriage.

CHILDREN AND MARITAL HAPPINESS

Certain scholars have carefully measured the adjustment of families which have children with that of families which do not. Bernard, Hamilton, Locke, and Terman have found no indication that having children contributed anything that differentiated the happy from the unhappily married couples. Landis and Landis found that chances for married happiness decreased as the number of children decreased.[2]

Paul H. Jacobson has contributed one of the most valuable recent studies. On the basis of a very careful investigation he concludes:

> It is easily apparent that the differential in divorce rate between "childless" couples and those with children is not uniform throughout married life. Rather, divorce is much more frequent among those without children in the early years of marriage, and the differential diminishes rapidly thereafter. The divorce rate for parent-couples climbs to a maximum of 15 per 1000 at duration 3–4 years, whereas the rate for couples without children reaches a peak of 44 per 1000 one year later. The chances for divorce among the "childless" fall off so much more rapidly after the peak that the ratio between the rates for the two groups drops from about 3½ after four years of marriage, to 3 by the tenth year, and 2 by the twentieth year. Indeed, after the thirtieth wedding anniversary, the two rates are practically identical.[3]

The Williamson study confirmed these findings that childless marriages did not necessarily prove to be unhappy. In fact husbands were happier when they had no children. The percentage of those having no children and having children who fall into the happiness group were 38.4 and 18.2 respectively which has a critical ratio of 2.7. Other studies, somewhat more refined, suggest that these conclusions may be modified. Burgess and Cottrell discovered that the question might be more adequately handled by investigating the relationship of having children and desiring them.[4] The following figure indicates the correlations they found in hap-

[2] Judson T. Landis and Mary Landis, *Building a Successful Marriage*, New York, Prentice-Hall, Inc., 1948, p. 434.

[3] Paul H. Jacobson, "Differentials in Divorce by Duration of Marriage and Size of Family," *American Sociological Review*, 15, 1950, pp. 235–244. Reprinted by permission.

[4] Ernest W. Burgess and Leonard Cottrell, *Predicting Success or Failure in Marriage*, New York, Prentice-Hall, Inc., 1939, p. 260.

piness ratings and desire for and having children. This figure indicates that for some men and women desire for children is associated with adjustment and for others having unwanted children is a factor associated with maladjustment. Rather than generalizing about the influence of children on family togetherness it is better to say that for some, perhaps for most, families, children are an added factor of happiness and for some they are an added cause of worry and frustration. On the basis of the Milbank Memorial Study, Robert B. Reed found an increase in marital adjustment with increasing success in controlling fertility according to the desires of the couple.[5]

Children contribute to happiness when they arrive in the number desired and at the time the couple desires them. There is no such thing

FIGURE 8. Desire for Children and Marital Adjustment*

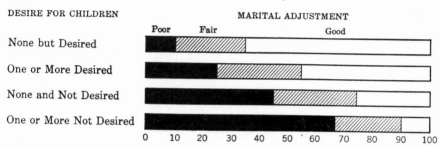

* Ernest W. Burgess and Leonard Cottrell, *Predicting Success or Failure in Marriage,* New York, Prentice-Hall, Inc., 1939, p. 260. Reproduced by permission.

as an optimum-sized family but when each family is planned in accordance with the wishes of the wife and the husband, greater happiness will result. Those couples who do not feel capable of assuming the responsibility of child-rearing find in children an additional source of anxiety, while those who want children may expect that they will add to their total adjustment.

If, then, the contribution of children to marital adjustment depends upon success in controlling fertility, we must explore the possibilities of that control. Children who are not wanted not only contribute to family disorganization but generally receive a poor psychological conditioning because of their rejection. Insistence that couples who are not ready for parenthood have children will impair the marriage. Sentimental indi-

[5] Robert B. Reed, *Social and Psychological Factors Affecting Fertility,* VIII, "The Interrelationship of Marital Adjustment, Fertility Control and Size of Family," New York, Milbank Memorial Fund, 1948, p. 423.

255

viduals who wish to foist parenthood on reluctant individuals may accomplish the very opposite of their ultimate goals. A short excerpt from a case history illustrates this point.

> I suppose that although our problem is a sexual one it has some roots far back in our marriage. Part of the trouble I lay at the door of a doctor who gave me some mighty bad birth control advice when we were first married. The result was that I got pregnant on my honeymoon and I have always resented that doctor and that pregnancy and I suppose I have rejected the child, too.[6]

Bossard comments on the situation in which young couples are pressured into being parents against their will:

> A final word should be said about parents who reject their children. Not all are heartless or selfish, as is often assumed. Many young people who become parents and reject their children are themselves victims of maladjustment; hence they are only the transmitters of what was done to them. Some of these parents may appreciate their own inaptitudes, so their fundamental unwillingness to be parents represents a reasoned judgment rather than a selfish whim. Again, some young people are high pressured into being parents, and their resentment against this pressure may find expression in their attitudes toward their children.[7]

Our emphasis then must be upon the education of the generation that must bear the responsibility of procreation so that they will be both mature enough to desire children and intelligent enough to rear well-adjusted children. This means more emphasis upon parent education and personality adjustment. Involved in this is an understanding of the contributions which children may make to the well-adjusted home. Bossard has studied the contributions of children in the home.

CONTRIBUTIONS OF CHILDREN TO PARENTS

Bossard begins his analysis by stating what he calls the Law of Interaction.[8] The law is stated thus: With the addition of each person to a family or primary group, the number of persons increases in the simplest arithmetical progression in whole numbers, and the number of personal interrelationships within the group increases in the order of triangular numbers. So:

---

[6] From a case study in the author's files.
[7] James H. S. Bossard, *The Sociology of Child Development*, New York, Harper Brothers, 1948, pp. 338–339. Reprinted by permission.   [8] *Ibid.*, pp. 145–149.

Number of persons...2, 3, 4, 5, 6, 7, 8
Number of personal relationships.........................1, 3, 6, 10, 15, 21, 28.

The relationships between a husband, wife, and one child are diagrammed this way:

But if two more children are added to the diagram expression, the
dynamic interaction of these five looks like this:

The result of this multiplication of interactions may be considered in
terms of our earlier discussion of the socialization of children. Obviously
from the standpoint of the child, the growing number of contacts with
diverse individuals gives the child a growing fund of experience with
others on which to base later social responses. It may likewise broaden
the perspective and total emotional capacity and life of the parent, provided that parent has the "ability to enlarge the capacity for such intimate relationships as the family makes possible."[9] A second aspect of
growth in family life is the "Expansion of Family Interests." Bossard lists
many of the new elements that become important upon the birth of a
child such as finance, insurance, home-ownership, assessment of the
community, religious education. Even more important is the new stake
the parent has in the "shape of things to come" because the world of
which he is a participating citizen will be the environment of his child.
Interests such as peace or public health which before had been given
nominal attention take on deeper significance. We many conclude that
the addition of children means the growth of a more profound general
philosophy of life.

The third point is the lasting emotional satisfactions derived from
parenthood. Here we quote Bossard directly:

> The child not only broadens the interests of parents in the community
> and social matters of all kinds, but gives to most parents emotionally
> satisfying interests of long duration. Nothing is perhaps more essential

[9] *Ibid.*, p. 149.

to a happy life than such interests. . . . Emotional exploitation of children is news; behind the news are innumerable parents who find in their interest in children deep and abiding satisfactions without exacting any crippling bondage. This is the essence of normal and happy parenthood.[10]

There are many women who, during their child-bearing years, are so content with their own personal achievements that any vision of their future needs is obscured. When they become older and lonely they may wish they had not concentrated so completely upon personal goals and had included children in their total life pattern.

A fourth concomitant of the rearing of children is the persistent stimulus to a more mature spiritual and intellectual life. Not only do children ask innumerable questions of philosophic or religious profundity, but they pose questions of value in terms of guidance situations. What shall I tell my daughter about drinking at sorority parties? What kind of training will best enable her to fit into our materialistic culture in terms of money stewardship? No parent may escape the consequences of the answers to both sets of questions. They will be indelibly reflected in later life decisions of the child. Consequently the parent must grow even though he is reluctant to face ethical or spiritual questions dormant since his own childhood.

Bossard stresses two other important contributions of children to parental growth; one is the growing insight into life's processes, and a second is an insight into the meaning of life itself. There is a final point which is implied but not directly stated by Bossard. This is the contribution of parenthood to the togetherness of husband and wife, irrespective of what the children directly contribute to the parents. With the introduction of children into the family the focus of attention shifts partially from an emphasis upon the pleasures or the needs of husband and wife to the needs of the child. This shift of emphasis may of course introduce new aspects of conflict if there is jealousy toward the child or if the parents' philosophies of child-rearing are very widely different. But in most cases both parents begin to plan for the child and the future. Furthermore, even if their own interests are rather widely dissimilar in other areas they plan for the child together, enjoy him together, and, if he is ill, worry together. The depth of their identification with the child gives this togetherness a special meaning. Thus, children may contribute much to the elimination of conflict by sublimating minor personal considerations to the larger concern with the child. Bossard concludes:

[10] *Ibid.*, pp. 151–152.

This, then, is the real end of life, that we receive, as it were, the torch from one generation, to carry it over to the next generation. This is what the child brings, in some varying form of expression, to each parent who has the capacity to perceive it.[11]

In establishing a frame of reference for the family, the conclusion is reached that children add many dimensions of value to the home and to the personalities of parents, contribute to the togetherness of the parents, and add to the general investment of citizens in their communities. This means that family planning is based on the realities of personality inter-action. With this background of appreciation of the contributions of children the problem of their spacing can now be discussed.

FACTORS IN FAMILY SPACING

There are many considerations which need emphasis in discussing family planning. The first important factor in the spacing of the family is that of timing the arrival of the first child to give it maximum psycho-logical security. This is not always easy because no matter when the first child comes, there is a certain quotient of inexperience which can be overcome only by trial and error. Nevertheless, the arrival of the first child should be postponed until the emotional nest is ready for him. It is unfortunate if the first child arrives so soon that he is a victim of the normal conflicts incident to early adjustment in marriage. Individuals with well-defined values will have conflicts because the man and the woman rarely have had identical backgrounds. If they quarrel in the course of compromising these differences they are not abnormal. But it is unfortunate if these conflicts affect the emotional security of their first child. It is therefore wise to postpone the coming of the first child until the first general adjustments of marriage have been completed.

FINANCES AND THE FIRST BIRTH

A second consideration involves finances. Very few young couples begin marriage with sufficient savings to be able to underwrite children immediately. If a couple have a child in the first nine or ten months of marriage this upsets their plans to lay aside sufficient funds to meet new expenses of marriage and, specifically, the expenses of a child. Today many new wives expect to work so that they may have the money to

[11] *Ibid.,* p. 156.

make a down payment on a house or a car, or to have a baby. The couple lay their plans in this way. If these plans are interrupted by a child, the parents will generally not welcome him as wholeheartedly as they would if his coming had been more in keeping with their schedule.

SEXUAL ADJUSTMENT AND FIRST BIRTHS

A third consideration involves sexual adjustment. The advent of pregnancy may mar the growth toward sexual adjustment. A client said recently:

> We really have never had time to get adjusted. My three pregnancies came so close together that, since the beginning of our marriage, I have been pregnant most of the time. I think that is one reason why we are so badly adjusted. The first pregnancy came before we had adjusted sexually and when I became pregnant we didn't make much progress.

The most extensive study of the interval between marriage and first birth has been made by Christensen in a study based on a sample of 1,670 marriages. This 1939 study involved Mormon individuals who lay great stress on early and large families. Christensen concluded:

(1) The modal interval between the marriage of parents and the birth of their first child was about ten or eleven calendar months.

(2) The trend from 1905 to 1935 was toward a lengthening of this interval.

(3) Heterogeneity between husband and wife, as to both age and premarital residence, was associated with the long time-intervals.

(4) In general, the older the couple at marriage the longer was the interval between that marriage and the birth of a first child.

(5) The occupations of farming and unskilled labor were associated with short intervals and the skilled and professional occupations with long intervals.

(6) Relief work was associated with disproportionately short time-intervals.

(7) Urban dwellers showed longer intervals than did the residents of rural communities.[12]

Anderson's study of the spacing of children of former Cornell University students reported that most of them had their first child in the second year of their marriage.[13]

[12] Harold T. Christensen, *Marriage Analysis*, New York, The Ronald Press Company, 1950, p. 363. Reprinted by permission.   [13] *Ibid.*, p. 363.

A couple who have saved enough so that financial strain does not undermine the joy of having a child, and who have adjusted psychologically and sexually so that the child does not threaten future growth in adjustment are ready for parenthood. On the other hand would-be parents should not wait too long. Their pattern of living should not become so fixed that it is difficult for them to adjust to an infant.

TIME-INTERVAL BETWEEN CHILDREN

A fourth consideration is the time-interval between children. There should be enough time so that the couple is ready financially for the second child. The first child should be old enough when the second pregnancy starts so that the mother does not have to lift and carry him everywhere. Again some time should elapse to allow the mother to regain her health. Obstetricians in general think that at least two years should elapse between births. Infant death rates are definitely higher when children are more closely spaced, probably because the mother has not fully recovered her strength. Another factor has to do with the relationship between the children. Children who are too far apart definitely do not have common interests or the degree of companionship which characterizes siblings born closer together.

TOTAL SIZE OF FAMILY

The fifth consideration has to do with the total number of children desired by a family. The following table shows the size of the family

TABLE 31. Average Number of Persons per Family Household in the United States, 1790–1950*

Year	Persons per Family	Year	Persons per Family	Year	Persons per Family
1790	5.7	1880	5.0	1920	4.3
1850	5.6	1890	4.9	1930	4.1
1860	5.3	1900	4.7	1940	3.8
1870	5.1	1910	4.5	1950	3.6

* Figure for 1790 from U. S. Bureau of Census, *A Century of Population Growth from the First Census of the United States to the Twelfth, 1790–1900*, 1909, p. 96; 1900–1920 from the *Fourteenth Census of the United States, 1920, Population, General Report and Analytical Tables*, 2, p. 1266; 1930 and 1940 from the *Sixteenth Census of the United States, 1940, Population, Families, Size of Families and Age of Head*, p. 4; 1950, 1951, *Bureau of the Census, Current Population Report*, Series, p. 20, No. 38.

from 1790 through 1950. Family size decreased from 4.1 in 1930 to 3.5 in 1951.

THE BIRTH RATE

The following figure indicates the birth rate itself. While it has increased since the war, this increase is not expected to continue because the generation born in the 1930's is a very small base for children in the 1950's and 1960's.

FIGURE 9. The Number of Births in the United States per 1000 Population, 1871–1950*

* Alfred J. Lotka, "Modern Trends in the Birth Rate," *Annals of the American Academy of Political and Social Science,* 188, 1936, pp. 2–3; Bureau of the Census, *Statistical Abstract,* 1943, p. 68. Provisional figures for 1943, 21.6, and for 1944, 20.3, per 1000 population from Bureau of the Census, *Monthly Vital Statistics Bulletin,* 7, No. 13, March, 13, 1945, p. 1. The 1946 figure of 23.3 from the *1948 Statistical Abstract,* Bureau of the Census.

DIFFERENTIALS IN THE BIRTH RATE

There are wide differences in the fertility rates of contrasting groups in society. Kiser and Whelpton's study by religious affiliation of 41,498 couples in 1947 showed that Jewish couples are the least fertile, producing about 25 per cent fewer children than Protestants. Protestants on the other hand are not as productive as Catholics who are 18 per cent more fertile.[14] Fertility rates also vary with education of parents. College graduates do not reproduce themselves. According to a 1948 report of the Metropolitan Life Insurance Company the following relationships existed between rural-urban dwelling and college attendance. The table shows that rural families have more children than urban and that non-college women are more fertile than college women. Fifty-four per cent of urban college wives were childless as compared to 33 per cent of non-college urban women. Birth rates also vary in accordance with occupa-

T A B L E 32. College Background and Educational Background as Related to Percentage of Childlessness for Women between 20 and 24*

	Rural	Rural Non-Farm	Urban
College educated	35.4	49.1	54.1
Non-college	23.4	26.3	33.0

* Metropolitan Life Insurance Company, "Childlessness Highest Among Urban Wives," Statistical Bulletin, January, 1948, p. 8. Reprinted by permission.

tional group and income. Until recently the higher the social rating of the occupation and the higher the income bracket the lower the fertility. But this trend is being reversed somewhat. Larger families among upper-class groups are now more common than previously. In speaking of this factor Christensen says:

> It is conceivable, however, that a reversal in some of the fertility differentials would be of benefit to society. From the standpoint of economic welfare it would be better if those who could most afford it would have more children, and those who could least afford it, fewer children. From the standpoint of cultural opportunity it would be better if the well educated would play a larger role in reproduction, and the uneducated a smaller role. Since economic success and higher education are at least partially selective, it follows that a reversal of present birth rate differentials in these areas would be eugenically beneficial. There is need for some kind of public policy and educational program directed toward these ends.[15]

[14] Clyde V. Kiser and P. K. Whelpton, "Progress Report on the Study of Social and Psychological Factors Affecting Fertility," *American Sociological Review*, April, 1947, pp. 175–186. [15] Christensen, *op. cit.*, pp. 358–359.

FAMILY PLANNING AND CONTRACEPTION

If it is wise to postpone the advent of the first child and to protect the health of the mother between births, it is important to know how this may be done. There are various methods of contraception or birth-control. The history of birth-control is as old as marriage itself but only today has science provided adequate methods. In discussing the various methods of birth-control we shall relate them to religious groups. These groups have varying attitudes toward contraception.

Birth-control is still a controversial subject. Recently the Roman Catholic Church reaffirmed its historic position, with certain clarifications. It declared that the only methods of contraception permitted were the rhythm and the temperature methods, both of which require the exercise of self-control; and that even these methods were not to be used indiscriminately but only for a "grave" reason such as serious economic stress or a condition of health which made child-bearing dangerous. No mechanical or chemical methods may be used, only the spiritual method of self-denial.[16]

THE TEMPERATURE METHOD

The temperature method of birth-control is based upon continence during the period immediately before and after ovulation. If one asks how one is to know whether or not ovulation has taken place, the answer is that a new method of using temperature charts assures this knowledge. We now know that temperature varies rather precisely with changes in the menstrual cycle as indicated in the following diagram.

FIGURE 10. Temperature and the Menstrual Cycle

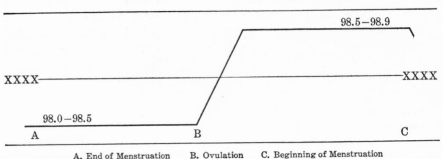

A. End of Menstruation   B. Ovulation   C. Beginning of Menstruation

[16] *The Tidings*, Catholic publication of the Los Angeles Diocese of Catholic Churches, November 14, 1951.

At the conclusion of each menstrual cycle the temperature falls to some point below normal (Point "C"). At ovulation it begins to rise and remains steady until the next menstrual period when it drops again. If a woman keeps a careful record of her temperature for several months she will be able to tell precisely the day when ovulation occurs, at Point "B." She is fertile after ovulation.

This method has helped those couples who were having difficulty achieving pregnancy so to time their coitus that they would have a maximum chance of insuring pregnancy. Furthermore it is a very inexpensive test of pregnancy, for every woman who keeps such a chart knows that if her temperature stays up for several weeks she is probably pregnant, unless some factor such as a cold or other infectious condition influences her condition.

THE RHYTHM METHOD

The second method which is approved by Catholics is the rhythm method, so-called because of the regularity of the menstrual cycle. This is the method which Pope Pius XI approved in his encyclical on marriage of December 31, 1930, when he said:

> Nor are those considered as acting against nature who in their married life use their right in proper manner, although on account of natural reasons of time and of certain defects, new life cannot be brought forth.[17]

This method depends again on exact knowledge of the menstrual cycle. This information may be obtained by keeping a careful record of the cycle for some months previous to marriage. When this is done the period when fertilization may take place can be predicted.

The ovulation period for a woman with a normal menstrual cycle of 28 days is from 12 to 16 days prior to the first day of menstruation. However, since the spermatozoa sometimes live for three days, three additional days must be added to the 16-day period, making it 19 days. In calculating the period of possible impregnation one counts back from the next expected period. Thus the time-interval when pregnancy would be possible is from 12 to 19 days before the first day of the next expected menstruation. Thus a woman who is on a regular 28-day cycle and expects to menstruate on November 28 can determine her fertile period

[17] T. S. Welton, *The Modern Method of Birth Control,* New York, Grosset and Dunlap, 1943, p. 148.

by counting back 19 days (or to November 9). Fertilization presumably is possible during this period. It is represented on a calendar like this:

FIGURE 11. Fertility and the Menstrual Cycle

NOVEMBER						
SUN.	MON.	TUES.	WED.	THURS.	FRI.	SAT.
		1	2	3	4	5
6	7	8	*First day of Fertility* 9	10	11	12
13	14	15	*Last day of Fertility* 16	17	18	19
20	21	22	23	24	25	26
27	*Expected Menstruation* 28	29	30			

The immediate objection to this plan is that it does not take account of irregularities in the monthly cycle. Specialists in the rhythm method however have worked out a way of meeting this problem—by keeping track of the degree of irregularity and compensating for it in the schedule. Thus, assuming that a woman with a 28-day cycle actually varies now and then by five days, the variation is taken care of by adding 5 days to the 7 which are ordinarily considered fertile or unsafe. That is, the unsafe period is 12 days in length and will end on November 22. One may thus adjust to any irregularity by incorporating into the schedule the maximum number of days of variation.

Couples must not expect too much certainty from the rhythm method. Anyone who practices it should seek the help of a competent physician in charting the calendar plan. Dickinson and Wood, after a lifetime of study conclude that:

> Those who have been taught that no method but observance of the safe period, the sterile period, is right, may give a year's study to a calendar marked with the date of each period, and then take advice as to whether the wife's regularity is such as to warrant a test of this method. It has not lived up to claims, as there are enough women who do not produce the egg on the usual calendar date near the mid-month (and with no way of telling who is uncertain) for the risk is still considerable.[18]

It is also true that ovulation may be stimulated or retarded by sudden surges of emotion and perhaps by intercourse itself. Again, the appearance of fraternal twins indicates that often two eggs are released in the same month and at different times. This may account for the number of children conceived during the so-called safe periods. Significant research is going on, and the rhythm method, when it is perfected, may offer a very adequate method of birth-control.

GENERAL ACCEPTANCE OF BIRTH-CONTROL

Only a generation ago Margaret Sanger was sent to prison for the "crime" of sending out birth-control information. Since then all but two states have legalized such information. The extent of approval of birth-control by the general public is indicated by the following table which summarizes findings of polls regarding various aspects of contraception. This table shows that as early as 1943 some 85 per cent of all women, and 69 per cent of all Catholic women, believed that birth-control information should be made available to married women. In 1947, 64 per cent of all women, and 57 per cent of Catholic women, stated that they would approve having government health clinics furnish birth-control information to married people who want it.

The meaning of this table is that the great majority of American women approve of birth-control, although only yesterday the mores condemned it. An even more persuasive proof of the acceptance of birth-control is the fact that women of all positions and educational attainment are having fewer children.

[18] Wood and Dickinson, op. cit., pp. 88–89.

TABLE 33. Findings of Polls of Public Opinion on Birth Control, 1936, 1943, and 1947, for Given Groups*

QUESTION AND RESPONSE	PER CENT OF GIVEN GROUPS				
	All	College	High school	Grades only	Catholic
1936. Do you believe in the teaching and practice of birth-control? (General population sample)					
Yes	63	—	—	—	—
No	23	—	—	—	—
Don't know	14	—	—	—	—
1943. Do you believe that knowledge about birth-control should not be made available to all married women? (Women, age 20–35, general population)					
Should be available	85	93	—	70	69
Should not	10	5	—	18	24
Don't know	5	2	—	12	7
1943. (If "should" above) Do you believe that knowledge about birth control should or should not be kept away from unmarried women? (Women, age 20–35, general population)					
Should not be withheld	70	—	—	55	59
Should be	23	—	—	34	34
Don't know	7	—	—	11	7
1947. Would you approve or disapprove of having government health clinics furnish birth-control information to married people who want it in this country? (General population)					
Approve	64	76	70	—	57
Disapprove	23	18	19	—	26
No opinion	13	6	11	—	17

* From Ernest W. Burgess and Harvey J. Locke, *The Family*, New York, The American Book Company, 1953, p. 454. Reprinted by permission.

GENERAL KNOWLEDGE OF BIRTH-CONTROL

How accurate is the birth-control information of the average American family? Dr. Earl Koos studied a typical small industrial community in the northeastern part of the United States to get an answer to that question. He discovered that one out of three couples either have no knowledge of modern birth-control methods or use methods regarded as inadequate by scientists. When those individuals, such as Catholics, who have religious objections to birth-control are eliminated from the sample, two out of five couples who would accept and use contraceptive methods do not have the necessary information.[19] Of the sample of 514 families, one-fifth (71 Catholic and 33 Fundamentalists) rejected birth-control on religious grounds. Of the remaining 410 families, who had no objection, 96 reported no direct information about contraceptive methods, 76 reported using methods of "limited or no value" and in some cases "potentially injurious." Thus, some 175 families did not know about birth-control or 33 per cent of the families involved in the whole study and 42 per cent of the 410 families who had no religious objection to the practice of contraception.

MECHANICAL AND CHEMICAL METHODS OF BIRTH-CONTROL

For those who in good conscience wish to use other types of birth-control, the methods recommended by gynecologists as most satisfactory are mechanical and chemical in nature. Ordinarily the safest method is a diaphragm coated with jelly which encloses the cervix and prevents the sperm from entering the uterus, but this method is not always practical. Actually the only safe procedure is for the woman to have a complete examination and allow the physician to prescribe the method best suited to her physical structure. Sometimes there are local conditions in the vaginal tract which indicate that the woman should use only a contraceptive jelly while the man uses a condom (a sheath worn over the penis to prevent the sperm from entering the vaginal tract at all). Coitus interruptus (withdrawal) is never advised because it is ineffective and psychologically frustrating.

Yarros made a study of 12,500 cases and found that not a single woman was injured in any way by the use of contraceptive devices recommended by competent physicians.[20] But some birth-control methods are dangerous. Caustic drugs may be injurious to tissue or rubbing metal devices may cause ulceration. The only safe rule for any couple to follow is to get their instruction from a physician. There is current so much "folk lore," stressing the success of this suppository or that type of douche, that double caution is advisable. Recently one member of a

[19] *Planned Parenthood News,* New York, No. 7, Spring, 1954, p. 5.
[20] Rachelle Yarros, *Modern Women and Sex,* New York, The Vanguard Press, Inc., 1953, p. 147.

discussion group held out for the use of the douche as the proper method, basing his arguments on the experience of two young couples he knew who had had perfect success with it. The next day another member of the class presented a case study of a bitter young woman who had become pregnant on her honeymoon because her mother had recommended the douche as the ideal method.

Whatever birth-control method is chosen, it should measure up to certain standards which have been rather carefully stated by Bowman:

1. It should be relatively effective, that is, as effective as modern medical science can make it. No method is entirely fool-proof. The methods most commonly recommended by informed physicians and reliable clinics, when used with intelligence and care, are nearly enough 100 per cent reliable to make possible the removal of all fear of unwanted pregnancy.
2. It should be relatively easy to use, simple and readily understood.
3. It should be readily available and relatively inexpensive.
4. It should be aesthetically acceptable to both parties and repugnant to neither.
5. It should permit normal, satisfactory, successful sexual adjustment.
6. It should have no harmful results. The contraceptive should contain and entail no chemical or mechanical irritant that may give rise to infection or poisoning.
7. It should be temporary, in the sense that its use may be terminated at will. Permanent sterilization, though it is a means of preventing conceptions, is not considered contraception.[21]

The temperature method, or the rhythm method, or chemical or mechanical contraceptive devices may all be regarded as means of promoting family adjustment and stability. Birth-control provides that sense of security in which a husband and wife may achieve maximum sexual joy without inhibiting fear of unwanted and unwise pregnancies. On the other hand, research is daily contributing to the fulfillment of the longing of husband and wife for children. In many cases careful study based on birth-control research has resulted in a baby when hope for one was almost gone. Everything possible should be done to determine whether or not sterility can be overcome. It has already been suggested that the use of the temperature method was helping some previously infertile couples to have babies. Since 1949 the number of infertility clinics in the United States has increased from 67 to 151 in 1954. In a nationwide

[21] Henry A. Bowman, *Marriage for Moderns*, New York, McGraw-Hill Book Company, Inc., 1948, p. 457. Reprinted by permission.

survey Dr. Mary Steichen Calderone discovered that among 13,051 patients treated some 3,026 pregnancies resulted or one out of four. Dr. Calderone believes that if the results of only the last five years had been reported the ratio would be higher because of improved methods and greater knowledge. Thus many couples who have been disappointed at not achieving parenthood may with help become parents.

STERILITY AND ADOPTION

No matter how competent the medical advice followed there will still be a number of families who will remain sterile. Fortunately, however, a sterile family need not always remain childless. There are many parentless children who need to be adopted and given a normal chance for healthy character development. In a sense the purpose of adoption is to bring together, under the most promising circumstances the homeless child and the childless adult. The mid-century White House Conference on Children and Youth came to the conclusion that about 38,000 children are adopted each year.

HESITATIONS ABOUT ADOPTING A CHILD

While barren couples may long for a child, many of them question the advisability of welcoming an adopted baby into their home. One of the questions which is often important to would-be adoptive parents is whether they have the capacity to accept fully and love as their own a child not related to them by birth or marriage. Many adoptive parents who later had children of their own have been asked whether or not there was any difference in the degree of love which they felt for their adopted and their natural children. In every single case these parents replied that they felt no such difference. When pressed as to what they would do if they had to make a choice almost all of them replied that they would probably keep the adopted child. The question was an invidious one but they went on, in their answers, to say that the reason they felt this way was that the adopted child had come to them at the time of their greatest need and loneliness.

Bearing a child or adopting a child does not necessarily make that child one's own except in a legal sense. The child becomes a part of the parent only when the parent has given to the child tender care, deep affection, and much time. Neither the personality of the child nor the nature of his adult values is determined at birth. Both are the products of interaction with others and in particular of interaction with parents. A child's bringing up is far more crucial to his personal happiness and to his worth as a member of society than his biological parentage. In every real sense the adoptive child is truly the child of the parents who share with him their lives, their ideals, and their values. Those childless couples who hesitate to adopt a child because they are afraid that they may never feel that such a child is really theirs do not fully understand the dynamics of personality growth.

Other couples may fear that the adopted child may turn out to be feeble-minded, handicapped, or delinquent. Of course it must be said that normal parents may have feeble-minded or retarded children. If an adoption is carried out through a recognized social agency, the chances of adopting retarded children are far fewer than are those of bearing one. Social agencies do not place retarded children for adoption. Every child is very carefully studied before being placed in a home. Testing procedures are now so adequate that few mistakes are made. Delinquency is the product of a great many environmental factors including both conditions in the home and in the society about the home. It is never inherited. Fears regarding future delinquency patterns are based on an erroneous notion of heredity or a lack of appreciation of the skillful management which goes into the placing of a child by a reputable agency.

A third fear which tortures some adoptive parents is that the natural parents may later demand custody of their child. A simple review of the laws governing adoptions should allay this fear. Adoptive parents need to investigate the specific laws of their state on this point but generally, if the seal of law is placed upon the new relationship between the child and the adoptive parents, legal responsibility is permanently established. Through the adoption process the child's natural parents generally waive all rights to the child and the adoptive parents assume all the rights and obligations of parenthood. However, parents should consult with a lawyer or social agency to clarify their rights when adopting a child. The child after adoption bears the name of his new family. This family has sole right to the custody of the child and to his services or earnings as a minor. Finally, the adopted child shares in the rights of inheritance.

As the result of careful study of problems that have risen in the past, the United States Children's Bureau has set up certain standards which should guide adoptive procedures:

1. The termination of parental rights is as important as the establishment of new parental ties by adoption and should be safely guarded.
2. Placement for adoption should be made only by an agency authorized to make such placements by the state department of public welfare.
3. Adoption proceedings should be in a court of record having jurisdiction over children's cases, in the home state of the petitioners for adoption and preferably in the local community in which they live and are known and where the child is properly before the court.
4. In every proposed adoption of a child the court should have the benefit of a social study and a recommendation made by the state department of public welfare, or by a local department of public welfare designated by the state welfare department.
5. Consent to adoption should be obtained from the natural parents, or if their parental rights have been legally relinquished or terminated, from a person or agency having legal responsibility for the child and the right to consent to adoption.
6. Court hearings should be closed to the public and the records, because of their confidential nature, should be protected.
7. A period of residence in the adoptive home, preferably for one year, should be required before the hearing on the petition, so that the suitability of the proposed adoption may be determined.
8. In the event a final decree is not entered, provision should be made for the removal of a child from a home found to be unsuitable and for his care and guardianship after his removal.
9. Safeguards should be provided in related laws, such as those affecting relinquishment of parental rights, regulations of child placing services and determination of guardianship and custody of all children, to assure the welfare of the child in all such matters as well as in the adoption proceedings and to define the rights and the obligations of the parents.[22]

Given these principles, we can study the exact procedure of an adoption and discover whether or not the interests of the child and of the new parents are safeguarded. After a couple has decided to adopt a child certain alternatives are presented. The prospective foster parents may visit a friend who is a doctor and ask him to use his good services in finding them a baby. They make it known in the community that any unmarried pregnant girl can expect them to take good care of her in return for her baby. These are called independent adoptions. For reasons that will be discussed later these methods are not recommended.

[22] *Essentials of Adoption Law and Procedure,* United States Children's Bureau, Publication No. 331, 1949, pp. 2–4.

The more acceptable method of adoption is through a recognized social agency. The couple calls and makes an appointment for an interview with one of the workers of the agency. During this first meeting they give their reasons for wanting a child and something of their background. In the course of this preliminary interview they fill in a first form which gives essential information regarding their place and type of residence, their citizenship status, their financial resources, their medical history, and physical descriptions of themselves and of any other persons living in the family. The worker describes the way the agency operates and discusses the remaining steps necessary before an application for a child may be entered.

After the initial interview and the completion of the first form a social worker is sent out from the agency to visit the home. She is interested in both the physical and the psychological attributes of the home. While some couples seem apprehensive about this visit, they should remember that the social worker is trained in making the parents feel at ease and never expects the extraordinary either in home facilities or in personality maturity. After this first visit to the home the agency studies the material it now has on the family and decides whether or not the couple seem to be good parental prospects. If the decision is a positive one, the couple is now sent an "Application for Child."

Following the receipt of the application the worker visits the home a second time and discusses any problems that may seem important to the couple or to the agency. A statement is then obtained from the couple's doctor explaining reasons for the inability of the couple to have a child of their own. This statement is put in the agency's files.

Some question whether such an exhaustive study is really necessary, but all of this information is important in matching the child and the parents in appearance, intelligence, religion, temperament, and personality. Every possible avenue is explored which may lead to a successful and happy relationship between the child and his adoptive parents.

Even more careful scrutiny is given the children who have been placed in the care of a placing institution. As soon as children enter the institution they have a very careful physical examination. This is soon followed by an equally careful psychological study. The children are also observed by several pediatricians and social workers. No child is ever placed until those who have supervised him are convinced that he has a reasonable expectation of success in the new home situation.

Introduction to the baby the agency has selected for them, needless

274

to say, is one of the very high points in the life of a childless couple. A special room is generally provided for this purpose. After the social worker "introduces" the baby to its possible parents, the couple and baby are left alone to get acquainted. The parents need not take the baby recommended to them, but they generally do. However, if they take the child home, they are only prospective parents for the next year. Technically they are on probation. If, during that year, the couple decide that they cannot manage this particular child or do not feel close to him for some other reason they do not have to keep him. During this year the couple is visited four times or so by a worker from the agency who observes the progress in the growing relatedness of child and foster parents. If this worker discovers that the parents and child are basically incompatible or for some other reason that it is not in the interest of the couple or the child to continue the relationship, the child may be removed from the home. It is, perhaps, unnecessary to add that this seldom happens because of the care with which the child has been placed.

At the end of the year the agency restudies the total situation and makes a recommendation for the guidance of the court which must approve the adoption.

When this final study has been completed the parents petition the court of jurisdiction for the adoption. The court considers the petition in a private hearing. The judge has a history of the child and his development, a copy of the home study and a recommendation of the state department of social welfare as well as the formal petition for adoption. If the judge, upon considering all of the evidence, favors the petition he issues a court order granting the adoption. The adoption is now legally consummated and the child belongs completely to the adoptive parents.

INDEPENDENT ADOPTIONS

An independent adoption is defined as an adoption which is negotiated directly between the natural parent or parents or their representatives and the adoptive parents. In many states independent adoptions are not permitted. In some states the law requires that the transaction take place within the legal framework provided by the state department of public welfare so that the one year waiting period and visits to the home are still required. What is not required is the very careful study of both foster parents and the child to be sure that they are matched to the degree that a happy relationship will result. As a result, the risk

275

in independent adoptions is great. How great is indicated in the conclusions reached by the Citizens Committee on Adoption of Children in California which studied independent adoptions over a two-year period. The conclusions, statistical and qualitative, were as follows:

> Statistical information was furnished by the Department (California State Department of Public Welfare) on 13,802 California Independent Adoption Cases Terminated in 1948. From these data it was learned that 44 per cent of the parents placed their babies in the year, but that intermediaries placed 56 per cent of them. A total of 60 per cent of all the mothers were 24 years of age and under. Unmarried mothers equalled 39 per cent. At the time of investigation by the State Department 45 per cent of the mothers were not acquainted with the couple who had petitioned to adopt their children.
>
> These four statements alone raised questions about the urgency of the need of these young, unmarried mothers for good services in making the decision to give away a child forever, and the necessity for knowing these children and the family adopting them. Of these 3,802 babies placed in independent adoption, 42 per cent were placed by married couples. This also raised questions about the reasons why families give up their children, the necessity for knowing these families and helping them to determine if this is the best plan for their family life.
>
> The fact that, following investigation, the State Department of Public Welfare recommended denial or dismissal for 23 per cent of the independent adoption petitions means that in one year 872 children were in adoptive homes which were not suitable for them, or their parents changed their minds about adoption, or they were not legally free for adoption, or their adoptive parents decided they did not wish to proceed with adoption. The result—uprooting of family ties, new adjustment, sorrow and heartache for 872 children, their natural parents and adoptive parents. Who knows if these changes in decision were right for the natural parents, the child, or adoptive parents, and if the services of a case work agency might not have helped before the second break in family ties was made? Who knows how many of these parents and children could have been helped by preventive services but who, for lack of such help, may later come as deeply disturbed people to social agencies.[23]

The advantages of agency placements as compared with independent adoption procedures (as shown by this study) are amply clear. Young couples eager for a baby should not be so eager as to neglect the warnings of this study. Carelessness in placing or receiving children in adoptive homes may mean much heartache and personality disruption later

[23] Mary Stanton, *Gleanings From Twenty-Two Months of Activity,* The Citizens' Adoption Committee of Los Angeles, June, 1952, pp. 11–12.

While couples adopt children because they have not been able to have any of their own, the giving of love to an adopted child sometimes results in a change in the sterility pattern. The adoptive mother often finds herself pregnant later. One study made indicated that in the cases of 273 mothers who had adopted children, 200 had a child within an average of approximately thirty-nine months after the adoption.[24] We do not know the reason for this. Some of the couples may have matured during this time so that they would have had a child anyway. In other cases the anxiety attendant upon not having a child may have diminished so sharply that pregnancy could take place. Again, it may be that the presence of a child somehow stimulates the endocrine glands so that fertility increases.

It is now rather universally recognized that an adopted child should be told that he is adopted and told very early in his relationship with his parents. One adoption agency releases the child to the parents with the understanding that the parents will tell the child he is adopted before he is three years of age. There are many positive ways in which this can be accomplished. Some mothers stress the fact that while other children just come, an adopted child is special because he has been "chosen." But the way the adoption is explained does not seem to be the important issue. The important fact for the emotional security of the child is that he shall be dearly loved; that every day of his life the tenderness and closeness of his relationship with his parents will assure him that he truly belongs. No word or phrase or illustration can ever substitute for emotional security based on feelings of closeness and love.

CONCLUSION

Both children and the desire for children contribute to family happiness. Careful spacing of children appears to be essential to the health and happiness of both siblings and parents. Hence the need for employing methods of birth-control—according to the dictates of conscience or religion. Because some married individuals will be permanently sterile, it is important to study adoption procedures.

PROJECTS

1. Take a census of the class to discover how many are only children, or first- or last-born in a larger family. Discuss the special problems in maturing that come to a child because of his ordinal rank in the family.

[24] Bowman, *op. cit.*, p. 443.

2. Ask a member of the sociology department to come to class for a discussion of population problems. Ask him about the contention of some eugenicists that the "best strains" are breeding themselves out of existence.
3. Ask a gynecologist to come to the class to discuss reasons for sterility, and to indicate the usefulness of the temperature and rhythm methods in assisting such couples in achieving a pregnancy.
4. If a discussion of religious approaches to birth-control develops, list the many positive points on which all religions agree.
5. Plan a field trip and visit several adoption agencies. Be sure that the visits are arranged so that individuals will be there who can explain thoroughly the work of the agency.
6. Ask a representative of the Public Welfare Committee of your state or of your county to come and discuss the problems of adoption with the class.
7. Discuss the question of what actually makes a child a real son or daughter of its parents.

READINGS

HENRY A. BOWMAN, *Marriage for Moderns*, New York, McGraw-Hill Book Company, Inc., Chapter 15.

LEE M. BROOKS and EVELYN C. BROOKS, *Adventuring in Adoption*, Chapel Hill, University of North Carolina Press, 1939.

JUDSON T. LANDIS and MARY G. LANDIS, *Building a Successful Marriage*, New York, Prentice-Hall, Inc., 1948, Chapter 17.

FRANCIS LOCKBRIDGE, *Adopting a Child*, New York, Greenburg Publishers, 1947.

HANNAH and ABRAHAM STONE, *A Marriage Manual*, New York, Simon and Schuster, Inc., 1952, Chapter 5.

V. P. WASSON, *The Chosen Baby*, Philadelphia, J. B. Lippincott Company, 1950.

THURSTON SCOTT WILTON, *The Modern Method of Birth Control*, New York, Grosset and Dunlap, Inc., 1943.

PAMPHLETS

Essentials of Adoption Law and Procedure, U. S. Children's Bureau, No. 321, 1949.

The ABC of Foster Family Care for Children, U. S. Department of Labor, U. S. Government Printing Office, 1936.

CHAPTER 15

The Process
of Reproduction*

INTRODUCTION: YOUNG PEOPLE NORMALLY EXPECT THAT
THEIR LOVE WILL RESULT IN A FAMILY. THEY MAY LOOK FORWARD
to children with mixed emotions because of anxiety or fear associated with
the process of reproduction. But reproduction is the most normal event
in life. The human body has been developing its capacity to reproduce
for millions of years. No chemical or physical process is so complex or
remarkable as that involved in reproduction. The intricate interplay of
psychological, glandular, nutritional, and muscular factors is a masterful
achievement of nature. Young people need to know the facts associated
with childbirth so that this knowledge will dissipate the vague fears or
tensions they must have. In understanding reproduction it is essential
to be familiar with the properties of the reproductive cells, the ovarian
cycle, the process of fertilization, nidation (the implantation of the
fertilized cell in the uterine wall), the growth sequence of the fetus, and
the birth process itself. Such an understanding generally builds confidence and eliminates in some degree unnecessary worry.

* Written with Dr. Nadina Kavinoky, M.D., Past-President, National Council on Family
Relations.

FIGURE 12. The Ovarian Cycle in Mammals*

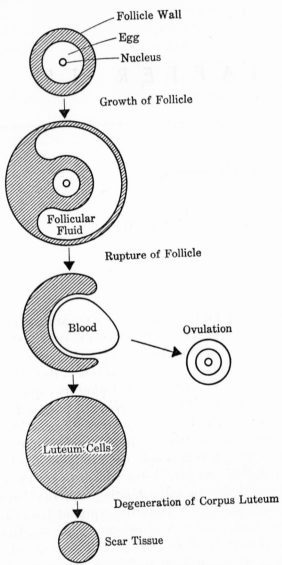

* Source: Lester George Barth, *Embryology*, New York, The Dryden Press, 1949, p. 21. Reproduced by permission.

THE REPRODUCTIVE CELLS

The cells which become ova or sperm are called germ cells. In human beings they develop directly from the tissues of the developing ovary or testis.[1] During the development of the egg and sperm cells there is a reduction in the number of chromosomes. In human beings the normal somatic cell contains 48 chromosomes but the reproductive cell (gamete) has but 24. When the male and female cells join, the zygote that is formed has 48 chromosomes. The egg develops within a follicle in the

FIGURE 13. The Pituitary and the Ovarian Cycle*

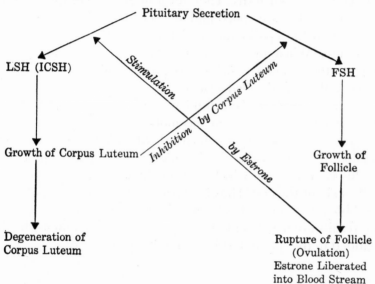

* Source: Lester George Barth, *Embryology*, New York, The Dryden Press, 1949, p. 23. Reproduced by permission.

ovary called the Graafian Follicle as illustrated in Figure 12. This follicle grows in size as the egg matures. As the egg is maturing, pituitary hormones become more concentrated and eventually liberate the egg by breaking down the follicle wall. The space previously occupied by the egg is now filled by a special kind of cell (the Luteum cells) and the follicle is now called the Corpus Luteum. If fertilization occurs the Corpus Luteum becomes active and remains active throughout pregnancy but if the egg dies the Corpus Luteum degenerates. Figure 12 from Barth illustrates the ovarian cycle in mammals.

[1] Lester George Barth, *Embryology*, New York, The Dryden Press, Copyright, 1949, p. 14.

281

The growth of the Graafian Follicle is stimulated by a hormone secreted by the pituitary FSH or Follicle Stimulating Hormone. The growth of the Corpus Luteum is stimulated by a second hormone from the pituitary designated LSH or Luteum Stimulating Hormone. The relationship of these hormones to the ovarian cycle is indicated in Figure 13 from Barth.

MALE REPRODUCTIVE CELLS

The male reproductive cells are called sperm. They are produced in the male gonads called testis. They form in very small tubes within the testicles. These tubes are coiled and are very long. The sperm pass from these tubes into the epididymis, and then into the vas deferens, while still immature. When orgasm occurs the sperm are mixed with the secretions of the seminal vesicles and prostate gland. These secretions are a whitish, thick fluid called semen.

The sperm is a tadpole-like cell microscopic in size, being about 1/500 inch long. It has some power of locomotion because of a long tail that lashes about, driving the sperm forward. Mammalian sperms contain a hormone-like substance called hyaluronidase which plays a part in fertilization. This is an enzyme which may facilitate fertilization by breaking down jellies about the egg. Thus in experiments in the artificial insemination of rabbits, if a seminal fluid containing low concentration of sperm is used the results are negative; but if a sperm extract containing hyaluronidase is added to the sperm, fertilization takes place.

INSEMINATION

In sexual intercourse the sperm are deposited in the vaginal canal. Each ejaculation contains about three hundred million sperm and if the concentration of sperm is less than 40 million per milliliter sterility is indicated.[2] The ascent of the sperm through the uterus to the fallopian tubes is very rapid.[3] This rapidity of ascent is thought to be due to the action of the sperm's flagellum, to uterine and tubular contractions, and to celiacy movements of the oviduct-epithelium.[4] How much time is required for the sperm to travel to the tube is not exactly known but

[2] *Ibid.*, p. 45.   [3] *Ibid.*, p. 52.
[4] Hans Selye, *Endocrinology*, Aeta Endocrinologica, Université de Montreal, Montreal, Canada, 1947, p. 816.

Selye reports that mobile sperm were found in the tube in a dog and a guinea pig twenty minutes after copulation.[5]

THE PROCESS OF FERTILIZATION

Many sperm, it is thought, reach the surface of the egg at about the same time. However, when one sperm begins to penetrate the cellular wall of the ovum a "wave of negativity" develops throughout the ovum which excludes all other sperm.[6] The egg reacts to the sperm by forming a fertilization cone which engulfs it.[7] The tail of the sperm drops off and the nuclei of the egg and sperm move together and fuse. The chromosomes pair off so that the 48 single chromosomes contained in the separate sperm and egg now become 24 pairs in the zygote (the fertilized egg). The first cell division then takes place. At fertilization some remarkable changes occur. There is a great increase in the rate of oxygen consumption by the fertilized egg, probably 500 per cent.[8] There is a measurable increase in heat production. The cell membrane becomes more permeable to allow for a freer exchange of substances through the membrane. The viscosity of the protoplasm of the cell increases—which perhaps is essential for cell division. The joining with the sperm vitalizes the egg and sets in motion new and dynamic processes.

PREGNANCY

When the egg is fertilized in the oviduct it must move to the uterus if a normal pregnancy is to occur. If for some reason the egg is implanted in the wall of the fallopian tube this condition is called an ectopic or tubular pregnancy and requires surgery as the body cannot maintain a growing fetus in this location. In human beings implantation in the uterus usually occurs between the sixth and ninth day after mating.[9] The implantation consists of the zygote burying itself in the uterine wall and is called nidation. The fertilized egg secretes a gonotropic hormone which stimulates the Corpus Luteum to increase in size and to persist throughout pregnancy.[10] The Corpus Luteum then supplies the progesterone and estrone essential for the maintenance of the uterine wall. It also prevents further ovulation and inhibits contractions of

[5] *Ibid.*, p. 816.　[6] Barth, *op. cit.*, p. 46.　[7] *Ibid.*, p. 46.　[8] *Ibid.*, p. 47.
[9] Selye, *op. cit.*, p. 818.　[10] Barth, *op. cit.,* p. 260.

the uterus.[11] During the latter half of pregnancy the placenta itself produces both progesterone and estrogen and takes over the function of the ovaries, the Corpus Luteum, and the pituitary. In human beings the glandular extracts produced by the placenta must be supplemented by a vitamin K which is essential to early embryonic development in mammals.[12]

PRESUMPTIVE AND POSITIVE SIGNS OF PREGNANCY

What bodily changes indicate that a woman is pregnant? There are certain signs which are presumptive and others that are positive. The presumptive signs are morning sickness, cessation of menstruation, increased frequency of urination, increased size of the nipple, the breasts, the vaginal lining, and the abdomen, increased vaginal secretion, and higher temperature. One or the other or several may be present in other bodily states but when they occur all together they are highly indicative of pregnancy.

Signs which are almost indisputable are the heartbeat of the baby, the discernible shape of the fetus, fetal movements, and the appearance of the fetus in an X-ray.

TESTS FOR PREGNANCY

There are three old and two relatively new tests for pregnancy. Ascheim and Zondek demonstrated a test in 1928 which is 99 per cent accurate. Five mice are injected with the woman's urine six times in 48 hours. A sixth mouse is not injected, for comparison as a control. If the five mice develop indications of ovulation, it means that a pregnancy hormone is present in the injected urine. The Friedman test is similar but varies in that only one injection of urine is necessary and a rabbit is used instead of mice. This test is almost 100 per cent accurate. When a third animal, the South African clawed frog is used, pregnancy is established if the frog expells eggs in large number.

The first of the new tests is the temperature test which has already been described. A continued high temperature in the absence of a cold or infection after the normal time for menstruation has passed indicates pregnancy. This is often called the "poor man's Friedman test." A second test now used involves the presence of estrones in the saliva. The level

[11] *Ibid.*, p. 262.   [12] *Ibid.*, p. 264.

of estrone is apparently increased during pregnancy so that a chemical analysis which precipitates out the estrones in the saliva has proved to be a very effective method of determining pregnancy. Some work is also being done on ascertaining the sex of the child by a subtle means of staining the precipitate. Experiments indicate, however, that this test is not effective until after the sixth month.

MEDICAL PROGRESS AND REPRODUCTION

One of the reassuring factors in considering reproduction today is the significant progress of medical science in the last century. In 1882 a book called *"The Physical Life of Woman"* by George Napheys, a doctor, went into its third edition; 150,000 copies had already been sold. The publisher of the book declared that it "may justly claim to count among the classics of American literature." The volume was constructive in temper, and it probably contributed a great deal to women seventy-five years ago. We quote it now only to show the progress medical science has made. In speaking of the influence of habitual mental conditions of the mother on the child Dr. Napheys gives several interesting illustrations:

> Dr. Demangeon of Paris quotes, in his work on the Imagination, the *Journal de Verdun,* as mentioning the case of a child, born at Blois, in the eyes of which the face of a watch was distinctly seen. The image was situated around the pupil, and the figures representing the hours were plainly perceived. The mother had experienced a strong desire to see a watch while she was pregnant with this child.[13]
>
> Professor Dalton of New York states that the wife of the janitor of the College of Physicians and Surgeons of that city, during her pregnancy dreamed that she saw a man who had lost part of the ear. The dream made a great impression upon her mind, and she mentioned it to her husband. When her child was born, a portion of one ear was deficient, and the organ was exactly like the defective ear she had seen in her dream.[14]

The learned doctor had a solution for these problems.

> Unfortunately all parents are not beautiful. Yet all desire beautiful offspring. The body of the child can be influenced by the mind of the parent, particularly of the mother. . . . A Roman magistrate, little, ugly, and

[13] George H. Napheys, *The Physical Life of Woman*, Philadelphia, H. C. Watts Company, 1882, p. 187.   [14] *Ibid.*, p. 183.

hunchbacked, had by his wife a child exactly resembling the statue of Aesop. Frightened at the sight of this little monster and fearful of becoming the father of a posterity so deformed he went to consult Galen, the most distinguished physician of his time, who counselled him to place three statues of love around the conjugal bed, one at the foot, the others one on each side, in order that the eyes of his young spouse might be constantly feasted on these charming figures. The magistrate followed strictly the advice of the physician, and it is recorded that his wife bore him a child surpassing in beauty all his hopes.[15]

Napheys felt it was important to have beauty about not only at the time of insemination but also during pregnancy.

During pregnancy the mother should often have some painting or engraving representing cheerful and beautiful figures before her eyes, or often contemplate some graceful statue. She should avoid looking at, or thinking of ugly people, or those marked with disfiguring diseases. . . . She should avoid ungraceful positions and awkward attitudes as by some mysterious sympathy these are impressed on the child she carries.[16]

Such were the myths that governed the men who cared for our grandparents. Today such myths have been discarded. Beyond that, painstaking research has found the cause of many pregnancy disorders and these have been eliminated. Hospital facilities and their use have both increased. Consequently the infant death rate has declined from around 100 per 1,000 live births in 1915 to under 30 per 1,000 in 1950. The maternal death rate has declined from about 60 per 10,000 live births to 6.1 in 1950. Week in and week out, our medical scientists are studying ways of making childbirth safer. They have accomplished a great deal already.

DEVELOPMENT OF THE HUMAN EMBRYO

The human embryo develops in relationship to the placenta. (The early cell implants itself and forms roots in the uterine wall. These roots eventually become the placenta.) The placenta is a disc-shaped organ about nine inches in diameter and an inch thick. It is an extension of the umbilical cord. Where the placenta comes in contact with the uterica wall it has a great many root-like projections which spread out in all directions. These projections have thin membranes which lie in the lacunae (or lakes of blood) supplied by the mother for the nourishment

[15] *Ibid.*, p. 127.   [16] *Ibid.*, p. 141.

and for the elimination processes of the embryo. Until the third week the embryo receives no food from the placenta but feeds on "debris" that results when certain cells break down at nidation and also on a diffusion of products from the uterus.[17] After the third week the embryo receives food from the placenta.

THE PLACENTAL FUNCTION

The placenta carries many substances necessary to the fetus and some that are harmful. Ordinarily only small molecules can penetrate the placental screen of three layers of cells which is placed between the maternal and fetal blood streams.[18] Carbon dioxide and oxygen have no difficulty in crossing the placenta. Ammonia, urea, and uric acid pass through easily. Glucose, animo acids, and a few red blood cells pass. Sometimes larger molecular substances such as the anti-RH factor and the German measles germ penetrate and cause difficulty. The placenta thus not only is the channel for food but functions to defend the fetus from destructive influences.

THE GROWTH OF THE EMBRYO

In the five or six days in which this new cell is carried along the tube on its way to the uterus, the cell begins to divide into two, four, and more cells. By the time it arrives at the uterus it looks like a raspberry—although much smaller.

Due to the effect of hormones, another miraculous process is going on in the uterus itself. The lining cells begin to enlarge and fill with glycogen, a form of sugar, which nourishes the new life. More mucus is secreted, the blood vessels increase, and more blood is brought to the lining of the uterus. All this in preparation to receive, nurture, and permit the fertilized ovum to imbed and grow.

At this stage, if we could look inside the nest called the uterus, the embryo would look like a pearl on a maroon velvet background.

The mass of cells comprising the embryo at nidation is divided into three sections. One has a yoke-like substance to feed the embryo until enough capillaries and vessels surround it and form a pool through which oxygen, iron, and other food may be obtained. Another section starts the development of the placenta, the organ which in a few months will filter

[17] *Ibid.,* p. 276.   [18] *Ibid.,* p. 276.

287

the food from the mother's blood and carry it through the fetal blood vessels in the umbilical cord to the fetus. In a few weeks this will be a pale pink fluffy sac filled with fluid, all prepared to protect and nourish the embryo. The third part contains the cells which will develop into the fetus. These will divide into three major divisions thus beginning the grouping of the cells to form skin, bone, muscles, brain, and other nerve tissue which will form the various organ systems of the body. Each of these systems has cells with highly specialized functions.

The male and female sex organs originate from the same group of cells. The shape and organization of the reproductive organs, whether male or female, will depend on the sex-determining chromosome derived from the father's spermatozoa. All other physical and mental characteristics are derived from the chromosomes of both mother and father.

The growth and development of the different organs goes on for about 267 days from ovulation or 280 days from the beginning of the last menstrual period if it was in a 28-day cycle. During all this time the mother's body is not only giving nourishment to her child, but her hormones are continuing to help it grow. By the third month, many rudimentary organs are developed. They continue to grow and by birth the digestive system of the baby can digest milk and distribute calcium to the bones and nerves.

While the baby has been cuddled up inside of the sac filled with fluid, it has been protected by the fluid and by the muscles of the uterus and abdomen. These formed an original shock absorber. The muscle wall has developed and increased many times in size and power. This is necessary to achieve the birth process itself. In the vaginal canal, the tissues have become softer, more elastic, and lubricated. All of these many processes go on quite automatically and efficiently until the infant is ready to be born. What signal is given or what organ gives it is not known, but a signal is automatically given when it is time for birth. Mechanisms are set in motion and the birth process begins: Figure 14 shows the position of the baby prior to birth. About two weeks before labor the baby has settled and its position is lower in the pelvis. The process of lowering is called lightening.

THE BIRTH PROCESS AND LABOR PAIN

In late pregnancy small pains and pressure signify that the opening in the cervix is beginning to thin out, stretch, and open. The mother may

THREE FIGURES
EXPLAINING THE BIRTH PROCESS

Reprinted from the *Birth Atlas*
with the permission of the
Maternity Center Association, New York City

FIGURE 14. Fetus at Term before Beginning of Labor

FIGURE 15. Labor: Cervix Completely Dilated

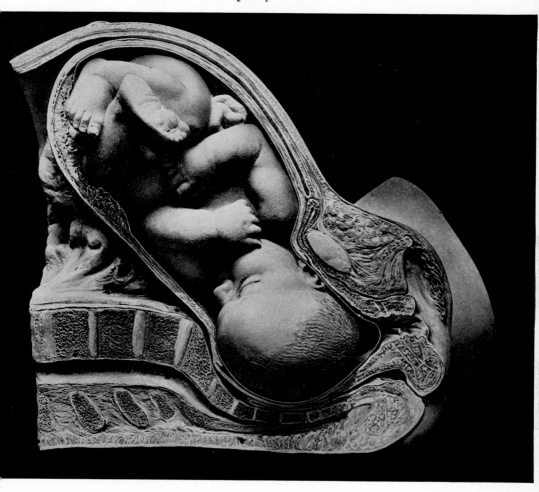

FIGURE 16. Labor: Birth of Shoulders

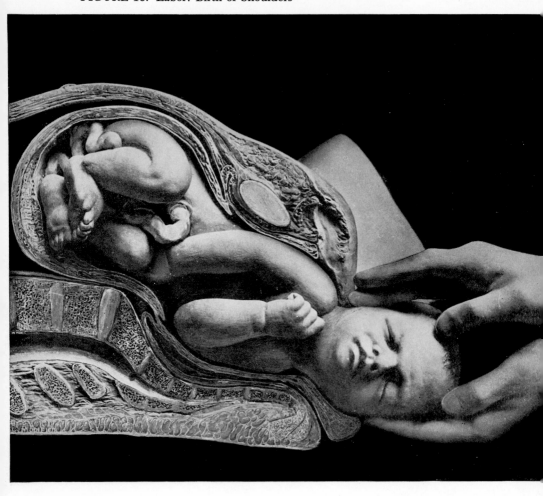

be conscious of scarcely anything more than a backache. When the opening has increased from ⅓ cm. to about 5 to 6 cm., or from ⅛ of an inch to about 3 inches, the rhythmic contractions of the uterus increase in frequency, strength, and discomfort. The manner in which the cervix dilates and prepares for the passage of the baby is indicated in Figure 15. The contractions last a minute or two, and the woman relaxes several minutes between contractions. The contractions become more frequent until the fetus is delivered.

The actual pain or discomfort which accompanies the birth process varies. Some women have accustomed themselves to falls and bruises and have developed the ability to grit their teeth. Others have not outgrown crying even at the anticipation of pain. Some weep and worry, and dread the birth process because of the descriptions given them by their mothers or friends. One such woman did not recognize her actual labor pains. Her idea of the torture she was expecting, the "terrible time" she had heard about, was so much more agonizing than the pains she was having that she failed to recognize that she was in labor.

There is no question that fear, apprehension, and tension increase the sensation of pain, and that the anxiety so often associated with labor prevents relaxation and rest between contractions.

The initial phase of labor involves a twofold muscular reaction of the uterus. The muscles at the lower end of the uterus develop during pregnancy to hold the heavy baby. These muscles keep the baby from descending for nine months. During the birth process they must relax and allow the cervix to expand so that the baby may pass through. Thus these muscles give way while the muscles that run longitudinally are contracting and forcing the fetus downward. If the mother is a victim of fear the lateral or horizontal muscles cannot relax and the other muscles must struggle against them. Fear thus not only causes pain but prolongs labor.

When the cervix is completely dilated the baby's head passes through the cervix and into the vaginal canal. As the head presents the largest diameter at birth, once the head is born the body follows easily. Figure 16 shows the doctor assisting during the final stage of the baby's birth. A few minutes after the baby is born the placenta is delivered. This is generally called the afterbirth.

Besides her emotional attitudes, a woman's nervous threshold also influences her ability to adjust to labor pains. The lack of Vitamin B and calcium often results in hypersensitive nerves. Inflammation of the reproductive organs increases the pain. Disproportion between the fetal

289

head and the mother's pelvis may prolong the labor. The only general statement we can make about labor pains is that they apparently differ with each individual case. Nevertheless a good attitude and knowledge of what is going on seem to lessen the discomfort.

Years ago, most women suffered during labor. Neither doctor, midwife, nor helping neighbor gave any sedative. Now a new era has arrived. Hospitals have trained anesthetists, and doctors and nurses understand the psychological need for reducing unnecessary tension. The mechanism in the reproductive system works so efficiently that 85 per cent of pregnant women give birth normally, 10 or 11 per cent have slight complications and 4 or 5 per cent have serious complications.

Complications in childbirth very often occur because of disease in other organs such as anemia (which is a lack of hemoglobin or iron in the blood), RH difficulties, or toxins which result from chronic disease in the head, lung, or diabetes. That is why the obstetrician checks the blood and examines the urine every few weeks. Most of the complications can be prevented and steps can be taken to relieve any abnormal situation so long as it is revealed by a thorough medical examination *before* pregnancy.

"CHILDBIRTH WITHOUT FEAR"

In this country and in England the theory of natural childbirth has become accepted largely through the efforts of Dr. Grantly Dick Read. This process is much misunderstood. It really means putting the patient at ease throughout the pregnancy so that she will not waste energy through fear. She learns to relax her muscles as well as her mind. However, Dr. Read gives anesthetics or sedatives to many of his patients.

There is no doubt that it is best for the mother to be relaxed throughout the birth process. If a patient's doctor thinks the mother should have a mild sedative or anesthetic, his advice should be followed—especially if stiches are necessary to help the pelvic organs return to normal size after delivery. Because there are many factors which must be considered at the time of birth it is not wise to be too rigid about sedatives. If the expectant mother chooses a well-trained doctor, she should give him her full confidence and intelligent cooperation.

Labor pains are due to hard contractions of the muscles of the uterus. There is no sensation of pain with the early contractions. Just before birth, the pains may last 30 to 40 seconds and come every minute or two. Thirty to 40 per cent of women can deliver their children without an anesthetic. Mothers seem to receive much satisfaction in consciously participating in the birth process. Joy and pride in the new baby appear on the mother's face almost before the last pain disappears. But whether a sedative is used or not, Dr. Read contributes much when he suggests that understanding the birth process and learning how to relax before birth takes place will contribute to ease of childbirth.

ROOMING-IN

Rooming-in is another new practice (or the revival of a very old one) which helps the father and mother learn how to care for their baby. The infant is placed in a crib next to the mother's bed in the hospital. Diapers and other necessary items are within her reach. She can easily swing over her bed the plastic box containing the baby. Under the guidance of a trained nurse, the new mother learns to feed, change, bathe and cuddle her baby. The father, when he comes in, also takes part in caring for the baby. Thus he gets to know his child from the start, and at the same time learns how to prepare its formula and change its diapers. All of this is possible because the nurses become teachers. More and more hospitals are using the rooming-in procedure.

Conditions today are quite different from those our parents knew. Courses in home economics, even the diets printed in our magazines and newspapers, have contributed to more intelligent nutrition. A higher standard of living has made nutritious food available. Home-nursing courses as well as courses in child care and development have helped mothers to become skilled and relaxed. Red Cross courses for prospective fathers have helped them understand both the process of pregnancy and labor as well as infant care. Learning these skills together has not only prevented problems between mother and father, it has created more fun all around. It is easier to learn the intelligent way than through trial and error.

NURSING

After a few hours of rest, many mothers are ready to nurse their babies. Many of them during pregnancy have gently massaged and exercised their nipples so that the infant can grasp them easily.

There is emotional satisfaction in being able to nurse the new baby—

291

pride in watching a baby thrive on the mother's milk, and the added satisfaction of holding the baby closely and cuddling it. This can and should also be part of bottle-feeding if the mother cannot nurse. However the sucking satisfaction seems to be greater in nursing. Moreover, nursing and the pelvic exercises are factors in helping the uterus absorb and discard the extra cells and shrink back to normal.

During the nursing period, the progesterone hormone is at a high level of efficiency. That is why many women do not menstruate for several months after giving birth. However, nursing mothers do sometimes menstruate, and no one can depend upon nursing as an effective means of birth-control.

POST-NATAL CARE

The reproductive organs return to normal in a matter of weeks. The stitches are usually healed in less than a week. But in the first few months after the birth of a baby, the menstrual periods may be very irregular. Some women start to menstruate at six weeks, others a month after they stop nursing. Here again, each individual case is different. The irregularity itself occurs because of the variation in the time necessary for the mother to re-establish a normal functioning of her endocrine glands.

During pregnancy and nursing, the progesterone hormone is more active. Slowly the estrogen phase comes back, and menstruation then becomes normal, followed by a greater desire for intercourse. Some women develop a greater capacity to respond sexually about a year after pregnancy than they had before they conceived. There is a maturing benefit from the increased hormone activity during pregnancy. Fertility generally also increases as a result of this great endocrine activity.

After the arrival of a baby, the contraceptive diaphragm, if it is used, should be refitted, since pregnancy may cause some change in the size and arrangement of the pelvic organs.

STERILITY

Sterility is a very real problem in our society. Dr. Overstreet recently reported that 17 per cent of couples in the child-bearing age group are unable to have children of their own. Two hundred couples apply for every child available for adoption, for only 33 per cent of infertile husbands and wives are being cured.

In order to evaluate the many factors which cause sterility a team of specialists is necessary. An internist must examine the heart, lungs, kidneys. A urologist must examine the male reproductive organs and analyze the sperm count, the mobility, the number of normal and abnormal forms. A gynecologist must examine the woman's reproductive organs. Emotional tensions are also studied. An endocrinologist checks the hormone functioning of both man and woman. Defects in the functioning of the pituitary, thyroid, and adrenals as well as of the ovaries and testicles should be corrected. This is sometimes difficult because some of the hormone preparations are very expensive and some are inadequate, not to mention the complicated interaction of the hormone-producing glands.

Fertility varies even in the same individual. Some women mature later than others. Those who mature late may not be able to conceive or may conceive only a few times. As a general rule, fertility decreases with age. Women rarely conceive after 48 or 50 years of age.

High strung, nervous men and women may have some difficulty conceiving. Emotional fears, aversions to sex and motherhood, over-emphasis on a career and too much or too little physical and sexual activity may all interfere with conception. Sterility can be avoided in many cases if the first pregnancy is planned soon after marriage; the mother usually conceives more quickly and has a healthier pregnancy, delivery, and recovery.

The desire for a car, a house, a job, or even a college degree may be greater than the desire for children in the early years of marriage, but if pregnancy is postponed too long it may be extremely difficult to attain. "Too long" varies with the health, sexual maturity, and reproductive organs of the woman. Some women are sterile, some become sterile in their early twenties, others in their late forties.

ABORTION AND STERILITY

There is much confusion and lack of knowledge about many matters of sex, particularly about birth-control and abortion. Birth-control, or contraception, is the prevention by mechanical or chemical means of the meeting of the sperm and the ovum. Abortion is the destruction of the fetus by surgery—in other words the prevention of birth *after* fertilization has taken place.

There are several types of abortions, and these should be clearly defined and understood. (1) Criminal abortion is an operation that is illegally performed to stop a pregnancy. Thousands of women annually die of hemorrhage or infection after a visit to an abortionist—a racketeer who performs an operation to terminate an unwanted pregnancy. Many women survive but suffer such damage to their reproductive organs that they are subject to inflammation, poor ovarian function, complicated labor in later pregnancies, or even sterility. Abortions may also give rise to guilt feeling, frustration, painful intercourse, and frigidity.

(2) Spontaneous abortion occurs of its own accord. The causes are not always known. It usually takes place in the early months of pregnancy and is not considered dangerous if medical care is sought immediately.

(3) Therapeutic abortion is surgical abortion performed in a hospital with the consent of a consulting committee of the staff to terminate a pregnancy which would endanger the patient's life. Such abortions are often recommended for women with tuberculosis or certain types of heart disease.

There are many factors to be considered before an abortion is performed (even a therapeutic abortion). A woman should realize that unless the operation is absolutely necessary and recommended by competent physicians, her health, her sexual relationships, her fertility, and even her life may be endangered.

CONCLUSION

Reproduction is not yet clearly understood. But every advance in scientific knowledge gives us new awareness of the way nature has equipped men and women so that life may go on. In this chapter some of the aspects of reproduction such as fertilization and the birth process have been described. Today young people, since they are informed about reproduction, are finding it possible to discard attitudes of fear and prepare realistically for parenthood.

PROJECTS

1. Visit the local health department and ask for statistics on mother and infant mortality. Chart the decline in deaths of both mothers and babies.
2. Ask an obstetrician to visit the class to discuss modern views of childbirth and to describe advances in modern obstetrics.

3. Ask some new mother who previously had the course in marriage to discuss the manner in which she dealt with her fears.
4. Visit a modern hospital and observe how this hospital provides for its mothers and babies.

VISUAL AIDS

Labor and Childbirth, Medical Films, Inc., San Francisco.

READINGS

LESTER GEORGE BARTH, *Embryology,* New York, The Dryden Press, 1949.

HENRY A. BOWMAN, *Marriage for Moderns,* New York, McGraw-Hill Book Company, Inc., 1948, Chapter 15.

GRANTLY DICK READ, M.D., *Childbirth without Fear,* London, William Heinemann, Ltd., 1947.

HANS SELYE, *Endocrinology,* Aeta Endocrinologica, Université de Montreal, Montreal, Canada, 1947.

CHAPTER 16

Achieving Sexual Maturity in Marriage

INTRODUCTION: THE ATTAINMENT OF SEXUAL TOGETHER-
NESS IS AN IMPORTANT FACTOR IN ACHIEVING COHESIVENESS IN
marriage. It is a climax to the process in which a man and a woman have
grown to share with and to trust each other. It is the most intimate form
of tender and loving communication. Optimum sexual satisfaction comes
only to those couples who have found optimum happiness in all other
areas of their lives. The mood and the extent of all other adjustment
determines the fullness of sexual expression. For this reason sexual success is almost always a function of adjustment in other areas of living.
That sexual satisfaction is something more than a phase of the reproductive function may be concluded because men and women desire to be
together physically without reference to the possibility of impregnation
and regardless of pregnancy. Sexual love both perpetuates the family
through reproduction and solidifies the marriage bonds.

PHYSICAL ASPECTS OF COITUS

There are many facts about the sexual capacity of human beings
which, if understood, would relieve young people of much of their
anxiety in approaching the physical side of marriage. The first is that
through millions of years nature has been perfecting the sexual organs

of man and woman so that they have become both more sensitive for pleasure and more adapted for complete union.

The penis becomes enlarged for coitus and extends forward at an angle which rather exactly matches the structure of the vagina of the wife. The glans, the end of the penis, is full of nerve endings and is one of the centers of sexual pleasure for the male. The two testicles, which hang in the sac or scrotum back of the penis, produce two things: the spermatozoa which fertilize the egg and the male sex hormones which circulate in the male's bloodstream and impel him toward sexual activity. Thus, male sex organs are not only structured for sexual intercourse, but manufacture materials which stimulate sensitivity and vigor.

The female sex organs are no less developed. The vagina consists of the vulva, or the outer lips, and the inner lips. At the upper junction of the inner lips is a small but important organ called the clitoris, which resembles a very small penis and in which there is also a concentration of nerve endings. The function of the clitoris is to promote enjoyment and orgasm. The clitoris is the most sensitive of all the female sexual organs and seems to have no other function than to provide sexual pleasure. The interior of the vagina is lined with a group of muscles which are perfectly structured for both childbirth and intercourse. These muscles have rugae or muscular folds which may expand to accommodate a large penis or contract to enfold a smaller one. They adjust to the male organ. Thus fear about difference in size is generally needless, for nature provides for this contingency. This means that not only are the male and female organs slanted to mate most closely, but their structure is adaptable so that the closest sort of physical union has been provided for.

It might seem that the closeness of the organs would cause friction in the back-and-forth motion of intercourse. But nature has provided for this contingency. The inner vulva contains glands which, during sexual stimulation, provide a lubricating fluid that not only enables the husband to make an easy entrance but facilitates a close but pleasurable union between the penis and the walls of the vagina. It is important that sufficient love play should precede the entrance so that there is a state of readiness on the part of the female structure to welcome the male organ.

DIFFERENTIALS IN MALE AND FEMALE SEXUAL-RESPONSE PATTERNS

A second characteristic of the male and female sexual systems is the differential in response patterns. This may be represented by the following figure.

297

FIGURE 17. Intensity of Male and Female Sexual Desire

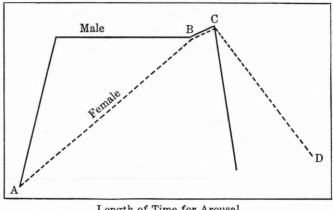

Length of Time for Arousal

A. Beginning of love play   C. Orgasm
B. Intromission   D. Detumescence

The male is very easily stimulated to sexual activity. This may be accomplished by a kiss, by some expression of tenderness, or even by the thought of his wife. He is then almost instantaneously ready for intercourse, but his wife does not respond so quickly to the same type of stimulus.

Kinsey has charted differences in erotic response between men and women. He used a threefold table to illustrate each of these differences —rated as definite and/or frequent, some response, and never. In the following adaptation of his findings we have combined the first two ratings and eliminated the "never" as this would obviously be the sum of the other two subtracted from 100 per cent.

These 14 items indicate the degree of difference which Kinsey illustrates in some thirty-three individual sets of data. In response to only three of these items (moving pictures, reading romantic literature, and being bitten) were as many females affected as males. Women then are not as prone to be sexually stimulated by psychological factors as are men. Women are aroused chiefly by tactile stimulation of erotic zones. Men may be aroused by both tactile and psychological factors.

Thus the female must be gradually roused by gentle caresses, many kisses, and fond words until she is ready for coitus. If we assume that the period from the first erotic impulse at "A" in Figure 17 to the time when the wife is sufficiently aroused for intercourse at "B," it might seem

298

T A B L E 34. Summary of Differences in Psychologic Factors in Sex Response for Men and for Women, by Per Cent*

EROTIC STIMULUS	By Females	By Males
1. Observing the opposite sex (clothes or nude)	58	72
2. Observing own sex	12	16
3. Observing portrayals of nude figures	12	54
4. Observing genitalia of opposite sex	48	Many
5. Observing own genitalia	9	56
6. Observing commercial moving pictures	48	36
7. Observing burlesque and floor shows	14	62
8. Observing portrayals of sexual action	32	77
9. Observing animals in coitus	16	32
10. Fantasies concerning other sex	69	84
11. Reading literary materials	60	59
12. Stimulation by erotic stories	14	47
13. Arousal from sadomasochistic stories	12	22
14. Responses to being bitten	55	50

* Adapted from Alfred C. Kinsey, *et al.*, *Sexual Behavior in the Human Female*, Philadelphia, W. B. Saunders Company, 1953, Chapter 16. Reprinted by permission.

that this difference indicates a difficult problem. But closer study of the facts indicates that this period of caressing, kissing, fondling, spoken appreciations and endearments is one of the most important in marriage. Such love play contributes to the general togetherness of the couple and makes coitus a time of meaningful joy. Far from being a mistake, this difference introduces into marriage a period of profound value.

We may assume that the same may be said of the period from "C" to "D." A man's feeling subsides very quickly after orgasm, but a woman's does not. This means that there is not only a need but an opportunity for further expression of love during this period of after-play.

SEXUAL ADJUSTMENT AND GENERAL MARITAL ADJUSTMENT

A second problem involved in achieving good coital adjustment relates to the totality of other adjustments. Man is the only animal in which psychological moods affect sexual functioning. In a man or a woman, thought or memory may influence glandular and emotional reactions. Consequently, conflicts over money or religion, neglect or discourtesies, quarrels and hurts will in time have an adverse effect on sexual harmony. While sexual difficulty is often caused by a lack of sufficient knowledge and a lack of acceptance of sex, it is also often caused by a failure in the general relationship of marriage. One reason why it appears that sexual adjustment is difficult to achieve is that failure in any one or several of the other major areas of adjustment is reflected in physical relationships. Generally a couple which has achieved a satisfactory cooperative framework in which to face all their other problems will find a minimum of difficulty in coming together sexually.

Some confirmation of this point of view is found in the research of Burgess and Wallin. They asked whether or not the sexual adjustment of a couple could be predicted from a knowledge of their general marital success. That sexual love is only a part of the total affectional pattern is indicated by the relationship they found between happiness scores and sexual-adjustment scores. Men with low happiness scores also had low sexual-adjustment scores. Wives with high happiness scores also had high sexual scores, and the women who had high happiness scores seldom fell into the low bracket of sexual scores (11.2 per cent).[1] This seems to indicate that good sexual relationships are barometers of the degree to which companionship and trust have been established.

This means that mutuality must pervade all the relationships in marriage if it is to be achieved physically. Marriages in which the principals are egocentric or neurotic, or use marriage either to satisfy personal needs or to satisfy dependency cravings, will miss the essential element of sharing. This lack will almost always be reflected sexually, for individuals without the experience of sharing other things will not share in sex either. A disturbance of relationship in social, economic, religious, or recreational areas will be a block as far as sexual togetherness is concerned. While there are couples who manage to find some sexual joy even though other aspects of their marriage are unhappy, we may say that the second general prerequisite to sexual harmony is a growing harmony in all the other phases of living together. On the other hand sex harmony also releases strains in other relationships so that there is a reciprocal action.

GLANDULAR FACTORS IN SEXUAL RESPONSE

The third and major problem in terms of sexual satisfaction is knowledge and acceptance of certain physiological factors. A couple need always to keep in mind that the man and the woman respond to a dif-

[1] Ernest W. Burgess and Paul Wallin, *Engagement and Marriage,* Philadelphia, J. B. Lippincott Company, copyright, 1953, p. 692.

ferent type of stimulus. The woman responds to gentle stimulation of lips, the neck, the ear lobes, and the breasts. The nipples, the lips of the vagina, and the clitoris are all especially sensitive. Nearly every part of the body is active during sexual play: the glandular system, the nervous system, and the muscular apparatus. The entire bodily mechanism comes to be more and more involved as passion increases. A male's excitable areas are generally localized, but the woman's erogenous zones are extensive and diffused. This makes for a different rhythm in the development of full sexual response, but as we have already pointed out, the male also has the capacity to sustain his passion over a long period of time and thus can enable his mate to reach the stage at which the sexual act will be satisfying to both.

But there is also a difference in terms of the degree to which the male and female are capable of responding at any given time. A male's sexual interest is subject to variation. His general state of health, his immediate energy or lack of it, the length of time since the last experience of coitus—all these have their effect. Such conditions also affect a woman, but because of the normal monthly cycle associated with preparation for pregnancy, her sexual desire sweeps in and out like the tides. She is also more sensitive to conflict and friction. But even more important is the relation of sexual desire to the menstrual cycle. Figure 18 indicates the relationship of hormones to the menstrual cycle of a woman.

This figure indicates that during all of the period between the menses, the little gland called the Graafian Follicle and Corpus Luteum, which encases the developing egg, secretes estrogen. Estrogen is a stimulant and so works upon the whole glandular system that during this period the female is predisposed to more sexual excitement. It is as though nature had provided not only that the egg should be produced during this period, but that the same organ which develops the egg should so influence the feelings of the female that she is eager and ready for impregnation. So, during the period after menstruation and before ovulation, the secretion of the estrogen hormone into the bloodstream makes the female more responsive to love overtures. It is during this period that most women experience orgasms of considerable intensity.

At ovulation the production of estrogen decreases, and the Graafian Follicle changes its form and function and becomes the Corpus Luteum. This small gland produces progesterone, a drug with a sedative influence, which by inhibiting too great excitement and diminishing in some degree the sexual response, promotes the motherhood function of the uterus and the body. The production of progesterone continues until the egg is either fertilized or dies. If the egg dies, the Corpus Luteum ceases to manufacture progesterone, and this brings on the menstrual flow. During the period when the hormone progesterone is active the emotional response of the female is that of a mother. During this period

FIGURE 18. Hormonal Curves of the Normal Menstrual Cycle*

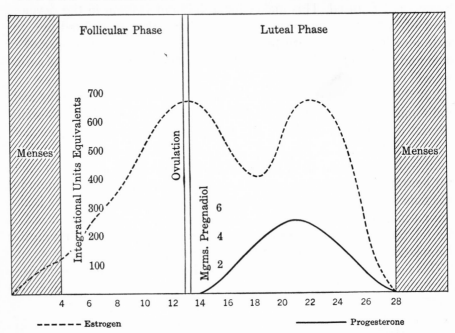

* Adapted from August A. Werner, M.D., *Endocrinology, Clinical Application and Treatment*, Philadelphia, Lea and Febiger, 1942, p. 305. Reproduced by permission.

she may not have an orgasm or the orgasm may be of considerably less intensity.

Thus after ovulation a woman's sexual response is modified by the hormone content of her system in such a way that her response is not as passionate as it is during the first period of her monthly cycle. Yet sexual relations during this period may be rewarding and meaningful even if the response is not so vigorous.

This means that a couple should not "worship" the orgasm. It is clear that from the standpoint of the endocrine system it may even be unwise to expect it. Furthermore, if too much stress is put upon achieving an

302

orgasm, a couple's love-making may become so artificial and so strained that the natural spontaneity of the act will be destroyed. Love-making and coitus ought to allow the emotions to be fully expressed, and too much concern that the act end in an orgasm or the orgasms be simultaneous may inhibit a couple from a full and free sexual expression. Sometimes the reward of intercourse will only be the tender closeness and the satisfaction of having given joy to the mate. Hannah and Abraham Stone have discussed this question thoroughly in their excellent book, *A Marriage Manual.* This book is written in the form of a conversation in which the patient asks questions and the doctor answers. The discussion of the effects of orgasm incapacity runs as follows:

First of all, I should like to stress the fact that if a woman responds actively to the sexual embrace and takes pleasure in the sexual union, her inability to reach an orgasm may not be of any serious import. Please understand that even if a woman does not attain an intense culmination, it does not mean that she does not derive a great deal of gratification from the sex act. Some women, indeed, are not at all aware of any orgasm problem until they learn about it from a conversation or book, and then they become greatly worried because they believe that they are not obtaining complete satisfaction from their sex experiences. As a matter of fact, some of the descriptions in the literature about the manifestations of the orgasm are often more poetic than real, and they sometimes lead men and women to expect sensations which are but rarely experienced.

If an actual orgasm deficiency exists, however, the effect of this condition upon the woman would depend largely upon the intensity of her sexual desires and the degree of her excitation at the time of the relation. If her sexual impulse is weak, or if she has been aroused but little, the absence of the orgasm will hardly have any harmful effects. On the other hand, if she has been very much stimulated, the failure to reach a climax may leave her in a state of frustration which may prove physiologically and emotionally disturbing. During erotic excitation there is a marked local congestion of the sexual organs as well as a general physical and emotional tension. With the completion of the act, if an acme is reached, there is a gradual release or detumescence, and this is followed by a sense of fulfillment and relaxation. In the absence of an orgasm however, the relief is not complete, and the woman may remain for some time in an unsatisfied and restless condition. Repeated experiences of this kind may eventually lead to various nervous or sexual disturbances.[2]

[2] Hannah and Abraham Stone, *A Marriage Manual,* New York, Simon and Schuster, Inc., copyright, 1952, pp. 265–267. Reprinted by permission.

ORGASMS AND SEXUAL HAPPINESS

What is the relation of orgasms to marital success? What percentage of times of intercourse must result in orgasm for the woman if the marriage is to succeed? There is some factual material on this point. From a study of 100 husbands and 100 wives, G. V. Hamilton concluded tentatively that at least 20 per cent of the copulations must end in orgasms for the female if the marriage is to be successful.[3] In a study of 792 couples Terman found that 8.3 per cent never achieved orgasm, 25.1 per cent sometimes did, 44.5 per cent usually did and 22.1 always did.[4] Orgasm apparently is one of the two sexual factors most importantly related to marital adjustment. Both of these studies indicate that it is perhaps unreasonable to expect that most women will achieve orgasm in every copulation. Orgasm capacity in women increases with age and marital experience. It is important that young people recognize this fact, lest they expect too much and set down as disappointing experience which is wholly normal.

LOVE PLAY AND SEXUAL ADJUSTMENT

The fourth problem in achieving sexual harmony is the development of love-play techniques which will bring the ultimate amount of pleasure to both the husband and the wife. Twenty-five years ago most of the books dealing with marital adjustment gave detailed instructions regarding various aspects of sexual play. This type of instruction often leads to strained procedures which are destructive both to sexual spontaneity and to personality fulfillment.

All delicate human achievements require experimentation and artistic improvisation. When Leonardo da Vinci painted a picture, he experimented with various colors, hues, and brush techniques until he achieved a masterpiece. His paintings are different from any other because they are unique combinations of line, color, and composition. Love-making is just such a delicate art. To achieve maximum creativity every couple must work out its own patterns of approach and response. To the extent that these patterns are standardized and do not express the couple's sincere and natural feelings, they are awkward and inhibiting.

[3] G. V. Hamilton, *A Research in Marriage*, New York, Lear, 1948 edition, Chapter 22.
[4] Lewis M. Terman, *Psychological Factors in Marital Happiness*, New York, McGraw-Hill Book Company, Inc., 1938, pp. 373–377.

Nevertheless, there are some general points which every couple should know, not as rules of procedure but as background information. The first of these is the assurance to the woman that any erotic gesture on her part is not only permissible but will increase both her husband's and her own pleasure during pre-play and during actual intercourse. Nothing that is right for the man to do is wrong for the woman. During the early part of the love relationship she may be somewhat timid about expressing her love, but after greater intimacy is achieved, she may take an active part. At times in fact, her initiation of love play will bring profound psychological pleasure to the male, in letting him know that he is wanted. Furthermore, the wife will wish to indicate to the husband those gestures of endearment which are most stimulating to her. The husband likewise will indicate to the wife what acts on her part are most pleasing to him. Strangely enough, such an important aspect of marital life as making love often receives the silent treatment even though both partners are relatively passionate and relatively emancipated from fear or repression. Nothing indicates so fully the degree of our cultural repression of sex as the stumbling way couples experiment sexually when frank discussion would solve any difficulties and add new understanding. It is a sign of the changing role of women in our society that they may look forward to being sexually active and share as creative partners.

What is right for the husband in terms of love play must also be permissible and desirable for the wife. But what is right? Young people entering married life are often troubled by fear of perversions or manipulations which are not generally discussed in adolescent conversation. In general nothing is wrong in sexual play which is not painful, which is aesthetically appreciated, and which does not substitute a type of foreplay for coitus itself. Furthermore, what is considered right during one period of the developing love relationship may not seem right at another. A couple will normally utilize a more varied repertoire of stimulating acts after they have been married ten years than earlier. The main criterion for love play is that it express the mutual desire of the couple and that it be spontaneous, creative, and tender.

If love play is varied, so is the time required for full tumescence of the male and female. Love play will vary according to variations in general sexual intimacy, in experience, in fatigue, and in frequency of intercourse. The ideal to be reached is the profound understanding of one another's reaction so that each responds to the other's need without hesitation.

A further point of information often sought by young people in pre-marital conferences is whether or not it is possible to determine at what period of love play coitus should begin. Men who are considerate of their mates are very often troubled by this point because they wish to begin intercourse only when their mates are ready. If a couple is able to communicate at all, there will be many ways in which the wife can indicate readiness, and her cooperation at this point often relieves the mate of considerable anxiety. Psychologically a state of deep excitation indicates such readiness. Physically the secretion of a mucoid from the glands of Bartholin makes the opening to the vagina moist and facilitates the penetration of the penis. The alert male will soon become aware of these signs and learn to time the consummation of the sex act without difficulty. The male may also want to know when an orgasm has taken place in the female. Ordinarily a strong orgasm can be felt by the penis because it consists of muscular vaginal contractions. At other times, when the orgasm is less marked, the male will know that it has occurred by a general relaxation of the whole body of his mate. In the male an orgasm is the ejaculation of the seminal fluid in a series of spasmodic contractions of the penis. A male's sexual excitement lessens very rapidly after his orgasm, and his general relaxation is unmistakable to his mate.

SEXUAL INHIBITIONS AND SEXUAL RESPONSE

The fifth general problem in achieving full sexual expression is that of overcoming sexual inhibitions. These are of different degrees and have their roots in different experiences for almost every person. Our society has shrouded sexual activity in secrecy. Children learn early that sex is some special type of experience which, even if it is discussed at home with Father and Mother, is not to be discussed with other children. When other children discuss it, they do so *sub rosa* and with a peculiar tone in their voice. This is the generalized experience of almost all children in our country. This heritage of Puritanism has caused a general repression of sexual expression. In addition, almost all young people have a history of personal incidents which have produced an accumulation of fear and wonder with regard to sexual intercourse.

Early experiences of masturbation or of heterosexual love play have also contributed a sense of guilt and shame. Severe punishment for quite natural sexual investigation leads to sexual fears for some. In many churches sex is linked to sin. In some cases long continued petting experiences have so conditioned an adolescent to saying "no" to his intense sexual drives that he cannot let go once marriage has taken place. More profound causes of sexual repression lie in deeply etched memories of an unhappy home which was sexually starved or indentifications with a mother or father who had been hurt by the other sex. There are innumerable specific psychological conditioning factors which may reduce the ability of individuals to respond satisfactorily.

In general, where a lack of sexual response exists, it is wise to consult two different types of specialists. In the first place a gynecologist should be consulted to determine whether or not any physical factor might account for the lack of response. If the gynecologist's examination proves negative, and he finds no physical reason for a lack of response, he may refer his patient to a marriage counselor. The counselor and the patient will explore then all of the processes of marriage reaction to determine whether or not the lack of response is due to other maladjustments in the marriage. The counselor will also determine whether or not the couple understand the physiological facts of intercourse and love-making. He may then explore the background of the patient to discover any traumatic experiences which might account for the lack of sexual feeling. If he discovers that the root of the difficulty is some repressed psychological pattern, he will probably refer the individuals to a psychiatrist for deeper therapy. Almost all couples have the potential for a gratifying sexual experience, but they may need the help of one or more of these specialists in order to overcome background impediments to sexual togetherness.

FEAR OF PREGNANCY AND SEXUAL RESPONSE

The sixth problem which frequently comes to the marriage counselor is a lack of response due to fear of pregnancy. Nothing is so constrictive of sexual freedom as the continual fear on the part of a woman that she may become pregnant when she does not feel ready for pregnancy. Locke found this a significant factor in his study. He quotes one divorced woman as saying, "I was scared all the time I'd get pregnant. I didn't like to have intercourse because I was scared. I had a child every year."[5] Here again a different approach is needed for different groups. For young people who are Catholics or who belong to other religious groups

[5] Harvey J. Locke, *Predicting Adjustment in Marriage: A Comparison of a Divorced and a Happily Married Group*, New York, Henry Holt and Company, copyright, 1952, p. 144.

which do not approve of the use of birth-control measures to delay the beginning of a family or to space or limit the family, the solution is to be found in a full understanding and appreciation of the philosophy of their church. The Catholic who does not feel ready to have children or mature enough to give them a good start in life should not marry until he is ready to accept the responsibilities of a Catholic marriage. Married Catholics who find themselves rebelling against the possibility of a large family must talk with their priests until they come to accept fully the philosophy by which they live. This in turn will eliminate fear of child-bearing and consequently give full freedom to sexual togetherness.

For Protestants and others who have no ethical feelings against birth-control, the selection of a reputable gynecologist and the willingness to follow his instructions implicitly as well as the understanding of the method of birth-control he prescribes will serve to eliminate fears of pregnancy. Sometimes this fear reaches the point where coitus inter-ruptus is practiced—the withdrawal of the penis just before ejaculation. Such a practice is universally unsatisfactory to both the female and the male and may lead to profound sexual dissatisfaction if not to neurotic reactions. If such a fear of pregnancy exists, it is well to face it very frankly and to deal with it honestly within the frame of ethical reference of the couple.

FATIGUE AND SEXUAL ADJUSTMENT

A seventh problem in achieving sexual completeness is that of con-serving enough psychic and physical energy so that there is a reserve for expenditure in coitus. One of the great modern enemies of good marital relations is fatigue. The investment by both male and female of most of their resources in the great struggle for power, prestige, and wealth leaves very few resources for any other development. Here, however, we are concerned only with the general depletion of the libido which comes from much anxiety over status or economic position.

Some gynecologists are very much concerned today over this problem as it relates to women in the working force of America. They have no prejudice against women working, but they report more and more cases of sexual incompatibility which seem to be caused by no more complex a factor than the serious depletion of strength caused by the stresses and strains of labor. They feel that women who sacrifice their sexual vitality by working are paying a very large price for added income because of innumerable tensions which must result. The same problem likewise occurs with men who suffer from a lack of potency because they are excessively involved either in work or in extra-curricular activity. Wilhelm Stekel introduces his two-volume work on *Impotence in the Male* with these words:

> In men love-inadequacy is increasing to an alarming degree, and impotence has come to be a disorder associated with modern civilization. Every impotent man forms the nucleus of a love tragedy. For impotence makes marriage impossible, or may be the cause of an ill-fated one; it also undermines the health of the woman and has an equally pernicious effect upon the mental life of husband and wife. The percentage of relatively impotent men cannot be placed too high. In my experience, hardly half of all civilized men enjoy normal potency. . . . The hypertrophic cultivation of the "will to power" has brought in its wake a situation wherein the majority of civilized men have neither time nor energy left for love.[6]

The problem here is so to budget energy and time that enough is left for marital relations and that this important phase of life is not a mere after-thought.

THE ENVIRONMENT AND SEXUAL RESPONSE

Related to this problem of energy is the problem of surroundings. Cleanliness of both body and environment is an essential factor in the total list of factors necessary for sexual gratification. A messy bedroom added to a home in disarray is not conducive to the beauty that ought to surround the sexual act. Strong body odors are not conducive to thoughts of endearment. Privacy is essential to complete abandon. A recent case illustrates the importance of this factor. A young couple came to the counselor because of a pronounced case of frigidity on the part of the wife. It was not too difficult to discover that the frigidity was rooted in her fear that her two sons who were old enough "to notice things" might wake up while the parents were having intercourse. They slept in the same bedroom. In another case, the wife's temporary frigidity was traced to the fear that her mother, sexually frigid herself, would walk into their home without knocking, and discover her and her husband making love.

[6] Wilhelm Stekel, *Impotence in the Male*, New York, Liveright Publishing Corporation, 1939, Volume I, pp. 1–5. Reprinted by permission.

PSYCHOLOGICAL SECURITY AND SEXUAL RESPONSE

The need for psychological security is of extraordinary importance to a woman. If she cannot feel that her husband truly loves her and would stand by her under any circumstances, she finds it difficult to give herself sexually to him. Where all of these conditions are met, the atmosphere is conducive for good sexual development.

LIFE PATTERNS OF SEXUAL RESPONSE

In discussing the developing love play of a couple, we have referred to the growing intimacy and the more complete surrender that comes after a period of sexual experimentation. We say a period advisedly because this period varies from months to many years. Many women report that "it took a few months for me to awaken sexually." Others report that their ability to respond developed gradually. One gynecologist reports that society has been so repressive of the female's sexuality that her development is in general about ten years behind that of her husband. Kinsey comments on this fact as follows:

> One of the tragedies which appears in a number of marriages originates in the fact that the male may be most desirous of sexual contact in his early years, while the responses of the female are still underdeveloped and while she is still struggling to free herself from the acquired inhibitions which prevent her from participating freely in the marital activity. But over the years most females become less inhibited and develop an interest in sexual relations which they may then maintain until they are in their fifties or even sixties. But by then the responses of the average male may have dropped so considerably that his interest in coitus with a wife who has previously objected to the frequencies of his requests, may have sharply declined. . . .[7]

While tragedy seems a strong word for this lack of harmony, Kinsey reinforces our point of the discrepancy between men and women in the rate of sexual interest at different age levels. The problem is to minimize the inhibitions and to develop such sexual acceptance that the wife will have early emancipation from inhibition and the husband consequently will not be thwarted in his sexual attentions to his wife.

It would seem that Kinsey's estimate was somewhat pessimisitic;

[7] Alfred C. Kinsey, W. B. Pomeroy and C. E. Martin, *Sexual Behavior in the Human Female*, Philadelphia, W. B. Saunders Company, 1953, p. 353. Reprinted by permission.

certainly it would be pessimistic for an alert young couple who focused on developing their love to its maximum extent. The present generation of young people have available to them many new books, many new courses in marriage, better counseling by doctors and ministers, so that the period of latency may be considerably reduced. It is also well to recognize the differential between a man's acceptance and readiness for full sexual participation and that of his wife. Understanding his wife's natural lag in sexual awakening would tend to relieve the husband of much anxiety about his love-making ability and his wife of self-doubt. The differential in the male's and the female's achievement of full sexual response may be indicated as follows:

F I G U R E 19. Male and Female Patterns of Sexual Response*

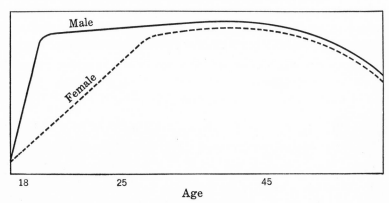

* Prepared by the author on the basis of interviews with gynecologists, case studies, and Kinsey's conclusions.

In interpreting this figure, we are assuming that if marriage occurs at eighteen, the man will in a few months develop completely his sexual powers. It is true that during the years new values will accrue to coitus, and the act will become more meaningful because of added togetherness in other areas of life. But as far as depth of passion is concerned, a man reaches the acme of his sexual prowess very early. The woman, on the other hand, will not ordinarily develop her full sexual capacity until she is twenty-five. The apt lover will recognize the differential and not inhibit her further by his misunderstanding of this basic fact.

A second observation on this life cycle of sexual response is directed toward the gradual decline that occurs after the age of forty. Potency does not suddenly diminish during either the male or female climacteric.

The change of life known in the female as the menopause occurs in most women between the ages of forty-five and fifty; a similar but less well defined change takes place in males at a slightly older age. In both instances the reaction is due to a combination of atrophy of the reproductive organs plus a psychological awareness of decreasing life function. In the woman, breasts gradually shrink, weight is gained in the abdomen, the voice may deepen, and hair may appear on the chin and neck. These changes may bring about a general nervousness and irritability. Generally most women go through this transition without medical treatment, although in cases of extreme tension both endocrine and psychological therapy prove helpful. In the male there may be a temporary loss of virility and fertility with prostate gland complications. Those men who have been most potent sexually may feel the most severe disturbances during this period, and some may resort to extra-marital affairs in an effort to compensate for their threatened loss of manhood.

Sexual activity should not be discontinued during these periods of natural change. Orgasms achieved during these trying months do much both to restore confidence and to relax tension. Knowledge of the fact that sexual desire and sexual satisfaction continue on about the same level after the climacteric may in itself be reassuring to both a man and a woman. The menopause is by no means the end of the love relationship, despite popular stereotype notions to that effect. Furthermore, the man and woman who have achieved a full and satisfying sexual togetherness may look forward to a far milder period of stress during the transition period. It is as though nature rewarded those who developed their physical possibilities.

While these various factors will tend to enhance the sexual adjustment of a man and wife by releasing their full sexual potential, it is important to stress the fact that after all of these factors are taken into consideration there will still be in some marriages some basic differences in intensity of sexual interest. Locke reports that while happily married men and women indicated "about the same" sex interest to a much greater extent than did divorced men and women, there were happily married couples who registered differences. In commenting on this Locke says:

> The informal material secured in the interviews reveals that husbands of the happily married occasionally had a stronger desire for intercourse than that of their wives. Other things in the marriage seemed to compensate for the relatively low sex interest of the wife.[8]

[8] Locke, *op. cit.*, pp. 141–142.

This seems to mean that, even though there is a difference in sexual desire, and accommodation can be made, providing other basic adjustments have been made in the marriage.

CONCLUSION

Nature has endowed men and women with very adequate sexual organs, but culture has not always given them wholesome attitudes. Still, if men and women realize the differences in their sexual rhythms and arousal patterns, if they are happy in other marital relationships, if they have some creativity in their love-making, if they overcome fears of pregnancy and insecurities, if they are healthy and not perpetually fatigued, if their home is orderly and their privacy assured, they may look forward to a lifetime of happy sexual interaction.

In all love-making which is on a high level of adjustment, there is much complementary interaction. The husband and wife receive the utmost pleasure from this interaction when they are assured of the complete fulfillment of their partner. In the mature sexual relation this effort to please the other brings profound psychological closeness between the two. The sexual act is thus both an expression and an undergirding of companionship love. Such mutuality is one of the most rewarding gifts of life.

PROJECTS

1. Take an anonymous ballot of the class to determine the degree of sexual instruction each has received from home, church, and school. Report on and discuss the results.
2. Discuss ways of sharing sexual information with children and discussing problems with adolescents so that sexual inhibitions may be ameliorated.
3. Pass a question box around the class and ask each student to drop in one or two questions regarding coitus which may have been troubling him.
4. Discuss the place of "bull sessions" in fraternities or sororities in terms of the adequacy of information shared in such groups.

READINGS

HAVELOCK ELLIS, M.D., *The Psychology of Sex*, New York, Emerson Books, Inc., 1938.

M. J. EXNER, M.D., *The Sexual Side of Marriage*, New York, W. W. Norton and Company, Inc., 1932.

313

ALFRED C. KINSEY, W. B. POMEROY and C. E. MARTIN, *Sexual Behavior in the Human Female*, Philadelphia, W. B. Saunders Company, 1953.

HARVEY J. LOCKE, *Predicting Adjustment in Marriage: A Comparison of a Divorced and a Happily Married Group*, New York, Henry Holt and Company, 1952.

HANNAH and ABRAHAM STONE, *A Marriage Manual*, New York, Simon and Schuster, Inc., 1952.

THEODORE H. VAN DE VELDE, M.D., *Ideal Marriage*, New York, Random House, Inc., 1930.

HELENA WRIGHT, M.D., *The Sex Factor in Marriage*, New York, The Vanguard Press, 1931.

CHAPTER 17

Achieving Religious Togetherness

INTRODUCTION: WHILE COMPANIONSHIP AND THE TRANS-
MISSION OF CULTURE ARE THE TWO CENTRAL FUNCTIONS WHICH
characterize the contemporary family, analysis of case-study material
reveals that there are other binding forces which can contribute to the
solidity of marriage. In this chapter the religious aspects of marriage will
be studied to discover how they may affect stability in the marital
union.

More than eighty-one million persons in the United States belong to
religious organizations. An additional large group of individuals do not
hold church membership but participate to some degree in religious
activities. A third group of adults no longer participate but as children
were associated with a church and received some degree of religious
education. Beyond this, all of us live in a democratic society whose laws,
spirit, and mores are largely an outgrowth of the close relationship of
religion to life during the most formative decades of the nation's
history. The influence of the Hebraic-Christian tradition is so pervasive
in our national laws, ideals, and customs that even the agnostic is largely
the product of a religious background.

It is reasonable to think that an institution with such a wide and his-

315

toric function in all human culture and in our own civilization has many influences upon the family.

THE RELIGIOUS CONTRIBUTION TO MORAL VALUES

Religion is a way of bringing some organization and meaning to the infinite number of experiences which happen to us in life. Religious values absorbed in the home give the individual a philosophy or a system of values which enables him to look at life with serenity and confidence. The White House Conference on Children in a Democracy stressed the contribution of the home by saying: "Here the foundations are laid for the moral standards that are to guide his conduct through life."[1] The later Midcentury White House Conference added that parents who have achieved personality integration on the basis of ethical or religious convictions are able to share these with their children.[2]

RELIGION AND HAPPINESS IN THE HOME

Stone studied the relationship between church participation and social adjustment of high-school and college youth in Washington. This study disclosed that two-thirds of the boys who said that they were active in religious activities also indicated that their home life had been very happy. On the contrary Figure 20 indicates that less than half of those who participated little in church activities considered their homes to be very happy. The figure indicates that the same conclusions were reached for girls.

Stone also found that those high-school and college students who took part in church activities tended to come from homes which were better adjusted than the homes of those who did not participate in religious activities, took part more frequently in school activities and had a larger circle of friends; and that high-school seniors who shared in church activities had a more wholesome attitude toward "helping their fellowman" and were worried less about problems than those who were not so active. On the basis of his study Stone concluded that young people who participate regularly in church activities will have fewer problems of ad-

[1] White House Conference on Children in a Democracy, Children's Bureau Publication No. 272 (Washington, 1942), pp. 185–186.
[2] Midcentury White House Conference on Children and Youth, *A Healthy Personality for Every Child, Fact Finding Report, A Digest,* Raleigh, N. C., Heath Publications Institute, Inc., 1951, p. 53 ff.

FIGURE 20. Percentage of WSC Students, Classified by Participation in Religious Activities, Giving Specified Answers to the Question, "Generally, how happy has your home life been?"*

Participation in Religious Activities	Number of Cases	"Very happy"	"Fairly happy"	"Fairly or very unhappy"
BOYS				
Very Much	88	66	28	6
Somewhat	219	58	37	5
Very Little	241	54	40	6
Not at All	158	48	40	12
GIRLS				
Very Much	128	73	21	6
Somewhat	325	74	22	4
Very Little	196	65	27	8
Not at All	50	58	30	12

* Carol Larson Stone, *Church Participation and Social Adjustment of High School and College Youth,* Washington Agricultural Experiment Stations, Institute of Agricultural Sciences, State College of Washington, Rural Sociology Series on Youth, No. 12, Bulletin 550, May, 1954, p. 15. Reproduced by permission.

justment in their homes, in their relationships with their peers (their own age group) and in school situations than do those who take little or no part in church activities.[3]

RELIGIOUS ACTIVITY AND MARITAL ADJUSTMENT

Locke's study indicates that religion is correlated with marital adjustment. He presents two tables which show the relationship between church attendance and marital adjustment. The following table for the last half of marriage shows that a much larger percentage of the divorced men and women attended church once a month or less while a much larger percentage of the married men and women attended church four or more times a month. This means that fairly steady church attendance is associated with happy marriage.

An analysis of Locke's figures also indicates that when both marriage

[3] Carol Larson Stone, *Church Participation and Social Adjustment of High School and College Youth,* Washington Agricultural Experiment Stations, Institute of Agricultural Sciences, State College of Washington, Rural Sociology Series on Youth, No. 12, Bulletin 550, May, 1954, p. 28.

TABLE 35. Regularity of Church Attendance of the Happily-Married and Divorced during Last Half of Marriage, by Per Cent, with Critical Ratios of the Difference of Per Cents*

MONTHLY ATTENDANCE	MEN			WOMEN		
	Married N 163	Divorced N 160	CR	Married N 166	Divorced N 182	CR
None	18.4	46.9	5.5	12.7	37.9	5.4
Once or less	28.2	28.1		29.5	27.4	
2 or 3 times	19.6	14.3		16.2	15.5	
4 or more times	33.8	10.7	5.0	41.6	19.2	4.6

* Harvey J. Locke, *Predicting Adjustment in Marriage*, New York, Henry Holt and Company, 1952, p. 241. Reprinted by permission.

partners belong to the same church they tend to be happily married while if they belong to different churches or if they do not belong to any church they tend to be in the divorced group. This is shown in the following table for men and women which compares those who were married and divorced, according to church affiliation.

When both were members of the same church 96 men and 95 women were happily married and only 45 men and 55 women were divorced. But when neither was a member of any church the proportion was reversed with only 19 men and 20 women in the happily married group as compared to 41 men and 42 women in the divorced group.

These statistics are collaborated by a recent report on a marriage-

TABLE 36. Comparison of Married and Divorced Men and Women in Relation to Types of Church Affiliation*

CHURCH AFFILIATION		Married	Divorced	Critical Ratio
One a member	Men	22	37	2.3
Other not a member	Women	26	48	2.37
Both members of same church	Men	96	45	5.4
	Women	95	55	5.21
Neither one members of any church	Men	19	41	3.3
	Women	20	42	2.66

* Harvey J. Locke, Adapted from data used in the study, *Predicting Adjustment in Marriage*, New York, Henry Holt and Company, 1952, but not reported in that study.

counseling experiment conducted by the Oklahoma City Family Clinic. This clinic, utilizing lawyers, ministers, teachers, business men, and doctors tries to effect reconciliations of couples having marital difficulties who are referred to it by judges and school teachers. The clinic had dealt with 250 couples at the time of the report. Forty per cent were separated, 11 per cent were divorced, 23 per cent had divorces pending. The Clinic was able to save 225 of these marriages or 9 out of 10.[4]

Only three of these families were attending church when they came to the clinic; the experience of the counselors was that participation in church activities was conducive to reconciliation. Reddick says:

> The Family Council has found that reconciliation becomes almost a certainty if they (the clinic) can persuade the couple to become active in church.[5]

SPECIFIC RELIGIOUS GROUPS AND MARITAL ADJUSTMENT

As society becomes increasingly diversified in its degrees of education, urbanization, and sophistication it is impossible for one single type of institution to meet all the needs of all the people. For some individuals liberal religion speaks with a foreign accent and for others an orthodox or conservative approach has lost all value. Consequently religious needs today can only be met by many different types of religious institutions. If it is true that we have many sects and many denominations, it is also true sociologically that these arose to meet different demands from different elements in society. All of them, however, cherish the home and all of them contribute in some ways to the preservation of a sense of sacredness of the home and to the cherishing of the marriage vows. Dr. Samuel Kincheloe has summarized the contribution of churches in general:

> However pessimistic anyone may be regarding the influence of churches in our society he must recognize that they are dealing with the formation of attitudes, opinions and, eventually, personalities, and doing so with impressive procedures. . . . Churches in our urban society have specialized in the transfer of a great tradition, a "gospel," and according to H. Paul Douglass, a veteran student of church life in America, have done so on a "very profound level."[6]

[4] DeWitt Reddick, "They Give Marriage a Second Chance," *Child Family Digest*, Volume X, Number 2, February, 1954.   [5] *Ibid.*, p. 43.

[6] Samuel C. Kincheloe, *The American City and Its Church*, Friendship Press, New York, 1938, p. 152. Reprinted by permission.

While the influence of the church is on a profound level it must necessarily be different to meet different needs. Whether the church is a small rural one-room type or a great city Cathedral, if people come consistently one may be sure both of them are serving basic human needs, and one of these needs is conservation of family life. The following material on churches deals with both their positive and their negative contributions to the family. However, as will be seen when the chapter is finished, the positive contributions are deep and significant.

The findings of Reddick, Locke, and Stone are valuable because they indicate statistically the importance of religion in family life. However, religious groups vary in their beliefs and attitudes, and consequently in their impact on family cohesion. It is important for the student to understand the different orientations of religious groups, and their contributions. In the following pages the association between specific religious approaches and marital adjustment will be presented in terms of case studies and statistical analysis.

The religious groups referred to in this study are not discrete denominational groups. The author is unwilling to name any particular denominations that "fit" the types described here. There is wide diversity even within denominations. Southern churches vary greatly from Northern churches of the same denomination. Many denominations in the East and Middle West are so different from sister churches on the West Coast that members who transfer from one section to another are not at home. Each individual church has its own history of conservatism or liberalism which sets it off as distinctive from other churches in the denomination. Hence it is more helpful to describe types of churches than to speak of Congregationalists, Methodists, Catholics, etc. The categories proposed here have been utilized in a study of religion and the family and have proved to be of some utility. Individuals who come from different religious groups may relate their own experience to the category into which it fits. The religious groups are placed on a scale; the categories are the sect, the orthodox-conservative, the authoritarian-institutional, the liberal, the Jewish, and the agnostic or non-church groups.

DESCRIPTIONS OF TYPES OF CHURCHES

The Sect Group. Sect churches are those which are characterized by emotional participation, emphasis on the supernatural, a withdrawal from life, and an otherworldly motivation. These groups tend to secure their members by a cataclysmic emotional experience of conversion. Their definition of happiness always has reference to a code of conduct which will earn eternal life by avoiding sin and by definite acceptance of a "truth" as revealed to that group alone. They interpret the Bible literally and only according to their own "revelation" of what the Bible means. Their hymns dwell on the sinful nature of man, the great moment of being "saved," high hopes of future "glory," and the evil of "worldly" pleasures. The church is the focus of family life and of life in general. Sects are as a rule extremely puritanical and tend to destroy any recreational life for the family. Members of sects may sacrifice family interests to church interests.

Sexual adjustment for young people reared in sect groups is likely to be very difficult. A report of the adolescent history of a girl reared in this type of church illustrates this impact:

> When M. . . . was fourteen years of age she was called upon to speak in Sunday School regarding the evils of dancing. M. . . . had no hesitancy in doing so. She was well informed. She knew all about the lascivious nature of natural man and natural woman and she knew what happened when those "natural" impulses were stimulated. She knew that dancing was a form of petting that stimulated sexual desire in both boys and girls. Dancing meant such close physical contact that it could be regarded in almost the same category as promiscuity. Without doubt it was one of the special tools of the devil to entice youth to sin. Therefore no good Christian boy or girl would ever give way to the temptation to join in Satan's dance. M. . . . gave this address with conviction and with sureness. It was received by the congregation as a sure testimony that "grace" had come to M. . . . What it meant in terms of M. . . . 's later marriage adjustment never occurred to that congregation. M. . . . was speaking "truth."[7]

The Conservative-Orthodox Group. The conservative-orthodox group has the same type of authority for its religious beliefs as the sect group. Members believe the Bible to be inspired and hold closely to a literal interpretation, although allowance may be made for some deviation in interpretation. In general, the denominations that tend to be subsumed under this heading are the older, more historic groups which still cling to an "orthodox" position but have mellowed to the point of associating with other groups, although they still insist on the uniqueness of their

---

[7] From a case study in the author's files.

"truth." These groups tend to be legalistic and to have a forbidding ethic, with much reliance for its enforcement on fear of future punishment. They also have a very imposing structure of "should nots" and regard happiness as the result of a rather rigid adherence to institutional codes. This group, however, tends to emphasize thoughtfulness in creed, and does not stress the highly emotional kind of conversion. Their members come as the result of a "letter" or by education in the creed.

This group tends to make much of doctrinal points of view and such outward forms of piety as prayer and church attendance. Sex is often linked with sin in the preaching and the educational work of these churches, which makes adjustment in marriage difficult. The following excerpt from a completed counseling record illustrates such a case:

> This case was referred by a lawyer in Chicago, who called to ask if the counselor would see a girl who had called on him to ask about preventing a divorce. The family consists of Marjorie, the wife; Henry, the husband; and two children, one four and the other twenty months. She had had Junior College training but the husband had only had four years of high school education. They lived in a duplex owned by her parents, who lived in the other half. The two sides were connected by a door which was never locked.
>
> The focal problem of this case was twofold: in-law trouble and sexual maladjustment. Ever since Marjorie and her husband had moved into the duplex the in-laws had taken over financially for them. They had provided financial help all through the marriage. Although this was done in a kindly way, it still proved to be a club. Marjorie and Henry had no sexual life whatsoever. They had had no sexual contact for over three months; they had had it seldom before that and it was so upsetting to Marjorie that she developed a migraine headache whenever her husband kissed or caressed her.
>
> Marjorie's early life had been very restrictive. She had a set hour to get into the house. She was not allowed to go to movies or to dance. So she lied about it and then lied again to get out of the lie. Her mother thought dancing very immoral and irreligious. Marjorie thought her mother went "hog wild" over religion. So Marjorie always had to go to her mother's church, which was of the conservative-orthodox type we have described, with great emphasis on the sin of dancing, card playing, movies, sex, and drinking. Furthermore, her mother insisted that this church only had the answer to the need for salvation and everyone outside it was condemned to hell.
>
> Marjorie was an only child, but she felt she had never been loved; in fact, she remembered wondering if she really would ever know what the mean-

ing of love was. Her mother would never allow her to kiss her or anyone else, on the theory that there were "bugs" which one would get. As a small child she remembered that she had not been allowed to see a boy baby until he was diapered. She never had seen a naked boy and felt very guilty because she often wondered what her father really looked like. In high school, when she discovered some things about sex she became very frightened. She was frightened not by the facts themselves but because her mother might find out that she knew these facts. Even though she was married and the mother of two children, she felt that her mother would be very much happier if she could feel that Marjorie knew nothing about sex. She knew that when she kissed her husband she made it as brief as possible lest her mother or father come in, which they did without knocking. All in all, her rigid religious and home background combined to inhibit her almost completely in the area of sexual acceptance and somewhat in the area of social adjustment.[8]

There were many important factors in this case; chief among them was an extreme dependence upon the parents which involved an acceptance of the general puritanism of the parents' religious group. This puritanism includes not only renunciation of sex but disapproval of activities such as card-playing, dancing, and going to the movies, which in our society are means of developing sociability, making friends and finding a mate. Marriage is difficult for a person who does not accept these activities. So is adjustment after marriage.

The Institutional-Authoritarian Group. The institutional-authoritarian churches tend to be the oldest. They have existed long enough to recognize the basic needs of personality and to take account of them in their philosophy of the family. They tend to emphasize authority, creed, and ritual. They regard the Bible and tradition as the sources of truth. They tend to be legalistic and dogmatic, and in their view conformity is the *sine qua non* of the good life. They generally stress the rewards of heaven or of hell as the result of good or evil living. They have a broad outlook on the family and stress its relationship to both the church and society. They generally accept the value of sexual life in marriage but are very emphatic about the evil of any pre-marital sexual experimentation. Members of these groups tend to be liberal in their views on gambling and drinking as long as they are not indulged in to excess. They do not proscribe card-playing, dancing, or movies. These churches tend to do the thinking for their members and set forth

[8] From a case study in the author's files.

conditions for divorce, use of birth-control, religious education of children and all other important family concerns. The following excerpt from a case study indicates how sharply this group influences the conscience of its members:

> Mary Mooney, age 23, white, first year of graduate school, came to see the marriage counselor because, as her wedding date approached, she began to feel that she would not be able to say "I do" at the altar. She had no doubt about her love for the young man, no doubt about their "fitness" as to education, recreational, or religious harmony. But she felt she was slipping away from the boy. As she was to be married in three weeks, she was most alarmed at this feeling of deep estrangement and fear of marriage to him. The first interview produced no indications of any emotional reaction which might account for this feeling, other than the normal trepidation of entering a new relationship. However, her emotional reaction seemed too intense to allow this to stand as a sufficient explanation of her feelings.
>
> In the second interview Mary immediately introduced the idea that there was something in her background of experience which made her feel that she did not want to get married. She went on to explain that she had allowed her fiancé to caress her and had taken deep pleasure in it. Two days later, she had experienced profound remorse and had gone into something of a depression as a result. She later talked it over with him and they agreed on no more caresses until after the marriage. Nevertheless, when they were alone, they could not seem to escape making love and each time she experienced the same profound pleasure and the same guilt feelings. In trying to discover the cause for such reactions to petting she explained that she had grown up in a _____ home, and had attended a _____ church and that she knew very explicitly that petting was a severe sin. As she talked about it she began to realize that it was her extreme feelings of guilt which were tending to separate her from her fiancé whom she loved dearly.[9]

The institutional-authoritarian group influences family stability by its great insistence upon the religious value of the family by its marriage ritual, and by its great power over the individual conscience. Some of the members of this church find it difficult to overcome the early linkage of sex with sin and conflict between the church's ideas on divorce, religious education of children, birth-control, and those accepted by society. Also the tendency to depend upon the church for the answers, rather than

[9] From a case study in the author's files.

upon the creative, problem-solving ability of each person, may cause maladjustments. This group of churches reinforces family cohesion by emphasizing family participation in the activities of the church.

The Liberal Churches. The liberal churches are differentiated from the others in that they accept no one authority for truth. They accept the Bible but they also depend on tradition, on science, and on human reason. They tend to accept divorce if they believe that it is in the interest of the developing personalities· of the individuals in the family. They also accept birth-control for the spacing of children, and grant the right of each member of the family to choose his own religion. They stress the realization of "eternal life" on earth rather than conformity to a moral code that will win entrance to heaven. They like to be considered "life-centered." Their members are secured by intellectual assent and they stress the intellectual side of religion, and the fellowship it provides, rather than emotional participation or dogmatic belief. Most of them put emphasis upon the full development of the various phases of human personality: physical and mental, social and religious. They fully accept most of the social customs such as card-playing, dancing, and going to the movies, but many of them have firm convictions against drinking and gambling. Many of them accept sex as a God-given aid to family togetherness and are developing ways of helping young people overcome ignorance in this field.

The Jewish Denominations. While all Christian denominations may be classified according to the types given, the Jewish groups have a somewhat unique heritage and must be considered separately. In general, the Jewish groups differ from all others in that they emphasize a rational rather than a supernatural, a democratic rather than an authoritarian approach; a "this-worldliness" as opposed to an "other-worldly" frame of ethical reference. There is very little asceticism in Judaism. Jews look on marriage as a way to find peace, to promote comradeship, to add to the enjoyment of life, and to perpetuate the race. "A man who has not a wife is not a complete man," says an ancient rabbi. Sex as such is accepted as a normal part of life and there are allusions to sexual intercourse in the Old Testament and in Rabbinical literature. Their rule has been continence before marriage and fidelity after marriage. Divorce is permitted under circumstances but "The Altar of God sheds tears for one who sheds the companion of his early years." Birth-control is accepted, but a family of children is one of the ideals of the group. All three branches of the Jewish church (orthodox, conservative, and reformed)

325

condemn interfaith marriage and regard such marriages as "driving a nail in the coffin of Judaism."

The Agnostic or Non-Church Groups. While the agnostics or non-church groups are religious groups only in a negative sense it is important to understand their concepts. Most of them have a humanitarian ethic which stresses good motives and sound living, but they do not believe it is necessary to refer such beliefs to any authority. Many of their members have carried this thought to its ultimate conclusion; one who has stated his point of view is Bertrand Russell:

> That man is the product of causes which had no prevision of the end they were achieving; that his origin, his growth, his hopes and fears, his loves and his beliefs, are but the outcome of accidental collocations of atoms; that no fire, no heroism, no intensity of thought and feeling, can preserve an individual life beyond the grave; that all the labors of the ages, all the devotion, all the inspiration, all the noonday brightness of human genius, are destined to extinction in the vast death of the solar system—all these things, if not quite beyond dispute, are yet so nearly certain that no philosophy which rejects them can hope to stand.[10]

The problem for young people who classify themselves as agnostics is one of values and motivations. Some navigators use the compass; others use the stars to guide them. But all have some means of establishing directions on the journey. The intellectual honesty of young people who state that they find themselves unable to accept some of the ideas of their forebears is admirable. But this is not enough. Such a declaration is only a negative statement of what one does not believe. How will these people weather the storms of life? By what values will they direct their family destinies? How will they compensate for the inspiration that comes to other individuals from worship? Adjustment to partners who have religious convictions may be a problem because of lack of communication and mutual interests.

The relationship of these religious groups to marital adjustment has been tested in a Los Angeles study of 420 husbands and wives.[11] The sample was obtained by utilizing a previous study made by Shevky and Williams of the characteristics of census tracts in Los Angeles County.

[10] Bertrand Russell, *Mysticism and Logic,* London, Longmans, Green and Company, 1919, pp. 47 and 48. Reprinted by permission.

[11] James A. Peterson, *The Impact of Objective and Subjective Religious Factors on Adjustment and Maladjustment in Marriage,* unpublished Ph.D. Thesis, University of Southern California, February, 1951.

The Shevky-Williams study rated the census tracts on the basis of two scales, one measuring socio-economic status and the other degree of urbanization.

The census tracts were then arranged in a grid, and nine social areas were constructed on this grid. While the Shevky-Williams study also indicated those areas which were high in segregation, this part of the investigation was not utilized by the religious study. The sample consisted of all white persons.

The sample of 420 persons came from the group with a central urbanization index. One-third of the sample came from low-rating socio-economic census tracts, one-third from medium-rating census tracts and the other one-third from high-rating social areas. Houses were picked at random within representative blocks in each of these areas. Two interviewers visited each home, one to interview the wife and the other to interview the husband.

Each couple was asked detailed questions regarding their religious background, present church participation and religious activities. In addition they were asked the special questions which make up the Locke Adjustment Scale.[12] When the interviewing was completed the answers were transferred to Holrith cards, and correlations were made between individual adjustment scores and religious factors. Comparisons were made regarding the impact of religious participation and membership in various types of churches in terms of marital adjustment. The Chi Square test was used as a measure of the significance of differences between these groups. This is a mathematical test which determines whether or not these differences might have been due to chance. A significance of .01 means that in 99 out of 100 times such a difference could not be due to chance.

Table 37 depicts the relation of high and low adjustment of men and women to religious types. The table indicates that men belonging to liberal religious groups have the highest level of adjustment while men belonging to institutional-authoritarian groups have the lowest level of adjustment. The high level of adjustment of the no-church group indicates some contradiction of the commonly held belief that those who are not members of churches fail in marital adjustment. The results for women are similar to those for men although women with no-church

[12] Harvey J. Locke, *Predicting Adjustment in Marriage: A Comparison of a Divorced and a Happily Married Group*, New York, Henry Holt and Company, 1951.

relationship have a somewhat lower adjustment score than men belonging to this group.

T A B L E 37. Relation of High and Low Adjustment of Men and Women to Religious Types (by Per Cent) *

N = 196 (MEN)   N = 186 (WOMEN)

	Sect Conservative-Orthodox	Institutional Authoritarian	Liberal	Jewish	No church-Agnostic	Chi Square
	PER CENT	PER CENT	PER CENT	PER CENT	PER CENT	
MEN						
Low-adjustment score	28	45	22	23	23	
High-adjustment score	72	55	78	77	77	22.21 Significant at .01 level
WOMEN						
Low-adjustment score	23	32	18	15	35	
High-adjustment score	77	68	82	85	65	11.157 Significant at .03 level

* Adapted from James A. Peterson, The Impact of Objective and Subjective Religious Factors on Adjustment and Maladjustment in Marriage, unpublished Ph.D. Thesis, University of Southern California Libraries, 1951, pp. 144–146.

DISAGREEMENT ON SEX AND RELIGIOUS BELIEF

It was important to see whether these differences in adjustment scores of men and women belonging to different religious types would be duplicated in other phases of family life. Questions were raised regarding disagreement on sexual matters and on guilt feelings regarding sexual relations. The two following tables indicate that there are important differences recorded in this pilot study along the lines suggested by the descriptions of the types. Table 38 compares church members by religious types on disagreement regarding sexual matters for both men and women. The liberal and no-church groups have the lowest degree of disagreement regarding sexual matters. Table 39, measuring the degree of guilt experienced by men and women of different religious types, indicates again that the liberal and no-church groups experienced less guilt than the others.

328

T A B L E 38. Comparison of Church Members by Religious Types in Terms of Guilt Feelings Regarding Sexual Relations*

	Sect Conservative-Orthodox		Institutional Authoritarian		Liberal		Jewish		No church-Agnostic	
	NO.	PER CENT	NO.	PER CENT	NO.	PER CENT	NO.	PER CENT	NO.	PER CENT
TOTAL	56		66		106		20		141	
Those who had some guilt feelings	16	29	14	21	12	11	2	10	9	6

* Adapted from James A. Peterson, *The Impact of Objective and Subjective Religious Factors on Adjustment and Maladjustment in Marriage,* unpublished Ph.D. Thesis, University of Southern California Libraries, 1951, p. 210.

T A B L E 39. Comparison of Church Members by Religious Types on Disagreement Regarding Sexual Matters Both Men and Women N = 414*

	Sect Conservative-Orthodox		Institutional Authoritarian		Liberal		Jewish		No church-Agnostic	
	NO.	PER CENT	NO.	PER CENT	NO.	PER CENT	NO.	PER CENT	NO.	PER CENT
TOTAL	56	100	66	100	106	100	20	100	141	100
No. who disagreed on sexual matters	14	25	21	31	20	18	5	25	13	9

* Adapted from James A. Peterson, *The Impact of Objective and Subjective Religious Factors on Adjustment and Maladjustment in Marriage,* unpublished Ph.D. Thesis, University of Southern California Libraries, 1951, p. 210.

GUILT OVER BIRTH-CONTROL AND RELIGIOUS MEMBERSHIP

A still further testing of the reactions of these religious types was made by comparing their guilt reactions to the use of birth-control. Here the statistical material bears out very strongly previous findings. Table 40 presents a comparison of church members by religious type in terms of

329

guilt feelings regarding birth-control. Again the liberal group and the no-church group show the lowest percentage of guilt feelings.

TABLE 40. Comparison of Church Members by Religious Types in Terms of Guilt Feelings Regarding Birth-Control N = 420*

	Sect Conservative-Orthodox		Institutional Authoritarian		Liberal		Jewish		No church-Agnostic	
	NO.	PER CENT	NO.	PER CENT	NO.	PER CENT	NO.	PER CENT	NO.	PER CENT
TOTAL	56		66		106		20		141	
No. who had some degree of guilt	7	12	13	20	4	4	4	20	3	2

* Adapted from James A. Peterson, *The Impact of Objective and Subjective Religious Factors on Adjustment and Maladjustment in Marriage,* unpublished Ph.D. Thesis, University of Southern California Libraries, 1951, p. 214.

These statistical conclusions indicate that there is a significant difference in adjustment to marriage according to membership in various types of religious groups. In terms of preparation for marriage and marriage adjustment, the student will want to review his religious background to see whether or not it may in some way present special problems for him. The student will wish to analyze such differences as may exist between himself and his intended mate, to discover whether or not those differences will be a special hazard to happiness in marriage. Case studies indicate some of the specific reasons why there is a difference in adjustment between religious groups. This material will now be presented.

TYPES OF RELIGIOUS INSTITUTIONS AND MARRIAGE ADJUSTMENT

The importance in marriage adjustment of membership and participation in these groups may be indicated by the following points:

(1) Members of those groups (sect-conservative or institutional-authoritarian) which are very zealous about their denomination are apt to bring stress into their marriage, if the partner is not a member, by constantly putting pressure on him to join and to participate.

(2) Members of those groups (sect-conservative-orthodox) which are "other-worldly" and ascetic sometimes have great difficulty in sexual

330

and social adjustment. The values to which they give allegiance and their life-time motivation are renunciatory of the "pleasures of the flesh." Consequently, problems of sexual and social adjustment arise unless both members of the marriage equally believe in this accent on their lives.

(3) Members of those groups (institutional-authoritarian) which may be described as rigidly ethical have a tendency to be so forbidding in pre-marital education that individuals carry into marriage such restraints that their sexual adjustment is often unhappy. However, this group sometimes achieves a better social adjustment because they accept smoking, movies, dancing, and controlled drinking.

(4) Members of those liberal groups who accept the sexual side of marriage and stress a "life-centered" approach sometimes fail to give their children and young people a sense of responsibility and value so that they enter marriage without determination to make it succeed.

(5) Members of those groups which condemn birth-control (institutional-authoritarian) may find themselves in conflict with their church or with their own consciences if they use this method of family planning. Many church members who develop these guilt feelings find that they interfere with their sexual adjustment.

(6) Inter-religious group marriages will be productive of conflict when the persons involved have differing attitudes toward such things as gambling, drinking, card-playing, movies, dancing.

(7) Inter-religious group marriages will be productive of conflict when they involve differing attitudes toward family planning and birth-control.

(8) Inter-religious group marriages will be productive of conflict when they involve competition about the religious education of the children.

(9) Inter-religious group marriages will be productive of conflict when they involve a major difference in degree of religious interest or religious orientation.

(10) Inter-religious group marriages may not achieve the highest degree of integration because the family is not unified in celebrating the great festival occasions in life.

THE POSITIVE CONTRIBUTIONS OF RELIGION TO THE FAMILY

Thus far we have discussed the ways in which religion may cause problems in marriage adjustment either by matching two very diverse religious types or by producing social and sexual inhibitions within the individual. In the concluding section we deal with specific ways in which religion contributes to family integration, family growth, and family happiness.

The Psychological Contributions of Religion. Man is not perfect. Life is often frustrating and irritating. Storms of temper and depressions born of fear and anxiety disturb most men and women. They react emotionally and hurt one another. One hour they are lovers and the next hour there is hostility between them. One of the most difficult lessons to learn in life is to accept our own imperfections. When this is done we are able to forgive others. Forgiveness promotes growth in togetherness in the family. Forgiveness is at the heart of all Hebraic-Christian beliefs. Hosea taught the Jewish nation to forgive as he forgave his erring wife and Jesus forgave those who drove nails into His hands and feet. Those who have listened since childhood to Jesus' insistance that we cleanse the inside of the cup and that no one is perfect are probably more humble than those who are non-religious. Self-examination in prayer stimulates growth and induces humility. And the person who is humble, who recognizes the grossness of his own egocentricity and the wilfulness of his own personal aggressions, may truly forgive others. Thus, religion helps overcome those egocentric blocks to happiness in marriage that are well-nigh universal.

The Character Contributions of Religion. The ideal of the church tradition is neighborliness and loving service. When the traveler fell among thieves it was a man with love in his heart who stopped and bound up the man's wounds and carried him to the inn. The ideal of loving service comes very close to the mutuality which contributes to happy marital relationships. Religion shifts the attention from the self to others. But it also takes motives into account. Attention to others which is part of a conscious effort to gain personal success or augment status is eventually productive of conflict. So Paul in his Hymn of Love says that even though one gives all he has, yes, even his body to be burned, if he does not have love, it is nothing. It is the love that is self-forgetting and spontaneous that makes the home a place of happy adjustment.

Religion helps marriage in that it tends to produce that type of character structure which is most productive of marital happiness.

The Contributions of Worship. Worship contributes to family unity by supplying a focus for family activity. Worship is a ritual, and like all

332

rituals tends to have a binding force when it is performed consistently and persistently. Anything which the family experiences together with satisfaction makes the family more of a unity. The rituals of dressing for church, walking or riding together to church, sitting together and then discussing the service are experiences which strengthen the bonds of togetherness.

Worship also contributes to the growth of the spirit of the family by consistently holding up to its members aspirations that demand growth. The ideals stressed by churches are brotherhood, reconciliation, peace, kindness, and redemption. In worship one endeavors to relate oneself to the meaning of existence and to the core reality of life. Hours of worship are hours of the uplifted heart and the questing spirit. The frontiers of conscience and mind are pushed outward and the concern for others is sensitized. This experience may bring to a man and a woman a sense of trust, of faith, and of destiny that changes meaningless drifting into purposeful living, that transforms the confused, ambivalent individual into a person with perspective. In saying this we are not unmindful of the morbidity of some overly puritanical faiths which are barren of beauty and destructive of tenderness. Nevertheless, worship of God, the searching of conscience in prayer, the singing of hymns of brotherhood, and the relating of our experience to ideal goals and aims constitute for many a moving and constructive growth experience.

The Contribution of the Religious Counselor. Religious counseling includes not only the Catholic confessional but also Protestant and Jewish counseling. Catholics ease the burden on their souls by "confessing" their sins. They are assured of pardon when they have done penance and have promised not to repeat their mistakes. In Protestant churches this experience takes a different form. Men and women go to the study of their ministers and "confess" there. Today many of the modern Protestant seminaries are training their ministers in techniques of pastoral counseling. These ministers are learning ways to implement their religious concern for their members by counseling them about family problems. People in trouble often turn to their priests or ministers. The modern minister also is being trained to recognize those problems which are so severe that referral is wise. A priest or a minister contributes to the balance of the troubled individual who feels guilty by allowing the troubled person to unburden himself and by helping him to achieve a sense of his own worth.

333

A major contribution of ministers, priests, and rabbis is the growing practice of pre-marital counseling in which a couple is helped to prepare more adequately for marriage.

The Contribution of Fellowship. Urban life is generally a lonely life. Bars are often inviting to individuals not because of the liquor they dispense but because of the company they provide—people with whom to laugh and talk. Churches have specific fellowship groups and some of these are directly focused on family life. Young married peoples' groups concentrate on ways of achieving better harmony in marriage, on discovering new recreational patterns, and on raising the ideals of their members. Such groups often have a therapeutic value for couples who may not have solved all of their adjustment problems. Many churches have discussion groups on child psychology, adolescent problems, and religious education. These groups bring to their members the best in modern thought about the rearing of children.

There are other groups in churches such as high-school, college or young adult groups in which more and more stress is put on wholesome recreation, on developing values in dating and courtship, and on the discernment necessary for wise marriage choice.

FESTIVAL OCCASIONS AND FAMILY COHESION

Christmas, Easter, Thanksgiving, Yom Kippur, may only be seasons of drinking and hilarity. But for some families they are periods when their own pleasures are somewhat determined by institutional practices and broader contacts. The story of Mary and her Baby in the manger, of the shepherds and the wise men bringing gifts, in its simple, moving beauty touches all of the family, adds to family appreciation of itself, and gives added dimension to the gifts which are shared. In like manner all festival occasions are among the high points of life and those who have a religious orientation seem to find deep beauty and meaning in them which is reflected in their family attitudes.

CONCLUSION

Worship, prayer, religious festival occasions, and church fellowship tend to increase reverence for life. People are thus led to view their hours on earth with a special sense of mission and a sense of responsibility for those close and far from them; to see that personality has an

334

eternal worth and that the family has a fundamental dignity that demands respect.

In this chapter certain of the important ways in which religion and religious participation are related to marital adjustment have been analyzed. It is impossible to generalize about the impact of a specific religious group because of the great diversity of influences compounded under the general title of religion. Therefore a typing of religious groups was made to help the student objectify the way his or her religion may have influenced his or her preparation for marriage, or may influence adjustment with a person of another religion. The concluding section dealt with the positive benefits of religion to marriage.

PROJECTS

1. Invite a Catholic priest, a Jewish rabbi, and a Protestant minister to discuss their points of agreement and of difference in their beliefs about the family.
2. If any member of the class knows of such a situation, let that member report on the problems which are causing conflict in a marriage between people of different faiths.
3. If any member of the class knows of such a situation, let that member report on a family in which differences due to religion have been happily solved.

READINGS

HENRY A. BOWMAN, *Marriage for Moderns,* New York, McGraw-Hill Book Company, Inc., 1949, Chapters VI, IX.

ERNEST R. GROVES, *Christianity and the Family,* New York, The Macmillan Company, 1943.

LANDIS and LANDIS, *Building a Successful Marriage,* New York, Prentice-Hall, Inc., 1948, Chapter XIII.

REGINA WESCOTT WEIMAN, *The Family Lives Its Religion,* New York, Harper and Brothers, 1941.

RECORDING

The Hazards of Inter-Faith Marriage is a twenty minute socio-drama illustrating the adjustment problems of those who belong to different religious faiths. It has an introduction to the socio-drama by James A. Peterson. Educational Recording Services, 5922 Abernathy Drive, Los Angeles 45, California.

Economic Contributions
to Marital Cohesion

INTRODUCTION: THE AMERICAN PEOPLE ARE THE MOST
FORTUNATE ECONOMIC GROUP IN THE WORLD. ON THE WHOLE, THE
average American has a higher living standard than any person has ever
had in history. Indeed, the average middle-class family today has a better
diet, better health care, more adequate housing, wider communication,
and more diversified recreational opportunities than the kings and nobles
of several hundred years ago. Yet as we get more and more, we seem to
want more and more; and money and its management are constant
sources of unhappiness in a large number of American families. On the
other hand, economic insight, cooperative planning, and management
skill reinforce the bonds of love and affection that hold families together.

CONFLICT OVER MONEY IN MARRIAGE

Innumerable surveys indicate the importance of money as a factor in
marital maladjustment. Wilson, in her study of college women, found
money and its management to be among the most frequent sources of
futility—with some 38 out of 50 women mentioning money as a problem.
Only parental relationships and sexual adjustment ranked higher—these
two being stressed by 40 out of the 50 women.[1]

[1] Pauline Park Wilson, *College Women Who Express Futility*, New York, Bureau of
Publications, Teachers College, Columbia University, 1950, p. 54.

336

The *Ladies Home Journal's* representative sample ranked money as the most important of all sources of marital conflict—in fact, three times as many women mentioned this factor as any other.[2] Locke found that a significantly higher percentage (80.6) of married than divorced men (35.1) rated their wives "very satisfactory" in managing the affairs of the home.[3] In Pace's study of 951 former University of Minnesota students, management of money ranked as the number one cause of marital conflict.[4] There is no doubt that skillful home management and financial planning contribute to marital adjustment, poor management and no planning to poor adjustment.

PSYCHOLOGICAL ASPECTS OF FINANCIAL PROBLEMS

Many of the problems described by individuals as economic in origin and nature are in reality psychological. Contests for dominance may be focused on economic issues. The casual observer and perhaps the partners themselves may ascribe their trouble to differences over money and its management but in reality these surface differences are, so to speak, a stage setting in which the more basic life drama is played out. Again, some individuals use buying as a device for easing feelings of frustration—buying a hat to make up for unhappiness is a classic example. Still, when this has been recognized and stated, the fact remains that there are problems of money and home management which cause conflict and these must also be studied.

ECONOMIC SECURITY AND MARITAL ADJUSTMENT
THE "CLASSICAL" STUDIES

In demonstrating the specific ways in which socio-economic factors are associated with marital adjustment, those studies generally regarded as "classic" in the field of family adjustment will be considered. Terman[5] studied 792 couples of early middle age from the upper-class or upper-middle class. Since more than 80 per cent were white-collar workers, generalizations based on his findings do not apply to the general popula-

[2] *Ladies Home Journal*, January, 1949, p. 26.
[3] Harvey J. Locke, *Predicting Adjustment in Marriage: A Comparison of a Divorced and a Happily Married Group*, New York, Henry Holt and Company, 1952, p. 282.
[4] Robert Pace, *They Went to College*, Minneapolis, University of Minnesota Press, 1941, p. 82.
[5] Lewis M. Terman, *Psychological Factors in Marital Happiness*, New York, McGraw-Hill Book Company, 1938.

tion. Terman found that insufficiency of income was frequently mentioned as a negative factor in marriage. Some 70.5 per cent of the husbands and 68.8 per cent of the wives checked this item. Inadequate income very definitely differentiated the high from the low happiness groups. Terman stated that it was the way in which income was handled rather than the absolute size of the income that was important in relation to marital happiness.

Burgess and Cottrell's study[6] included a sample of 526 middle-class couples who had been married six years or less. These couples were studied by means of questionnaires. By use of the statistical device of partial correlation, other major factors of adjustment were held constant. Burgess and Cottrell found that the economic factor was of almost no importance. Locke,[7] studying 846 happily married and divorced families in Indiana, asked his interviewees to indicate whether their income was very adequate, adequate, inadequate, or very inadequate. The happy group considered their income adequate, the divorced described theirs as inadequate. Locke also found that certain indices of security, namely possession of life insurance, possession of savings at marriage, and accumulated savings at the time of interviewing were all associated with good adjustment. Furthermore he found that the families on a higher level in terms of rent, life insurance, utilities, and luxuries were happier than those on a lower level.

WILLIAMSON'S STUDY

The most comprehensive study of the economic factors in marriage has been made by Williamson.[8] He studied three diverse social areas of Los Angeles. His sample included 420 persons and each of them was individually interviewed. His study was therefore not subject to the criticism leveled at other major studies—that the sampling was too limited. Williamson likewise used more careful differentiations of economic factors than did previous investigators. For this reason his study, while not conclusive, is highly valuable. Concerning the amount of income he concludes:

> This factor was found to be associated with marital success, although the results were not conclusive. Incomes of less than $463 [per month]

[6] Ernest W. Burgess and Leonard Cottrell, *Predicting Success or Failure in Marriage,* New York, Prentice-Hall, Inc., 1939.   [7] Locke, *op. cit.* p. 297.

[8] Robert Williamson, *Economic Factors Associated with Marital Adjustment,* unpublished Doctoral Dissertation, University of Southern California, June, 1951.

prevailed among the unhappy individuals. Conversely there was a larger percentage of happy husbands and wives in the income bracket of $463 and above. Although the differences did not reach a high level of significance, they were impressive compared to other studies, in which almost no relationship was found between income and marital happiness.[9]

His specific findings in terms of individual economic items are clearly set forth in Table 41. This table shows that an average income of over $445 a month, home-ownership, small indebtedness and insurance over $5,000 are associated with happiness in marriage.

T A B L E 41. Percentages of Happy and Unhappy Husbands and Wives Regarding Given Economic Items with Critical Ratios*

ITEM	HUSBANDS' RESPONSES			WIVES' RESPONSES		
	Happy	Unhappy	Cr	Happy	Unhappy	Cr
Amount of average monthly income (445 or less)	57.3	70.8	−1.7	61.2	75.4	−1.7
Renting (as against owning one's home)	27.9	50.0	−2.8	27.7	45.9	−2.3
Mobility (moving two or more times during the last 3 years)	34.0	52.4	−2.2	27.9	43.9	−1.5
Amount of savings ($600 or more)	72.4	49.8	2.0	75.0	51.3	2.2
Amount of indebtedness (less than $300.00)	81.6	57.8	3.3	79.2	54.7	3.4
Amount of insurance (over $5000.00)	63.9	55.2	1.0	72.6	53.1	−3.9

* Data adopted from Robert Williamson, *Economic Factors Associated with Marital Adjustment,* unpublished Doctoral Dissertation, University of Southern California, June 1951, p. 152.

Williamson developed what he termed a "security rating" of high, medium, and low derived from a composite of economic items. Williamson concludes:

> There was the highest proportion of happy husbands and a still higher proportion of happy wives among the highest security ratings. (Percentages for the husbands: 31.8 and 19.1, CR 1.7; for the wives: 36.5 and 16.1, CR 2.7.) Medium security was also associated with significantly happy marriages. (Percentages for husbands: 47.1 and 30.9, CR 2.1; wives: 47.1 and 25.5, CR 1.2.) Most critical, about twice as many of

[9] *Ibid.,* p. 143.

the unhappy marriages were found among the individuals with low security ratings. (Percentages for husbands: 21.2 and 50.0, CR —3.8; for the wives: 16.5 and 48.4, CR —4.2.)[10]

Williamson's findings seem to give moderate support to Locke's findings that security or a higher economic level is associated with marital happiness.

However, it is not only the question of what the mate is able to provide that is important. More important is the question of what his own background, his youthful training, and his family experiences have led him to expect as normal in the way of provision. Certainly those marriages are difficult in which a young woman from a wealthy background marries the son of a plumber or vice versa. For our idea of what is normal in the way of comfort-providing items, luxury items, food, and housing is contingent upon our family and social background.

ECONOMIC MANAGEMENT AND MARITAL ADJUSTMENT

It is important to investigate the use—or misuse—of money and its relation to marital adjustment. Money may be said to have been "earned" if by wise management the total overhead of a home is substantially reduced. If a wife, by studying weekly sales and watching price differences in various stores, spends 30 per cent less on food than she might have spent, she has "earned" that much. If she cleans her own dresses and shines her own shoes, the saving is likewise money "earned." Hence, wise management must be considered "earning." A family which had an unexpected and costly illness adjusted quite satisfactorily by combining trips and saving gasoline, by using two rooms instead of seven for study and recreation in the evening, by doing a good many tasks that had been done by others previously, and by making shopping an exercise in financial wizardry. The most important change to be observed in the family was not a lowering of its standard of living but an improvement in family unity.

BUDGETING

The term budgeting has had a very narrow connotation in the minds of the general public. Because of the concern for the "almighty dollar"

[10] *Ibid.*, p. 154.

budgeting has been thought of exclusively as a way of using that dollar more intelligently.

Each of us has six sorts of things in life which he may spend:

Time: days, weeks, months, years; vacation, minutes while waiting, and so on.

Energy: as expressed in interests whether these are physical, intellectual, social, spiritual or other.

Abilities: talents, aptitudes, skills, poise and so on.

Space: such as is within his control; walls and floor space in his own room and office, desk, drawers, shelves, closets, owned ground, seats at performances, there are many examples.

Property: tools, clothing, house, whatever one legally owns or controls.

Money: negotiable papers, cash excess materials which can be sold or traded, and so on.

This sixth resource is different from all the others. It is worthless in itself. It can be so spent as to increase the others. With it, we can often buy materials, inventions, or services which make our own time, energy, abilities, space or property go much further. Or it can be spent so as to decrease our resources considerably without rendering equivalent value. Examples are buying a house too large for our needs, sustaining a meaningless membership in an expensive club, subscription to a fat magazine with indifferent contents, and a hobby dealing with trivial things.[11]

Families sometimes sacrifice happiness and security because of environmental pressures for status. So many families "keep up with the Joneses" either consciously or unconsciously that the force of social competition is very marked. Advertising men are aware of this fact and use it to make sales. When television first became popular, one firm's advertisements proclaimed that children who did not have a set were underprivileged. In our materialistic culture we often buy for purposes of ostentation rather than for pleasure or usefulness. Money and things have become synonymous with success. Some wives who do not have the latest refrigerator, washing machine, dryer, garbage-disposal unit, deep freeze, television, radio, car, mangle, etc. may feel inferior to those who have these things. Today such women do not depend upon their education, or charm, or kindliness to win position. They buy it. Some husbands, too, find that the size of the car they drive makes a greater impression than their character or the wholesome growth of their families.

[11] Regina Wescott Weiman, *The Family Lives Its Religion,* New York, Harper and Brothers, 1941, p. 116. Reprinted by permission. See also pp. 176, 177.

In such a social-economic environment one values in a mate initiative and the desire to get ahead—and accumulates things as if they were a substitute for personal growth or family happiness.

The way income is managed has some bearing on marital adjustment. The family that is always overburdened with debt, never able to meet an economic crisis, anxious and strained at the thought of taxes or Christmas is not likely to be too well adjusted. A good credit rating is commendable and is very useful. But the family that is making so many installment payments that it cannot afford enough milk or a trip to the beach has mortgaged itself too deeply. To carry on family life without any financial plan may be as unwise as allowing the financial outlay to be dictated by competition for status. On the other hand, to follow a budget too rigidly may also bring maladjustment.

The virtue of a budget is that it necessitates the thinking through of family values—it also reflects that thinking. The family which sets its sights early upon long-range goals—a home, foreign travel, retirement income—is likely to achieve them. The children's education and the family security should be provided for in an adequate savings or insurance program. Where no long-term values are projected, no outstanding achievement of family goals or security can result. Likewise decisions about the amount of income to be devoted to individual family pleasure and the amount to be allotted to the community chest, the Red Cross, the church, war savings bonds, etc. are important, for they reflect the attitudes we have toward money and income. In the home that is sensitized to human need beyond its walls there is a continuous feeling of stewardship. The family council that decides to cut down on the allowances of each individual for recreation for a month in order to help tubercular Italian children or an orphanage is teaching spiritual values in a dynamic way. Budget sessions in a family may serve as schools in decision-making and at the same time create ties which bind the family more closely together.

Thus a budget involves far more than just planned spending. Equally important are the factors of planned saving, of long-time goals, of individual needs and family unity. A budget of a family with outdoor recreational interests will be much different from the budget of a family that is interested in art, music, and literature. One interest is not better than another, merely different. Some wives, perhaps most wives, will get their greatest pleasure from time-saving equipment and from clothes; for others a new assortment of oil paints and money to be used to participate in art groups and to make trips will take precedence. It is generally recommended that a budget be based on past expenditures. In plotting these expenditures there must be an earnest endeavor by the family group to meet the dynamic interests of each of its members. Budgeting may then contribute to family unity and to personality growth.

A Model Budget. It has been suggested in this discussion that every family work out a budget to meet the needs of the individual members of the family. However, there is some value in presenting a budget which

TABLE 42. Budgets for a Family of Four (Man, Wife, Boy 13, Girl 8) at Three Income Levels, at September, 1948, Prices in San Francisco*

EXPENDITURES	ANNUAL COST IN DOLLARS			PERCENTAGE OF TOTAL COST		
	Executive	*White-collar Worker*	*Wage Earner*	*Executive*	*White-collar Worker*	*Wage Earner*
TOTAL COST	$12,849.24	$5,208.47	$4,111.22	100	100	100
Income and payroll taxes	1,864.80	439.74	275.82	14.5	8.5	6.7
Federal income	1,740.26	378.74	215.82	13.6	7.3	5.3
State income	64.54			.5		
Unemployment	30.00	30.00	30.00	0.2	0.6	0.7
Old-age insurance	30.00	30.00	30.00	0.2	0.6	0.7
Total consumption items	10,984.44	4,768.73	3,835.40	85.5	91.5	93.3
Food	2,222.98	1,623.15	1,408.51	17.3	31.1	34.3
Meals at home	1,524.90	1,281.54	1,325.27			
Guests at home	171.79	63.00	43.69			
Meals away	526.29	278.61	39.55			
Clothing	1,586.01	666.68	428.05	12.8	10.8	10.4
Man	435.67	187.71	119.77			
Wife	750.22	234.29	126.88			
Boy of 13	207.27	137.45	106.43			
Girl of 8	192.85	107.23	74.97			
House operation	1,081.53	170.59	131.65	8.4	3.3	3.2

* Heller Committee for Research in Social Economics, *Quantity and Cost Budgets for Three Income Levels,* Berkeley, University of California Press, 1949. Reprinted by permission.

represents average expenditures and thus provides a general pattern for planning. No young married couple should adhere slavishly to any given budget. The preceding budget developed in San Francisco by the Heller Committee for Research in Social Economics, may, however, suggest the various items which must be considered and suggest also a way of planning. This budget is taken from one of the studies of what families in three occupational groups in an urban community have actually spent. The costs of items apply to 1948.

THE PROBLEMS OF THE WORKING WIFE

Wives work in two areas. Some of them work at home as homemakers and others work away from home as wage-earners. The problems of each of these groups will be considered as well as the special problems involved in trying to combine the two kinds of work.

PROBLEMS OF THE HOMEMAKER

Despite the electric iron and the deep freeze most women must work if they are to maintain a home. The amount of time required in this work is indicated in a study by Folsom for urban and rural wives in Table 43.

T A B L E 43. Distribution of All Household Time (by Per Cent) *

	Farm Homes	City Homes
Meals and dishes	43	33
Housecleaning	14	13
Washing and ironing	10	8
Mending and sewing	9	6
Other house care	6	3
	82	63
Care of children	10	24
Purchasing, management and others	8	13
Total	100	100

* Adapted from Joseph Folsom, *The Family and Democratic Society*, New York, John Wiley and Sons, 1943, p. 580.

The most interesting difference here is the difference between the time spent on the care of children in rural and in urban homes. Evidently the freedom of the farm and the more ample space in rural areas takes part of the burden from the rural mother. That children raise many problems

344

for the urban mother is clearly indicated in a study by Ruth Linquist. She asked 306 mothers to indicate the chief sources for (*a*) fatigue, (*b*) worry, and (*c*) friction in their lives. The majority of the mothers put at the top of the list in each of the three categories not housework, or marriage problems, or financial concerns but child-rearing.[12] Kamarovsky comments on this problem:

> Among women who are not career-minded and whose dissatisfactions were not expressed with an eye to a totally different role, mothers of young children with little or no domestic help seem to be a particularly problem-ridden group. Overwork, tired muscles, constant and almost exclusive association with young children and monotony are among the most frequently mentioned grievances.[13]

If rearing children or homemaking is to be satisfying and rewarding for the wife, some relief from the monotony of constant association with her children must be found. Domesticity and child-training are cohesive factors when they are enjoyable. Young couples need to plan their recreational life and their sharing of tasks with a view to eliminating the factors so frequently mentioned as grievances.

PROBLEMS OF THE EMPLOYED WIFE

The wife who works outside the home has special problems. One of these is to adjust to the attitudes of her husband. Unless he understands her double responsibilities and is cooperative in meeting the pressures of running the home on a reduced schedule, the working wife may quickly become frustrated. If the husband's concept of the role of woman is such that he cannot tolerate the thought of a wife earning money, that idea will undoubtedly lead to friction. Again, if he is insecure he may regard the success of his wife's occupational venture as a threat to his own ego. On the other hand, if he regards her contribution to the family income as a constructive help and reciprocates by lending a willing hand about the house, no problem is likely to occur. While the question of a man's attitude toward his wife's working is of great importance, there are other factors of equal weight. One of the taunts thrown at women who work is the assertion that they cannot be good mothers. This depends

[12] Ruth Linquist, *The Family in the Present Social Order*, Chapel Hill, University of North Carolina Press, 1931, p. 35.
[13] Mirra Kamarovsky, *Women in the Modern World*, Boston. Permission to quote granted by Little, Brown and Company, copyright, 1953, by Mirra Heyman, p. 107.

upon the woman. If a woman likes her work, she may be able to give her children more affection than if she were tied down at home. One does not have to spend hours and hours with children in order to assure them of security. The essential need is to share a great number of happy experiences and to have a secure relationship with them. On the other hand, if the mother comes home fatigued and irritable, this offsets any economic assistance her employment may yield for the family. Thus no generalization as to the desirability of women's working is possible. Much depends upon the temperament, the vitality, and the capacity of the individual woman. Her employment may add value to affectional relationships at home or detract from them. It is unfortunate, of course, if the mother's perspective is so shallow that she works only in order to supply her children with things that she herself never had. Neither maturity nor affection can be purchased, and this bitter lesson is sometimes learned too late. On the other hand, as Mavity points out, many women today have no alternative to working; this is the price they pay for having children since the family income will not support them otherwise. Kamarovsky shows that the outstanding point about working wives is the low earnings of the husbands.[14]

The question is more acute when a woman wants to invest her life in a career rather than in a family. There may be some basic insecurity in her attitude toward rearing children or she may simply have such an interest in some vocational field that she does not want to be burdened at all by children. Then, too, not every woman can be an adequate mother. But such women are few. Marriage normally implies having children. Most husbands marry with this expectation, and even the husband who does not have a great interest in children at the beginning of marriage often develops it later. If a career woman marries with the intention of remaining childless, this fact should be made clear before marriage. On the other hand, there is no good reason why a woman cannot combine a career with motherhood provided she has the strength and the emotional equipment for both. It is something of an anomaly that many girls who are highly trained in college, and make brilliant starts in their chosen profession are expected to give up their work when they marry. Many women have much to contribute to science, to art, to literature. It is difficult to believe that marriage, *ipso facto*, must eliminate the possibility of making such contributions.

If, on the other hand, a couple organize their marriage on the basis of

[14] *Ibid.*, p. 167.

346

the wife's working, certain alterations in family habit patterns must be made. The selection of reliable domestic help is of first magnitude. The willingness of the husband to participate in family chores must be assumed and realized. Mavity comments on this point:

> The postwar husband feels no ignominy in running the washing machine or taking clothes to the Laundromat, starting dinner, or pushing the vacuum cleaner. Executive efficiency in the household is not a sex attribute, and many men who take the common-sense view that they should share in the housework if their wives share in the production of income, have demonstrated that freedom from hide-bound traditional procedures can be turned to good account. They see the problems of household management with fresh eyes. They discover shortcuts, tighten schedules, and invent improved procedures. "Woman's work was never done," perhaps because she followed deep-rutted grooves and did not try to invent new methods of getting the work done more quickly.[15]

The family time budget must be planned with as much care as the financial budget (if not more) so that a maximum number of hours may be spent in family activities. In fact when the wife works and a time budget is used, the total time invested in family activities is often greater than when the wife does not work and therefore uses her husband's free hours to get away by herself or with him.

The general acceptance of women in the working force may be regarded as a lever for better adjustment in marriages. When a woman had no alternative to marriage, there was little she could do if there was great unhappiness in the home. Today the situation is changed. The successful experience of "Molly the Riveter" during the war gave women a new confidence in their ability to support themselves and their children as well, if need be. Consequently if they stay married today, it is because they are happy in marriage. This means that a man can no longer run roughshod over his wife's feelings or needs. She is in a bargaining position which means that he must expend greater effort to make the marriage last. In the long perspective this fact should make for the permanence of marriage, even though conflict over wives working may be a factor in the current unprecedented divorce rate.

Many students wonder whether the wife should work while her husband is still in college. This has nothing to do with the question of careers for women, because many college girls have no wish for careers.

---

[15] Nancy Mavity, "The Two Income Family," *Harper's Magazine*, December, 1951, p. 60. Reprinted by permission.

They are willing to work, however, until their husbands graduate and get jobs, and beyond that until they have built up sufficient reserves to buy a home and start a family. Again, the old problem of the attitude of the husband must be considered. If he regards his wife's working as a blow to his ego, his attitude should be courageously faced before any final plans are made. If he agrees that the wife should work, they still ought to live as though they had only one income. The wife's income can then be saved, to be applied as a down payment on a home or simply kept in the bank as a form of insurance. If they spend all they make during the time the woman works, they will become accustomed to the standard of living their joint income makes possible. Then when the wife stops working to have a baby, they will be in the position of having to adjust to a smaller income and greater expenses. Such an adjustment is difficult. Sometimes, too, during the early years of marriage when the husband wants all the wife's affection and interest, he may be jealous of her contacts and the stimulation associated with her work. If he is jealous, and if his jealousy takes the form of harping about her neglect of duties around the house, especially such duties as cooking and cleaning, the wife may feel guilty because she is not fulfilling the role she has accepted.

The basic point of this discussion is that there is no such thing as a "woman's place." Men and women are involved in a spectacular social change by which the status of women is undergoing more radical transformation than it has in the last five thousand years. The woman who leads this procession may marry a man who is threatened and bewildered by her new role; and often she does not have any firm convictions herself about the meaning of her action. We are moving from a very, very old concept of woman's rights and place to a very modern one. This generation is still involved in experimentation. Young people should realize that what is basically important is not the criticism of what they do but their adjustment to each other. If this adjustment is good, they need not be concerned with the value judgments of others. They should also realize that there are few available patterns to guide them. This is a period of change, but that change also has much promise of happiness and marital success.

WISE BUYING

The average college man in America will earn between a quarter of a million and half a million dollars during his entire working life. If he buys wisely and saves wisely, he will be able to provide adequate nutrition, good clothes, a comfortable home, medical care, excellent educational opportunities and stimulating vacation and recreational experiences for his family. However, in the Pace study, 35 per cent of the respondents found it difficult to keep out of debt, 40 per cent expressed a need for information on economic planning, and more than 50 per cent revealed that they had no plan for spending intelligently. There are many ways in which each of the budgeted items may be reduced. Some of them are: (a) buying in the off-season of demand, i.e., buying school clothes in early summer instead of in September when the demand is at its peak, (b) buying items in the period when the supply is high and prices low, i.e., buying corn in July but not in November, (c) buying at sales or buying items on sale, i.e., every week-end large grocery stores put certain items on sale to attract customers, (d) buying when possible for cash instead of by installments, thus saving carrying charges, handling charges, and interest, (e) buying quality instead of appearance or because of sales propaganda. These are but a few of the many ways the good home manager learns to "earn" money by wise buying. Every student should study carefully books on consumers' economics. The "Executives' Quiz" which follows this chapter is an interesting test which covers many items of wise buying as well as other factors in intelligent home management.

PROVIDING FOR FUTURE SECURITY

Families use different methods of planning for future security. Involved in that planning are measures designed to assure adequate resources for the education of children, for sickness or accidents which might mean the loss of employment as well as burdensome costs, for retirements, and for security in old age. A large number of families are now covered by Social Security. The benefits from Social Security survivors' insurance are shown in the table on page 350. These particular benefits accrue to the widow and children if the breadwinner who is insured dies. The differences in benefits come about because of the differences in salary and in the amount deducted from the salary. Social Security also provides old-age benefits but the payments are generally not high enough to maintain a decent standard of living unless supplemented by other funds. Nevertheless Social Security has provided a base for a general security not hitherto possessed by many families.

T A B L E 44. Monthly Social Security Survivors' Benefits

Average Monthly Wage	Widow and One Child under 18	Widow and Two Children under 18	Widow and Three Children under 18	One Child Alone under 18	Two Children Alone under 18
$150	$ 86	$115	$120	$43	$ 72
200	98	130	150	49	81
250	109	145	150	54	91
300	120	150	150	60	100

Most families supplement the protection afforded by Social Security by taking out health, accident, and life insurance. The type of insurance one should purchase depends upon its purpose. If its only purpose is to protect the family against the possible death of the breadwinner, term or ordinary life insurance is the most economical type to buy. If, however, its purpose is to provide both protection and savings for the purchase of a home or for the education of children, then an endowment policy is generally chosen. This kind of policy does not give as high protection per dollar paid in premiums but it offers the best investment of any type of life insurance. Insurance is complex and the services of a competent insurance counselor will help young couples avoid costly mistakes in their insurance program.

GOVERNMENT BONDS AS A FORM OF SAVINGS

Troelstrup thinks that endowment insurance as generally purchased by parents to provide for the education of their children is uneconomical because of the low return it offers.[16] He recommends rather a combination of term insurance for protection and the purchase of government bonds as a savings program for educational funds. Government bonds are recommended because the principle is secure and the interest is adequate. Series "E" bonds pay as high as 3 per cent interest. If a family invests $18.75 each month for 10 years it will have accumulated in principle and interest $2,498.98.[17] Almost every company has a service by which it will deduct the cost of a bond each month and deliver the bond to the worker. Buying government bonds gives the purchaser a

[16] Arch W. Troelstrup, *Consumers Problems*, New York, McGraw-Hill Book Company, Inc., Copyright, 1952, p. 293.   [17] *Ibid.*, p. 294.

satisfying feeling of sharing in the financing of his country's democratic enterprises, in its protection, and in its future.

CASH RESERVES

In addition to planning for life-time security it is wise to be prepared for minor emergencies which occur in all families. An adequate budget will spread out over the entire year such major expenditures as insurance, taxes, Christmas spending, vacation costs, medical and dental expenses. But there are other emergencies such as unexpected trips when a member of the husband or wife's family becomes suddenly ill or dies, costs involved in moving because of promotion to a new and perhaps better job, and many other possibly expensive items which cannot be budgeted. For this reason most financial advisors recommend a savings fund immediately available or a maintained surplus in the checking account equal to two months' salary. This sum is generally adequate to meet most emergencies not covered by health, accident, or unemployment insurance. A further benefit of such a margin is the sense of security it gives the family.

INDIVIDUAL NEEDS AND DEMOCRATIC MANAGEMENT

Family financial planning ought to result in two achievements, (a) adequate provision for the individual needs of the members of the family and (b) adequate provision for the basic needs of the family as a whole. Such plans should help each person develop his potentialities and his feeling of independence and security. When a family budget does not provide allowances for every member, it is too tight and may become a source of friction instead of a means to greater cohesiveness. Likewise the budget is not adequate unless it provides well for the general needs such as food, housing, and transportation of the whole family. This dual goal helps the family keep in mind two purposes; the goal of individual personality fulfillment and the goal of family cohesion.

CONCLUSION

The way money and security are handled may weaken or strengthen individual growth and family unity. A budget should be a medium whereby the family plans together for the achievement of individual and family goals. The budget will not in itself solve every problem of finance for the family. Wise buying practices as well as wise planning for the future require careful practice and study. Study must be given also to ways of adjusting to the problems that arise when a wife works. Society is in a period of transition. The shifting roles and values do not make for automatic adjustment. The couple who can intelligently plan their time and the use of their money will discover that the effort used to do so will be a positive factor in their growing happiness.

THE EXECUTIVES' QUIZ

In modern families both the husband and the wife must be good executives if their families are to be happily adjusted. The following checklist enables families to test themselves on their ability in home management. Students looking forward to marriage may use this quiz as an outline to follow in achieving good home management. (Originally this appeared in *Program Notes,* published by the National Association of Manufacturers.)

How Good a Purchasing Agent Are You?

1. Do you use advertisements and catalogs to compare prices?

   Always_____   Usually_____   Seldom_____

2. Do you examine quality as well as price?

   Always_____   Usually_____   Seldom_____

3. Do you buy in quantities whenever it means a saving?

   Always_____   Usually_____   Seldom_____

4. Do you check your supplies of food staples, clothing, and household articles, so you can buy them when the market is most favorable?

   Always_____   Usually_____   Seldom_____

5. Do you plan well-balanced menus and make up shopping lists before going shopping, so you can take advantage of special bargains?

   Always_____   Usually_____   Seldom_____

6. Do you carry with you a list of family clothing sizes, measurements of beds, windows, floor, and wall spaces, color combinations, etc., to save you time when unexpected sales are discovered?

   Always_____   Usually_____   Seldom_____

7. Do you keep records, either mental or written, of taste appeal of food brands or the wearing qualities of dry-goods brands?

Always_____ Usually_____ Seldom_____

How Good a Secretary-Treasurer Are You?

8. Do you maintain a good credit rating with the stores in your town?

Always_____ Usually_____ Seldom_____

9. Do you see to it that your bills are paid on time?

Always_____ Usually_____ Seldom_____

10. Do you keep accurate accounts of family income and expenditures?

Yes_____ Partly_____ No_____

11. Do you budget your income, allowing a reserve for vacations, taxes, insurance and replacement of major items such as your automobile?

Yes_____ Usually_____ No_____

12. Do you save a definite portion of income for your future security, retirement and pleasure?

Yes_____ Usually_____ No_____

13. Do you invest your savings and reserves wisely where they will produce interest?

Yes_____ Usually_____ No_____

14. Do you keep your valuable family papers in a safe place—birth certificates, savings bonds, an inventory of household goods with your fire insurance policy?

Yes_____ Partly_____ No_____

15. Do you have files of recipes, and household helps that others in your family can use as well as yourself?

Yes_____ Some_____ No_____

How Good a Plant Manager Are You?

16. Do you plan your home arrangement for the greatest convenience and comfort?

Yes_____ Partly_____ No_____

17. Do you plan the work about the home, assigning to each member jobs most fitted to him?

Always_____ Usually_____ Seldom_____

18. Do you schedule the work so it can be accomplished with minimum effort, leaving time for recreation?

Always_____ Usually_____ Seldom_____

19. Do you have your refrigerator, vacuum cleaner and other motor equipment oiled and cleaned regularly?

Regularly_____ Sometimes_____ Seldom_____

20. Do you examine furniture and clothing for needed attention at the beginning of spring and fall seasons?

Always_____ Usually_____ Seldom_____

21. Do you plan major painting, papering, and redecoration far enough in advance?

Always_____ Usually_____ Seldom_____

How Good a Personnel Executive Are You?

22. Do you call a meeting of all your family frequently to plan your future together?

Frequently_____ Sometimes_____ Seldom_____

23. Do you study the skills and natural inclinations of your family members and encourage their development?

Always_____ Usually_____ Seldom_____

24. Do you have a plan for your children's further education?

Yes_____ Partly_____ No_____

25. Do you call their attention to books, lectures, films, concerts, and exhibits? Encourage stimulating discussions?

Yes_____ Usually_____ No_____

26. Do you keep up with psychology and cultivate common sense to help your husband and children with their personal problems?

Yes_____ Usually_____ No_____

27. Do you maintain a well-stocked medicine chest for giving first aid?

Always_____ Usually_____ No_____

28. Do you check regularly on the safety factors in the house, avoiding such dangers as cluttered stairways and open electrical outlets?

Constantly_____ Sometimes_____ Seldom_____

29. Do you create an atmosphere within your family of working as a team?

Yes_____ Partly_____ No_____

How Good a Public Relations Director Are You?

30. Do you keep on good terms with your neighbors?

   Always_____   Usually_____   No_____

31. Do you work out complete details when you entertain—the extra house touches, menus, chores for each member of the family?

   Always_____   Usually_____   Seldom_____

32. Do you encourage members of your family to take part in school, church, and civic activities? Do you vote?

   Frequently_____   Sometimes_____   Seldom_____

33. Do you make a conscious effort to deserve the reputation in your community as a "fine family"?

   Always_____   Usually_____   Seldom_____

Now count up your answers. For each check in the left-hand column, allow yourself 3 points. Count 2 for each check in the middle column and 1 for each check in the right-hand column. If your score is 81 to 99 points, you're excellent. But 50 or better is good.

READINGS

RAY E. BABER, *Marriage and the Family*, New York, McGraw-Hill Book Company, Inc., 1953, Chapter 12.

HARVEY J. LOCKE, *Predicting Adjustment in Marriage: A Comparison of a Divorced and a Happily Married Group*, New York, Henry Holt and Company, 1952, Chapter 13.

ARCH E. TROELSTRUP, *Consumer Problems*, New York, McGraw-Hill Book Company, Inc., 1952, Chapters I, II, III, and IV.

PAULINE PARK WILSON, *College Women Who Express Futility*, New York, Contributions to Education, No. 956, Bureau of Publications, Teachers College, Columbia University, 1950, Chapter V.

Recreational Contributions
to Family Life

If I had my life to live over again, I would have made it a rule to read some poetry and listen to some music at least once a week; for perhaps the parts of my brain now atrophied would then have been kept alive through use. The loss of these tastes is a loss of happiness, and may possibly be injurious to the intellect, and more probably to the moral character, by enfeebling part of our nature. CHARLES DARWIN

INTRODUCTION: SIGNS ACROSS THE NATION STATE: "THE FAMILY THAT PLAYS TOGETHER STAYS TOGETHER." THERE IS NO one of the various aspects of life, recreational, educational, religious, or economic, that in itself is the magic key to marital happiness. A blend of achievement in all of them insures the fullness of creative life that is the family goal. Of all these, recreation has been the one most often overlooked in the literature on preparing for marriage. Only one book in those canvassed for this study contained more than a brief reference to the basic importance of recreation in marital adjustment. A superficial glance at our environment is enough to convince us of the need for recreation. Properly developed, recreation is a major force for family cohesion.

Many of us are destined to live and work in the great, gray canyons

356

of cities where there is neither sunshine nor grass, where the sirens howl and crowds mill like cattle. There we worship the great gods of Speed, Efficiency, and Noise. Our compass becomes the clock and our horizon is always a deadline. The tempo of the business world, of the social world, of the political world moves faster and faster, and man runs, anxious and driven, through the shadowy canyons. Small wonder that half of our hospital beds are filled with those who could not stand the smoke, the tension, the bustle, the nervous derelicts burned out by the friction of such an accelerated and unlovely life.

But not everyone succumbs to the pace of modern life. Consider John Smith, for example. He seems very serene in the midst of the bustle of his office, calm when crises come, relaxed at the beginning and at the end of the day. Men in his office look at him and say, "I wonder what John's secret is, he is never harried." There is not one, but several answers. But one of them is John's recreational life. In the middle of the week, he leaves his office early, he meets his wife for dinner, and they explore the various restaurants of different nationality groups. Sometimes they stay after dinner and dance to a Swiss accordion, sometimes they leave after a leisurely meal and see a play or hear a concert or visit friends. But the mid-week ritual is never missed. On week-ends, John is out in his garden, or playing with a group of children who have come to know that they have fun at John's house on Saturdays, or is on a picnic or a ski trip with his family. John occasionally goes to church on Sunday, but on other occasions he may take his family to the beach or on a long drive. John is not overcome by the vastness of urban complexities; he uses these to enrich his life. He is not overcome by the nervous pressures of his occupation because he has a balanced existence. He has perspective. He knows that his economic life is important, that his contribution of energy and of his time is essential, but he does not give all of himself. He renders unto Caesar what is Caesar's but he keeps for his family and for his God that which is theirs. As a result John Smith will not die of a premature heart attact, he will not have ulcers, he will not burn out. He will enjoy it all, laugh a great deal, and look back on his life as a worthwhile investment. Recreation not only gives him balance, it makes his other efforts worthwhile.

Though the authors of books on the family have not paid too much attention to recreation, those who have studied family adjustment have asked questions about its importance. Dr. Harvey Locke in his study asked two significant questions; the first ran as follows:

In leisure time both husband and wife prefer to be "on the go," both prefer to stay at home, one prefers to be "on the go" and the other to stay home.[1]

The second dealt with agreement on recreation: the couple was asked to check, on a six-point scale, the degree to which they felt they agreed. When Locke came to determine the importance of his findings in terms of their predictive value, that is, how the answers to these questions were related to marital adjustment, he put the answers to all his adjustment questions in rank order of their importance in differentiating the happily married and the divorced. There were some thirty-four, leisure time rated in sixth place; while the agreement question rated in twenty-sixth place. This seems to indicate that differences in doing things together are of more importance than what is done. Furthermore it appears that differences in preferences for the use of leisure time are highly important in determining the adjustment of a man and wife. On the other hand, Williamson found that agreement on recreation was one of the most significant differences between the well adjusted and the poorly adjusted groups in his sample. (See Table 21 on page 153.) Williamson's study corroborates our conclusion that recreation is one of the major factors in marriage adjustment.

What is recreation? We need to think about this because of the common misuse of the term. The Twenty-Second National Recreation Congress defined recreation as "any form of activity in which an individual feels a sense of freedom, and of self-forgetfulness, and to which he gives himself wholeheartedly because of the satisfaction he gains by participating." The important thing about recreation is not the "what" but the "how." Many individuals work so hard at what they think is recreation that they are completely exhausted physically and psychologically by their effort. This is work. Other individuals regard recreation as another way of competing in life. They must win, and if they do not win, the game is a failure. They are using recreation to bolster their flagging egos. They have never learned that "how" one plays determines its usefulness. Of course, we play to win but, if one is red-faced and sullen after losing a golf game, it has little creative value for him. The same thing is true of those who only watch sports events. Rabid followers of one school or one team often come near to apoplexy when their

[1] Harvey J. Locke, *Predicting Adjustment in Marriage: A Comparison of a Divorced and a Happily Married Group*, New York, Henry Holt and Company, 1952, p. 374.

team loses. The result of such an overemphasis on winning has changed some college sports into cut-throat competition, has made amateurs almost professionals, and has turned sport into big business. This is far removed from play or the spirit of play and points up the importance of analyzing the way America spends its leisure time. For the degree to which we have lost the ability to play directly influences the degree to which fun can bind the family closer together. We will find that America has become a stadium of spectators instead of a nation of participators.

RECREATION TODAY

A California Senate committee charged with the responsibility of making recommendations regarding hunting and fishing made a complete study of leisure-time activities in California. The results showed that Americans were spending 20.9 per cent of their leisure hours consuming tons of newspapers; 18.8 per cent listening to the radio; 17.3 per cent attending movies; 11 per cent hunting and fishing; 10.4 per cent attending sports events; 6.6 per cent playing outdoor games and sports; 5.3 per cent playing cards and other indoor games; and 3.7 per cent going to the theatre. The remaining percentage was not accounted for in any way. This survey indicated that 76.4 per cent of total leisure time was spent passively watching others perform in one way or another. The trend towards vicarious, usually sedentary, recreation is all too obvious. This means that we were being amused or entertained by others. Only 22.9 per cent of our leisure was occupied in actual participation. The only exercise the spectator got was in applauding others.

But this was before television. In 1954, there were over 30 million television sets in the nation serving about seventy million viewers. The figures given above did not include this new threat to activity. What is happening to leisure-time activities in those homes where television has introduced its all conquering presence? In Syracuse, New York, a survey to determine the interaction of radio and television revealed that radio was still taking 3.07 hours a day in addition to some 4.52 hours devoted to television. The public is now devoting over seven hours a day to radio and television. Much of the time devoted to listening to the radio or looking at television is also devoted to performance of mechanical household tasks. The hours of 6:00 to 9:00 a.m. and 4:30 to 6:30 p.m. are peak hours for car radio listening. Television has further contributed to non-participating activity. Television has had other important influences on the family but we will study these later. Here we are chiefly concerned with the fact that the American public has lost its sense of play and has become merely the cheering section.

There are more subtle effects that must be noted. Because we have lost the "readiness for play" we spend those hours with friends or with a group in destructive or, at least, non-constructive activities. Parties are dull unless one has so much to drink that the dullness is banished. The art of conversation is often so much forgotten that it takes three or four highballs to make talk exhilarating. The family has no pattern for fun and tries to make up for its lack by buying fun at some commercial amusement zone. Thus much that today is called recreation might be better described as "wreck-creation."

Recreation ought always to be Re-Creation. Then it may bring the psychological rewards of relaxation, reduced tensions, improved motivation; the physical rewards of better posture, better muscle tone, more adequate timing of responses; and the social rewards of new friendships, deeper fellowship, new patterns of interaction. Re-Creation involves change for the better in health, in personality, and in social grace. These changes come about when one feels a sense of freedom and gives oneself completely to the game or activity. One is then for a time forgetful of all worries, dedicated completely to the task at hand, and exhilarated by the fun one is having. It is our task to see how this type of play may influence the family.

RECREATION AND FAMILY PATTERNS OF INTERACTION

What happens while the family is engrossed in a game of parchesi or ring-toss or tennis may influence what happens when it is planning the budget or discussing the family diet. There are personality clashes, competitions for status, difficulties in waiting for one's turn at speaking or moving or playing. The same personalities are involved. But the spirit of the occasion is different. The family organizing a game or the married couple setting out to play tennis are the same individuals who have been pondering the budget, but their orientation is different. Now they are intent on having a good time. Memories of past good times come to their aid. Their expectation is that if there are clashes they will be resolved with humor or at least with a minimum of difficulty. And when the conflicts do arise these expectations of fun—and the good-humored

360

solutions of the past help the couple or the family settle the conflict without too much difficulty. The whole spirit of the game influences their interaction. Consequently, they deal with these personality problems as something new and interesting. It is true that recreation may restore a family unity that has been sadly shredded by routine.

How does it do this? Thomas and Znanicki, in their study, *The Polish Peasant,* concluded that every individual has a need or a wish for new experience. That which is repeated comes to be also drab. But play is never drab. In play a couple finds new stimulus, and if their play is full of adventure, it supplies the answer to this fundamental need of personality. A marriage marked by constant creative adventuring, in talk and in activities, in the home and outside it, will not be habit-worn and dry, but a union in which new interests and constant fun intensify togetherness. So recreation contributes to the couple's real unity by adding appreciation and by multiplying common interests.

PSYCHOLOGICAL CONTRIBUTIONS OF RECREATION TO MARRIAGE

Unless one partner is completely submissive or unless a couple is very dependent, they are bound to have conflicts. As has been pointed out, it is never easy for a person reared in one sort of family, with its particular set of expectations, to be joined to another person with an entirely different history. And if partners are full of life and energy, there will be many occasions when the gears grind. Again, few of us pass through childhood and adolescence or face the business of life without developing some hostilities. The outlet for hostility is aggression. We tend to express this aggression in irritation, annoyance or even anger at our partners, and, later, at our children. The very closeness of the partner produces tension. Many marriages break under the strain of aggressions which are expressed too violently and too perisistently in the family circle.

Nevertheless these aggressions must somehow be expressed. If they are not verbalized or brought to the surface, serious strain is introduced into marriage. The family needs to develop a method of handling aggressions intelligently.

One answer to this problem is suggested by Dr. Karl Menninger, who, speaking before the American Association of Health, Physical Education and Recreation in Los Angeles, on April 10, 1952, had this to say:

Uncontrolled aggressions within us are major causes of mental illness. Adequate play is a means of channeling off excess aggressions. Play is one of the best antidotes for low morale and other conditions that might lead to mental illnesses.

In competitive family play, aggression is part and parcel of the activity. We take out our feelings in the game. We are, in a restricted way, carrying on a duel. Our needs to get even, to batter down, to let out latent hostility against our mates are all part of the motivation in a bridge game or a golf game. But the expression of those feelings is generally modified by the spirit of the game itself. We do get rid of the feeling but in a way that is not divisive of family unity.

Hard physical effort such as scaling a mountain or hiking a great distance or lugging a canoe around a portage or playing a hard fought set of tennis—all these enable us to release some of the aggressions built up within us. We invest ourselves in these activities and when they are finished there has taken place a kind of catharsis that has value.

There is a type of psychological help for children called play therapy which is based on the definite recognition that creative play enables the child to release feelings hitherto inhibited. In the same way the play of husband and wife releases pent-up feelings and clears the way for more positive feelings.

RECREATION AND FAMILY INTERACTION

Recreational events are the "sunshine among shadows," the highlights of sometimes gray marital experience. But every experience in the family influences all other experiences. When a couple solves difficulties in a game, this provides them with a new pattern for solving difficulties in other areas. After several such recreational experiences the budget-planning session will be conducted in a little different atmosphere; with more gaiety and good humor.

The budget session will be conducted in a different atmosphere because those who participated in the game have come to think of each other in a different way. We say "think" but we should rather say "feel," for recreational experiences produce rather profound emotional changes.

What is this new interactive pattern? It has many ingredients. Instead of the picture of opposition and competition we have now a picture of the mate who cooperates in having a good time. There is a sense of "withness" rather than a sense of "againstness" which is so prevalent in many families. Again the buoyancy that goes with recreation changes the emotional approach to the rest of the marriage. If marriage is limited merely to facing problems, life is indeed a serious business. But if these problem-solving sessions are interspersed with fun sessions the mood of the recreational hour carries over. Consequently the "tone" of the interaction is changed. Zest and enthusiasm have been introduced into this marriage and they cannot be compartmentalized and restricted to the picnic, the game, or the trip; they "spill over" into the rest of the marriage.

RECREATION RESULTS IN FAMILY COHESION

Recreation in the sense of joyful, spontaneous participation not only gives a different tone to family interaction but changes the positions of those in the family. It reduces social distance. It results in greater solidarity. Of course anything that a couple does together that they view positively binds them closely together. Family rituals, admiring a new baby, handling a knotty problem of finance successfully, agreeing on a new purchase or on how to handle a mother-in-law or worshipping together or sharing a good meal brings them together more and more. But recreation contributes to cohesion in a special way.

When two people play together their mood is one of appreciation. They tend to say: "I had a wonderful time playing golf" or "It was a nice dance" or "Didn't we enjoy that bridge game?" When the activity has been spiced with laughter or very zestful participation there is a hang-over of happy memory. This extends to those who have shared the activity with them. The husband identifies his joy with his wife who made it possible or at least who participated with him. One then does not tend to say as in a contemporary song, "I cannot understand why in a world full of peaches I had to choose a lemon," but one says, "Yes, that's my wife and my companion in life."

Balzac says that "there is a monster that devours everything in marriage who must constantly be vanquished, his name is habit." So many marriages have been blighted by routines in which each partner comes to take the other one for granted or to think of the other as an uninteresting person that rule-of-thumb advice to families having difficulty is to go on a trip or take a second honeymoon.

363

PHYSICAL CONTRIBUTIONS OF RECREATION TO MARRIAGE

George Bernard Shaw, who lived to a great old age, contended that he got his exercise attending the funerals of his friends who exercised. But, Shaw to the contrary, good health is related to recreation. Good health is also related to happy marriages, while constant illness or poor vitality are associated with marital maladjustment.

The sluggish, anemic, devitalized individual can hardly be stimulating to a member of the other sex. Active recreation sends the individual's blood coursing through his arteries. When it returns to his lungs it is well purified because he is breathing deeply. His muscles harden, and every gland, bone, and sinew renews its youth. When he eats, it is with a natural hunger that makes eating a happy experience. His grace of movement and his attractiveness of form improve. His sexual capacity is augmented, and he becomes a more inviting sexual partner. Some gynecologists believe that much of the sexual frustration of modern women is due to their diet and lack of exercise. If they had a more normal physical routine, they would have sufficient energy to share vigorously in sexual pleasures. Not the least of the contributions of happy, zestful, outdoor participation in sports or games is the achievement of a more adequate body to carry on a more adequate life.

THE CONTRIBUTION OF RECREATION TO PARENT-CHILD INTERACTION

Wieman, in her chapter on "Fun," summarizes with great acuity the contribution of recreation to parent-child relationships:

> Creative interaction is a novel relationship where parents and children are equals under the immediate authority of the rules and courtesies of the game. This is more of a test for us parents than we always realize. For one thing, the children have the opportunity to observe how we interact with others when we are not the immediate authorities and cannot run things. The converse side of this is that we parents now having to obey orders taste the experience of our children who usually are the only ones who must do as they are told. We are reminded how it feels not to be boss but to be bossed. For another thing, quite often it is the children who excell in games or sports, and they then have the opportunity to observe us in the inferior position. Can we qualify as "good sports"? Third, it becomes apparent to the children what each of us parents values most in fun. We may be childish and think that winning

is the big thing, or we may be mature and believe that playing *together* counts more than anything else.

Of course, these possible values in creative fun are lost if we parents either pretend an interest in the fun or feign an indifference to losing or to acting under a unfavorable rule when the children sense that we actually do care.

But the two best values that come out of the relation of equality required in fun are these: First, the parents, being relieved of management and responsibility, can release aspects of themselves usually subdued or inhibited. They can react more nearly with the full self and with joyful spontaneity. Second, the parents have a generous opportunity to balance their usual commands, requests and guiding standards with such graces as can be expressed through kindly jokes, through gracious subordination to the guidance of a child who plays well, and through tactful reinforcement of the child who is daringly experimenting or courageously holding to his own intention against the advice of others.[2]

We may add to this concise description of the values of family play the observation that the points made earlier regarding the contribution of recreation to the psychological adjustment between husband and wife apply equally to the relationship to parents and children.

The value of play in character building is more and more understood by leaders of recreation. Neumeyer says:

In recent years recreation leaders have become definitely interested in character building, because of the close relationship between the child's play and his character. Possibly the greatest opportunity of a child's character lies in the proper attitude toward play and in the habits formed. . . .

Recreation by means of games and sports is a valuable medium for lessons in gentlemanly and honorable sportsmanship. To win honestly, lose graciously, and to cooperate generously have made men out of selfish and cowardly individuals. Self-imposed discipline has moral values. Mastery over self fits a person to exert greater control over others and to meet critical situations more adequately.[3]

Finally, enthusiastic participation in games and play provides for children as well as for their parents an outlet which is highly necessary. There is no more basic need for child development than intensive and exertive play.

[2] Regina Wescott Wieman, *The Family Lives Its Religion*, New York, Harper and Brothers, 1941, pp. 176–177. Reprinted by permission.
[3] Martin H. and Esther S. Neumeyer, *Leisure and Recreation*, New York, A. S. Barnes and Company, 1949, pp. 159–160. Reprinted by permission.

PLANNING FAMILY RECREATION

There is no set form of recreation that gives the same stimulus to different types of individuals. A form of play that commands the entire allegiance of one family may be anathema to another. The first consideration in the choice of recreational activity is that it meet the needs of the individuals who are participating. A quiet game may provide as valuable results as a violent one. Dr. Menninger in the speech mentioned earlier said that "a chess game to one man may be as effective a relief as some violent sport like basketball to another."

The study made by Lehman and Witty and the National Recreation Association, published under the title of *The Psychology of Play Activities*, stressed the varieties of play. In endeavoring to discover the favorite leisure-time pursuit of thousands of children and youth under twenty-two they discovered that looking at the Sunday funny papers, reading books and newspapers, chewing gum, playing catch, drawing, running and romping, going to the movies, watching others participate in sports, participating themselves in games, riding in automobiles, playing cards, and many other individual interests were checked.[4] The final statistics indicated that less than 50 per cent of the group participated in any one special activity. This means that no one should attempt to find satisfaction in a sport or hobby simply because it is popular. He should rather follow his own inclination. One individual will prefer chess, another tennis, another will simply concentrate on conversation.

Recreational life should be an expression of an individual's interests and talents. While it is not necessary for every person to be a champion, one will probably not enjoy those sports or games in which he is hopelessly awkward or clumsy or in which his participation means an almost certain loss of status and a constant effort just to keep up with the others instead of a sense of freedom in participating. The development of some skill in trout-casting, serving a tennis ball, bidding a hand in bridge or in carrying on a conversation naturally adds to the enjoyment of the experience. Those who do very poorly in one area may do well in another. Whatever one chooses, one's recreational interests ought to have the possibility of life-long enjoyment. Continuity makes for skill, for long-term friendships with partners, and for a host of happy memories.

It really makes little difference what hobby or what sport a family

[4] H. C. Lehman and P. A. Witty, *The Psychology of Play Activities*, New York, A. S. Barnes and Company, 1927.

chooses. The important thing is that it represent an interest which will integrate the group and contribute to the growth of each member. It is the attitude of play associated with the activity that is important. If the activity ever comes to be thought of as a duty, or as work it had best be quickly dropped. The degree of happiness and enthusiasm marking the participation of each member of the family is the final test of its value.

Having considered these general principles of choice we come to the question of exactly what leisure-time activities a woman and a man may take part in together. It was thought until quite recently that the physical endowments of a man and a woman are so different that they had best be separated for recreational pursuits. Today's stress on co-educational play has resulted in the awareness that both girls and boys may enjoy most activities. This is of value because skill and interest are developed in activities which both may enjoy throughout life. Certainly there is an absurd contradiction in the suggestion that a woman may stand beside a man in a factory and do the same work he is doing but not play beside him on a volley-ball court.

Some students say that some leisure-time pursuits are very expensive financially and that they therefore will not have the resources to do these things after marriage. But this is generally an excuse and not a fact. The equipment for recreation is within oneself, and community-wise there are so many free opportunities that, irrespective of financial status, one may have a very full experience at any age. Marjorie Greenbie has described what is needed for recreation more poignantly than anyone else. She says:

> Because happiness is so personal, there is only one place for a man to begin his search for it, and that is in himself. The doctors of leisure now talk of equipment for the use of spare time, endowments for community recreation, swimming pools, workshops. All these things are good. But the primary equipment for leisure consists in the possession of two eyes, two ears, two hands and two feet, with the addition of numerous other items such as a heart, a memory, and a tongue—so long as they are all your own, and not mortgaged to any mass interest, mass habit, mass advertising, or mass hooey whatsoever. One can get along with a fraction of this equipment, if one really runs it one's self, for one's own satisfaction. But some personal possessions of this sort are fundamental, and if a man has all the Lord usually provides, he has so much equipment that it is any wonder he ever puts himself out to get any more.[5]

[5] Marjorie B. Greenbie, *The Arts of Leisure*, New York, McGraw-Hill Book Company, Inc., 1935, p. 5. Reprinted by permission.

367

What is needed for a full recreational life is not a full purse but a bountiful imagination and a desire to make of one's married life a rewarding adventure in sharing many stimulating activities.

THE IMPACT OF TELEVISION ON FAMILY LIFE

No subject has so intrigued both the research sociologists and the armchair observers during the last five years as the question of the impact of television upon the future of the family. Watching television has become a favorite recreation of a great many families in America. Has it been productive of closer relationships in the family or has it been divisive? A few tentative answers will be given to that question.

TELEVISION AND RECREATION IN THE HOME

One of the elements in family disintegration is "flight from the home." Does television tend to bring the family back? A series of interesting studies indicate that it may have the tendency. Dr. Edward McDonagh studied an anonymous community in Southern California to ascertain new family habits due to television. This study focused on a community large enough, and with sufficient range of social groupings, to be valid for wide generalization. Out of some 800 families, ranging from the professional class to the unemployed, the study staff selected a television-owning group and a non-television group, nearly identical in education, social, and economic composition. Personal interviews were conducted by trained interviewers, who employed a carefully compiled questionnaire.

That the "flight from the home" has been arrested is demonstrated by

TABLE 45. Difference of Television on Family Visiting*

	TELEVISION FAMILIES		NON-TELEVISION FAMILIES	
	Number	*Percentage*	*Number*	*Percentage*
More	4	4.2	24	25.5
Less	63	66.3	16	17.0
Same	28	29.5	54	57.5

* Data from Edward C. McDonagh, "Television and the Family," *Sociology and Social Research*, November-December, 1950, Vol. 35, No. 2, p. 121. Reprinted by permission.

this table which shows a change in visiting habits of television and non-television families. Sixty-three per cent of the television families were visiting other families less often as compared to 16 per cent of the non-television families.

New York University, corroborating with Cunningham and Walsh, a New York agency, in a continuing study of an anonymous community located 40 miles from New York, sent 16 researchers to interview some 3,007 television families and many non-television families. Their "census" showed that 16 per cent of the members of television families are away from home in the evening in contrast to 25 per cent of the non-television families.

If it is true that families spend more time at home after buying a television set, it logically follows that some of their activities outside the home have diminished. A clue to such a major shift of family life may be seen in reports of attendance at movies. Dr. McDonagh found an appreciable decline:

T A B L E 46. Movie Attendance and Television*

	TELEVISION FAMILIES		NON-TELEVISION FAMILIES	
	Number	*Percentage*	*Number*	*Percentage*
More	3	3.2	13	13.9
Less	76	80.0	24	25.5
Same	16	16.8	57	60.6

* Adapted from Edward C. McDonagh, "Television and the Family," *Sociology and Social Research*, November-December, 1950, Vol. 35, No. 2, p. 121. Reprinted by permission.

The Videotown Census shows that twice as many members of non-television families attend movies as do members of homes having television sets.

What has happened to radio listening in the family since the advent of television? This question also has received careful scrutiny by the researchers. McDonagh reported as in Table 47 on the increase or decrease in radio listening: 84 per cent of the television families listened less to radio as compared to 12 per cent of the non-television families. These findings are corroborated by a study made in the Middle West for the John Meck Industries of Plymouth, Indiana, and reported in July, 1950.

TABLE 47. Radio Listening and Television*

	TELEVISION FAMILIES		NON-TELEVISION FAMILIES	
	Number	Percentage	Number	Percentage
More	0	0	17	18.1
Less	84	88.4	12	12.8
Same	11	11.6	65	69.1

* Adapted from Edward C. McDonagh, "Television and the Family," *Sociology and Social Research*, November-December, 1950, Vol. 35, No. 2, p. 120. Reprinted by permission.

TABLE 48. Radio Listening in Families Owning Television*

	High Income	Low Income
Listen about the same	22.2	14.3
Listen less	77.8	85.7

*Adapted from data from *Broadcasting* magazine, July 10, 1950, p. 3. Reprinted by permission.

Relatively few families are all at home together before 5:00 p.m.; hence television is making its bid precisely at the hour when the family gathers! What relative difference is there between the behavior of radio families and television families in respect to family participation when listening? The Princeton University study is the only one which has analyzed this difference statistically, and its findings are perhaps the most impressive of any research findings to date. This study shows that 91.6 of television families listen together as compared to 27.4 of radio

TABLE 49. Family Listening to the Same Program*

	Radio	Television
Family listens together	27.4	91.6
Family does not listen together	72.6	8.4

* Adapted from data from *Broadcasting* magazine, December 11, 1950, p. 40. Reprinted by permission.

families. This means that there is a new togetherness in the family—a finding borne out by individual comments gathered by the University of Southern California and Princeton surveys. Typical comments from

370

television homes were: "The family now stays home all the time and watches the same programs—turn it on at 3:00 p.m. and watch until 10:00 p.m. We never go anywhere—my husband was awfully restless and never wanted to stay at home, but now he wants to watch the sports contests on TV." Sixty-six per cent of those who answered the questionnaires drawn up by Dr. Michael stated that "it was their frank opinion that TV served to bring all of the family closer together."

Television tends to monopolize life. Perhaps a better way to express it would be to say that it brings the world into the living room. In consequence family participation in many other forms of experience has decreased. The Opinion Research Corporation of Chicago in a study conducted for General Foods Corporations and the National Restaurant Association discovered that one-fifth of TV-owners go out to dinner less than previously. Fewer families entertain guests than they did before putting up their video antennas. Mack's survey indicated that they are attending sports events 24 per cent less, traveling to bars and taverns less, and playing records considerably less.

Another significant finding is that the family is using television to entertain, but this medium of entertainment is not always appreciated. In an interview one woman vitriolically told the author:

> Sure people use it to entertain. Last week we drove 35 miles through very heavy holiday traffic to see some old friends. We wanted to know about their children, their work, about other friends. What did they do? They turned on the television as soon as we got there and it stayed on for two hours. It was the most boorish, uncouth thing that ever happened. After two hours of it we drove 35 miles home.

And a doctor who has very few spare hours in which to cultivate friendships contributed this statement:

> My wife and I of course rarely have an evening. Recently whenever we do go out the people in homes make us watch television in silence. We want to talk. We have now made an invariable rule that, if we do go to a friend's house and they have a television antenna, we quietly turn around and go the other way.

Television cuts down conversation, the intimate face-to-face communication that sociologists believe is so important in the formation of attitudes and friendships. Dr. McDonagh found a decrease in conversation. Sixty-two per cent of television families are talking less as compared with 15 per cent of non-television families.

TABLE 50. Talking and Television*

	TELEVISION FAMILIES		NON-TELEVISION FAMILIES	
	Number	Per Cent	Number	Per Cent
More	8	8.4	13	13.8
Less	59	62.1	14	14.9
Same	28	29.5	67	71.3

* Data from Edward C. McDonagh, "Television and the Family," *Sociology and Social Research,* November-December, 1950, Vol. 35, No. 2, p. 120. Reprinted by permission.

On the basis of this finding he concludes:

> It may not be too great a generalization to say that television is bringing the family members together in the home, but not necessarily in a face-to-face relationship. In the evening in many homes the television set is making the family an audience rather than an intimate group characterized by much spontaneous talking and confiding. . . . In some families where they admit "a common interest since television," it is conceivable that television offers the subject of much conversation.[6]

Dr. Michael of Princeton concludes:

> Such answers begin to show a reversal of trend that started with the automobile, motion pictures, and even multiple radio sets . . . to separate the family unit for entertainment. Television is bringing the family together more often for home enjoyment. This may well prove to be one of the most significant influences of the medium.[6]

In some disorganized American families, television may be giving boys and girls a home life they never had before.

TELEVISION AND THE AGED

More positive is the contribution of television to the older members of the family who have done their work in life and find their last decade or two filled with an exasperating number of empty hours. Such persons may have looked forward to retirement only to find it strangely empty of meaning. Many are unable to participate in the vigorous pastimes of their more virile years. Furthermore a great many more individuals are

[6] William B. Michael and Jerry N. Jordan, "Analysis of the Effect on Living Habits in Families with TV Sets More Than a Year," *Television Magazine*, May, 1949, p. 13.

living longer than before. For older persons television has much promise. Television is so virile, so enthusiastic, and so varied in its fare that a great many older people are finding it the answer to a long-felt need. For them, television provides a source of education and entertainment. Undoubtedly it will become of increasing value to those who can no longer go to the ball game or the church service but may attend both at home.

CONCLUSION

One of the major trends of contemporary family life is the shift from home recreation to commercialized entertainment. This shift is accompanied by more and more watching and less and less participation. Furthermore, commercialized recreation tends to fragment the family by its organization on an age-level basis. Television has added to the limitation of activity, in that it requires only the minimum exertion of twisting a dial. On the other hand, television does bring the family together in the living room. It gives the family a core of common experiences which are binding in nature. It is particularly valuable to the shut-ins, the ill and the aged who may find the television screen a window upon the world.

PROJECTS

1. Have each member of the class list his leisure-time interests which will later contribute to binding the family together.
2. Discuss commercialized recreation and analyze what percentage of recreational time each member of the class gives to it.

READINGS

E. Draper, *Entertaining is Fun,* New York, Doubleday, Doran and Company, 1941.

Marjorie Greenbie, *The Arts of Leisure,* New York, McGraw-Hill Book Company, Inc., 1935.

Martin H. and Esther S. Neumeyer, *Leisure and Recreation,* New York, A. S. Barnes and Company, 1949.

S. R. Slavson, *Recreation and the Total Personality,* New York, The Associated Press, 1946.

Contributions of Conflict
to Family Cohesion

INTRODUCTION: AFTER THE HONEYMOON, MOST COUPLES
FACE SOME CONFLICT DURING THEIR PERIOD OF ADJUSTMENT.
These conflicts arise because of the necessity of bringing two distinct
personalities into alignment. Marriage always imposes the obligation
of compromising on some wishes, some habits, and some values which
have been held sacred by one of the partners. The fact that two individuals come from different families and from different segments of a
heterogeneous culture means that there must necessarily be problems
in adjusting their life patterns. In this chapter we are concerned with
the ways of achieving pair harmony and cohesion.

Conflict may be viewed in two ways: in the negative sense, conflict
may be dreaded as a threat to marital stability. Those who have come
from homes in which conflict has been continuous and disruptive may
vow that they will sacrifice anything for harmony. Indeed in a recent
discussion group on adjustment in marriage, a wife objected bitterly
to the thought that there might be any positive outcome as the result of
conflict. She said:

> The idea of marriage ought always to be an ideal of harmony. I resent
> any suggestion that conflict can bring anything but broken hearts and
> social distance into the relationship between a husband and a wife.

Later she said that in her home she had been victimized by twenty-five years of never-ending conflict so that in her own marriage she wanted peace at all costs. But her parents' conflicts had never been adjusted. It was always a compromise with incompleteness. While the actual details of this marriage are not available, it is probable that the basic conflicts were never clarified or ventilated.

The second way to view conflict is to regard it as both a tribute to character depth and a means to the promotion of a final family cohesion. Individuals with values so superficial that they can easily adjust to anyone or to any situation generally have little of worth to share. It is the person with strong convictions and well-oriented values who comes into conflicts with others. So the very strength of some early family disturbances is an indication of the strength and resources which each of the partners will ultimately contribute to the partnership. Thus, "peace" may mean not only the absence of conflict but also the absence of personality substance. While it is not necessary to conclude that conflict is thus the prerequisite for every full marriage, it is often the harbinger of a union of deep meaning and finally of steady direction. Again, conflicts may be the stepping-stones to a marriage of maximum togetherness combined with a maximum development of personality for both partners. The ideal of marriage is not to eliminate areas of conflict but rather to face them courageously so that new values and new solidarity will appear. Some couples involved in an inter-faith marriage solve their problem by dropping out of all religious participation. Likewise, some men try to solve the problem of conflict over the use of money by simply turning over their checks to their wives and allowing the wives to decide how the money shall be used. They eliminate the conflicts by never discussing them. The problems are solved by default. For the yielding individual, something of meaning has been sacrificed and the total family configuration of values has become weaker because of it. This type of resolution of conflict is a form of withdrawal which eventually weakens the structure of family unity and certainly weakens the interests and values of those in the family. On the other hand, in some matters about which one or both partners do not feel strongly to overlook or forget the problem is not damaging. Many minor conflicts are solved in this way.

We are speaking here of the normal types of conflict which are contingent upon normal differences in temperament, cultural patterns, ritualistic systems, and expected roles in the family. Where conflict is

375

rooted in severe neurotic needs, therapeutic help is essential as has been indicated in a preceding chapter. When the causes of conflict in the contemporary family have been established, it will be possible to develop ways of dealing with the conflicts that will promote family cohesion.

GENERAL CAUSES OF FAMILY CONFLICT

The more recent studies of marriage indicate the relative importance of areas of conflict. In Table 51, page 377, taken from Locke's study, it will be noted that much conflict centers about the traditional functions of the family—economic, recreational, social, religious, and sexual. There are important differences between the married and divorced samples. For instance only one item was checked by more than 20 per cent of the happy men but 13 items were checked by more than 20 per cent of the divorced men. The happily married and divorced differed significantly in the following five categories: (1) affectional and sex relationship, (2) socially disapproved behavior, (3) economic problems, (4) individualistic, and (5) miscellaneous difficulties.

DIFFERENCES IN PERSONALITY CONFIGURATIONS

Individuals expect different things from marriage because of their diverse experiences in the homes in which they grew up. They expect different patterns in marriage because they come from different regions, nationality groups, or social classes which have different definitions of marriage and family life. In our chapter on economic considerations in wise marriage choice, some attention was paid to the importance of clashes resulting from differences in work, status, and the use of money.

Other research findings seem to indicate substantial differences in various types of marital behavior in the various social classes. Kinsey's research, for example, shows radical differences in sexual behavior, and in sexual morality, among men of different social classes.[1] Because of the nature of his research, Kinsey's findings must be regarded as hypothetical, but they indicate that from lower social classes men have a greater intensity of sexual drive and less control of that drive than men from the middle and upper classes.

[1] Alfred C. Kinsey, W. B. Pomeroy, and C. E. Martin, *Sexual Behavior in the Human Male*, Philadelphia, W. B. Saunders Company, 1948.

376

TABLE 51. Per Cent of Happily-Married and Divorced Checking Items as Serious Marital Difficulties, with Critical Ratios of the Difference of Per Cents*

ITEM	MEN			WOMEN		
	Married N = 111	Divorced N = 123	CR	Married N = 125	Divorced N = 147	CR
A. Affectional and sex relationships.						
1. Mate paid attention to (became familiar with) another person	2.7	65.9	10.1	5.6	73.5	11.3
2. Lack of mutual affection (no longer in love)	4.5	60.2	9.0	1.6	61.2	10.3
3. Adultery	0.9	43.9	7.7	1.6	55.1	9.6
4. Unsatisfying sex relations	8.1	46.3	6.5	5.6	32.7	5.6
5. Venereal disease	0.0	1.6		0.8	12.2	3.7
6. Unsatisfied desire to have children	2.7	8.1	1.8	8.8	3.4	1.9
7. Sterility of husband or wife	0.9	3.3		4.8	0.7	2.1
B. Economic difficulties						
1. Mate's attempt to control my spending money	9.0	26.8	3.5	7.2	21.1	3.2
2. Other difficulties over money	14.4	34.1	3.5	19.2	38.1	3.4
3. Nonsupport	0.0	7.3	2.9	0.0	49.0	9.1
4. Desertion	0.0	20.3	5.0	0.0	27.2	6.3
C. Socially disapproved behavior						
1. Drunkenness	2.7	26.0	5.0	1.6	56.5	9.7
2. Gambling	2.7	6.5		3.2	26.5	5.2
3. Mate sent to jail	0.0	4.9	2.4	0.0	16.3	4.7
D. Individualistic behavior						
1. Do not have mutual friends	10.8	38.2	4.8	6.4	25.2	4.2
2. Selfishness and lack of cooperation	6.3	22.0	3.4	12.0	29.9	3.6
E. Miscellaneous items						
1. Interference of in-laws	17.1	52.8	5.7	20.0	29.9	1.9
2. Ill health	3.6	13.8	2.7	15.2	10.2	
3. Constant bickering	5.4	48.0	7.3	8.8	34.7	5.1
F. Undifferentiating items						
1. Different amusement interests	28.8	34.1		20.0	28.6	
2. Religious differences	6.3	8.1		4.8	7.5	
3. Cruelty to step-children	0.0	0.0		0.0	0.0	
4. Other reasons	6.3	12.2		15.2	19.0	
G. No difficulties at all	38.7	0.0	7.6	27.2	0.0	6.8

* Data from Table 12 in Harvey J. Locke, *Predicting Adjustment in Marriage: A Comparison of a Divorced and a Happily Married Group*, New York, Henry Holt and Company, 1952, pp. 75–76. Reprinted by permission.

Another investigation studied practices in child-training. A study of upper-middle- and upper-lower-class Chicago families showed that they differed markedly in their regulations regarding movie attendance, the enforcement of an afternoon nap, learning to wash dishes, cook, and sew, the age considered proper for weaning, training in bowel and bladder control.[2] These differences are reflected in the way individuals react when they are faced with these specific problems. The following excerpt from the case of Harry and Margaret illustrates what happens in terms of child-training. Harry said:

> I came to you because I am losing respect for my wife. She gives in to the children at all times. When I get home I like a little order and at least some peace. In our home we always respected the wishes of Father when he got back from the office. But it isn't so with my kids. When I get home they climb all over me. They even sass me. They won't eat what is put before them and if I insist my wife says that modern child training methods are against forcing children to eat. The same thing happens when I reprimand them for being nasty or swearing. She says they need to get this out of their system. I think once in a while children need to learn to repress some things. I had to and it hasn't hurt me any. In fact I think I get along better because I learned to respect the wishes of others. No matter what it is my kids do my wife acts as though they were gods. I think she just doesn't want to run the risk of alienating them by making them behave.

But Margaret had an entirely different point of view:

> My husband doesn't understand children at all. Just because he was raised with the switch he thinks that's the best way. But our little girl had polio when she was four and she needs all the love and all the encouragement she can get. We quarrel about their freedom because he wants them to learn to be quiet and mannerly. We quarrel about their eating because he wants them to learn to eat anything we happen to have on the table. We quarrel about their discipline because I think it's good for them to express themselves and get their feelings out in the open but he says it's disrespectful. If he were a little more tender and understanding the children would love him more. They try to reach him by romping but he can't even respond to that. I think if he had been raised with more love and less severity he could love his children more and I want them to grow up to be loving persons.[3]

[2] Allison Davis and Robert J. Havighurst, "Social Class and Color Differences in Child-Rearing," *American Sociological Review*, 11:698–710, 1946.
[3] From a case study in the author's files.

Both of these parents wanted the best for their children. Both thought they knew exactly what the best was. That best was the pattern of training in which they had been reared. This illustration could be duplicated in dozens of case histories where basic differences in values or life patterns are related to social, class, or family backgrounds. The factor of inter-class marriage is important because it accentuates conflict. As Burgess and Locke point out, "the United States has wide cultural differences in folkways by regions, by rural and urban areas, by various nationality stocks, and by social classes.[4] Over 50 per cent of the population in this country moved between 1940 and 1950. As individuals come into new neighborhoods and into new regions, it is inevitable that they will marry persons who have grown up with a different set of values and expectations regarding child-rearing, sexual life, and other phases of matrimony. Since differences in personality configuration due to membership in different social classes or to residence in different regions are basic, they have very real potentialities for conflict.

VALUES AND MARITAL CONFLICT

Values are objects, or actions, or ideas which are viewed as having worth for an individual. They, too, vary with our cultural backgrounds. How important are differences in values, beliefs, customs, or family patterns in causing difficulty in the family? Of course there are some specific conflicts over certain traditional problems which seem important. Locke found that:

> Conflict over drinking, reading, sports, and parties was reported by a larger per cent of divorced men; conflict over drinking was reported by one fourth of the divorced and by one seventh of the married. For women, the activities where conflict was reported by a larger per cent of divorced than married were: going to church, drinking, and sports; drinking as a source of conflict was reported by one half of the divorced and by one fifth of the married.[5]

The importance of values, beliefs, ethical attitudes, and moral concepts has been strikingly indicated in an unpublished Ph.D. dissertation

[4] Ernest W. Burgess and Harvey J. Locke, *The Family, From Institution to Companionship*, New York, The American Book Company, 1953, p. 497. Reprinted by permission.
[5] Harvey J. Locke, *Predicting Adjustment in Marriage: A Comparison of a Divorced and a Happily Married Group*, New York, Henry Holt and Company, 1952, pp. 260–261. Reprinted by permission.

379

by Dr. Leland Ellis Glover. The following table illustrates the importance of values and beliefs to young people as well as the concern caused by differences between themselves and their prospective mates. Beliefs, values, and attitudes constituted the most important problem area (35.3 per cent) while the values included in dating and courtship were an

T A B L E 52. Consensus of 218 Students Who Were Counseled on Difficulties by 36 Teachers of Marriage and the Family*

Rank	TITLE OF AREA OF CONCERN	Number of students	Per cent of 218 students	Area number
1.	Beliefs, values, attitudes, ethical and moral concepts	77	35.3	8
2.	Situations in dating, courtship, engagement	62	28.4	3
3.	Differences between self and prospective mate	53	24.3	5
4.	Money matters	40	18.4	9
5.	Attitudes toward parents and relatives	35	16.	1
6.	Feelings of insecurity and inadequacy	35	16.	6
7.	Sex adjustment, excluding homosexuality, of unmarried student	31	14.2	12
8.	Rearing of children or child	29	13.3	15
9.	Marital discord between self and mate	25	11.5	7
10.	Need for information relative to organs of reproduction or the reproductive process	20	9.2	4
11.	Marital discord between student's parents	20	9.2	13
12.	Spacing of children	18	8.3	16
13.	Physical or mental defects, known or suspected, in self, mate or prospective mate, or in a relative	11	5.6	2
14.	Legal implications of student's activities	6	2.6	10
15.	Venereal diseases	6	2.6	14
16.	Homosexuality	6	2.6	11

* Adapted from Leland Ellis Glover, The Teacher of Marriage and the Family as Counselor, unpublished Ph.D. Dissertation, University of Southern California, 1951, p. 87.

important second category (16.0 per cent). Psychological problems were also prominent (24.3 per cent), whereas differences between prospective mates troubled many students (24.3 per cent). In commenting on the meaning of this table, Dr. Glover said:

> Students in the study who were counseled by their teachers indicated that the problems about which they were concerned most in common involved their beliefs, values, attitudes and ethical and moral concepts. They implied, thereby, their philosophical confusion and their need for clarification of their ideas and ideals. Therefore, it is recommended

first, that teachers of marriage and the family should have a thorough knowledge and understanding of philosophers and religions, and second, that beliefs, values, attitudes, ethical and moral concepts as they apply to marriage and living in the family should be given considerable attention in the life-problems-centered course.[6]

These findings also suggest the confusion among young people confronted by the wide diversity of values in our society. If students have such concern for values, it is inevitable that these values will be important in marital adjustment. Twenty-four per cent of the students were concerned enough about differences between themselves and their prospective mates to seek counsel They were aware of the potential of such differences for conflict in marriage. Every marriage counselor has dealt often with the task of helping couples adjust to differences concerning the training of children, the discipline of children, the use of money, the importance of luxuries, church attendance, drinking, gambling, and a great many other items. Because our society is so heterogeneous, most marriages must face a number of these differences.

INTER-PERSONAL RELATIONSHIPS AND MARITAL CONFLICT

Conflicts which are the result of social relationships outside the immediate family are also important. A problem often arises over choice of friends. With reference to this Locke says:

> The number of friends a husband and wife have in common is highly associated with marital adjustment, particularly for women. A wife who reported that she had "almost no" friends in common with her husband was much more likely to be in the divorced than in the happily married group, and, if she reported only "a few" friends in common with her husband, there was a fair probability that she would be in the divorced rather than in the married group.[7]

Locke gives the following excerpt from the life-history of a divorced man to illustrate how chances of success in marriage seem to be reduced unless the husband and wife have mutual friends:

> We got along quite well, and I enjoyed married life. In fact I think I will marry the girl I am now going with. The main trouble with my marriage

[6] Leland Ellis Glover, The Teacher of Marriage and the Family as Counselor, unpublished Ph.D. Dissertation, University of Southern California, 1951, p. 248.
[7] Locke, op. cit., p. 234.

was that my wife resented the amount of time I spent with my friends. These were boyhood chums. I used to play basketball and go out evenings with them. She always wanted to do something else. She did not want me to hang around with them. They were perfectly fine fellows, and I resented this attempt on her part to keep me away from them. One quarrel gradually led to another, and we finally separated. Her in-laws kept interfering, too, since she had been a little spoiled when she was a child. They took her side. Later on, when she had a child by another man, and we went through with divorce, her folks agreed that I was in the right.[8]

Another problem involving outside social relationships is that of in-laws. It has been said that it is not two individuals who marry but rather two families. This has been truer in the past than it is today although the statistics indicate that complications arising from in-law relationships are still important.

Landis and Landis asked couples who had been married for an average of 20 years to list their most serious problems in achieving happiness; the women mentioned in-law relationships second and the men listed them third.[9] In a follow-up study, 544 couples who were in the early years of marriage were asked the same question. These couples gave the in-law problem first place in their list of difficult situations. The following figures give specific statistical details of these 554 marriages.[10] When the

FIGURE 21. Happiness and In-Law Relationships*

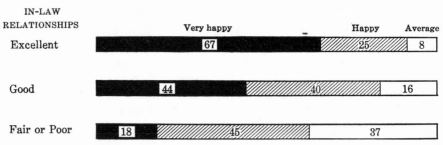

* Judson T. Landis and Mary Landis, *Building a Successful Marriage*, New York, Prentice-Hall Inc., 1948, p. 289. Reproduced by permission.

in-law relationships were excellent, 67 per cent of the marriages were happy, but when the in-law relationships were poor only 18 per cent of the couples were happy.

[8] *Ibid.*, p. 235.
[9] Judson T. Landis and Mary Landis, *Building a Successful Marriage*, New York, Prentice-Hall, Inc., 1948, pp. 287–288. [10] *Ibid.*, p. 289.

It is essential in interpreting these percentages to recall the point made in Chapter 6 regarding the problems associated with dependencies in marriage. Part of the in-law adjustment problem is a reflection of that basic psychological difficulty. Another part of the problem of the in-law is derived from differences in family customs, rituals, and values which separate the parent-in-law and the child-in-law.

One of the tasks of the early years of marriage is the establishment of a deep emotional relationship between the partners, and it is easy for either party to resent any obvious display of deep attachment for outsiders. If dependency by a partner does exist, it may prove exasperating to the other mate, particularly if the young people live with or near the parents on whom one is dependent.

Finally, one should bear in mind that the stereotype of in-law relationships is one of the most powerful of our day and that, consequently, even when there would otherwise be no great problem, fears and uncertainties based on that cultural stereotype may actually produce difficulties.

Still another type of domestic conflict arises from interest in "the other woman" and, increasingly, in "the other man." Here the emotional difficulty stems not from an old tie to earlier friends or to the family but from new relationships. We are not referring here to gross infidelity but merely to that perennial situation in which one partner pays what is regarded by the other as too much attention to some one else. Levy and Munroe discuss this problem as follows:

> There is also the question of glamour outside of marriage. An old song runs:
>
> > If in your heart one corner lies
> > That has no room for me
> > You do not love me as I deem
> > True love should ever be . . .
> > You do not love me, no!
> > Bid me goodbye and go.
>
> To this exacting young lady I reply: "Bushwah." No man is so deeply in love with his wife that he loses his eye for a pretty pair of legs wherever he finds them—unless he's the sort of man who never notices his wife's legs either. A lady with a worried air said to me: "Whenever I'm feeling particularly keen about my husband I start behaving like a school girl with other men, kissing in the moonlight and that sort of nonsense. I fall for sweet nothings like a ton of bricks. Does that mean I don't love my husband?"

383

Not at all. Happily married people are by no means impervious to the romantic attractions of outsiders. Indeed, I sometimes think that the woman who has developed strong sex feelings in the arms of her husband is somewhat more susceptible to other men than the woman to whom sex has proved a disappointment. Moreover, however attractive a husband may be, he is ipso facto, not a new story, and we have already described the contribution sheer novelty makes to the love relationship. If we were picking reading matter for a winter in Little America we would take with us the Bible and Shakespeare and the Iliad. We recognize and enjoy their permanent value. Here at home the most highbrow literati are not above chuckling over an ephemeral paragraph in the *New Yorker*. Flirtations are ephemeral, but many married folk find them amusing and seem to be none the worse for them.

When the marriage is really stable, however, these extra-marital adventures are not compulsive. We can take them or leave them with small disappointment. We can be pleasantly thrilled about the other woman without for a moment considering throwing over our marriage for her or even changing our affection for our wife. . . .[11]

But if one partner is the least bit insecure or jealous, such adventuring causes rifts that are hard to heal. Many marriages apparently are not "really stable" and consequently are damaged by flirtations or even a passing interest in other individuals.

Conflict is present in most marriages. It may be the result of egocentric or neurotic tendencies in one or both marriage partners; it may be caused by romantic attitudes which predispose the individuals to expect the impossible; or it may be the result of diverse value structures. Finally, there are many types of inter-personal relationships such as friendships, relations with in-laws, and flirtations which seem to be productive of trouble. An analysis of constructive ways of facing such conflict patterns is thus in order.

CONFLICT AND TENSION

There is a difference between conflict and tension. Conflict is an overt struggle of any sort and about anything. Tension may be defined as unsolved conflict.[12] Tensions are the product of frustrations, or of conflict situations in which the vital interest of one person is never openly admitted, recognized, or discussed. If, in a series of problems, no solution

[11] John Levy and Ruth Munroe, *The Happy Family*, New York, Alfred A. Knopf, Inc., 1946, pp. 78–80. Reprinted by permission. [12] Burgess and Locke, *op cit.*

FIGURE 22. Development of Social Distance Between Alfred and Miriam Donaven*

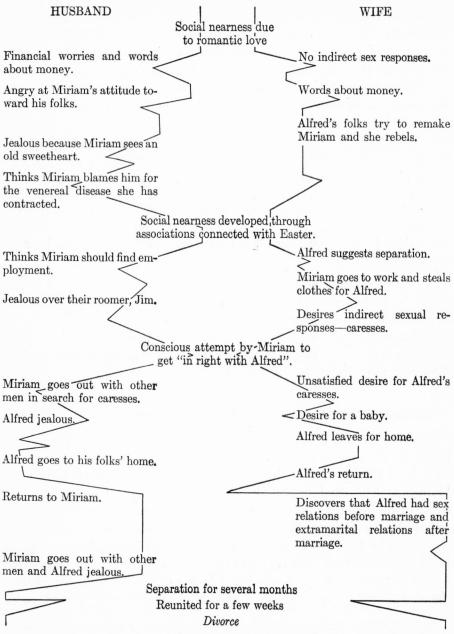

HUSBAND   WIFE

Social nearness due to romantic love

Financial worries and words about money.

No indirect sex responses.

Angry at Miriam's attitude toward his folks.

Words about money.

Alfred's folks try to remake Miriam and she rebels.

Jealous because Miriam sees an old sweetheart.

Thinks Miriam blames him for the venereal disease she has contracted.

Social nearness developed through associations connected with Easter.

Thinks Miriam should find employment.

Alfred suggests separation.

Miriam goes to work and steals clothes for Alfred.

Jealous over their roomer, Jim.

Desires indirect sexual responses—caresses.

Conscious attempt by Miriam to get "in right with Alfred".

Miriam goes out with other men in search for caresses.

Unsatisfied desire for Alfred's caresses.

Alfred jealous.

Desire for a baby.

Alfred leaves for home.

Alfred goes to his folks' home.

Alfred's return.

Returns to Miriam.

Discovers that Alfred had sex relations before marriage and extramarital relations after marriage.

Miriam goes out with other men and Alfred jealous.

Separation for several months
Reunited for a few weeks
Divorce

* From Ernest W. Burgess and Harvey J. Locke, *The Family, From Institution to Companionship*, New York, The American Book Company, 1953, p. 517. Reproduced by permission.

385

is reached, the tension increases and causes social distance and withdrawal to take place. Waller uses a term, "the process of alienation," to describe the growth of increasing instability and social distance due to a series of tensions.[13] Mowrer indicates the manner in which conflict and tension result in the development of social distance in "The Diary of Miriam Donaven."[14] Burgess and Locke have diagrammed this development as shown in Figure 22. Burgess and Locke summarize this case as follows:

> An analysis of this case reveals tensions over money matters, the failure of the wife to adjust her conduct to the expectations of the husband's mother, the failure of the husband to give indirect sexual responses in the form of caresses, and sexual incompatibility. These tensions seem to have their roots in differences in the cultural background of the couple. The diagram indicates that, while temporary periods of social nearness occurred, the trend was toward increasing distance between husband and wife.[15]

A careful scrutiny of Burgess and Locke's diagram will reveal almost all of the factors studied so far in the chapter as explanatory of conflict in marriage. No one item of conflict ever exists by itself. There is an interdependence of response and alienation that makes it very hazardous to attach importance to single factors. They are important, nevertheless, if we remember that they are parts of a whole.

PERSONALITY RESOURCES FOR MARITAL ADJUSTMENT

Whether or not a couple have indifferent or determined attitudes regarding the success of their marriage is important. Whether they invest their total loyalty or only a part of it in the new venture is important. Many marriages that might otherwise have succeeded have failed because of the tentative manner in which one partner has entered into the union. If the friction caused by a mother-in-law or a secretary is cushioned by the secure feelings that result from a complete transfer of loyalty and affection, that friction can be absorbed. If a wife knows that her husband will always be on her side in any quarrel with his mother, she can afford to be more generous. She will be more lenient, more

[13] Willard Waller (Revised by Reuben Hill), *The Family: A Dynamic Interpretation*, New York, The Dryden Press, 1951, pp. 539–557.

[14] Ernest R. Mowrer, *Family Disorganization*, Chicago, University of Chicago Press, 1927, pp. 231–250.   [15] Burgess and Locke, *op. cit.*, p. 516.

understanding, and more tolerant of the mother-in-law. But even more basic is the fact that if friction does develop, facing the problem as a pair or a team brings the couple closer together. This is our first insight into the constructive handling of conflicts. It is the goal that is important. If the problem is faced by the couple as a unit and if they focus on achieving an outcome which will contribute most to their togetherness, no matter how strong the disagreement, the outcome will be constructive. It is when the couple is divided and the real problem is a struggle between their egos that social distance develops.

It is this willingness to abandon self-interest for the common good which gives both stability and motivation to the struggle for cohesion in today's marriage. Christensen speaks strongly about the effect of selfishness in some marriages.

> Marriage is a cooperative adventure that fails when family members become self-centered rather than group centered, when they look towards "rights" and "privileges" rather than "obligations" and "contributions." Whether one looks at husband-wife relationships or those between parents and children, he will see that failure is almost invariably tied up with the selfishness of someone. There is too much emphasis on "I" and "me" rather than "we" and "us." Successful marriage is a process of give and take, but there are too many today who try to do all of the taking and none of the giving.
>
> In short, married mates prove most adjustable when they have a spirit of mutually accepted responsibility and cooperation, when they are realistic about the task before them, and when they are determined that they shall not fail. Success here does not spring from romanticizing alone, nor from temporizing, nor from exploiting; rather, it comes first and foremost from the attitude of regarding marriage as a challenging job and accepting it as a partnership.[16]

It is, then, the total investment of one's affectional, emotional, and intellectual self in the task of making the marriage succeed that gives a secure framework in which conflict and difficulties can be faced.

OVERT MARITAL CONFLICT AS A MECHANISM FOR ACHIEVING MARITAL ADJUSTMENT

By stressing the need for unselfish dedication of both partners to their marriage, we do not mean at all to overlook the fact that a marriage is

[16] Harold T. Christensen, *Marriage Analysis*, The Ronald Press Company, 1950, pp. 313–314. Reprinted by permission.

never fully successful unless each partner achieves the full development of his own potentialities. While it is important to emphasize unselfishness and understanding as basic qualities in achieving marital compatibility, it is also important to stress selfhood. Often submission and ego-repression are the costs exacted in the name of unselfishness. These impoverish any human relationship and lead ultimately to hostility and social distance. One must be completely honest in one's dedication to one's mate at the altar; one must not reserve anything on any tentative basis. But one must also be prepared to be emotionally honest. If one is upset, or chagrined, or hurt, to interiorize these feelings is only to cause a long-lasting and basic tension. When one feels anger, it is wise to express that anger honestly and openly. If it is kept under cover, it will be sure to appear in sexual withdrawal or irritability or under some other unfortunate guise.

Overt emotional conflict has many values. "Blowing up" may often release tensions which have stood in the way of a more enduring and more basic solution to the problem. The emotional release of feelings resulting from frustrations also brings the problem to the attention of the couple in such a dramatic way that it must be faced and cannot be forced underground again. Most of us in this day of change, loneliness, and tension have deep hostilities and daily frustrations. Wise is the husband or the wife who can recognize the need on the part of his or her mate for an aggressive expression of feeling. Duvall and Hill say:

> The modern couple will expect that in marriage they have a place of security and intimacy where they are free to behave like human beings with the normal variety of emotions. The workaday world, organized as it is, does not permit the frank expression of resentment, vanity, jealousy, and selfish ambition along with tenderness and love, all of which exist in the normal person. The individual must control his annoyances and his affections, he must often act like something more than human to get along in our complex industrial society. If he flies off the handle at his boss he may lose his job. There needs to be some place, however, where the individual can give vent to his annoyances and be himself, and that place seems to be in marriage. If there is that kind of cantankerousness in a marriage, the couple should chalk it down as proof that their marriage is performing one of its main functions—providing a place to let off steam and re-establish emotional balance. If a marriage is so fragile that it must be maintained by the same kind of artificial manners

that keeps an office force functioning, it is pretty precariously based. One insightful authority has stated in positive terms, "one of the functions of marriage is to weave a rope of relationships strong enough to hold each person at his worst."[17]

Indeed, the basic acceptance of the partner "at his worst" is the precondition for growth in togetherness. If there is either a lack of acceptance of the mate or a subtle effort to handle him or her so that those aspects that are not acceptable will be eliminated, the inevitable result will be a defensiveness which will be a barrier to the growth of closeness. But if anger, sorrow, grief, hatred, and resentment can be freely expressed, then the emotions of tenderness and love are more likely to find full and free expression. The individual who represses all negative emotions finds it equally and increasingly difficult to express positive feelings.

DISCUSSION AS THE SOLUTION FOR CONFLICT

To stop on the note of a full and free emotional expression would be to leave the matter half-ended. Some conflicts may be resolved by the honest expression of emotions, but this is not true of conflict rooted in cultural values or social relationships. After the air has been cleared of tension, the couple needs to go on to a sane and intelligent discussion of the causes of that tension. There needs to be persistent and patient exploration of the basic roots of the differences that brought about the frustration. Often these roots have no relation to the matter at issue. The focal point of difficulty quite often obscures the more basic frustration. But couples who have learned how to talk together will sooner or later root out the cause of tension. The cue is communication of both ideas and feelings. Rewarding insight will come to the couple who are able to discuss their perplexities and irritations. It is for this reason that so many items dealing with discussion are included in the pre-marital test. There is no solvent for conflict more valuable than talking, and talking with a mate who is genuinely interested in knowing how the partner feels. If a couple cannot talk about problems or expectations, they need very soon to recognize this limitation and to practice on small matters until facing greater issues together comes more easily.

[17] Evelyn M. Duvall and Reuben Hill, *When You Marry*, Revised edition. Reprinted by permission of D. C. Heath and Company, Boston, copyright, 1953, pp. 187–188.

DEMOCRATIC FAMILY STRUCTURE AND PROBLEM-SOLVING

If a couple are profoundly dedicated to their marriage, if they are honest with each other emotionally and intellectually, and if they have achieved the capacity for intelligent discussion, they will make progress in solving conflicts constructively. However, in this process they will discover that they must work out some type of structure for their relationship so that ego-maximizing and the struggle for power will not engage energies which ought to go into constructive problem-solving. They must decide whether the husband or the wife is to be dominant or whether they will work together on a democratic basis of equality. In the past the patriarchal type of family organization, in which the father took the lead and made the decisions, was nearly universal. The changing role of women in today's world and the complexity of the conflicts to be faced raise the real question whether this type of organization will prove effective in the families of the future. What seems to be effective today for the adjustment of differences between partners and the solution of the problems continuously presented by our culture is the most fluid and flexible relationship a couple can achieve, a marital structure, in other words, which allows for the highest degree of give and take. This seems to be the equalitarian, democratic type of marriage in which both partners share in decision-making. Locke attempted to discover whether or not there was a difference between a married and a divorced sample in terms of democratic and individualistic behavior. Happily married and divorced persons were asked whether the lead was more often taken by the wife than by the husband, by the husband more often than by the wife, or by both equally in making family decisions, disciplining the children, handling family money, affectionate behavior, religious behavior, recreation and meeting people. His conclusion is as follows:

> The above analysis emphasizes the value attached by many persons, particularly women, to democratic behavior, in the family. The happily-married tended to feel that equality between husband and wife was present in their marriages, while the divorced felt that it was relatively absent.[18]

Another study gives a certain justification for holding this position. Yi-Chuang Lu reached similar conclusions in his investigation of the

[18] Locke, *op. cit.*, p. 266.

relationship of dominant-equalitarian-submissive behavior to marriage adjustment. He made an intensive study of some 603 husbands and wives selected from the Burgess-Wallin sample of 1,000 couples. As Burgess and Wallin had already studied the marital adjustment of these couples it was only necessary for Lu to develop a scale by which to measure dominant-equalitarian-submissive roles and then to relate persons playing these roles to the adjustment scores. An index was developed consisting of sixteen items which had been selected out of 52 previously constructed questions.[19] After the dominant-equalitarian-submissive scores of these 603 couples were determined, they were then related to the marriage-adjustment scores by means of the two following tables and were tested for statistical significance by means of the Critical Ratio formula (CR). A Critical Ratio of 2.0 was taken to mean that the statistic had a significance that could not be the result of chance. For both husbands and wives an equalitarian role was associated with the highest rating or adjustment.

T A B L E 53. Marital Roles and Husband's Marriage Adjustment*

| Marriage adjustment | Marital Role | | | | | | Number of cases |
| | Husband more dominant | | Equalitarian | | Wife more dominant | | |
	PER CENT	CR	PER CENT	CR	PER CENT	CR	
Poor	41.5	2.2	30.4	—	28.1	—	135
Fair	34.5	—	32.1	—	33.4	—	290
Good	29.8	—	39.9	1.8	30.3	—	178
TOTAL							603

* Yi-Chuang Lu, "Marital Roles and Marriage Adjustment," *Sociology and Social Research*, July-August, 1952, V. 36, No. 6, p. 365. Reprinted by permission.

In interpreting these data Lu says:

An examination of Table 1 [53] reveals that a negative relation exists between the husband's dominant role and his marriage adjustment. A larger proportion of those with "poor" adjustment fall in the "husband-more-dominant" group and a smaller proportion are found in the "equalitarian" and "wife-more-dominant" groups. In the husband-more-

[19] Yi-Chuang Lu, "Marital Roles and Marriage Adjustment," *Sociology and Social Research*, July-August, 1952, V. 36, No. 6, p. 365.

dominant group, only 29.8 per cent of husbands have made a good adjustment in marriage (CR 2.2) and 41.5 per cent a poor adjustment in marriage. The better the husband's adjustment with his wife, the higher the percentage of such cases falling into the "equalitarian" group. In the "equalitarian" group, 39.9 per cent of husbands make "good" adjustment with their wives and only 30.4 per cent are poorly adjusted. The critical ratio of the difference between 39.9 and 30.4 is 1.8 which approaches significance. In the wife-more-dominant group, however, practically no difference is found in the husbands of the three degrees of marital adjustment.[20]

T A B L E 54. Marital Roles and Wife's Marriage Adjustment*

Marriage adjustment	Marital Role						Number of Cases
	Husband more dominant		Equilitarian		Wife more dominant		
	PER CENT	CR	PER CENT	CR	PER CENT	CR	
Poor	43.0	—	22.2	—	34.8	2.2	135
Fair	31.0	−2.4	33.3	2.5	35.7	2.9	255
Good	33.8	−1.7	42.3	4.2	23.9	—	213
TOTAL							603

* Yi-Chuang Lu, "Marital Roles and Marriage Adjustment," *Sociology and Social Research,* July-August, 1952, V. 36, No. 6, p. 365. Reprinted by permission.

In interpretation of this data Lu says:

The figures in Table 2 [54] indicate a definite relation between the husband's dominance in the marriage and the wife's poor marital adjustment. Of those wives who make "poor" adjustment in marriage, 43 per cent of their husbands are dominant. . . .

In the "equalitarian" group there is an even more significant relation between the equalitarian role and the wife's good adjustment in marriage. Of those wives who make a "poor" adjustment in marriage there are only 22.2 per cent playing equalitarian roles. . . . And of those wives who make good adjustment in marriage, an even higher proportion, 43 per cent play the "equalitarian" role. The critical ratio of the difference between 22.2 per cent and 42.3 per cent is 4.2.

If we turn to the "wife-more-dominant" group we find that a positive relation exists between the wife's dominance and her poor or "fair" adjustment in marriage. The data at least indicate a negative relation be-

[20] *Ibid.,* p. 366. Reprinted by permission.

tween the wife's more-dominant role and her good adjustment in marriage. . . .[21]

This material, according to our interpretation of it, indicates that a democratic, equalitarian type of marital structure yields the highest degree of adjustment. For many marriages, however, this would not be true. Social, religious, and economic backgrounds help to determine expectancy of role.

CONTRIBUTIONS TO THE DEMOCRATIC FAMILY

A study of the relationship of parental authority patterns to teenage adjustments provides additional insights into the contribution of the democratic structure both to individuals and to family life as a whole. This study involved 4,310 high-school seniors, one-third of all high-school seniors in the State of Washington. The hypothesis of the study was that teenagers reared in the democratic family suffer from "fewer serious personal adjustments and enjoy all-around happier homes than do young people reared in an atmosphere dominated by their parent's wishes or commands."[22] This hypothesis was upheld by the data. The authors concluded that a comparison of democratic and authoritarian families shows the superiority of the former in terms of parent-teenage adjustment because teenagers in democratic families have fewer major problems and have a closer relationship with their parents than do boys and girls from authoritarian homes.[23]

Figure 23 records the reactions of boys and girls who were asked to respond to the question, "When I am the age of my father or mother I would like to be exactly like him or her, somewhat different or different?" This question is a very crucial one, for it measures the degree to which the boy or girl accepts the patterns of the home, their closeness to their parents, and their respect for them. Among both boys and girls, a substantially higher percentage of those who had been raised in a democratic family wanted to be exactly like their father or mother. For boys the difference in percentage was 47.2 per cent compared to 23.3 per cent and for girls 60.5 per cent compared to 23.5 per cent. In interpreting

---

[21] *Ibid.*, pp. 367–368. Reprinted by permission.
[22] Paul H. Landis and Carol L. Stone, *The Relationship of Parental Authority Patterns to Teenage Adjustments,* Rural Sociological Series on the Family, No. 3, Washington Agricultural Experiment Stations, Institute of Agricultural Sciences, State College of Washington, September, 1952, p. 2.   [23] *Ibid.*, p. 28.

these figures it is important to note that the degree of identification, the extent to which the boy or girl will adopt the way of life of the parents, depends on the degree of democracy in the home.

FIGURE 23. Responses of Teenagers, by Sex and Family Administrative Pattern, to the Question, "When I am the age of my father or mother I would like to be":*

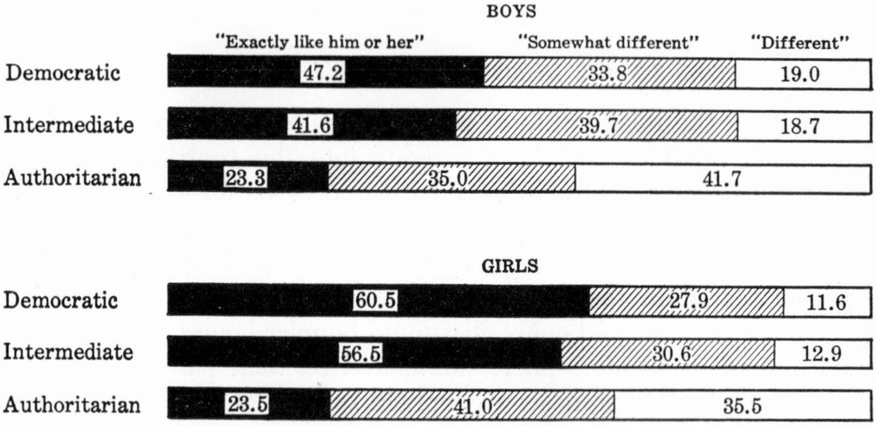

BOYS

	"Exactly like him or her"	"Somewhat different"	"Different"
Democratic	47.2	33.8	19.0
Intermediate	41.6	39.7	18.7
Authoritarian	23.3	35.0	41.7

GIRLS

Democratic	60.5	27.9	11.6
Intermediate	56.5	30.6	12.9
Authoritarian	23.5	41.0	35.5

* Paul H. Landis and Carol L. Stone, *The Relationship of Parental Authority Patterns to Teenage Adjustments*, Rural Sociological Series on the Family, No. 3, Washington Agricultural Experiment Stations, Institute of Agricultural Sciences, State College of Washington, September, 1952, p. 17. Reproduced by permission.

The principal thesis of Landis and Stone is that the growth of creative individuality of children and youth is one of the prime purposes of modern family living and that such individuality is essential to purposeful adjustment in modern society. Landis and Stone feel that "the superiority of the democratic family probably lies in the fact that, by and large, it substitutes cooperation for commands."[24] Cooperation undoubtedly gives larger place for individual development and growth of ability to make decisions. That democratic living is more cooperative and less repressive is shown in Table 55, which emphasizes the differences in disagreements between teenagers and parents in democratic families as compared to authoritarian families. Two times as many teenagers living in authoritarian homes frequently disagreed with parents as those living in democratic homes.

[24] *Ibid.*, p. 28.

TABLE 55. Percentage of Teenagers Checking Items on Which They "Frequently Disagree" with Parents, Classified by Type of Family Administrative Patterns*

AREAS-OF DISAGREEMENT	Sex	FAMILY ADMINISTRATION PATTERN		
		Democratic	Intermediate	Authoritarian
My spending money	Boys	20.2	28.8	39.4
	Girls	16.0	22.7	38.6
My friends	Boys	3.6	9.4	11.1
	Girls	3.9	10.4	23.1
My choice of clothes	Boys	6.6	9.2	11.9
	Girls	5.4	9.3	14.3
My attitude toward my parents'	Boys	8.9	13.2	24.7
	Girls	11.5	15.8	34.1
My outside activities	Boys	13.8	22.7	27.8
	Girls	13.8	19.5	28.5
My school work	Boys	21.6	28.4	31.8
	Girls	8.0	12.7	15.6
My future plans	Boys	13.5	17.5	20.2
	Girls	12.1	19.5	25.5
My share of the work around the house	Boys	26.2	24.7	40.4
	Girls	27.4	27.6	40.3
My social life	Boys	8.2	15.8	22.7
	Girls	9.1	12.8	27.2

* Paul H. Landis and Carol L. Stone, *The Relationship of Parental Authority Patterns to Teenage Adjustments*, Rural Sociological Series on the Family, No. 3, Washington Agricultural Experiment Stations, Institute of Agricultural Sciences, State College of Washington, September, 1952, p. 22. Reprinted by permission.

ADJUSTMENT OF DEMOCRATIC FAMILIES

The greater adjustment of teenagers living in democratic families is emphasized again in Table 56 which shows that teenagers from democratic homes have fewer family problems than those from authoritarian homes. However, this table also reveals that democratic families as a whole are happier than authoritarian families. There is only one-third the quarreling in the family (9.9 per cent compared to 27.8 per cent.) Children from democratic homes get along better with their parents. Only 5.7 per cent of boys and 8.4 per cent of girls checked getting along with parents as a problem compared to 17.2 per cent of boys and 24.2

395

T A B L E 56. Percentage of Teenagers Living in Democratic, Intermediate, and Authoritarian Families Checking Family Problems Listed*

PROBLEM	Sex	FAMILY ADMINISTRATIVE PATTERN			CR between Dem. and Auth.
		Democratic	Intermediate	Authoritarian	
Quarreling in the	Boys	9.9	11.8	27.8	7.90
family	Girls	12.7	16.2	37.0	9.21
Getting to use the car	Boys	22.3	25.0	34.8	4.58
	Girls	11.7	14.3	11.4	—
My folks under-	Boys	10.0	12.5	16.2	3.07
standing me	Girls	13.4	16.7	28.3	5.92
I have to work	Boys	12.0	21.6	27.0	6.44
to buy things	Girls	8.2	11.3	18.8	5.08
Getting Mother to un-	Boys	4.2	5.7	10.6	4.24
derstand my prob-	Girls	6.5	12.1	26.3	8.62
lems					
Getting along with	Boys	5.7	10.6	17.2	6.30
my parents	Girls	8.4	10.8	24.2	13.59
Having no regular	Boys	5.7	8.2	16.9	6.16
allowance	Girls	8.6	12.6	21.2	5.79
Getting Dad to un-	Boys	10.4	10.9	17.7	3.53
derstand my prob-	Girls	12.5	16.0	20.6	3.57
lems					
Afraid I can't	Boys	13.4	14.0	17.9	2.04
afford college	Girls	10.2	12.5	16.3	2.94
I don't have any	Boys	4.4	5.3	8.3	2.68
privacy at home	Girls	2.6	7.1	17.8	8.22
Having a happy	Boys	7.8	10.5	12.1	2.55
home life	Girls	9.9	8.9	17.1	3.45

* The total check list contained sixty-three items. Only those checked by at least 10 per cent in one category, and which showed statistically significant differences, are reproduced here.

Paul H. Landis and Carol L. Stone, *The Relationship of Parental Authority Patterns to Teenage Adjustments*, Rural Sociological Series on the Family, No. 3, Washington Agricultural Experiment Stations, Institute of Agricultural Sciences, State College of Washington, September, 1952, p. 24. Reprinted by permission.

per cent of girls from authoritarian homes. Other revealing comparisons are to be found in the responses to such statements as "Wish I could live by myself," "I want to leave home," and "My parents are always quarreling." These items indicate that in general family adjustment the democratic family is superior to the authoritarian family. It would appear that in our society democratic home relationships make for more creative individuals and for better adjusted homes.

TABLE 56. Percentage of Teenagers Living in Democratic, Intermediate, and
(Cont.) Authoritarian Families Checking Family Problems Listed*

Problem	Sex	Family Administrative Pattern			CR between Dem. and Auth.
		Democratic	Intermediate	Authoritarian	
Understanding my	Boys	5.7	8.2	10.1	2.75
folks	Girls	7.4	12.0	15.8	4.29
Family always worried	Boys	6.9	7.5	10.4	2.08
about money	Girls	8.2	10.0	15.6	3.74
Wish I had my	Boys	6.2	6.9	11.4	3.10
own room	Girls	11.4	12.2	15.6	2.01
Don't have much	Boys	6.8	7.9	11.4	2.68
spending money	Girls	4.7	7.1	15.0	5.66
Mother has to work	Boys	7.0	6.9	6.8	—
	Girls	10.4	11.2	14.6	2.02
Treated like a child	Boys	4.8	6.1	11.6	4.27
at home	Girls	5.0	7.2	14.4	8.31
Folks ridicule	Boys	3.1	4.5	9.3	4.50
my ideas	Girls	2.2	3.1	14.3	7.20
Wish I could live	Boys	2.7	2.2	9.1	4.79
by myself	Girls	3.2	3.7	14.1	6.36
My parents are	Boys	2.5	3.0	8.1	4.42
always quarreling	Girls	3.4	5.2	13.5	5.95
Can't bring friends	Boys	2.3	3.5	8.3	4.73
to my home	Girls	3.1	4.9	13.3	6.01
Don't like the	Boys	4.3	5.6	9.1	3.29
house we live in	Girls	6.9	7.7	12.4	3.05
I want to leave home	Boys	2.2	2.3	9.1	5.35
	Girls	2.8	2.6	12.4	5.94

THE FAMILY COUNCIL

One of the ways in which many young couples are consciously structuring their relationship democratically is by providing a stated time when difficulties may be faced and new family opportunities may be explored. Many call this the family council. During these talks the monetary and time budgets of the family are prepared or revised, recurrent problems are discussed, and individual needs are considered. While problem-solving cannot be completely institutionalized, some form of continuous communication promotes family cohesion and certainly reduces family tension.

CONCLUSION

In this chapter we have reviewed some of the complex factors involved in conflict or tensional situations. These conflicts and tensions have been regarded not as threats but as opportunities to achieve greater closeness in marriage as well as avenues to self-realization for each marriage partner. Constructive approaches to conflict situations were found in a dedication to the success of the marriage, in emotional freedom and honesty of expression, in the development of ability to discuss creatively, and in the achievement of a democratic family structure which facilitates problem-solving. We have tried to show that conflict is inevitable and continuous, that it has its source in our culture, but that it may lead to new ways of achieving unity. Burgess and Locke say:

> It is through conflicts and their solution that a family sets up and achieves goals, that a division of labor and cooperative action is developed, and that individual members come to subordinate their individual interests to what is considered the welfare of the whole family. Where all conflict is lacking family stagnation will take place. The dynamic, progressive family is constantly facing, discussing, and cooperatively solving its problems; consequently, conflict in this sense may be considered normal and functional.[25]

A FINAL WORD

This book has presented many ways in which marriage today may result in happiness. In the first part, the student was given an opportunity to investigate those background circumstances and experiences which might have conditioned him or her in such a way as to have an adverse effect on marital adjustment. It was suggested that by reviewing our past we could alter inhibitions and achieve more healthy attitudes. The emphasis was upon becoming a mature and marriageable person.

In the last part, psychological and sociological factors that influence marital choice and adjustment were analyzed so that the student might be better prepared when he or she faces the necessity of making similar choices or adjustments. In all of these sections, problem-solving was regarded as a means to togetherness and as a way of enriching the dynamic bond between a man and his wife.

In conclusion, a word can profitably be said for using all the resources

[25] Burgess and Locke, *op. cit.*, p. 514.

which are now being marshaled in the interest of better family living. Most families reach whatever degree of cohesion or happiness they achieve as a matter of chance. If husbands and wives gave only one-tenth as much time to discussing and planning the future of their relationship as they do to their business or even to their social life, their marriages would grow in meaning and cohesion. Many couples spend more time keeping their automobiles clean than in keeping their romance shining. We have said that contemporary social trends make it necessary for those who wish to be happy to plan consciously for that happiness. But we have also suggested that these same trends may mean that the contemporary couple may find new patterns of achievement in marriage which were not possible under the more rigid mores of several generations ago.

PROJECTS

1. Select any two members of opposite sex in the class. List on the board ten or fifteen important areas which will involve decisions in marriage such as child-training, budget-making, vacations, etc. Then ask each of the two to indicate their present ideas about each of these areas of interest.
2. Have a sharing session in which various members of the class indicate their own habits or ways of solving conflicts. Which of these ways will be detrimental in marriage?

VISUAL AIDS

Jealousy McGraw-Hill Marriage Series
McGraw-Hill Book Company
In Time of Trouble McGraw-Hill Marriage Series
McGraw-Hill Book Company

READINGS

ERNEST W. BURGESS and HARVEY J. LOCKE, *The Family, From Institution to Companionship,* New York, The American Book Company, 1953, Chapter 18.

HAROLD T. CHRISTENSEN, *Marriage Analysis,* New York, The Ronald Press Company, 1950, Chapter 10.

JUDSON T. LANDIS and MARY LANDIS, *Building a Successful Marriage,* New York, Prentice-Hall, Inc., 1948, Chapter 10.

YI-CHUANG LU, "Marital Roles and Marriage Adjustment," article, *Sociology and Social Research,* University of Southern California Press, Los Angeles, California, July–August, 1952, Volume 32, Number 6.

PAUL H. LANDIS and CAROL L. STONE, *The Relationship of Parental Authority Patterns to Teenage Adjustments,* Rural Sociological Series on the Family, No. 3, Washington Agricultural Experiment Stations, Institute of Agricultural Sciences, State College of Washington, September, 1952.

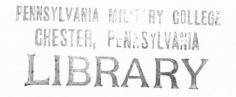
400

Appendices

The Billig Stretch

(Exercise to Relieve Menstrual Pain and Cramps)

Stand with left side toward wall or other firm support, feet together and about eighteen inches from wall, knees locked in hyper-extension, hips "tucked" under.

Place left arm against wall, shoulder height, with palm of hand, forearm, and elbow in firm contact with wall.
Place right hand against hollow of right hip joint.
Slowly and deliberately push hips forward and toward wall, as far as they will go—and then just a little bit farther.
Slowly return to starting position.
At all times keep knees locked and shoulders at right angle to wall.

Three times to right. Three times to left. Three times daily.

[1] Eleanor Metheny, *Body Dynamics*, New York, McGraw-Hill Book Company, Inc., 1952, p. 219. Reprinted by permission.

Ante-Nuptial Agreement
of the Catholic Church

To be signed in duplicate in the presence of the priest by the parties entering a mixed marriage, and by two witnesses.

To Be Signed by the Non-Catholic Party

I, the undersigned, not a member of the Catholic Church, wishing to contract marriage with the Catholic party whose signature is also hereinafter affixed to this mutual agreement, being of sound mind and perfectly free, and only after understanding fully the import of my action, do hereby enter into this mutual agreement, understanding that the execution of this agreement and the promises therein contained are made in contemplation of and in consideration for the consent, marriage and consequent change of status of the hereinafter mentioned Catholic party, and I, therefore, hereby agree:

1. That I will not interfere in the least with the free exercise of the Catholic party's religion;

2. That I will adhere to the doctrine of the sacred indissolubility of the marriage bond, so that I cannot contract a second marriage while my consort is still alive, even though a civil divorce may have been obtained;

3. That all the children, both boys and girls, that may be born of this union shall be baptized and educated solely in the faith of the Roman Catholic Church, even in the event of the death of my Catholic consort. In case of dispute, I, furthermore, hereby fully agree that the custody of all the children shall be given to such guardians as to assure the faithful execution of this covenant and promise;

4. That I will lead a married life in conformity with the Law of God and the teaching of the Catholic Church regarding birth control, realizing fully the attitude of the Catholic Church in this regard;

5. That no other marriage ceremony shall take place before or after this ceremony by the Catholic priest.

In testimony of which agreement, I do hereby solemnly swear that I will observe the above agreement and faithfully execute the promises therein contained, and do now affix my signature in approval thereof.

_____
Signature of the non-Catholic party

_____
Address

_____
City or Town

To Be Signed by the Catholic Party

I, the undersigned, a member of the Catholic Church, wishing to contract marriage with the non-Catholic party whose signature is affixed above to this mutual agreement, being of sound mind and perfectly free, and only after understanding fully the import of my action, do hereby enter into this mutual agreement, understanding that the execution of this agreement and the promises therein contained are made in contemplation of and in consideration for the consent, marriage and consequent change of my status, and I, therefore, hereby agree:

1. That I shall have all my children, both boys and girls, that may be born of this union, baptized and educated solely in the faith of the Roman Catholic Church. I understand that in case of my death, or in the event of a dispute, the custody of all the children shall be given to such guardians as to assure the faithful execution of this covenant and promise;

2. That I will practice my Catholic religion faithfully and will strive, especially by example, prayer and the frequentation of the Sacraments, to bring about the conversion of my consort;

3. That I will lead a married life in conformity with the Law of God and the teaching of the Catholic Church regarding birth control, realizing fully the attitude of the Catholic Church in this regard;

4. That no other marriage ceremony shall take place before or after this ceremony by the Catholic priest.

_____
Signature of the Catholic party

_____
Address

_____
City or Town

403

Signed in the presence of:

Witness

Witness

I, the undersigned, do hereby attest that the parties whose signatures are affixed to the above agreement and promises appeared before me personally on the given date, and fully understanding the import and meaning of the aforementioned agreement and promises, freely entered into this agreement and signed the above in my presence.

Pastor—Assistant

Date:————————————

TWO COPIES of this form should be filled in and sent to the Chancery. One copy, when duly signed, dated and sealed by the Chancellor, will be returned to the priest to be kept in the parish archives: the other copy will be retained in the Chancery. See "Synodus Dioecesana Sancti Ludovici Septima—1929" (Page 54 No. 95 under 2).

Trends in Family-Life Education

INTRODUCTION: MANY SOCIAL RESOURCES ARE TODAY
AVAILABLE TO YOUNG PEOPLE WHO NEED HELP AND ADVICE.
Courses in junior high schools, high schools, colleges, and churches are
preparing students for the wise choice of a mate and for adjustment in
marriage. Red Cross and special hospital courses prepare them for
parenthood. Extensive sociological and psychological research undergird
the work of teachers and counselors. Both family-life education and
marriage counseling are growing in scope and in value.

The first functional course in preparation for marriage was instituted
at the University of North Carolina in 1925 as the result of a petition of
a committee of senior men to the President of the University, Dr. Harry
W. Chase. The course was taught by Ernest W. Groves of the Sociology
department who later, in 1933, wrote the first textbook in the field, a
volume simply entitled, "Marriage." Since that time, courses in functional aspects of the family have become so popular that today they are
given in more than 700 colleges and universities while the importance of
family-life education has come to be so widely recognized that it has
spread to elementary schools, junior high and high schools, junior colleges, and adult educational groups.

FAMILY-LIFE EDUCATION ON THE ELEMENTARY LEVEL

Emphasis on education for family life at the elementary level has
been accentuated by a recognition of the formative nature of experience
during these years. Some school systems have an integrated program in
which education for family life is given in every grade. The Montebello
school system of California asked Dr. Leland Glover to assist it in work-

ing out such an over-all plan. Today in this school system education for family life begins in kindergarten and extends through high school. In discussing the need for family-life education on the junior high-school level, Helen Jensen says:

> Many students are not reached because the courses (in high school) are limited to seniors and are usually elective. Students leaving high school before the senior year miss the course entirely. With the increasing number of married students attending high school, it seems that the information gleaned from such a course comes too late to be of real value. With puberty occurring in the early junior high-school years, it appears to be more feasible that at this level students should have instruction and guidance in personal problems.[1]

Jensen interviewed 221 junior high-school students and surveyed another 531 of the same age group.[2] She found that the six major problems of junior high-school students were of the sort with which family-life education is concerned. They were:

(1) grooming
(2) boy-girl relationships
(3) sex education
(4) personality, and
(5) child-adult relationships[3]

Jensen states that many high-school students feel that they need help in these matters before they reach high school. No survey has been made to determine the national scope of family-life education in the junior high-school field. It is at best sporadic but growing throughout the country.

FAMILY-LIFE EDUCATION IN HIGH SCHOOL

Family-life education in high schools is conducted formally and informally. Formal courses which touch upon various phases of preparation for marriage are those in physiology, social living, family life, family living, senior problems, and personal adjustment. Informal instruction is part of the effort of physical educators, coaches, deans, and counselors. The most recent study of trends in family-life education was made by Kirkendall who had 68 persons representing 19 states from Connecticut

---

[1] Helen Kane Jensen, *Integrating Into the Curriculum the Physical and Social Adjustments of the Boys and Girls in a Junior High School,* unpublished Master's Degree Thesis, University of Southern California, July, 1954, p. 1.   [2] *Ibid.,* p. 3.   [3] *Ibid.,* p. 3.

to California fill out a survey form. The most important finding of the survey was that some 75 per cent of the respondents reported that fears that sex discussion might lead to "unwholesome experimentation" are decreasing.[4] Fifty per cent of the group felt that free discussion of sexual matters was increasing and another 35 per cent thought that it was beginning. Sixty-five per cent of the respondents felt that sex education was improving in scope, in that emphasis on considering sexual attitudes a normal part of education for marriage was growing.[5] Another 48 per cent said that stress on counseling as part of marriage education was increasing and 31 per cent said it was starting. Fifty per cent reported that community and faculty acceptance of family-life education was increasing and another 40 per cent said such acceptance was beginning.[6] Fifty per cent thought that the integrated approach in which all departments deal with related matters pertaining to family life was increasing and 28 per cent said the integrated approach was beginning. In California, almost every high-school student is required to take a year's course called Senior Problems. Approximately one-third of the course is devoted to preparation for effective adjustment in marriage.

In 1944, the United States Office of Education codified a series of principles and chose the term, "family-life education," in preference to the one previously used, "social-hygiene education," as a more fitting title for this instruction. In 1945, the state legislature of Oregon pioneered a statewide integrated program by passing an act requiring sex education in the secondary schools. Many other states are now following suit.[7] Several good texts are now available in the field of family living for high-school students, and summer institutes and courses in the communities for training teachers are increasing in scope and number.

FAMILY-LIFE EDUCATION IN THE COLLEGES

Training for effective family living has developed more extensively in the colleges than at any other level. Henry Bowman surveyed 1,370 colleges and junior colleges in 1948–49 for the American Social Hygiene Association to determine the extent of marriage education. Six hundred and thirty-two of the 1,270 schools that returned the questionnaire reported at least one course in their curriculum. Bowman thinks that some 50,000 students or 2 out of every 100 college students have enrolled in

---

[4] Margie Robinson Lee, "Current Trends in Family Life Education," *Marriage and Family Living*, Volume XIV, No. 3, August, 1952, p. 203.
[5] *Ibid.*, p. 203.   [6] *Ibid.*, p. 204.   [7] Jensen, *op. cit.*, p. 10.

such courses.[8] Seven hundred and sixty-five instructors teach these courses; 70 per cent are men and 30 per cent are women.

A more recent and detailed study is the one made by H. L. Manheim in 1954 of marriage preparation courses in Southern California colleges. Manheim divided these schools into two groups; Group I refers to junior colleges and Group II refers to colleges and universities. Questionnaires were returned by 88 per cent of the junior colleges and 90 per cent of the colleges and universities. The following table shows the number of courses given by these schools. Only 33 per cent of the colleges and universities and 14 per cent of the junior colleges had not included in the curriculum one or more courses in family life.

T A B L E 57. Number of Marriage Preparation Courses Offered by Junior College and College Institutions*

NUMBER OF COURSES	GROUP I		GROUP II		TOTAL	
	Number	Per Cent	Number	Per Cent	Number	Per Cent
0	4	14	8	33	12	23
1	20	72	10	42	30	57
2	2	7	2	8	4	8
3	2	7	1	4	3	6
4 or more	0	0	3	13	3	6
TOTAL	28	100	24	100	52	100

* Henry L. Manheim, *Marriage Preparation Courses in Southern California Colleges,* unpublished paper, June, 1954, p. 5.

These courses are taught in many different departments and by individuals trained in different fields. Departments of sociology have the greatest number of courses with departments of home economics running a close second.

A wider diversity of teaching techniques is employed in the field of family life than in perhaps any other educational field. Seventy-three per cent of the respondents in this study reported the use of movies, 5 per cent the use of slides and film-strips, and 15 per cent the use of models, charts, and other visual aids. Most of the instructors supplement their lectures with discussions, "buzz sessions," and outside speakers. Table 59 indicates that only 10 per cent of the teachers limit their presentation to lecturing.

[8] Henry A. Bowman, *Marriage Education in the Colleges,* American Social Hygiene Association, Pub. No. A-770, p. 5.

TABLE 58. Departments Offering Family Life Courses*

DEPARTMENT	GROUP I		GROUP II		TOTAL	
	Number	*Per Cent*	*Number*	*Per Cent*	*Number*	*Per Cent*
General studies *or* Orientation	1	3	1	3	2	3
Health education	0	0	3	9	3	5
Home economics	7	23	10	30	17	26
Human relations	1	3	0	0	1	2
Psychology	1	3	3	9	4	6
Religion	0	0	5	15	5	8
Science	3	10	0	0	3	5
Social science	5	17	0	0	5	8
Sociology	9	31	11	34	20	31
No department	1	3	0	0	1	2
Not stated	2	7	0	0	2	3
TOTAL	30	100	33	100	63	100

* Henry L. Manheim, *Marriage Preparation Courses in Southern California Colleges,* unpublished paper, June, 1954, p. 7.

TABLE 59. Various Teaching Techniques in Family Life Courses*

TEACHING METHOD	GROUP I		GROUP II		TOTAL	
	Number	*Per Cent*	*Number*	*Per Cent*	*Number*	*Per Cent*
Lecture only	0	0	6	19	6	10
Lecture and discussion	11	36	20	62	31	49
Above methods, plus panels, buzz groups, etc.	5	17	2	6	7	11
All above plus outside resource persons	5	17	4	13	9	15
Not stated	9	30	0	0	9	15
TOTAL	30	100	32	100	62	100

* Henry L. Manheim, *Marriage Preparation Courses in Southern California Colleges,* unpublished paper, June, 1954, p. 15.

CONTRIBUTIONS OF COLLEGE MARRIAGE COURSES

Marriage education is one of the most recent additions to the college curriculum. Very few attempts have been made to evaluate the contributions of such courses scientifically. Two such attempts have been made. Gilles and Lastrucci used the Bell Adjustment Inventory, the

Mooney Problem Check List, a one-hundred-item test of factual information and a fifty-item open-end projective test of the sentence-completion type to evaluate contributions of a family life course. The authors concluded that changes in student behavior did take place; they also noted that the changes in information were appreciably greater than the changes in attitude and personal adjustment.[9]

A second recent study was that of Wilbur Clark at the University of Southern California which utilized an eighty-five-item instrument to measure changes in information, opinions, and sexual readiness resulting from participation in a marriage course. Clark gave his test to two classes, one in education for marriage and one in American history, at the beginning and at the end of the semester. There were 101 students in the marriage course, that is, the experimental group, and 94 in the American history class, or the control group. These two groups were matched for age, college class, religious affiliation, and marital status but they were not matched for sex, as there were more men than women in the history class, more women than men in the marriage class. Clark divided each group into those who made high scores on the test and those who made low scores.

By condensing Clark's tables, it is possible to summarize his findings. In the following table only the movement of students from the low division to the high division for the experimental and the control groups is given. The extent to which the percentage increased in the top division indicates the degree to which the students have a greater total preparation for marriage, a greater sexual readiness, more information, and more accurate opinions about marriage. The "experimental test" is the first test given to the marriage students at the beginning of the semester; the "control test" is the first test given to the history students at the beginning of the semester. The "experimental retest" and "control retest" are the tests given to the marriage students at the end of the semester.

The "Marriage Readiness" score includes all items and is a general score indicating the degrees of readiness for marriage.

While only 39.6 per cent of the experimental students were in the upper division on the test at the beginning of the semester, at the end of the instruction period 63.4 per cent made such scores. The change in the control group was negligible and statistically not significant. The "Marriage Opinion" score describes students' feelings in certain areas

[9] D. V. Gilles and Carlo L. Lastrucci, "Validation of the Effectiveness of a College Marriage Course," *Marriage and Family Living*, XVI, February, 1954, pp. 51–55.

which are not regarded as factual in the presentation of class material. The judgment as to which "opinions" were correct and the indicated movement toward marriage readiness constituted the subjective judgment of Clark and the teacher of the marriage class. There was considerable change in the experimental group as contrasted with the control group. The "Marriage Information" score has to do with the mastery of items generally regarded as true by authorities in the field. No significant change was recorded here. In fact, the control group changed more than the experimental group. In this respect this study varied from the Gilles-Lastrucci study and may reflect different emphasis in the two classes. The "Sexual Readiness" score measures changes in attitudes toward sexual and reproductive phases of marriage. The changes recorded here were most significant as indicated by a CR of 3.4 while the control group varied scarcely at all. A subjective evaluation form was given the students of this marriage class at the end of the semester, and their evaluation paralleled Clark's more objective analysis.

TABLE 60. Comparative Test and Retest Scores of a Marriage Education Class (Experimental) and a History Class (Control) for Marriage Readiness in Terms of the Per Cents of Each Class Falling in the Top Division of Test Scores*

Area of Study	Experimental Test	Experimental Retest	CR	Control Test	Control Retest	CR
Marriage Readiness (Total score)	39.6	63.4	2.4	14.9	18.1	—
Marriage Opinion score	63.4	82.27	2.1	36.6	30.8	−.7
Marriage Information score	66.3	72.3	.8	27.7	40.4	.9
Sexual and Reproductive Readiness score	56.4	81.2	3.4	53.2	54.3	—

* Wilbur W. Clark, *A Study of Opinions and Information of a College Class before and after Taking a Marriage Education Course as Compared with a Control Group*, unpublished Masters' Degree Thesis, University of Southern California, August, 1954, pp. 28–35.

More studies of this nature need to be made so that teachers of marriage courses can scientifically evaluate their efforts and improve their methods. These studies by Gilles-Lastrucci and Clark indicate that marriage courses do make significant contributions both to the formation of wholesome attitudes and to the acquiring of essential information.

COUNSELING SERVICES FOR THE FAMILY

Dr. Napheys, writing in the eighties, recalled with approval a type of enforced marriage counseling which was apparently used as a means of preventing divorce:

> It is said that in Zurich, in the olden time, when a quarrelsome couple applied for a divorce, the magistrate refused to listen to them at first. He ordered that they should be shut up together in one room for three days, with one bed, one table, one plate, and one cup. Their food was passed in by attendants who neither saw nor spoke to them. On the expiration of the three days, it was usual to find that neither of them would want a separation.[10]

Marriage counseling has made some progress from the "olden time."

One of the most progressive developments of recent years has been the increase in counseling agencies which serve the family. We have mentioned previously the new type of training for ministers. Many social agencies are specially equipped to deal with the problems of marriage. No couple need be without help when in difficulty. Glover's study indicates the many resources young people have at their disposal.

Table 61 indicates the diversity in the backgrounds of individuals to whom students turn for help. Of interest is the high percentage of students that turn to their boy or girl friends for assistance. Next in rank are certain members of the immediate family. While talking with these individuals cannot properly be regarded as counseling, such persons have an important function to perform in listening and giving advice, so that they need adequate knowledge to share. The growth of parent-education classes helps to make the contributions of mothers and fathers more effective. Adult-education classes are also contributing insight to parents so that they may be wise in dealing with their children in these decisive matters.

With such a wide variety of individuals engaged in one form or another of the helping process, it is important that the student have some criterion by which to judge the qualifications of those to whom he may turn for guidance. For if, as the result of counseling experiences, he has more guilt, or more dependency, or is more confused, he will neither have grown nor be willing to turn to others who might be more competent. Human personality is very complex. To discuss problems in-

[10] George H. Napheys, *The Physical Life of Women*, Philadelphia, H. C. Watts Company, 1882, p. 93.

TABLE 61. The Relative Roles of Selected Persons as Counselors of College Students in the Areas of Concern According to Responses by 1265 Students in 47 Colleges, in Rank Order of Frequency of Responses*

Rank		Person	Total Responses	Per cent of Total Responses
1.		Girl-friend	601	18.0
2.		Boy-friend	574	17.2
3.		Mother	571	17.1
4.		Father	321	9.6
5.		Teacher of Marriage and Family Course	218	6.5
6.		Sister	205	6.1
7.		Spouse	142	4.2
8.		Brother	127	3.8
9.		Doctor	121	3.6
10.		Minister	105	3.1
11.		Priest	56	1.7
12.		Cousin	51	1.5
13.		Aunt	49	1.5
14.		Psychologist	48	1.4
15.		Psychiatrist	35	1.0
16.		Home economist	23	0.7
17.	(a)	Sociologist	20	0.6
17.	(a)	Vocational specialist	20	0.6
19.		Uncle	18	0.5
20.	(b)	Biologist	12	0.4
20.	(b)	Social worker	12	0.4
22.	(c)	Lawyer	6	0.2
22.	(c)	Rabbi	6	0.2
24.		Dentist	3	0.1
		TOTALS	3344	100.0

* Adapted from Leland Ellis Glover, *The Teacher of Marriage and the Family as Counselor,* unpublished Ph.D. Dissertation, University of Southern California, 1951, p. 87.

volving the relationship of two personalities obviously requires much information and training. To whom, then, may one turn for adequate help?

The qualifications of marriage counselors were the subject of prolonged discussion at the 1944 meeting of the National Conference on Family Relations. A summary of its findings follows:

Qualifications: The person who seeks to become a marriage and family counselor should be one who is intellectually mature and emotionally

413

stable. Although age is not a criterion of maturity, the very young adult might find difficulty in convincing others that he is fitted to counsel. Personal experience in marriage would be an asset. Those with a natural aptitude for counseling should be encouraged; methods need to be developed to screen out those unsuitable for counselors before much special training is given.

Training: The marriage counselor deals with the total personality and finds the most pressing problems in the area of family inter-relationships. The counselor must be able to probe beneath surface problems to trace maladjustments to their source. He, therefore, needs training primarily in the area of human development and personal inter-relationships, including those of a psycho-sexual nature. Nevertheless, clients also come for particular information; the counselor therefore, must have a wide general background of information in many fields, such as budgeting and laws relating to family life. Also the counselor will be faced with problems that call for the specialized services of a lawyer, physician or psychiatrist and he must be able to recognize the signals for such referrals.

Since the program of training will be highly specialized in certain fields it can best be given as graduate work. The student should come into this graduate work with an undergraduate degree in sociology or psychology or should be required to cover these fields in some other way.

At present no one university department is prepared to monopolize the training. The nearest approach is found in some departments of social work or psychiatric social work which are especially well adapted to give the background courses. Other courses needed, especially in the psycho-sexual field, are now rarely offered. Many of these cut across traditional departmental lines and call for specially organized classes oriented to marriage and family relationships. The content of training needed by a marriage and family counselor is indicated under the departments which logically would provide the instruction.

Psychology: The central core of training should be in the structure and development of human personality, with emphasis on the significance of the formative period of childhood and youth. This is important in the diagnosis of adult maladjustments as well as in the analysis of parent-child relationships. The theories of personality should be thoroughly covered. The counselor needs thorough training in psycho-sexual inter-relationships, since many problems, arise here and this is an area that the counselor should make pre-eminently his own. The counselor should also be acquainted with psychological tests, although any extensive testing and interpretation should, if possible, be done by a trained clinical psychologist.

Social Anthropology, Biology, Sociology and Religion: Background training to give perspective and understanding of present-day family life is needed. The marriage counselor should be familiar with primitive and contemporary social life and with the culture of local ethnic groups with which he may deal. This knowledge of the relativity of culture will give objectivity, free the counselor from devotion to his own culture and make clear the structure of American society.

The counselor should study enough biological science to appreciate the meaning and significance of the human organism. He should know the facts of human heredity and the eugenic program advocated for the security and improvement of the race.

Sociology should make clear the development of American social life, including the family, and the common social problems of those who marry, become parents, are courting or who have given up the idea of marriage. The significance of class and section as they influence marriage should be stressed, since the counselor must always be prepared to take these cultural differences into account. The counselor should also be familiar with population trends and the factors affecting marriage and birth rates. The counselor must also have a clear conception of the Catholic, Protestant and Jewish philosophies of marriage.

Economics, Home Economics, Law, Medicine, Psychiatry: Related fields of knowledge, including those in which referrals to other services must be made, should be thoroughly covered.

An important field of related knowledge is economics, as applied to family living. The counselor especially needs to be familiar with problems of credit, budgeting, buying and household management.

The counselor should also know the principles of domestic law, with special attention to marriage laws, annulment, and divorce, including personal financial responsibilities. For legal services, however, referral also should be made to a lawyer.

The counselor needs certain training in the field of medicine and psychiatry to give an awareness of difficulties that should be referred to a physician or a psychiatrist. This should cover (1) embryology as it reveals the development of the sexual structure, (2) endocrinology especially as related to adolescence, fertility, pregnancy and climacteric, (3) obstetrics and gynecology, (4) representative health programs of preventative medicine, and (5) available resources for safeguarding and improving the health of communities and individuals. Included should also be discussion of human sexology emphasizing the normal and also giving attention to such abnormal expressions of sex as the counselor is most likely to encounter in his conferences. Psychiatry should add to the background of the counselor modern psychiatric theories and an understanding of the principal mental diseases and their characteristic expression. The counselor should have part of his training in clinics as this would give insight not to be gained in the classroom.

Technical skills of several types are needed. The student in training should be taught principles of interviewing and should have practice in diagnosis and treatment of representative cases under proper guidance, either of a professional counselor or as a student apprentice with some organization giving a well-developed counseling service.

In order to extend his services to group guidance, the counselor should be trained in handling informal group discussions and in the use of visual aids.

In order to make full use of community resources the counselor should be familiar with the allied services found in typical communities such as social agencies, mental hygiene societies and clinics, child guidance centers, legal and medical services, psychiatric clinics and public health services. He should know how to make full use of these facilities in order to concentrate upon his own special field of marital and family inter-relationships.[11]

The student may well wonder where help of this nature can be obtained. These standards represent the ideal, and few individuals or centers conform to all of them. However, there are certain agencies which maintain very high standards and which come close to fulfilling these requirements. Before mentioning these, we urge the student to remember some of these qualifications and to look into the educational and experimental background of whoever is chosen as counselor.

Family Service Organizations. The Family Service Association of America is a national organization of social-work organizations which are staffed by trained social workers (and psychiatric social workers) skilled in meeting family problems. Most large cities in the United States have such organizations, which are generally supported by the community chest and charge only nominal fees for counseling. The Catholic, Jewish, and Protestant church groups maintain family service units in most large cities. In the Los Angeles area, the Family Service gives help to ap-

---

[11] "The Training of Full Time Workers on Marriage and Family Counseling," *Marriage and Family Living*, 6, 1944, pp. 70–71. Reprinted by permission.

proximately 2,400 families a year. This society maintains five district offices and an administrative office and describes the service as follows:

Family Service of the Los Angeles area is ready to help when:

A man and his wife cannot get along together and wonder why;
A family feels lost because the mother is upset, ill, or hospitalized;
Parents and children misunderstand each other;
An aged person needs to make new plans because of tension at home;
A person feels unsure of himself at work.

It handles other family problems, too, but this list indicates the range of its interests. Some of the most penetrating literature on family problems and counseling techniques has come out of Family Service groups.

Mental-Hygiene Clinics. Many states and cities now maintain mental hygiene clinics. These clinics are equipped to deal with childhood, adolescent, or marital problems. Such clinics are staffed with psychiatrists, psychologists, psychiatric social workers, and physicians who are qualified to help solve marital problems of whatever nature. Many cities also maintain child-guidance clinics. These are useful when problems of parent-child conflicts or personality disturbances are involved. Some of these are tax-supported and some are supported by public subscription. In any event they are at the disposal of all citizens of the area they serve and are, in general, very competent.

Veterans' Counseling Agencies. The Federal Government has taken a profound interest in the welfare of the ex-serviceman and provides him with various types of counseling: vocational, personality, and marital. All veterans may avail themselves of these services. These clinics maintain a high level of professional ethics and are usually competent to deal with the problems presented.

Marriage-Counseling Centers. In some large communities there are nonprofit organizations which devote their whole attention to marital or premarital counseling. Some of the better known of these are the American Institute of Family Relations of Los Angeles, the Marriage Council of Philadelphia, the Marriage Consultation Center of the Community Church of New York, the Counseling Service of the Boston Y.M.C.A. If no counseling service is available in a particular community, those in need may write to one of the three following national organizations for recommendations:

American Association of Marriage Counselors, Janet F. Nelson, Ph.D., Secretary, 563 Park Avenue, New York 21, New York

Family Service Association of America, 192 Lexington Avenue, New York 16, New York

National Council on Family Relations, 1126 East 59th Street, Chicago 37, Illinois

Local or School Resources for Students. Local clinical assistance is often available to students. Most health services of universities maintain in residence a psychiatrist whose function is to help students confronted with emotional difficulties. If the health services do not provide psychiatric service the head of the psychology department generally can make recommendations. In some universities a clinical psychological service is maintained which is available to students and to the community as a whole. The dean of the college is usually able to refer to a suitable counseling service any student who has to make a difficult decision or has to meet a disturbing situation. Today, no student, no individual, need blunder through a complex situation, for resources sufficient to meet these problems are available.

READINGS

ERNEST W. BURGESS and LEONARD S. COTTRELL, *Predicting Success or Failure in Marriage*, New York, Prentice-Hall, Inc., 1939.

ERNEST W. BURGESS and HARVEY J. LOCKE, *The Family, from Institution to Companionship*, New York, The American Book Company, 1953, Chapter 22.

SIDNEY GOLDSTEIN, *Marriage and Family Counseling*, New York, McGraw-Hill Book Company, 1945.

HARVEY J. LOCKE, *Predicting Adjustment in Marriage: A Comparison of a Divorced and a Happily Married Group*, New York, Henry Holt and Company, 1952, Chapter 15.

CARL R. ROGERS, *Counseling and Psychotherapy*, Boston, Houghton Mifflin Company, 1942.

LEWIS M. TERMAN, *Psychological Factors in Marital Happiness*, New York, McGraw-Hill Book Company, Inc., 1938.

RECORDING

"Principles of Family Life Education" is a forty minute lecture by James A. Peterson discussing purposes, methods and materials for family life education. Educational Recording Services, 5922 Abernathy Drive, Los Angeles, 45, California.

INDEX

Index

Date Due

NOV 2 '71			
DEC 16 '71			
MAR 15 '72			
APR 20 '72			
NOV 23 '72			
AUG 22 '73			
DEC 1 '76			
APR 29 '77			
OCT 3 0 1977			
APR 2 9 1981			
JUN 1 1983			
MAR 3 0 1988			
DEC 2 2 1995			
DEC 2 0 1996			